The Philosophy of Adam Smith

Adam Smith's contribution to economics is well-recognised but in recent years scholars have been exploring the philosophical aspects of his works. *The Philosophy of Adam Smith* contains essays by some of the most prominent philosophers and scholars working on Adam Smith today. It is a special issue of *The Adam Smith Review*, commemorating the 250th anniversary of Smith's *Theory of Moral Sentiments*. Contributors to this volume include Stephen Darwall, Fonna Forman-Barzilai, Patrick Frierson, Charles L. Griswold, Ryan Patrick Hanley, Alice MacLachlan, Bence Nanay, Angelica Nuzzo, D.D. Raphael, Ian Simpson Ross, Emma Rothschild, Geoffrey Sayre-McCord, Arby Ted Siraki and Robert Urquhart, who discuss:

- The phenomenology of moral life
- Sympathy, moral judgment and the impartial spectator
- Issues such as aesthetics, value, honour, resentment, praise-worthiness, cosmopolitanism and religion

Vivienne Brown is Professor Emerita of Philosophy and Intellectual History at The Open University, UK. She is the author of *Adam Smith's Discourse: Canonicity, Commerce and Conscience* and numerous articles in a range of disciplinary and interdisciplinary journals. She is the founding editor of *The Adam Smith Review*.

Samuel Fleischacker is Professor of Philosophy at the University of Illinois-Chicago, USA. He works on moral and political philosophy, and is the author of *A Third Concept of Liberty: Judgment and Freedom in Kant and Adam Smith*, and *On Adam Smith's* Wealth of Nations: *A Philosophical Companion*. From 2006 to 2010, he was President of the International Adam Smith Society.

The Adam Smith Review

Published in association with the International Adam Smith Society
Edited by Vivienne Brown
Faculty of Social Sciences, The Open University, UK

Book Reviews

Edited by Fonna Forman-Barzilai
Department of Political Science, University of California, San Diego, USA

Editorial Board

Books available in this series:

The Adam Smith Review Volume 1
Edited by Vivienne Brown
(Published in 2004)

The Adam Smith Review Volume 2
Edited by Vivienne Brown
(Published in 2006)

The Adam Smith Review Volume 3
Edited by Vivienne Brown
(Published in 2007)

The Adam Smith Review Volume 4
Edited by Vivienne Brown
(Published in 2008)

The Philosophy of Adam Smith
The Adam Smith Review, volume 5:
Essays commemorating the
250th anniversary of The Theory of
Moral Sentiments
*Edited by Vivienne Brown and
Samuel Fleischacker*
(Published in 2010)

The Philosophy of Adam Smith

The Adam Smith Review, volume 5:
Essays commemorating the
250th anniversary of
The Theory of Moral Sentiments

Edited by
Vivienne Brown and Samuel Fleischacker

Routledge
Taylor & Francis Group

LONDON AND NEW YORK

IASS

First published 2010
by Routledge
2 Park Square, Milton Park, Abingdon, Oxfordshire OX14 4RN

Simultaneously published in the USA and Canada
by Routledge
711 Third Avenue, New York, NY 10017
First issued in paperback 2014

Routledge is an imprint of the Taylor and Francis Group, an informa business

Typeset in Times New Roman by Taylor & Francis Books

British Library Cataloguing in Publication Data
A catalogue record for this book is available from the British Library

Library of Congress Cataloging in Publication Data
A catalog record has been requested for this book

ISSN: 1743–5285
ISBN 978-0-415-56256-0 (hbk)
ISBN 978-1-138-80702-0 (pbk)
ISBN 978-0-203-84618-6 (ebk)

Contents

Notes on contributors

Stephen Darwall is Andrew Downey Orrick Professor at Yale University. He has written widely on the history and foundations of ethics. His books include *The Second-Person Standpoint, Welfare and Rational Care, The British Moralists and the Internal 'Ought'*, and *Impartial Reason*. With David Velleman, he edits *The Philosophers' Imprint*.

Fonna Forman-Barzilai is Associate Professor of Political Science at the University of California, San Diego, where she teaches political theory and the history of modern thought. She is author of *Adam Smith and the Circles of Sympathy: Cosmopolitanism and Moral Theory* (2010) and is Editor of *The Adam Smith Review*, from Vol. 6.

Patrick R. Frierson is an Associate Professor of Philosophy and Garrett Fellow in the Humanities at Whitman College. Publications include *Freedom and Anthropology in Kant's Moral Philosophy* (Cambridge University Press, 2003) and numerous articles and reviews. Presently, Frierson's historical research includes a monograph on Kant's conception of the human being and another using Smith's moral philosophy to develop a new approach for environmental ethics.

Charles L. Griswold is Professor of Philosophy at Boston University. His publications include *Adam Smith and the Virtues of Enlightenment* (Cambridge University Press, 1999) and *Forgiveness: A Philosophical Exploration* (Cambridge University Press, 2007). With the support of a Fellowship from the American Council of Learned Societies, he is writing a book on Rousseau and Smith.

Ryan Patrick Hanley is Associate Professor of Political Science at Marquette University. He is the author of *Adam Smith and the Character of Virtue* (Cambridge University Press, 2009), and the editor of the 250th Anniversary Edition of *The Theory of Moral Sentiments* recently published by Penguin Classics.

Alice MacLachlan is an Assistant Professor of Philosophy at York University (Canada). Her current research topics include forgiveness, resentment and apology. She received her PhD in Philosophy from Boston University in 2008. Previously she completed her MA at Queen's University (Canada) and her BA at Cambridge University (UK).

Bence Nanay received his PhD in 2006 at the University of California, Berkeley, and he is now Assistant Professor of Philosophy and Adjunct Assistant Professor of Biology at Syracuse University. He has published mainly on philosophy of mind, philosophy of science, and aesthetics. He is the editor of *Perceiving the World* (Oxford University Press, 2010).

Angelica Nuzzo is Professor of Philosophy at the Graduate Center, CUNY and Brooklyn College. She has been Fellow at the Radcliffe Institute for Advanced Studies at Harvard (2000–01) and recipient of an Alexander von Humboldt Fellowship (2004–05). Her latest book is *Ideal Embodiment: Kant's Theory of Sensibility* (Indiana University Press, 2008).

D.D. Raphael is Emeritus Professor of Philosophy at Imperial College, London. He was much involved in the Glasgow Edition of the Works and Correspondence of Adam Smith and is joint editor of *The Theory of Moral Sentiments* (1976). His latest book, *The Impartial Spectator* (2007), is a study of Adam Smith's moral philosophy.

Ian Simpson Ross was born in Dundee, Scotland, and attended the Universities of St Andrews, Oxford and Texas. He is Professor Emeritus of English, University of British Columbia, also Fellow of the Royal Society of Canada, and has written books on Lord Kames (1972), William Dunbar (1981), and Adam Smith (1995, 1998). With E.C. Mossner, he edited Smith's *Correspondence* (2nd edn, 1987). His 2nd edn of Smith's biography is due to be published in July 2010.

Emma Rothschild is Jeremy and Jane Knowles Professor of History at Harvard, and Director of the Joint Centre for History and Economics. She is the author of *Economic Sentiments: Adam Smith, Condorcet and the Enlightenment* (2001), and *The Inner Life of Empires* (forthcoming, 2011).

Geoffrey Sayre-McCord is the Morehead Alumni Distinguished Professor of Philosophy at the University of North Carolina, where he has taught since 1985. Sayre-McCord's research interests are in metaethics, moral theory, the history of moral philosophy, and epistemology. He is the editor of *Essays on Moral Realism* (Cornell, 1989).

Arby Ted Siraki is a doctoral candidate in the Department of English at the University of Ottawa. His dissertation, entitled 'Adam Smith and the Problems of Eighteenth-Century Aesthetics', examines Adam Smith's contribution to and perspective on the aesthetic debates of his age.

Robert Urquhart teaches economics at the University of Denver. He has written on a number of figures in early political economic thought, including Steuart, Hume, Tucker and Locke, as well as Smith. He has also written a book on the concept of incommensurable choice, *Ordinary Choices: Individuals, Incommensurability, and Democracy* (2005).

Preface

The papers in this volume were presented at the conference, 'The Philosophy of Adam Smith', held at Balliol College, Oxford, 6–8 January 2009, in commemoration of the 250th anniversary of the publication of Adam Smith's *Theory of Moral Sentiments* (1759). The conference was organised jointly by *The Adam Smith Review* and the International Adam Smith Society.

Adam Smith attended Balliol College as a Snell Exhibitioner during the 1740s. Even though Smith later criticized the lack of teaching at Oxford at that time, it was a period during which his reading and private studies laid the foundations for his later work. We are grateful to Dr John Jones, Senior Fellow, and Dr Anna Sander, Lonsdale Curator, Balliol College, for compiling an exhibition on Smith's time at Oxford to mark the occasion.

We are also grateful to the reviewers who read and commented on the conferences papers. Without their invaluable work our task of selection from so many interesiting papers would have been that much harder.

We also wish to thank those whose financial support made this conference possible: the Mind Association, Routledge, the University of Illinois at Chicago (USA), and the Arts Faculty and Economics Department at The Open University (UK).

We are extremely grateful to Sally O'Brien, the conference administrator, for organising the conference so efficiently, and to the staff at Balliol College, especially Howard Chirgwin and Natalie Perry, for looking after us so well.

Vivienne Brown would like to acknowledge the following institutions for welcoming her as a Visiting Academic for the period during which she completed her editorial work on this volume: Centre for the Study of Mind in Nature, Oslo, Norway (summer term, 2009); and the Faculty of Philosophy, Oxford, UK (academic year, 2009–10).

Finally, we would like to thank all the speakers and delegates for making this conference – perhaps the largest conference on Adam Smith's philosophy thus far convened – such an interesting and enjoyable occasion.

Vivienne Brown
Samuel Fleischacker
July 2010

Introduction

Samuel Fleischacker and Vivienne Brown

I

Adam Smith published *The Theory of Moral Sentiments* (TMS) in 1759 (final, sixth edition in 1790), to great acclaim. It was translated three times into French and twice into German before the end of the century,[1] and was widely read – by Hume, Burke, Lessing, Herder, Kant and Thomas Jefferson, among others.[2] TMS was regarded for a long time as a major accomplishment in its own right, a contribution to moral philosophy of no less importance than those of Shaftesbury, Butler, Hutcheson or Hume, and it set the stage for Smith's subsequent fame – it spread his name so widely that many people were eager to read *An Inquiry into the Nature and Causes of the Wealth of Nations* (WN) when it appeared 17 years later.

Nonetheless, TMS eventually fell out of the accepted canon of great works in moral philosophy, and is today rarely taught in philosophy curricula. Exactly why that is so is a bit of a mystery. Perhaps it is seen as lacking by the standards of argumentation expected of philosophers after Kant, or perhaps it has been eclipsed by Smith's own economic masterpiece. In recent years, however, there has been a revival of interest in TMS. Smith, many now think, has an intriguing conception of sympathy, different from and perhaps superior to Hume's, and a unique view of the nature of moral judgment and conscience. Having been interpreted, along with Hume, as a proto-utilitarian, Smith is now often understood to be one of the earliest *critics* of utilitarianism. And Smith's views on justice and religion have been re-examined and held up as a nuanced alternative to those of Hume, as well as to other views of his time. This re-assessment of Smith's moral philosophy was stimulated by the publication of the scholarly edition of TMS in 1976 as part of the definitive Glasgow Edition of Smith's Works and Correspondence (1976–87), but it has been gathering momentum over the last decade or so (we list some of the contributions to this renaissance in the bibliography).

And 2009, which marks the 250th anniversary of the first publication of TMS, opened with what was probably the largest conference ever held on that book, sponsored by the International Adam Smith Society and *The Adam Smith Review*, and held in Balliol College, Oxford, where Smith himself was

The Philosophy of Adam Smith. The Adam Smith Review, 5: 1–11 © 2000 The International Adam Smith Society, ISSN 1743–5285, ISBN 978-0-415-56256-0.

a student in the 1740s. This volume comprises essays based on talks and papers presented at that conference, selected with an eye towards the range of issues of philosophical interest that may be found in TMS, and to its continuing relevance to debate over those issues today. We hope it will fan the flames of the burgeoning interest in TMS as a philosophical work, and perhaps restore the book to the place it once had, among the canonical works of moral philosophy studied in colleges and universities.

We have also included a lovely memoir of Smith by his modern biographer, Ian Simpson Ross (Ross 1995). This memoir, 'Adam Smith's smile: his years at Balliol College, 1740–46, in retrospect', was presented as an after-dinner talk at the conference, providing new insights into Smith's time at Balliol College.

In this Introduction, we summarize Smith's life and the major themes of TMS, then sketch the main lines of argument that concern our contributors.

II

Although Ross's memoir captures Smith's personality better than any summary of the events in Smith's life could do, perhaps a sketch of those events will nevertheless be useful.

Adam Smith was born into a modest family in Kirkcaldy, Scotland in 1723. He was educated at schools in Kirkcaldy, after which he attended Glasgow University where he studied under Francis Hutcheson, Professor of Moral Philosophy. Smith then went to Balliol College, Oxford, with the award of a Snell Exhibition designed for students intending ordination into the Scottish Episcopal Church – although, at least by the time he left, Smith had no interest in becoming a clergyman. Smith's stay at Oxford was an important time of private study and intellectual development, but he disliked Oxford and was critical of its slack approach to teaching. In 1746 he returned to Scotland and in 1748–51 he gave a series of lectures on rhetoric, literature, jurisprudence and the history of science at Edinburgh; on the basis of his rhetoric and literature lectures, he has been called the first professor of English. In 1751, he moved to Glasgow as Professor of Logic at the university, and in 1752 he was elected to the Chair in Moral Philosophy earlier held by his teacher Francis Hutcheson. From some of the lectures he gave in this position came his first book, *The Theory of Moral Sentiments* (1759) and the early versions of many of the ideas that went into the *Wealth of Nations*. In 1764, he left Glasgow University to serve as a tutor to the young Duke of Buccleuch, a stepson of Charles Townshend, then President of the Board of Trade. In this capacity, Smith travelled to France and Switzerland meeting many *philosophes*, including Voltaire, and others who later came to be known as Physiocrats. He returned to Britain upon the death of one of his pupils, spending almost a decade largely at home in Scotland in the preparation and writing of *An Inquiry into the Nature and Causes of the Wealth of Nations* (WN). Throughout his life, Smith participated actively in Scotland's lively intellectual circles. A particularly close friend of David Hume, he was also well acquainted with most of the other major figures in the Scottish Enlightenment, including James Boswell, the chemist Joseph Black, the historian William Robertson, and the social and political thinker Adam Ferguson. After WN's publication in 1776, Smith took up a position as a Commissioner of Customs in Edinburgh – somewhat surprisingly, given his famous opposition to tariffs – which he retained, apparently enjoying his work, until his death in 1790. He wrote to La Rochefoucauld in his later years (Smith 1987, *Corr.* Letter 248, 1 Nov. 1785) that he still had 'two other great works upon the anvil' – 'a sort of Philosophical History of all the different branches of Literature, of Philosophy, Poetry and Eloquence' and 'a sort of theory and History of Law and Government' – but he never published a book after TMS and WN, and he insisted that most of his unpublished notes be burned prior to his death. These instructions apparently did not apply to several early writings on literature and the history and philosophy of science, which were published in a small volume after his death (Smith 1980 [1795]). In the nineteenth and twentieth centuries, student notes on his lectures on law and government and his lectures on rhetoric and *belles-lettres* were discovered and published as well (Smith 1978, 1983).

Who was Adam Smith? A moral philosopher dabbling in social and economic analysis? A pioneering social scientist with a background in moral philosophy? An Enlightenment *belle-lettrist*, whose writings about both moral philosophy and economics are just parts of a larger body of work? For a long time, as we have seen, Smith's work has hovered on the margins of the philosophical canon, and while many economists claim him as the father of their discipline, few of them now actually study WN.

Smith's curiously eccentric relationship to the more technical aspects of philosophy may be at least partially explained by a central thread running through all his work: an unusually strong commitment to the soundness of the ordinary human being's judgments, and a concern to fend off attempts, by philosophers and policy-makers, to replace those judgments with the supposedly better 'systems' invented by intellectuals. In one of Smith's earliest writings, he is concerned to refute the notion that the ordinary person objectifies secondary qualities (Smith 1980: 141–2); in the 'History of Astronomy', he characterizes philosophy as a discipline that attempts to connect and regularize the data of everyday experience (Smith 1980: 44–7); in TMS, he tries to develop moral theory out of ordinary moral judgments, rather than beginning from a philosophical vantage point above or beyond those judgments; and a central polemic of WN is directed against the notion that governments need to guide the economic decisions of ordinary people. Perhaps taking a cue from Hume's scepticism about the capacity of philosophy to replace the judgments of 'common life', Smith represents one of the first modern philosophers to be suspicious of philosophy itself – at least of philosophy as conducted from a foundationalist standpoint, outside the modes of thought and practice it examines. Smith brings out the rationality already inherent in common life, mapping it from within and correcting it, where necessary, with its own tools, rather than trying either to justify or to criticize it from an external standpoint. It is consistent with this attitude that he hoped to bring philosophy, literature, and the social and natural sciences into one large whole, treating each of these disciplines as equally an outgrowth of ordinary human thought and interests. Smith's corpus aims in good part to break down distinctions between different types of theorizing, and between 'theoretical' and 'ordinary' thought. This intellectual aim is not unconnected with, and no less important than, his political interest in guaranteeing to ordinary individuals the 'natural liberty' of thought and action he believed they rightly possess.

It is also not unconnected with the growth of his philosophical reputation in recent years. As the idea that there is any single right methodology by which all philosophy should be conducted has lost its hold, and as philosophers of many sorts have taken a greater interest in working with scholars in other disciplines, the virtues of a philosopher who long ago saw his work as continuous with ordinary thought, and with the work of historians and literary theorists, shine ever more brightly.

III

We are faced with a question about what kind of work TMS is. This is not an easy question to answer. Modern conceptions of disciplinary demarcation were not well developed in the eighteenth century, and this holds true for demarcations within what is now regarded as 'philosophy'. Much of the argument in TMS concerns moral psychology and moral phenomenology, and this raises difficult issues about the relationships among the empirical, normative and meta-ethical aspects of Smith's theory. Furthermore, in view of Smith's broader intellectual interests – he was a classic Enlightenment polymath – the boundaries of the subject matter presented in TMS are perhaps wider than would be included in a philosophical treatise now. For example, Smith includes illustrations of his principles from works of literature, especially drama; he provides allusions from historical and classical sources; and he comments on current social and political developments and events. The challenge of a philosophical engagement with TMS thus involves some complex issues of genre, in addition to the difficulties of trying to understand and evaluate what Smith wrote.

The Theory of Moral Sentiments is primarily about the making of moral judgments. Smith draws on many sources – including Aristotle, a variety of Stoics, Francis Hutcheson and Bishop Butler – for elements of his views, but above all engages in a running dialogue with Hume. At the core of the book is a theory of sympathy, subtly different from Hume's, a view of moral judgment drawn from that account of sympathy, and an exploration of the importance of sympathy and the moral sentiments in society. According to Smith we sympathize with others by imagining what we would feel in their situation. When the feelings we have as a result of this process match the ones they themselves seem to be having, we approve of their feelings; otherwise we disapprove. In many cases, if not in all, this sympathetic approval and disapproval amounts to a moral judgment: we judge the feelings an agent has on taking a certain action as appropriate when we sympathize with them and as inappropriate when we do not. And since each of us seeks the sympathy of the people around us, we *want* to have the feelings they expect us to have: to live up to their standards for approval. At the same time, we know that others are often misinformed about the facts of our situations, or biased by their relationships to us or the people we are acting upon. So we construct in our imaginations an 'impartial spectator' whose sympathies set the standard for true moral approval and disapproval. Our neighbors do the same, and in this way moral standards arise. What begins as the set of interactions by which people give and seek one another's sympathy eventually leads to impartial-spectator standards for the sympathy on which proper moral judgment can be based.

Smith draws a remarkably wide range of implications from this core account. He shows how our sympathy with the intentions on which a person acts is different from our sympathy with the people affected by those actions, and thereby allows a role for consequences in moral judgment while fending off any wholesale consequentialism. He derives an entire theory of justice from our uneasy, and divided, sympathy with people moved by resentment. He includes a place for moral rules as a guide to the way we should act, in recognition of the facts that people often deceive themselves about their own feelings and are therefore led to inappropriate results if they rely on the impartial spectator process alone, and that many people are not up to the demands of engaging with the impartial spectator and so need to rely on rules in order to live decent lives.

Smith also connects his moral theory with a variety of broader issues. He remarks on the way morality can justify certain kinds of religion, although he never explicitly says that any religion is *true*. He also offers hints of an aesthetic theory, some rich political observations, and the beginnings of some thoughts about economics. Smith's emphasis on a morality of intention rather than a morality of consequences lends itself to a political view on which there is little that government can do to improve us morally; he is rightly seen as a believer in minimal government, opposed in particular to the government establishment of religion. And his conception of the goal of winning other people's approval leads him both to suggest that material goods do not matter much to happiness and to warn that social status is naturally *seen* as central to happiness: people often seek wealth instead of goodness, he says, as a way of winning approval. Smith argues that what we *really* seek (or *should* seek) is to be worthy of approval – to be praiseworthy and not just to be praised – and this leads him to reflect critically on the pursuit of social status and wealth.

The co-presence of these different elements raises questions about the nature of the philosophical argumentation of the TMS. Philosophers such as

Kant and Hegel were influenced by Smith, and modern philosophers have attempted to explicate and defend Smith's fundamental claims. But scholars of literature, economics and intellectual history have also taken a great interest in TMS, sometimes suggesting that it is misconstrued if seen as a contribution purely to philosophy.

IV

These issues of interpretation are represented in the essays in this volume, which fall, broadly, into three categories. The first category is mainly interested in Smith's moral phenomenology – his emphasis on the role moral feelings and judgments play in everyday life. Such essays accept that one of the distinctive characteristics of TMS is the social embeddedness of its account of moral judgment and its sharply drawn, astute examples of everyday moral circumstances. The second category addresses Smith's arguments by concentrating on their normative and meta-ethical aspects. This involves addressing the core philosophical 'system' of TMS and how it might be appraised or defended according to modern standards of philosophical debate. And the third category addresses some of the discrete topics to which Smith applies his core view: issues about aesthetics, religion, politics and economics, as well as morality.

To begin with the first group: In their essays, David D. Raphael and Emma Rothschild elaborate the nature and significance of Smith's skill as a moral phenomenologist. Expanding on his earlier work (Raphael 1985, 2007), Raphael argues in 'The virtue of TMS 1759', that the vivid examples with which TMS is laced explain the success of the book, adding that the fact that this stylistic feature was particularly prominent in the first edition – later editions having added material to respond to various philosophical objections Smith received from his colleagues – is a virtue of that edition that has not hitherto received enough attention. In '*The Theory of Moral Sentiments* and the inner life', Rothschild presents an almost directly opposite view: that it is the final, 1790 edition of TMS, not the first one, that is most packed with concrete examples. She argues that Smith came over time increasingly to understand his project as an attempt to illuminate our inner lives, and simultaneously to recognize that he could only do that by 'illustrations' that turn our attention to the experience of other people. Consequently, the final edition of TMS 'is very much more full of people and events' than the 1759 edition (p. 28): Smith's revisions to the book consist largely, by his own account, in expanding its use of concrete examples. Rothschild suggests that this great attention to concrete cases brings Smith's work closer to that of an historian than are the writings of most philosophers, but notes also that the historical dimension of Smith's account of morality makes it susceptible to the charge of relativism.

The philosopher best known for integrating philosophy with history – for arguing that all ideas develop out of, and must be understood as responses to, particular historical contexts – is of course Hegel, and Angelica Nuzzo's contribution to this volume argues for Smith's kinship with and influence on Hegel. To make this argument, Nuzzo emphasizes Smith's interest in concrete illustrations in much the way that Raphael and Rothschild do. In 'The standpoint of morality in Adam Smith and Hegel', Nuzzo argues that Hegel, who explicitly cites Smith's *Wealth of Nations* in his *Philosophy of Right*, implicitly also indicates there that TMS is the proper philosophy of what he calls the sphere of 'civil society': the realm in which morality, abjuring the purely abstract form that it has for Kant, comes to embrace the social practices around it and work through them. For Nuzzo, Hegel was accordingly attracted to precisely what is *unsystematic* – concrete, and socially and historically located – in Smith's account of morality.

The second group of essays engages with issues pertaining to the core normative and meta-ethical arguments of TMS. Two areas of debate are particularly important:

1 *Sympathy*: Given that Smithian sympathy depends more on the workings of our own imaginations than on information we get from the people with whom we sympathize, can we really share feelings with other people?
2 *Moral judgment*: To what extent do our judgments reflect the judgments of actual spectators around us rather than the judgment of the impartial spectator? (Do we seek praise or praiseworthiness?) Are such judgments relativistic or absolute? How does Smith's account allow us to condemn slavery or infanticide if our society does not – how does it even make sense of the idea that this could be the right view to hold?

Charles L. Griswold focuses on the first of these issues in 'Smith and Rousseau in dialogue: sympathy, *pitié*, spectatorship and narrative'. Known widely for his warm and thorough defence of Smith (Griswold 1999), Griswold here raises some Rousseauan questions about the intelligibility of the distinctive notion of sympathy on which Smith rests so much. Can we really enter into the feelings of people very different from ourselves – a man sympathizing with a woman in childbirth, to take one of Smith's own examples – or do we always remain more locked up in ourselves than Smith wants to admit? Griswold pits Smith against Rousseau, who had lesser hopes for our ability to sympathize, and raises the question whether Rousseau's view was more plausible.

These claims are implicitly disputed by Bence Nanay who urges us not to ask of Smithian sympathy that it carry out tasks for which it was never designed. In 'Adam Smith's concept of sympathy and its contemporary interpretations', Nanay situates what Smith calls 'sympathy' in the context of modern philosophical debates over the nature of sympathy and empathy, arguing that we misconstrue the Smithian notion if we read too much of our contemporary concerns back into that idea. He proposes that Smithian sympathy is best construed as a *proto*-sympathetic state, on which full-blown accounts of sympathy and empathy can be built.

Other authors take up the second issue, about moral judgment. The question of whether people pursue praiseworthiness as well as praise – and of what praise-worthiness consists in – comes up repeatedly. Stephen Darwall and Geoffrey Sayre-McCord address this theme directly. Darwall has long argued that a notion of equal dignity plays a foundational role in Smith's ethics (for example, Darwall 2006), but in 'Smith's ambivalence about honour' he takes up a competing conception of 'honour', with historical roots in the feudal world Smith was trying to leave behind, that he thinks has a lingering place in Smith's writings. The desire for praiseworthiness leads us to care about equal human dignity, but the desire for praise grounds a hierarchical honour code. Smith recognizes the dangers of the latter but is unable fully to free his account from its influence: Darwall shows how a tension between an honour-based and a properly moral notion of respect shapes, especially, Smith's view of resentment.

Sayre-McCord wrestles with the general problem of how, on Smith's account, we can ever transcend the influence of the 'irregular' factors – which include but are not limited to the influence of customary notions that Darwall discusses – that go to shape our conception of praiseworthiness. In 'Sentiments and spectators: Adam Smith's theory of moral judgment', he traces the many ways in which Smith's impartial spectator is not, and seems not meant to be, an ideal figure, like Roderick Firth's 'ideal observer' (Firth 1952). At the same time, he argues, Smith does not intend for us to correct for the failings of the impartial spectator by appeal to some more basic principle of moral judgment, like the principle of utility. For Smith, the impartial spectator is more fundamental to moral judgment than any such principle. How, then, do we correct for its limitations? By turning it on itself, Sayre-McCord suggests: by using the idea of being an impartial spectator, on a higher level, to correct for the actual impartial spectator we use in daily life. Drawing on Smith's claim, against Hutcheson, that any moral sense we have must be itself subject to moral scrutiny, Sayre-McCord maintains that for Smith the standards of judgment that we actually happen to accept at any one time can always be assessed for their adequacy at a higher level. Sayre-McCord sees this recognition of the essential corrigibility of moral notions as a great insight, which allows Smithian moral judgment to transcend the social circumstances that originally give rise to it.

But not everyone considers the cultural and historical situatedness of Smithian moral judgments to be a problem. Fonna Forman-Barzilai, in 'Smith's anti-cosmopolitanism', finds social and political advantages in the fact that Smith does *not* focus just on the nature we share with all other human beings, instead recognizing the importance to us of our historical context. In urging us to be concerned above all with the duties we owe to people in our local communities, rather than our relationship to human beings in all places and times, Forman-Barzilai suggests, Smith sets more realistic expectations for us than do many contemporary political theorists, who suppose too readily that we all can, because we all should, become cosmopolitans.

Alice MacLachlan takes up one of the same topics that Darwall addresses: Smith's account of resentment. In 'Resentment and moral judgment in Smith and Butler', she agrees that there is a sharp tension in that account, although she describes it rather differently than Darwall, correlates it with Smith's different treatments of resentment in Parts I and II of TMS, and argues that it derives from the internal logic of resentment itself. She also shows how Smith's view of resentment both echoes and adds to the important insights of Joseph Butler, in his sermons on resentment, earlier in the eighteenth century.

The third group of essays focuses on particular aspects of TMS, rather than its overall view. Two long-standing questions about TMS concern its relationship to WN (the so-called 'Adam Smith Problem' posited an inconsistency between the two books) and whether Smith was a religious sceptic or believer. Robert Urquhart addresses the first of these questions in 'Adam Smith's problems: individuality and the paradox of sympathy', but offers a new twist on it. He sees a tension between a socially oriented and an individualistic strand in Smith, and a corresponding influence from Aristotle on the one hand and the Stoics on the other, that can be found in TMS itself as well as between TMS and WN. Ryan Patrick Hanley revisits the question of whether Smith was a believer or a sceptic about religion, and gives a novel answer to it in 'Scepticism and naturalism in Adam Smith'. Using Hume's notion of 'natural belief', Hanley forges a 'third way' between attributing either radical religious scepticism or theism to Smith. In 'Adam Smith's solution to the paradox of tragedy', Arby Ted Siraki finds an answer in Smith's account of sympathy to the 'paradox of tragedy' – the question of why we take pleasure, at the theatre, in other people's pain – that haunted much other writing on aesthetics in the Scottish eighteenth century. In the course of doing this, Siraki contributes to the still rather sparse literature on Smith's aesthetics.

Patrick Frierson applies elements of Smith's moral system to contemporary discussions of intrinsic value, showing how Smith can improve on the more common Kantian and Moorean approaches to this topic. Smith enables us to locate a middle ground between subjectivist and objectivist accounts of intrinsic value, Frierson argues in 'Smithian intrinsic value', while allowing for a greater range of ways in which such value can be relevant to our lives than do otherwise similar views among contemporary philosophers.

Frierson and Siraki illustrate the degree to which the central insights of TMS can shed light on an array of issues that continue to be debated among philosophers. Urquhart and Hanley bring out the subtlety of TMS, the fact that it contains a rich array of resources for responding to many of the criticisms made of it.

V

What unites all the essays in this collection is a commitment to working out carefully the structure of Smith's arguments. Many of our contributors – Darwall, Sayre-McCord, Siraki and MacLachlan, especially – find an argument implicit in various passages of Smith which they then try to make explicit for him. Others – Hanley and Urquhart come to mind – bring together what Smith's view may have been from remarks in various places in TMS, or Smith's other writings. This kind of work helps bring out the overall shape of Smith's views; Smith himself often gives telling illustrations of his points rather than laying out their structure systematically. And some of our contributors delight precisely in the fact that Smith's views resist strict systematization: that seems to be part of what Raphael, Rothschild, Nuzzo and Forman-Barzilai find to praise in TMS.

Whatever their view of Smith's methods, all the contributors bring out the continuing life of Smith's insights and arguments. Descartes and Locke and Hume and Kant continue to be *used* by philosophers, not just studied for their historical relevance. Smith's philosophy, by contrast, has been studied largely from an historical perspective. Scholars in intellectual and social history, political theory and literature have brought out the role that Smith's ideas in TMS have played in the history of civic republicanism, the birth of the social sciences, and the secularization of the modern world, but increasingly scholars from a range of fields in the humanities and social sciences also now recognize the current relevance of TMS. The editors of this collection see this also beginning to happen in philosophical work on TMS. Something is surely missing from the legacy of a philosopher if he or she is not treated *as* a philosopher – someone whose ideas remain relevant to those who reflect on moral or metaphysical or epistemological questions today. One way of honouring Smith's TMS, 250 years after it was written, is to treat it as a set of arguments that still invite philosophical engagement. The essays in this volume, we believe, do just that.

Notes

1 Tribe (2002) provides the definitive bibliography of Adam Smith.
2 See Raphael and Macfie (1976), Introduction to the Glasgow edition of TMS, pp. 25–33, for a summary of the reception of TMS. Smith's influence on Kant is summarized in Fleischacker (1991). For Jefferson's interest in the book, see his letter to Robert Skipwith of 3 August 1771 (Boyd 1950, 1: 79).

Bibliography

Boyd, J., Bryan, M.R. and Butterfield, L.H. (eds) (1950) *The Papers of Thomas Jefferson*, 28 vols, Princeton, NJ: Princeton University Press.
Brown, V. (1994) *Adam Smith's Discourse: Canonicity, Commerce and Conscience*, London and New York: Routledge.
Darwall, S. (2006) *The Second-Person Standpoint: Morality, Respect, and Accountability*, Cambridge, MA: Harvard University Press.
Firth, R. (1952) 'Ethical absolutism and the ideal observer', *Philosophy and Phenomenological Research*, 12: 317–45.
Fleischacker, S. (1991) 'Philosophy in moral practice: Kant and Adam Smith', *Kant-Studien*, 82: 249–69.

—— (1999) *A Third Concept of Liberty: Judgment and Freedom in Kant and Adam Smith*, Princeton, NJ: Princeton University Press.

—— (2004) *On Adam Smith's* Wealth of Nations*: A Philosophical Companion*, Princeton, NJ: Princeton University Press.

Fricke, C. and Schütt, H.-P. (eds) (2005) *Adam Smith als Moralphilosoph*, Berlin: de Gruyter.

Griswold, C.L. (1999) *Adam Smith and the Virtues of Enlightenment*, Cambridge: Cambridge University Press.

Haakonssen, K. (1981) *The Science of a Legislator: The Natural Jurisprudence of David Hume and Adam Smith*, Cambridge: Cambridge University Press.

Hanley, R.P. (2009) *Adam Smith and the Character of Virtue*, Cambridge: Cambridge University Press.

Montes, L. (2004) *Adam Smith in Context: A Critical Reassessment of Some Central Components of His Thought*, Basingstoke: Palgrave Macmillan.

Montes, L. and Schliesser, E. (eds) (2006) *New Voices on Adam Smith*, London and New York: Routledge.

Otteson, J.R. (2002) *Adam Smith's Marketplace of Life*, Cambridge: Cambridge University Press.

Raphael, D.D. (1985) *Adam Smith*, Oxford: Oxford University Press.

—— (2007) *The Impartial Spectator: Adam Smith's Moral Philosophy*, Oxford: Oxford University Press.

Raphael, D.D. and Macfie, A.L. (1976) Introduction to Adam Smith, *The Theory of Moral Sentiments*, Oxford: Clarendon Press.

Ross, I.S. (1995) *The Life of Adam Smith*, Oxford: Clarendon Press.

Smith, A. (1976–87) *The Glasgow Edition of the Works and Correspondence of Adam Smith*, 6 vols, Oxford: Clarendon Press.

—— (1976 [1759]) *The Theory of Moral Sentiments*, D.D. Raphael and A.L. Macfie (eds), Oxford: Clarendon Press; vol. I of the The Glasgow Edition. Liberty Press imprint, 1982.

—— (1978) *Lectures on Jurisprudence*, A.L. Meek, D.D. Raphael and P.G. Stein (eds), Oxford: Clarendon Press; vol. V of The Glasgow Edition. Liberty Press imprint, 1982.

—— (1980) *Essays on Philosophical Subjects*, W.P.D. Wightman and J.C. Bryce (eds), D.D. Raphael and A.S. Skinner (gen. eds), Oxford: Clarendon Press; vol. III of The Glasgow Edition. Liberty Press imprint, 1982.

—— (1983) *Lectures on Rhetoric and Belles Lettres*, J.C. Bryce (ed.), Oxford: Clarendon Press; vol. IV of The Glasgow Edition. Liberty Press imprint, 1985.

—— (1987) *Correspondence of Adam Smith*, E.C. Mossner and I. S. Ross (eds), 2nd edn, Oxford: Clarendon Press; vol. VI of The Glasgow Edition. Liberty Press imprint, 1987.

Tribe, K. (gen. ed.) (2002) *A Critical Bibliography of Adam Smith*, H. Mizuta (advisory ed.), London: Pickering & Chatto.

Vivenza, G. (2001) *Adam Smith and the Classics*, Oxford: Oxford University Press.

Part I
Moral phenomenology

The virtue of TMS 1759

D.D. Raphael

Our conference is intended to commemorate the publication of the first edition of *The Theory of Moral Sentiments* in 1759 (Smith 1976, TMS). I have therefore focused my contribution mainly on that edition.

To speak of the virtue of TMS 1759 is, in a way, paradoxical, for the most substantial change that Adam Smith made in the sixth edition was to add a new Part VI on 'The Character of Virtue'. Earlier editions include a distinction between 'amiable and respectable virtues', an extensive discussion of two particular virtues, justice and beneficence, and an historical survey of philosophical theories about the nature of virtue in general; but there is no detailed account of Smith's own view of the general concept of virtue. That comes only in the sixth edition.

The first edition has a further defect, concerning sympathy. Smith deals with this in a long note added to the second edition, answering critical queries posed by David Hume and Sir Gilbert Elliot. Their queries are not so closely related as Smith seems to think. Hume's point is that Smith's theory depends on the false supposition that sympathy is always pleasant; Elliot's concern is that basing moral judgment on social attitudes does not allow for conscientious dissent from majority opinion. Hume's criticism is given in a letter dated 28 July 1759, asking Smith to deal with it in his projected second edition (Smith 1987, *Corr.* Letter 36). Elliot's criticism was given in a letter that has not survived, but the gist of it can be inferred from Smith's reply, dated 10 October 1759, which is accompanied by a copy of the statement that he had sent to Hume (*Corr.* Letter 40). That statement, with some minor adjustment, also formed the note added to the second edition of the book, published in 1761.

When Smith reports Hume's criticism in the second edition, he purports to defend his original view, but his defence includes an addition that goes beyond the original view. The original view described two elements in moral approval: (1) sympathy with the feeling of the person affected by an action, and (2) a consequential feeling of approval or disapproval of the action. (In some places Smith says, confusingly, that the apparent two elements are simply different descriptions of a single element.) The defence in the note of the second edition speaks of three elements: (1) sympathy with the feeling of

The Philosophy of Adam Smith, The Adam Smith Review, 5: 15–24 © 2010 The International Adam Smith Society, ISSN 1743–5285, ISBN 978-0-415-56256-0.

the person affected, a sympathy that can be pleasurable or painful, depending on the character of the feeling shared; (2) awareness of that sympathy; and (3) a feeling of approval or disapproval, which includes the pleasure of knowing it is a shared feeling.

Since the first edition contains two serious defects, why am I ready to speak of its virtue? Because of two commendable qualities. One is the character of its language, relatively simple and at times strikingly vivid, so that the book is a pleasure to read and can be easily understood. The other commendable quality is that the role given to sympathy is distinctly original and quite persuasive. These are the things that made the book popular among the literary public at its first appearance.

I have in the past suggested that Smith wrote the new Part VI because he realized that he had failed to live up to his statement, in the final Part, that there are two main topics for moral philosophy, the nature of virtue and the nature of moral judgment (Raphael 1992: 103, 109; 2007: 10–11). In the original version of his book he deals at length with the second topic but says comparatively little about the first topic. He distinguishes virtue from propriety, classifies virtues into the amiable and the respectable, and gives careful consideration to the leading virtues of justice and beneficence; but he does not produce a theory about the concept of virtue as such, comparable with his elaborate theory about the origin and character of moral judgment.

Professor Samuel Fleischacker has expressed dissent from my suggestion that Smith wrote the new Part VI to repair an omission which he recognized late in the day (Fleischacker 2006: 249). Fleischacker queries this because the final Part of the *Moral Sentiments*, in the early editions as well as in the sixth, gives far more space to the topic of virtue than to the topic of moral judgment. Fleischacker says there are 50 pages on virtue and 13 on moral judgment. His figures presumably relate to the pages of the modern Glasgow Edition (Part VII, Sections ii and iii). In the actual first edition of 1759 (Part VI, Sections 2 and 3) there are 74 pages on virtue and 31 pages on moral judgment. The apparently greater difference in the modern edition (roughly 4:1 as against 2.5:1 in the first edition) is due to some long editorial notes, but that does not affect the nub of Fleischacker's case.

What needs to be said, however, is that the final Part of the *Moral Sentiments* surveys the *history* of the philosophic treatment of the two topics. It is not written as a statement of Adam Smith's views. In the sixth edition Smith allies himself with the propriety theory of virtue and claims to improve on predecessors in giving a measure for judging the propriety of feeling, namely 'the sympathetic feelings of the impartial and well-informed spectator' (TMS VII.ii.1.49). But he also, in all editions, regards the propriety theory as inadequate because virtue is often more than propriety and commands greater esteem than propriety taken alone (TMS VII.ii.1.50). A little later in the final Part Smith refers to the difference between his theory of virtue and Hume's theory, which, he says, 'coincides' with the propriety theory. He writes:

> According to this [ie. Hume's] system ... virtue consists not in any one affection, but in the proper degree of all the affections. The only difference between it and that which I have been endeavouring to establish, is, that it makes utility, and not sympathy, or the correspondent affection of the spectator, the natural and original measure of this proper degree.
> (TMS VII.ii.3.21)

Smith plainly thinks that his own view of virtue is to be found in earlier Parts of the book, not in the final Part.

The title page of the book in the first three editions names the book simply as 'The Theory of Moral Sentiments', but the fourth edition (followed by the fifth and sixth) supplements this with a long alternative, describing the subject-matter: 'The Theory of Moral Sentiments, or an Essay towards an Analysis of the Principles by which Men naturally judge concerning the Conduct and Character, first of their Neighbours, and afterwards of themselves'. The long addition says explicitly that the book is about *judgment*. So I stick to my view that in the original version of the book Smith does not live up to his thesis in the final Part that there are two main topics for moral philosophy, the nature of moral judgment and the nature of virtue. I think that my view receives some support from the very title of the new Part added to the sixth edition, 'Of the Character of Virtue'.

In Smith's correspondence with his publisher Thomas Cadell about a possible sixth edition there is no mention of this substantial addition until 31 March 1789. A letter of 21 April 1785 is primarily concerned with the possibility of a new edition of the *Wealth of Nations*, but Smith added a sentence about the *Moral Sentiments*: 'If a new edition of the theory is wanted I have a few alterations to make of no great consequence which I shall send to you' (*Corr.* Letter 244, p. 281). He returned to the subject on 14 March 1786 in a letter, only an extract of which survives. It is concerned with the period of copyright available at that time: 'I should be glad to know in what degree of demand the theory of Moral Sentiments still continues to be. The eight and twenty years property are now near expired. But I hope to be able to secure you in the property for at least fourteen years more ... ' (*Corr.* Letter 257, p. 293).

These letters clearly imply that a new edition would not contain anything very substantial in the way of additional material. Unlike them, Smith's next letter on the matter, dated 15 March 1788, does speak of substantial addition, but not of a whole new Part:

> ... I am at present giving the most intense application. My subject is *the theory of moral Sentiments* to all parts of which I am making many additions and corrections. The chief and the most important additions

will be to the third part, that concerning *the sense of Duty* and to the last part concerning *the History of moral Philosophy*.

(Corr. Letter 276, pp. 310–11)

Only after a further year, on 31 March 1789, do we hear anything of the new Part on the character of virtue.

> Ever since I wrote to you last I have been labouring very hard in preparing the proposed new edition of the Theory of Moral Sentiments. ... Besides the Additions and improvements I mentioned to you; I have inserted, immediately after the fifth part, a compleat new sixth part containing a practical system of Morality, under the title of the Character of Virtue.
>
> *(Corr.* Letter 287, pp. 319–20)

It seems that the idea of this further, and even more substantial, addition came to Smith in the course of making the changes described in the letter of 1788. There he had said that his corrections and additions would affect his discussion of the history of moral philosophy. I think that his attention to this final Part of the book is probably what led him to see that he had written there of two main topics and that he had not dealt adequately with the second of them.

A delightful letter from Hume, dated 12 April 1759, tells Smith of the immediate success of the first edition of the *Moral Sentiments*:

> Supposing, therefore, that you have duely prepared yourself for the worst by all these Reflections; I proceed to tell you the melancholy News, that your Book has been very unfortunate: For the Public seem disposd to applaud it extremely. It was lookd for by the foolish People with some Impatience; and the Mob of Literati are beginning already to be very loud in its Praises. Three Bishops calld yesterday at Miller's Shop in order to buy Copies, and to ask Questions about the Author: The Bishop of Peterborough said he had passed the Evening in a Company, where he heard it extolld above all Books in the World. You may conclude what Opinion true Philosophers will entertain of it, when these Retainers to Superstition praise it so highly. ... Millar exults and brags that two thirds of the Edition are already sold, and that he is now sure of Success. You see what a Son of the Earth that is, to value Books only by the Profit they bring him. In that View, I believe it may prove a very good Book.
>
> *(Corr.* Letter 31, p. 35)

Hume is, of course, being ironic when he says that true philosophers will take a very different view from bishops and that the book will prove to be very good (only) in being profitable to the publisher. Yet I think he makes these ironic remarks with tongue in cheek; that is to say, he himself does not have a particularly high opinion of the *Moral Sentiments*. Why do I think that? Well, compare the beginning of this letter with the beginning of Hume's letter on receiving a copy of the *Wealth of Nations*. The letter on the *Moral Sentiments* begins: 'Dear Smith, I give you thanks for the agreeable Present of your Theory'. That is all, quite simple. The letter on the *Wealth of Nations* begins at much greater length:

> Euge! Belle! Dear Mr Smith: I am much pleas'd with your Performance, and the Perusal of it has taken me from a State of great Anxiety. ... I shall still doubt for some time of its being at first very popular: But it has Depth and Solidity and Acuteness, and is so much illustrated by curious Facts, that it must at last take the public Attention.
>
> (*Corr.* Letter 150, p. 186)

What a difference. The initial words of the *Wealth of Nations* letter are worth some attention. The first word is Greek, the second Latin. They illustrate the familiarity of educated men of the eighteenth century with the classical languages, but they do a little more than that. The word 'euge' is not easily found in the most prominent works of ancient Greece: 'eu', meaning well, is very common, but not together with the enclitic 'ge', added for emphasis. The word 'belle' is familiar to us as the feminine of 'beau' in modern French, but in classical Latin it is the adverbial form of the adjective 'bellus', which can mean beautiful but is more commonly a synonym of 'bonus'. So Hume's opening words mean something like 'Well done! Splendid!', with the extravagance of his feelings discreetly veiled in the words of dead languages known to both of them.

It is not really surprising that Hume should be impressed by the *Wealth of Nations* but not by the *Moral Sentiments*. He himself had written both about ethics and about economics. On ethics he took particular pride in his *Enquiry concerning the Principles of Morals*, which he described in *My Own Life* as being, in his opinion, 'of all my writings, ... incomparably the best' (Hume 1778 [1776], para. 10). This is primarily a literary judgment: Hume cannot have thought that the *Enquiry concerning Morals*, as a contribution to knowledge, was superior to the *Treatise of Human Nature* or, for that matter, to his *History of England*. Still, the judgment must to some extent refer also to the content of the *Enquiry*. So Hume had no reason to think that Smith's book on ethics was especially notable. Indeed he might well have thought that Smith's reliance on sympathy as the key concept for ethics was less helpful than his own view of the role of sympathy. In Hume's ethical theory the moral judgment of a spectator of an action arises from sympathy with the happiness or unhappiness that the action causes. Smith's theory, by contrast, makes the spectator's judgment depend on sympathy with the agent's motive. Hume's view has more point.

On economics, however, comparison between the two thinkers presents a different picture. Hume had written essays on economic topics but had not produced a major theory about economic action in general. Nor had anyone else. The *Wealth of Nations* was truly revolutionary and Hume pays tribute to that quality in his letter.

On ethics Hume thought that he himself had done pretty well and so his praise of the *Moral Sentiments* is restrained. Indeed the specific merit of that book is not immediately apparent. When I first read it, as one of Selby-Bigge's British Moralists, I was not greatly impressed, as I was by Richard Price and by Hume himself. It was only much later, after having spent many days on editing and thinking about the *Moral Sentiments*, that I came to appreciate its worth as a signal contribution to ethics.

I doubt if the praise of the book by the bishops was due to an appreciation of its philosophical merit. It is more likely that they were pleased by its handling of conventional moral thought in clear language and by its acceptance of Christian theology. Likewise, when Hume's inamorata, Madame de Boufflers, said that she would have liked to translate Smith's *Theory of Moral Sentiments* into French because 'il a des idées si justes de la sympathie' (cited in Minto 1868: 13), she probably had little idea of the main role of sympathy in the work. She was no doubt impressed by the colourful examples of sympathy portrayed in the first chapter of the book, and she evidently did read the whole of it; but it is most unlikely that she saw the novelty of Smith's use of the concept of sympathy in his theory.

A reader who certainly did appreciate the originality of Smith's theory was Edmund Burke. He was well placed to form a judgment since he had published, a couple of years earlier, a philosophical discussion of the distinction between the sublime and the beautiful. Indeed that was the reason why Hume had sent him a copy of Smith's book: in his letter to Smith of 12 April 1759, Hume says he has sent copies to five people, including 'Burke, an Irish Gentleman, who wrote lately a very pretty Treatise on the Sublime'. (The word 'pretty', at that time, was a wider term of admiration than it is today.) Burke gave a detailed opinion of the work in a letter to Smith and also in a review which he included in the first issue of his *Annual Register* (1759). As might be expected from a writer on aesthetics, Burke took account of the style as well as the substance. In the letter he says:

> I am not only pleased with the ingenuity of your Theory: I am convinced of its solidity and Truth; ... I am particularly pleased with those easy and happy illustrations from common Life and manners in which your work abounds more than any other that I know ... Besides so much powerful reasoning as your Book contains, there is so much elegant Painting of the manners and passions, that it is highly valuable even on that account.

> (*Corr.* Letter 38, pp. 46–7)

The *Annual Register* review likewise compares the work to painting. It describes the book as 'one of the most beautiful fabrics of moral theory, that has perhaps ever appeared. ... His language is easy and spirited, ... it is rather painting than writing' (Burke 1759: 485).

The 'elegant painting' of which Burke writes is indeed part of the virtue of the first edition of the *Moral Sentiments*. An early example comes in Smith's illustrations of sympathy:

> When we see a stroke aimed and just ready to fall upon the leg or arm of another person, we naturally shrink and draw back our own leg or our own arm; and when it does fall, we feel it in some measure, and are hurt by it as well as the sufferer. The mob, when they are gazing at a dancer on the slack rope, naturally writhe and twist and balance their own bodies, as they see him do, and as they feel that they themselves must do in his situation.
>
> (TMS I.i.1.3)

Another striking example is the picture of envy felt by the ambitious son of a poor man:

> The poor man's son, whom heaven in its anger has visited with ambition, when he begins to look around him admires the condition of the rich. He finds the cottage of his father too small for his accommodation, and fancies he should be lodged more at his ease in a palace. He is displeased with being obliged to walk a-foot, or to endure the fatigue of riding on horseback. He sees his superiors carried about in machines, and imagines that in one of these he could travel with less inconveniency.
>
> (TMS IV.1.8; punctuation as in 1st edn)

Burke's record of his opinion in his letter to Smith has the further merit of adding a note of criticism to his words of praise:

> I have mentioned something of what affected me as Beauties in your work. I will take the Liberty to mention too what appeared to me as a sort of Fault. You are in some few Places, what Mr Locke is in most of his writings, rather a little too diffuse. This is however a fault of the generous kind, and infinitely preferable to the dry sterile manner, which those of dull imaginations are apt to fall into.
>
> (*Corr.* Letter 38, p. 47)

Burke is not the only person to describe Smith's work as 'diffuse'. J.R. McCulloch wrote a *Sketch of the Life and Writings of Adam Smith* and then used it as a prefix to his edition of the *Wealth of Nations*. John Rae, in his *Life of Adam Smith*, reports a conversation in which McCulloch spoke of Smith's composition of his two books:

> One of the party said the habit of dictating always bred a diffuse style, and McCulloch supported this view by the example of Adam Smith,

whose *Wealth of nations*, he said, was very diffuse because it had been dictated, while his *Theory*, which was not dictated, was admirable in style. But in reality there is probably more diffuse writing in the *Theory* than in the *Wealth of Nations*, which is for the most part packed tightly enough.

(Rae 1895: 260–1)

I take the word 'diffuse' in these comments to mean long-winded, using more words than are necessary to express one's thought: that at any rate is implied by Rae's contrast with being 'packed tightly'. For my own part I find Part VI of the *Moral Sentiments*, written long after the *Wealth of Nations*, more long-winded than the rest of the book, most of which was in the first edition.

The first edition of *The Theory of Moral Sentiments* represents part, not the whole, of Adam Smith's lectures as Professor of Moral Philosophy. Nowadays the term 'moral philosophy' tends to be used as a synonym for ethical theory, but in the Scottish universities of the eighteenth century it had a wider meaning, as did the term 'logic'. The Professor of Logic at Glasgow University taught not only formal logic but also the theory of knowledge and metaphysics, while the Professor of Moral Philosophy taught natural theology, ethical theory and 'jurisprudence', the latter term covering the general principles of law, politics and economics.

The original version of the *Moral Sentiments* is not a transcript of the second part of Smith's lectures, but there is plenty of evidence that it is built upon a text of the lectures. Apart from the testimony of two contemporaries at Glasgow University, John Millar and James Wodrow, the book itself in a couple of places contains phrases that must hail from a lecturer: 'it has been observed on a former occasion', 'the propriety of humanity and justice has been explained upon a former occasion', 'as I have observed upon a former occasion', 'which I have explained upon a former occasion' (TMS IV.2.7, 9; VII.iii.1.2 (two instances)). There is also a manuscript fragment of part of a lecture on justice, written by an amanuensis but with a few corrections in the hand of Adam Smith himself (as can be confirmed by comparison with manuscript letters). These corrections attest to the authenticity of the fragment as the work of Smith. It corresponds pretty closely to passages in the *Moral Sentiments*, though the book version alters the order of topics and expands some of the exposition, while continuing to use much of the original wording (TMS Appendix II; reprinted from Raphael 1969).

If, as I have suggested, the new Part VI was intended to repair a deficiency, providing a theory of virtue to match the theory of moral judgment, it is not altogether successful. The theory of moral judgment is an elaborate hypothesis, in terms of psychology, of the origin and development of moral judgment. It begins with the reaction of a spectator observing a beneficial or harmful action and reflecting upon its motive. He imagines what his own motive and action would be if he were in the same sort of situation, and expresses his conclusion with a feeling of approval or disapproval. That enables him to judge, favourably or unfavourably, the actions of other people. He does this in the role of a spectator and knows that he himself can be judged by others as spectators of his conduct. He can then exercise his imagination still further by supposing himself to be the spectator of his own actions, and can thus form disinterested judgments about his own past or contemplated conduct. The theory depends upon the use of the imagination and the concept of sympathy in the sense of having the same sort of feelings that one finds manifested in the language and behaviour of other people.

Part VI does not provide a comparable theory of virtue. It certainly elaborates Smith's account of prominent individual virtues, prudence, beneficence (or benevolence), and especially self-command, but not the general concept of virtue. That is to say, it lays out the principal content of virtue[1] but not a theory of its psychological foundation and development. However, since Smith turned his thoughts to this topic so much later than to moral judgment, he may not have had in mind the same sort of account. Part VI does give a touch of a different sort of unifying theory in claiming that self-command adds a lustre to all the virtues.

I return to TMS 1759. It presents the gist of part of Smith's lectures on moral philosophy. The lectures began with a discussion of natural theology as the foundation of ethics, then proceeded to ethics itself, and ended up with 'jurisprudence', which was taken to include economic theory. TMS is a polished version of the second part of the lectures. Comparison of the surviving fragment of the lecture on justice with the treatment of justice in TMS suggests that the book builds upon the lectures but rearranges the order of topics and extends the content of the subject-matter.

A similar conclusion, not surprisingly, can be drawn about the relation between Smith's lectures on economics, as presented in the student reports of those lectures, and the published version of the same topics in the *Wealth of Nations*. It is to be expected that the book in this instance would go well beyond the Glasgow lectures, because it was bound to take in the effect of Smith's encounter with the French *économistes* and his reading of further source material during his retirement in Kirkcaldy. The longer of the two student reports is of special interest because it is virtually verbatim and so enables us to make a detailed comparison between Smith's thought on economics in 1762–3 and in 1776.

The publication of Smith's ethical thought in 1759 suggests that he thought he had reached finality on that topic. His students could read the book, with little to be added in lectures, which henceforth could concentrate on jurisprudence and economics.

Note

1 It does not include justice, either because justice had already been described at some length in the original version of the book (TMS II.ii.1–2) or because justice

will have been given especial treatment in the manuscript of the 'theory and History of Law and Government' (*Corr.* Letter 248, p. 287) destroyed along with others at Smith's dying request.

Bibliography

Burke, E. (1759) Review of A. Smith, *The Theory of Moral Sentiments, Annual Register*, pp. 484–9.

Fleischacker, S. (2006) '*On Adam Smith's* Wealth of Nations: response', *The Adam Smith Review*, 2: 246–58, V. Brown (ed.), London and New York: Routledge.

Hume, D. (1778 [1776]) 'My Own Life', in *The History of England, from the Invasion of Julius Caesar to the Revolution in 1688*, vol. I, London.

Minto, Countess of (1868) *A Memoir of the Right Honourable Hugh Elliot*, Edinburgh: Edmonston and Douglas.

Rae, J. (1895) *Life of Adam Smith*, London: Macmillan.

Raphael, D.D. (1969) 'Adam Smith and "the infection of David Hume's society"', *Journal of the History of Ideas*, 30: 225–48.

—— (1992) 'Adam Smith 1790: the man recalled; the philosopher revived', in P. Jones and A.S. Skinner (eds), *Adam Smith Reviewed*, Edinburgh: Edinburgh University Press.

—— (2007) *The Impartial Spectator*, Oxford: Oxford University Press.

Smith, A. (1976) *The Theory of Moral Sentiments*, D.D. Raphael and A.L. Macfie (eds), vol. I of The Glasgow Edition of the Works and Correspondence of Adam Smith; Oxford: Clarendon Press, corrected reprint, 1991.

—— (1987) *The Correspondence of Adam Smith*, E.C. Mossner and I.S. Ross (eds), vol. VI of The Glasgow Edition of the Works and Correspondence of Adam Smith; Oxford: Clarendon Press, corrected 2nd edn, 1987 (1st edn, 1977).

The Theory of Moral Sentiments and the inner life

Emma Rothschild

The Theory of Moral Sentiments has had a long and involuted history, over the two hundred and fifty years since its first publication in 1759. I would like to suggest that it is also an historical work, in three different senses: first, as a work which depends, to an extent which increased over the successive editions, on historical illustrations; second, as a work in which historical information is of importance to moral judgments; and third, as a work which is suggestive, or inspiring, for historical scholarship.

The celebration of *The Theory of Moral Sentiments* at the University of Oxford is itself odd, and even eery, from the historical perspective of Smith's own life. Smith encouraged his readers to sympathize with the dead, and there is no evidence that he changed the dismal view of Oxford that he expressed to his family at the age of seventeen, reiterated in the *Wealth of Nations* in 1776, and returned to once more in the entry he included in the index he added to the *Wealth of Nations* in 1784; '*Oxford*, the professorships there, *sinecures*' (Smith 1784, Index, unpag.; Letter 1 to William Smith of 24 August 1740, Smith 1987, *Corr.*: 1). There is some evidence, even, that Smith's views were reciprocated by the university, to the extent that the university had a corporate point of view. It is certainly the case that the Clarendon Press, the Oxford University Press which is now the custodian of so much of Smith's continuing renown, under-took a small but diligent vendetta against Smith, over the entire period from the publication of the *Wealth of Nations* to his death in 1790. The Vice-Chancellor of the time, George Horne, was the leading figure in the campaign, with a celebrated open letter to Smith, published by Clarendon Press in 1777, about his account of Hume's death; Smith wrote later that this had brought upon him 'ten times more abuse' than the *Wealth of Nations* (Horne 1777; and see Letter 208 to Andreas Holt of October 1780, *Corr.*: 251). The Vice-Chancellor's letter was republished in second and third editions in 1777, and in a fourth edition in 1784. In his subsequent *Letters on Infidelity*, also published by Clarendon Press, Horne was identified on the title page as the author of the letter to Smith; in this later work he added a very good and slightly paranoid description of Smith, as 'wary and modest' (Horne 1784: 8).

The Clarendon Press continued the vendetta in 1790, in a pamphlet in opposition to the essayist Vicesimus Knox, who had followed the *Wealth of*

The Philosophy of Adam Smith, The Adam Smith Review, 5: 25–36 © 2010 The International Adam Smith Society, ISSN 1743–5285, ISBN 978-0-415-56256-0.

Nations in describing the university's professorships as 'Sinecures' – 'I believe Europe cannot produce parallels to Oxford and Cambridge, in opulence, buildings, libraries, professorships, scholarships, and all the external dignity and mechanical apparatus of learning. If there is an inferiority, it is in the PERSONS ... ' – and who was accused of participating in the 'common errors of Voltaire and of Smith' (Knox 1781: 356; [Anon.] 1790: 5). The minor Oxford publishers contributed to the common enterprise, and so did the larger milieu of Oxford printing. One of the most effective of all Smith's early critics, the poet William Julius Mickle, was the proof-corrector for the Clarendon Press, and his brother was an Oxford printer. Mickle's dissection of Smith's writings on the East India Company was published in Oxford, buried within a long historical introduction to his translation of the Portugese epic, *The Lusiad* (Mickle 1778: clxi-clxxxi; [Anon.] 1794: xxxvii). Smith's writings on Hume were in particular, for Mickle, something like the sounds of a frog: 'And Smith, in barbarous dreary prose,/ Shall grunt and croak his praise'.[1]

I

The Theory of Moral Sentiments is at first sight the least historical of all Smith's writings. Smith's enduring preoccupation, in Dugald Stewart's account, was 'the study of human nature in all its branches, more particularly of the political history of mankind' (Stewart 1980: 271). The *Wealth of Nations* is a notoriously historical work, full of pieces of information about the price of wheat in 1202, or the copper content of coins during the second Punic war; 'particular facts', or 'long digressions' about 'the history of a law, or an institution', in Jean-Baptiste Say's description (Smith 1976b, WN I.xi.p.10, V.iii.61; Say 1803: v–vi, xxv). For Walter Bagehot, it was 'a very amusing book about old times' (Bagehot 1881: 295). The *Essays on Philosophical Subjects*, published posthumously by Smith's friends in 1795, is also, in large part, a work in the history of science, or on the principles of philosophical enquiry, 'illustrated by the history' of astronomy, ancient physics, ancient logic and metaphysics (Smith 1980, EPS, title pages, 31, 106, 118.) The two extended series of Smith's lectures which have since been published as the *Lectures on Rhetoric and Belles Lettres* (1983) and the *Lectures on Jurisprudence* (1978) are historical surveys, of language and law; the *Lectures on Rhetoric* are in part a guide to 'historicall Composition', and to the 'History of Historians' (LRBL ii.31, 45).

The *Theory of Moral Sentiments*, which was published in 1759, was by contrast an almost entirely unhistorical work. The reader of the first edition had to proceed as far as page 58 before arriving at a proper noun; and another few pages before coming to the name of an historical figure (the royalist poet Cowley, with his 'grave, pedantic and long-sentenced love') (Smith 1759: 62). The work is not particularly abstract. It is full of stories, or descriptions of sentiments. It is even 'a little too diffuse', as Edmund Burke wrote to Smith, with all its 'easy and happy illustrations from common

Life and manners' (Letter 38 from Edmund Burke of 10 September 1759, *Corr.*: 46–47). But the illustrations are for the most part not historical. The word 'history' occurs only three times in the book; twice in relation to the experience of reading history, and once in the last paragraph, in which Smith announces his own future inquiry into the history of jurisprudence (Smith 1759: 164, 267, 551).

It is this unhistorical sense which changed, I would like to suggest, in the course of the thirty years over which Smith added to, subtracted from, and in general deconstructed the book. *The Theory of Moral Sentiments* became a substantially more historical work, in a sequence of revisions which is associated, in interesting respects, with Smith's ideas of the inner life.

The omnipresent metaphor of *The Theory of Moral Sentiments* is of vision or seeing, as Vivienne Brown and others have shown (Brown 1994). Smith used the words 'eye' and 'eyes' 38 times in the 1759 edition; he referred 67 times to the verb 'to see', and 31 times to spectators. The image of moral experience, in the book, is of looking or glimpsing, at oneself or at others. But there is a related metaphor, of insideness or interiority, which is also omnipresent. The experience of moral judgment consists of looking at the inner life; of seeing inside, or seeing that which cannot be seen. The inner life is within, and therefore invisible. To have moral sentiments is to have looked, in as clear a light as possible, at the outside events of life, and to have imagined the life within.

The image of light and vision is ubiquitous in eighteenth-century philosophy, and the image of trying to see the unseeable, or that which is in darkness because it is within, was one of the continuing preoccupations of the critics of the French Enlightenment. The philosophers of the French Revolution, for Joseph de Maistre, were like a child, who when he is given a toy, 'breaks it, *to see inside*. It is thus that the French have treated the government; *they have wanted to see inside*' ('Lettres d'un Royaliste savoisien', quoted in Descostes 1894: 2, 328). But for Smith, too, the related metaphors of seeing and insideness posed continuing difficulties. These difficulties were associated, in part, with the overall enterprise of *The Theory of Moral Sentiments*, of founding a system or science of morality (in Burke's description) on the 'whole of Human Nature' (Letter 38 from Edmund Burke, *Corr.*: 46). A system in which morality was founded on powers of judgment which were placed inside individuals by God, who is all-seeing, would pose no such problems; and Smith's *Theory*, to the extent that it was understood, as it clearly was by Dugald Stewart and Sophie de Condorcet, as attempting to provide an unmetaphysical 'foundation of Morals', can be included in the works of enlightenment which De Maistre so disliked (Stewart 1980: 287, 290; see Rothschild 2001: 68). But there were other and less metaphysical difficulties that Smith encountered, in relation to the image of seeing inside, and they were difficulties to which he returned in all his successive revisions of the *Theory*.

Smith altered *The Theory of Moral Sentiments* in many different ways, of which the most conspicuous was the sub-title that he added in the fourth edition of 1784: *Or, An Essay towards an Analysis of the Principles by which Men naturally judge concerning the Conduct and Character, first of their Neighbours, and afterwards of themselves*. This was an odd adjustment, in respect of an 'essay' which extended to 551 pages in 1759, and had increased to 898 pages in 1790. It is an example, to use the Oxford expression, of Smith at his most 'wary and modest'. But it established several important characteristics of the work: that it was about human nature; that it was concerned with both outside or visible events ('conduct') and inside events ('character'); and that it asserted a sequence over time in moral judgment, in which individuals start by judging other people, and then judge themselves. In the new Advertisement to the 1790 edition, Smith explained that 'a good many illustrations' of his doctrines had 'occurred' to him over the preceding 30 years, and the changes he made were for the most part illustrations; illustrations, in particular, of the judgment or evaluation of the inner life.

Smith returned again and again, in the revisions, to the double metaphor of seeing and insideness. The idea of the 'man within' is not present in the 1759 *Theory of Moral Sentiments*. It is introduced in a small way in the 1761 edition, and in an ostentatious way in 1790, where there are 22 references to the 'man within', together with various demi-gods, judges, vice-gerents, and other 'inmate[s] of the breast' (Smith 1761: 208, 213; and see the anticipation of the 'man within' in Smith 1759: 132, 281, 283). The idea of 'other people' – Smith uses the expression an amazing 84 times in the 1790 *Theory* – is also far more important in the later editions. He tinkered almost obsessively with the language of vision and insight. There is an awkward reference to eyes – 'we must look at ourselves with the same eyes with which we look at others' – which he removed in the second edition; and a passage to do with mirrors – 'Unfortunately this moral looking-glass is not always a very good one' – which he also removed (Smith 1759: 257, 260). There are more eyes in the 1790 than the 1759 edition; almost twice as many. The two 'Raskolnikov' passages in the *Theory* – where Smith describes the remorse of the criminal, for whom 'solitude is still more dreadful than society', and who 'could not think without terror and amazement even of the manner in which mankind would look upon him, of what would be the expression of their countenance and of their eyes' – were revised and rearranged (TMS II.ii.2.3 and III.2.9; see Smith 1759: 184–7 and 250–3).[2]

The cumulative effect of Smith's revisions and additions is to make *The Theory of Moral Sentiments* a far more diffuse and more historical work; a work with more 'illustrations', as he announced. If the substantial new passages added to the 1790 edition (the passages to which Smith draws attention in his Advertisement) are considered as a distinct work, then it is a work which is very much more full of people and events than the 1759 *Theory*. I counted 88 proper nouns of persons in the 1759 edition, with a preponderance of references to ancient and modern philosophers; and 95 additional proper nouns in the principal new passages of 1790, many of them the names of historical persons of modern times. Smith added the names of

Queen Anne, Catherine de Medici, Isabella of Spain, Joanna of Castille, and the novelist Mme. Riccoboni, among others, as well as Idame, Jocasta, Niobe, Olympia and Venus.[3]

There are explicit references to history and historians in the new additions: the disregard of 'contemporary historians' for the lives of the 'obscure and insignificant', including 'men of letters'; the propensity of later historians to fashion their 'narratives' without recourse to 'authentic documents'; the responses of observers to historical painting (or historical engraving, the illustrations of illustrious men); and the uses of history in moral reflection ('examine the records of history', and the lives 'you may have either read of, or heard of, or remember') (TMS III.3.31, VI.iii.5, VII.ii.1.31). But the change is most evident in Smith's style; his 'copious and seducing composition', in Dugald Stewart's expression, or the 'variety and felicity of his illustrations' (Stewart 1980: 291–2.)

Smith's historical turn can be understood within the changing circumstances of his own life, and of the philosophical universe in which he lived. In moving from theory to historical inquiry, and from a *Theory* to an *Essay*, or to an *Inquiry* (the *Inquiry into the Nature and Causes of the Wealth of Nations*) he was making much the same move as David Hume, in his *Treatise*, his *Essays* and his *History of England*. The Scottish 'science of man', as Nicholas Phillipson and J.G.A. Pocock have shown, evolved from a natural to an historical science (Pocock 1999: 199–221; Phillipson 1989: 137–41; 2009). Historical inquiry was itself becoming a more elaborate, and, in Smith's opinion, a more venal subject (LRBL ii.41, 70; Pocock 2006). His closest associates, including Hume, William Robertson and Adam Ferguson, as well as Voltaire, Turgot, Condorcet and others of his French acquaintances, wrote works of history; essays on history or sketches of history. In the years following the initial publication of *The Theory of Moral Sentiments*, Smith was deeply involved in thinking about historical composition and historical evidence, in connection with his lectures on rhetoric of 1762–3, and in writing historically, in his *Essays*, in the *Wealth of Nations*, and in the ever-impending history of jurisprudence.[4]

But there is a more specific sense, as well, in which Smith's historical turn in *The Theory of Moral Sentiments* can help to illuminate his understanding of moral judgment; and was one of the ways, even, in which he tried to understand the complicated idea of insight into the inner life. For Smith was collecting names and stories because he was concerned, as he said in his Advertisement, to provide more illustrations of his theory, or his analysis. But he was also providing a description of the moral judgments which individuals make. Individuals, in Smith's description, make judgments, in their own lives, on the basis of illustrations. They observe their friends and relations, and they also trade places in fancy with mythical or fictional or historical people, people they have heard about or read about, in 'history or romance' (TMS III.4.9). The 'illustration' of historical stories is itself a kind of illumination, or light; a light in which it is almost possible to see, or to imagine, the interior darkness of the inner life. There is something of Wittgenstein's gaze in the 1759 *Theory of Moral Sentiments*, or of the Wittgensteinian eyes of the owls in the Antwerp night zoo, in W.G. Sebald's description: 'the fixed, inquiring gaze found in certain painters and philosophers who seek to penetrate the darkness which surrounds us purely by means of looking and thinking' (Sebald 2001: 3). But there is also light; in Smith's own expression, 'the day-light of the world and of society' (TMS III.3.39).

II

The second suggestion I want to make has to do with what Dugald Stewart called the 'foundation of Morals' (Stewart 1980: 290). The foundation of moral judgment, in all the successive versions of *The Theory of Moral Sentiments*, is to be sought in the world which surrounds the individual: conversation, society, intimate friendships, family relationships. Smith emphasized the intimacy of moral society in his new sub-title of 1774; how men judge the 'Conduct and Character, first of their Neighbours'. But a moral theory which is founded on local and intimate relationships is subject to two serious criticisms, both of which were apparently made to Smith in 1759 by Hume's friend Sir Gilbert Elliot. Elliot was one of the sources of the Deist Cleanthes, in Hume's *Dialogues concerning Natural Religion*, and his objections to Smith, in a letter which has been lost, seem to have been, first, that a morality which is entirely without unworldly foundation is fickle and insecure; and second, that a morality founded on intimate observations – the observations of one's own society, or one's own neighbours – is inevitably a local or parochial morality, in which even virtue is a condition of 'public opinion' (Letter 40 of 10 October 1759 to [Gilbert Elliott], *Corr.*: 48–9; Raphael and Macfie 1976: 16). The two objections are related, in that if the principles of moral judgment are placed in nature by God, who is all-seeing, then God can place a universal or un-local morality in all individuals. But the second objection, about parochialism (or relativism, in modern terms), is serious even in respect of an entirely unmetaphysical morality, and it is one with which Smith seems to have been much concerned.

The multiplicity of references to 'other people', almost all of which Smith added in the 1790 edition of the *Theory*, provide one way of averting the dangers of local morality. So do the references to distance; 'to view ourselves at the distance and with the eyes of other people' (TMS III.1.5). Smith's description of the uninterrupted custom of infanticide, and its influence on the 'imaginations' of Athenians, is an illustration of the ways in which even philosophers come to tolerate horrible inhumanity, with the support of 'far-fetched considerations of public utility' (TMS V.2.15). The story that Smith added to *The Theory of Moral Sentiments* in 1761, about the response of a 'man of humanity in Europe, who had no sort of connexion with that part of the world', to the news that 'the great empire of China, with all its myriads of inhabitants, was suddenly swallowed up by an earthquake', is an illustration of the faintness of moral sentiments, over large distances in space and time; the man of humanity would take his repose or his diversion, and sleep 'with the most profound security'. The experience of moral judgment, in Smith's description, consists in observing and being observed, imagining and being imagined, in the easy exchanges of daily life and manners. But it is not at all easy to observe or even to imagine the 'hundred millions of [our] brethren' in China; or a distant moral world (TMS III.3.4; Smith 1761: 211–14).

These questions of distance and judgment were of intense interest to Smith and Hume, in their own little society of enlightenment. *The Theory of Moral Sentiments* was published, 250 years ago, at a moment of virtually worldwide war, in which the British, after the *annus horribilis* of the early defeats of 1758, in the Seven Years' War of 1756–63, were entering a new age of distant empire. Smith's and Hume's enlightened Scottish friends were deeply involved in the new settlements of the postwar world, from East and West Florida to Grenada, and to Bihar, Bengal and Orissa. They lived in a new world of information about distant societies, and of influence on the lives of distant individuals. It was a world, too, in which the philosophical questions that Smith asked in 1759 and 1761, about uninterrupted custom, and connections to distant catastrophes, were of new and immediate consequence.

There were dozens of Scottish officials, within Smith's and Hume's closest circles of friends, who were the rulers of slave societies, and the owners of slaves; even the owners of slaves at home in Scotland (Rothschild forthcoming, 2011). Smith was interested in the politics of slavery (and anti-slavery), and the very first controversy, in print, over the *Theory of Moral Sentiments* – the first work in which Smith was named in the title – was a defence of the continental colonies, by the American publicist Arthur Lee, published in London in 1764, in which Smith was accused of having 'exalted into heroes' the African slaves, and 'debased into monsters' the American colonists (Lee 1764: iv, v, 13, 30).

One of Smith's favourite students, the son of his friend William Cullen, was the counsel for the slave-owner, in the celebrated case, Knight vs. Wedderburn, that ended slavery in Scotland in 1778. Smith was himself invoked by the counsel for the slave. 'Well has Dr Smith in treating of this subject expressed the Indignation of a generous mind at that Cruelty & oppression which is the disgrace of modern times', Allan Maconochie wrote in his memorial of 1775 for Joseph Knight (Maconochie 1775: 34). Robert Cullen, on behalf of the owner, argued that the liberal position, in the modern world, was rather to consider the customs of other, distant, and almost universally slave-owning societies; it was indeed 'illiberal to limit all ideas of justice to the regulations of their own particular society', and in order to 'correct their local prejudices', a 'regard became due to the laws of other countries' (Cullen 1777: 51; and see Rothschild forthcoming, 2011).

The foundational difficulty of Smith's system in *The Theory of Moral Sentiments*, or the dilemma of local and intimate morality, was in these circumstances of immediate political importance. For if morality is social and conversational, then how is it possible to be critical, as Smith himself was, of the almost uninterrupted customs of one's own society? If it is illiberal to be concerned only with the ideas of justice of one's society, then is it also liberal to be illiberal? If morality is conversational, how is it possible to have conversations with individuals in China, or to hear their distant cries?

Smith's historical illustrations, I would like to suggest, were part of his answer to these vexing questions. They constituted a sort of virtual conversation, on the basis of ever more information, about the 'other people' of history, geography, theatre and romance. The enduring difficulty of the Scottish science of man was to be at one and the same time a (natural) science of the universal characteristics of all human individuals, and an (historical) science of the particular circumstances in which these characteristics are manifested. It is the same sort of difficulty as the difficulty of universal and parochial morality, and it is a difficulty which Smith sought to resolve, in both instances, with historical illustrations, and particular facts.

III

The last suggestion I want to make is more speculative. Smith's historical illustrations, his stories and episodes and observations, are of importance, as I have tried to show, to his understanding of moral judgment as an elaborate, diffuse process of glimpsing, as though through the obscurity of circumstance, the outer and inner lives of other people. I have also suggested that his own method or style, his pell-mell piling up of different kinds of illustrations, is both a way of making a philosophical argument, and a description of the process of moral judgment itself. But this is almost exactly what historical inquiry is like, in the evocation of some of the greatest historians.

The ancient historian Barthold Niebuhr wrote in 1810 that the object of historical investigation was the *Innere*, or the 'inwardness of the ordinary life' of antiquity; an insight into events as they were seen by individuals at the time, as Goethe wrote to Niebuhr in 1812, in which 'the Past can be made present to the inward eye and imagination'. The historian's achievement, in this view, is to dispel the clouds or the mist (the *Nebel*) that separate us from the past, and to make it possible to glimpse, as though in a clear light, the individuals of those other times, 'living and moving'.[5] This metaphor of historical understanding, of seeing how it really was in the past, as though through the clouds of distance, is of importance, still, for modern historians; and Bernard Bailyn has used Niebuhr's language of an 'unglimpsed world', which is 'obscured from view by clouds', of the 'depiction of interior worlds', and their relationship to the 'exterior world' of historical events (Bailyn 1982: 22; 1985: 10, 13).

Smith's theory of sentiments, and his historical, pell-mell method, are in this respect of interest and potential utility to historians. Historians are continually importing theories from other, more abstract subjects, and philosophy is not a particularly sought-after source at the moment. But I would like to propose *The Theory of Moral Sentiments* as a source of these imports, or exports.

There are various kinds of history in relation to which *The Theory of Moral Sentiments* would be of interest. The most obvious would be the history of the human mind, or of moral sentiments. This sort of inquiry was of intense concern to David Hume, especially in his accounts, in the essays which he published in his *Political Discourses*, and later in his successive collections of essays, of how moral sentiments change with circumstances, and of how individuals, in commercial societies, become milder and more moderate.[6] The history of the 'descent' of the conscience was of continuing interest throughout the nineteenth century: the genealogy of morality (Nietzsche 1994: 4, 12). The anthropologist Lucien Lévy-Bruhl, who was the 'master' of the twentieth-century history of mentalities, was an historian of the development of national consciousness, and of the 'restitution of sentiments', in respect of the history of moral conscience; morality and the science of morals (Lévy-Bruhl 1903: 229).[7]

But it is not only in respect of these large inquiries into the history of mentalities that Smith's theories may be of interest to historians. For many sorts of historians are involved, as Smith was, in an effort to evaluate the inner lives of other people (in this case past people) on the basis of diffuse and diverse evidence. They are engaged in judging the inner on the basis of the outer, or of the circumstances of ordinary life. Smith's conception of the process of evaluation, in *The Theory of Moral Sentiments* as in the *Wealth of Nations*, has been described as one of *tâtonnement*, or of arriving at judgments of value on the basis of a multitude of individual and 'inter-subjective' judgments (Rothschild 2001: 235–46; Wiggins 1991: 80–1).[8] This is also the historian's procedure, on the basis of evidence which is always incomplete.

The Theory of Moral Sentiments is Smith's continuation, as Nicholas Phillipson has shown, of David Hume's great enterprise, in the *Treatise of Human Nature*, of a science of man (Phillipson 2009). It is in the spirit of Hume's injunction, in the prologue to the *Treatise*, to 'glean up our experiments in this science from a cautious observation of human life, and take them as they appear in the common course of the world, by men's behaviour in company, in affairs, and in their pleasures' (Hume 1978: xix). Even moral sentiments, for Smith, were the outcome of the cautious observation of human life; which is also an experiment in historical observation, and historical imagination.

Notes

1 For him shall Russell rant and rave,
  In hobbling rumbling lays;
  And Smith, in barbarous dreary prose,
  Shall grunt and croak his praise.
  ('On the Death of David Hume', in Mickle 1808: 144)
2 TMS II.ii.2.3, III.2.9; and see Smith (1759: 184–7, 250–3).
3 The three proper names of women in TMS 1759 are all of fictional characters: Monimia, Palmira and Phaedra (TMS 1759: 32, 33, 177).

4 Smith also came close, in his correspondence towards the end of his life with the Austrian reformer Count Windisch-Grätz, to the respect for established institutions which was later described as 'historicist'; in this case, the institutions of legal 'style books', or 'these collections, which are the produce of the wisdom and experience of many successive generations' (Ross and Raynor 1998).

5 'Einleitung zu den Vorlesungen uber die Römische Geschichte October 1810', in Niebuhr (1828a: 1, 92–3); letters from Goethe of 17 December 1811 and 23 November 1812, in Niebuhr (1852: 1, 345, 358); Niebuhr (1828b: 1, 6).

6 See especially 'Of Refinement in the Arts' ('Of Luxury'), 'Of Interest', 'Of the Balance of Trade', and 'Of the Protestant Succession', in Hume (1987).

7 On the restitution of 'the state of mind of our ancestors', and on 'our master Lucien Lévy-Bruhl', see Febvre (1968: 17).

8 The image of *tâtonnement*, with its allusion to feeling one's way in darkness, is not entirely well-suited to Smith's own figurative language of glimpsing and light. But the use of the image by economists since Turgot, has placed an emphasis, rather, on the distinctively Smithian idea of the uncoordinated and uncoerced aggregration of individual valuations (or sentiments).

Bibliography

[Anon.] (1790) *A Letter to the Rev. Vicecimus Knox* [sic], Oxford: Clarendon Press.

[Anon.] (1794) 'Anecdotes of William Julius Mickle', in W. Mickle, *Poems and a Tragedy*, London: A. Paris.

Bagehot, W. (1881) 'Adam Smith as a Person', in W. Bagehot, *Biographical Studies*, London: Longmans, Green.

Bailyn, B. (1982) 'The challenge of modern historiography', *American Historical Review*, 87: 1–24.

—— (1985) *History and the Creative Imagination*, St. Louis, MI: Washington University.

Brown, V. (1994) *Adam Smith's Discourse: Canonicity, Commerce and Conscience*, London: Routledge.

Cullen, R. (1777) *Additional Information for John Wedderburn of Ballendean, Esq; Defender; against Joseph Knight, a Negro of Africa, Pursuer June 1777*, [Edinburgh]: n.p.

Descostes, F. (1894) *Joseph de Maistre avant la Révolution: Souvenirs de la société d'autrefois, 1753–1793*, Moutiers-Tarentaise: F. Ducloz.

Febvre, L. (1968) *Le problème de l'incroyance au 16e siècle: La religion de Rabelais*, Paris: A. Michel.

[Horne, G.] (1777) *A Letter to Adam Smith LID on the Life, Death and Philosophy of his friend David Hume Esq, By one of the People called Christians*, Oxford: Clarendon Press.

[——] (1784) *Letters On Infidelity. By the Author of a Letter to Doctor Adam Smith*, Oxford: Clarendon Press.

Hume, D. (1978) *A Treatise of Human Nature*, Oxford: Clarendon Press.

—— (1987) *Essays Moral, Political, and Literary*, E.F. Miller (ed.), Indianapolis, IN: Liberty Classics.

Knox, V. (1781) *Liberal Education*, 2nd edn, London: Charles Dilly.

[Lee, A.] (1764) *An Essay in Vindication of the Continental Colonies of America, From A Censure of Mr Adam Smith, in his Theory of Moral Sentiments. With some Reflections on Slavery in general. By an American*, London: Becket and Hondt.

Lévy-Bruhl, L. (1903) *La morale et la science des moeurs*, Paris: F. Alcan.

Maconochie, A. (1775) 'Memorial for Joseph Knight', National Archives of Scotland, CS235/K/2/2.

Mickle, W. (1778) 'The History of the Rise and Fall of the Portugese Empire in the East', in Luis de Camöens, *The Lusiad; or, the Discovery of India. An Epic Poem*, transl. Mickle, 2nd edn, Oxford: Jackson and Lister.

—— (1808) *The Poetical Works of William Julius Mickle*, T. Park (ed.), London: J. Sharpe.

Niebuhr, B.G. (1828a) *Kleine historische und philologische Schriften von Barthold Georg Niebuhr*, Bonn: E. Weber.

—— (1828b) *Römische Geschichte*, 2nd edn, Berlin: G. Reimer.

—— (1852) *The Life and Letters of Niebuhr*, S. Winkworth (ed. and trans.), London: Chapman and Hall.

Nietzsche, F. (1994) *On the Genealogy of Morality*, C. Diethe (trans.), Cambridge: Cambridge University Press.

Phillipson, N. (1989) *Hume*, London: Weidenfeld and Nicolson.

—— (2009) 'Smith, Hume and the science of man in Scotland', lecture delivered at Glasgow University, 1 April 2009.

Pocock, J.G.A. (1999) *Barbarism and Religion: Narratives of Civil Government*, Cambridge: Cambridge University Press.

—— (2006) 'Adam Smith and history', in K. Haakonssen (ed.), *The Cambridge Companion to Adam Smith*, Cambridge: Cambridge University Press, pp. 270–87.

Raphael, D.D. and Macfie, A.L. (1976) Introduction to A. Smith, *The Theory of Moral Sentiments*, D.D. Rapahel and A.L. Macfie (eds), Oxford: Clarendon Press.

Ross, I. and Raynor, D. (1998) 'Adam Smith and Count Windisch-Grätz: new letters', *Studies on Voltaire and the Eighteenth Century*, 338: 171–87.

Rothschild, E. (2001) *Economic Sentiments: Adam Smith, Condorcet and the Enlightenment*, Cambridge, MA: Harvard University Press.

—— (forthcoming, 2011) *The Inner Life of Empires*, Tanner Lectures delivered at Princeton University, 19–20 April 2006.

Say, J.-B. (1803) 'Discours préliminaire', in J.-B. Say, *Traité d'Economie Politique, ou simple exposition de la manière dont se forment, se distribuent, et se consomment les richesses*, Paris: Deterville.

Sebald, W.G. (2001) *Austerlitz*, London: Penguin Books.

Smith, A. (1759) *The Theory of Moral Sentiments*, London: A. Millar.

—— (1761) *The Theory of Moral Sentiments*, 2nd edn, London: A. Millar.

—— (1784) *An Inquiry into the Nature and Causes of the Wealth of Nations*, 3rd edn, London: W. Strahan and T. Cadell.

—— (1976a) *The Theory of Moral Sentiments*, D.D. Raphael and A.L. Macfie (eds), Oxford: Clarendon Press.

—— (1976b) *An Inquiry into the Nature and Causes of the Wealth of Nations*, R.H. Campbell and A.S. Skinner (eds), Oxford: Clarendon Press.

—— (1978) *Lectures on Jurisprudence*, R.L. Meek, D.D. Raphael and P.G. Stein (eds), Oxford: Clarendon Press.

—— (1980) *Essays on Philosophical Subjects*, W.P.D. Wightman (ed.), Oxford: Clarendon Press.

—— (1983) *Lectures on Rhetoric and Belles Lettres*, J.C. Bryce (ed.), Oxford: Clarendon Press.

—— (1987) *Correspondence of Adam Smith*, E.C. Mossner and I.S. Ross (eds), Oxford: Clarendon Press.

Stewart, D. (1980) 'Account of the Life and Writings of Adam Smith, LL.D', in A. Smith, *Essays on Philosophical Subjects*, Oxford: Clarendon Press.

Wiggins, D. (1991) *Needs, Value, Truth*, Oxford: Basil Blackwell.

The standpoint of morality in Adam Smith and Hegel

Angelica Nuzzo

In evaluating a change of orientation in recent scholarship on Adam Smith and taking his cue from the so-called 'Adam Smith Problem', Stephen Darwall proposed a reading of *The Theory of Moral Sentiments* as 'sympathetic liberalism' (Darwall 1999). On this view, Smith's moral sentimentalism in its distinctive difference from David Hume's and Francis Hutcheson's and in its proximity to some Kantian concepts, lays the foundation, via a theory of jurisprudence, for his political and economic liberalism. The 'Adam Smith Problem' famously regards the apparent incompatibility between Smith's sentimentalist virtue ethics and his seemingly egoistic libertarian economics.[1] The problem, formulated for the first time at the end of the nineteenth century, dominated the scholarship until a few decades ago. Recently, it has been dismissed as an utter misunderstanding[2] but it continues to inspire historical studies dedicated to placing Smith's moral theory in the context of the history of moral philosophy (exploring his ancient Stoic sources, his debt to the Renaissance humanistic idea of virtue, his relation to Rousseau, and his anticipations of Kant) as well as systematic inquiries which, like Darwall's (also Brown 1992/3; Fitzgibbons 1995; Griswold 1999; Muller 1995), aim at establishing the link between the sentimentalist ethics of the *Theory* and the economic ideas of the *Wealth of Nations* – a link that Smith himself never explicitly discussed.

In this essay, I address the question of the relationship between Smith's ethics and his economic views from an indirect historical perspective. I frame this problem as a chapter of the history of the reception of Smith's thought in German nineteenth-century philosophy taking as a case in point Hegel's interpretation of Smith in his *Philosophy of Right* (1986c [1821]). Starting with Georg Lukacs' pioneering work on the 'young Hegel' that saw in Smith the 'turning point' of the evolution of his social and political thought, Hegel's early interest in Smith's economic liberalism (and more broadly in the Scottish Enlightenment) has been the topic of several important historical works (Lukacs 1948; Riedel 1969; Waszek 1988, 1995).[3] There is, however, no contribution – either historical or systematic – on the impact that Smith's *ethics* and the *Theory* may have had on Hegel.

My present aim is to offer some suggestions in this direction, thereby rectifying the dominant view according to which Hegel valued Smith exclusively

The Philosophy of Adam Smith, The Adam Smith Review, 5: 37–55 © 2010 The International Adam Smith Society, ISSN 1743–5285, ISBN 978-0-415-56256-0.

for his economic ideas – in particular, for his analysis of the division of labour in society, for his insights into the mechanisms of the market, and generally for his 'political economy'. Hegel was familiar with these ideas from a careful early study of the *Wealth of Nations*.[4] From at least 1803/4 onwards[5] he integrates them into his political philosophy in various ways until Smith's lasting influence crystallizes in the crucial concept of 'civil society'. Hegel introduces this concept for the first time in 1817/18 in his Heidelberg lectures on political philosophy (Hegel 1983) but he gives it final systematic form only in the 1821 *Philosophy of Right* (Riedel 1962; Waszek 1995). Opposing the widespread view that limits Hegel's appreciation of Smith to the political economy of the *Wealth of Nations*, I argue that Hegel was well aware of the deep interconnection between moral philosophy and economics in Smith's thought. *The Theory of Moral Sentiments* was translated into German in 1770 and was well known to writers such as Gotthold Ephraim Lessing, Immanuel Kant and Friedrich Schiller, among others, as well as being reviewed in important philosophical and literary journals of the time.[6] Hegel comments on this work in his *Lectures on the History of Philosophy* (1986d). My present argument, however, will not be historical but systematic. I suggest that in his presentation of 'civil society' in the *Philosophy of Right* Hegel transforms or translates Smith's economic ideas along with his sentimentalist ethics. The context of Hegel's notion of 'civil society' provides the systematic connection between the two. Hegel's explicit mention of Smith's (along with Say's and Ricardo's) 'political economy' at the outset of the 'System of Needs' is often underlined and commented on (1986c [1821], hereafter R; §189 Remark). However, that the development of the structures of civil society also makes room for a type of morality that deeply resonates with Smith's moral theory – with his idea of sympathy and the impartial spectator – and that such morality sustains the articulation of the economic activity of civil society are two points curiously but consistently missed by interpreters. Here I shall frame the discussion of Hegel's idea of a morality proper to civil society as if he were responding to and appropriating Smith's moral philosophy. This interpretive 'speculation' is not meant to support a historical claim but to achieve three results. First, it rectifies a systematic issue regarding the structure of civil society in Hegel and the role that (a certain type of) morality plays in it; second, it discloses the broader concerns that lead Hegel to mention Smith's political economy in this sphere; and finally, it confirms from an indirect Hegelian perspective some contemporary readings of Smith's sentimentalist ethics.

In discussing this connection, I will establish two claims, one on the relation between ethics and political economy, the other on the specific character of Smith's moral theory. First, I contend that for Hegel civil society is the sphere in which the economic relations among individuals are made possible and sustained by a morality based on 'sentiments' such as sympathy, resentment and justice. This, I submit, is Hegel's appropriation and transformation of Smith's doctrine in *The Theory of Moral Sentiments*. To put this point in a different way, I claim that Hegel sees Smith's *Theory* and his *Wealth of Nations* – his sentimentalist ethics and his political economy – as two interconnected and interdependent aspects of modern civil society.[7] Ultimately, I suggest that viewed in Hegel's perspective the 'Adam Smith Problem' is not a specific problem of the interpretation of Smith's philosophy but is the chief problem of modernity itself – an issue to which Smith gave voice like no other philosopher before. Second, I claim that at the level of 'ethical life' within the structures of civil society Smith's *Theory* appears to Hegel as a valuable concrete alternative to Kant's too abstract morality. On Hegel's view, within 'ethical life' it is the virtues and duties of Smith's sentimentalist ethics, not those of Kant's formalistic deontology, that shape the life of individuals as economic agents and citizens of the modern world. While Kant's position, on Hegel's interpretation,[8] does not differ substantially from the abstract neutrality of an 'ideal observer',[9] Smith's theory is fruitful precisely because it is a moral position developed *from within* social life – it is, properly, a moral 'standpoint'. It is a moral position that has nothing to do with detached and disinterested impartiality and has all to do with the possibility of endorsing sympathetically, as it were, the standpoint of the agent. Read in this way, the value that Smith's sentimentalist ethics displays for Hegel over Kant's morality may help us illuminate an important aspect of Smith's philosophy, confirming Darwall's attempt to distance Smith from 'impartial spectator' positions such as Hume's and Hutcheson's. Unlike Darwall, however, who points to Smith's anticipation of Kantian themes, I shall insist on the proximity between Smith's moral theory and Hegel's in opposition to Kant's.[10] Significantly, such proximity in my view is due precisely to the necessary link between morality and economics.[11]

In the first section of this essay, I briefly outline how, generally, Hegel's *Philosophy of Right* relates to Smith's *Theory*. My aim herein is limited to laying out the conditions for the discussion to follow. In the second section, I present the problem of the 'standpoint of morality' within 'ethical life' examining Hegel's development of a morality proper to civil society. I will argue that such morality comes significantly close to Smith's moral philosophy. In this context I discuss the relationship between Smith's 'sympathy' and 'impartial spectator' and Hegel's notion of 'recognition' with regard to the analogous role that they play in shaping the morality proper of civil society, that is, in constituting a social 'we'.

Smith's *Theory of Moral Sentiments* and Hegel's *Philosophy of Right*

Part VII of *The Theory of Moral Sentiments* contains a history of moral philosophy. Herein Smith offers a typology of philosophical thinking about practical rules that can be encountered throughout the history of moral philosophy. He distinguishes ethics, casuistry and jurisprudence. This distinction is based on the degree of precision and accuracy with which rules of morality are defined. While 'the rules of justice are the only rules of morality which are precise and accurate [...] those of all the other virtues are loose, vague, and indeterminate' (Smith 1976, TMS VII.iv.1). Ethics does not prescribe determinate rules of action but concerns the 'sentiments' on which the virtues are founded, the specific internal feelings or emotions that constitute the 'essence' of the virtues, and the different types of virtuous conduct. In fulfilling these tasks ethics is, more precisely, moral psychology (and rhetoric). Smith's *Theory* is intended as a fundamental contribution to ethics understood in this way. Thereby it is placed in the tradition of the 'ancient moralists' who have described those sentiments and virtues 'in a general manner' (TMS VII.iv.3). 'Sympathy' is, for Smith, the means by which we share our moral sentiments. Unlike ethics, casuistry attempts the impossible task to 'lay down exact and precise rules for the direction of every circumstance of our behaviour' (TMS VII.iv.7). It denies the 'common sentiments of mankind' (TMS VII.iv.12) and rationalizes, instead, the problem of virtue. Casuistry, on Smith's account, is utterly useless and 'ought to be rejected altogether' (TMS VII.iv.34).[12] The two 'useful parts of moral philosophy' are 'Ethics and Jurisprudence' (TMS VII.iv.34). Only a theory of justice can provide exact rules of behaviour. Those rules, however, are prescriptions for 'the decisions of judges and arbiters', not 'for the conduct of good men' (TMS VII.iv.8). Justice, for Smith, is a 'negative virtue', which does not concern benevolence and is not addressed to the ethics of the individual. It considers 'only what the person to whom the obligation is due, ought to think himself entitled to exact by force; what every impartial spectator would approve of him for exacting, or what a judge or arbiter [...] ought to oblige the other person to suffer or to perform' (TMS VII.iv.8). Sentiments do play an important role in jurisprudence. The specific sentiment that constitutes the basis of justice is 'resentment'. Resentment is the political analogue to (or the political specification of) moral sympathy (resentment is sympathy with the sufferer); it is the sentiment whose gratification is punishment. The 'natural rules of justice independent of all positive institutions' which 'ought to run through and be the foundation of the laws of all nations' (TMS VII.iv.37) occupy a fundamental part of the *Theory*. On Smith's view, the ancients lacked any important insight into jurisprudence, which is a properly modern discipline. Hugo Grotius is Smith's main reference in matters of jurisprudence. It is to Grotius – or better to a planned continuation of Grotius's efforts on the basis of his sentimentalist ethics and the concept of natural justice it entails – that Smith turns in the conclusion of the sixth edition of the *Theory*. In sketching out his philosophical programme, Smith announces that *The Theory of Moral Sentiments* will be followed by a theory of jurisprudence in which an account will be given 'of the general principles of law and government [...] not only in what concerns justice but in what concerns police, revenue, arms, and whatever else is the object of law' (TMS VII.iv.37). The *Wealth of Nations* will stand at the other end of this philosophical enterprise.

The view of moral philosophy sketched out at the end of the 1790 *Theory* confirms the results of the scholarship on Smith's sources and influences. Historically, the *Theory* is set in the aftermath of the ancient tradition of virtue and community – in particular of Stoic ethics – that considers man as a social being, but also in the aftermath of the later humanistic theory of virtue of the Renaissance (Brown 1992/93; Fitzgibbons 1995: 22; Darwall 1999: 146; Teichgraeber 1981: 113–14). These traditions, however, are taken up by Smith within the peculiar framework of modern jurisprudence. Roman law had already modified the ancient moral tradition in light of a marked focus on the individual. It is only with Grotius and Pufendorf that modern jurisprudence provides a framework of justice and political institutions able to accommodate the emergent individualism. Thus, it has been rightly noted that 'Roman law and natural jurisprudence […] were Smith's intellectual starting points' (Darwall 1999: 151 discussing Muller 1995: 58) – they are the starting point and framework of his sentimentalist ethical theory, of his moral and political egalitarianism, and of his political and economic liberalism.

In its systematic structure and general philosophical programme Hegel's 1821 *Philosophy of Right* belongs to a very different tradition. What is interesting, however, is the way in which systematic and programmatic differences generate the context for a fruitful reception and transformation of Smith's ideas that go to the heart of the connection between ethics, jurisprudence and political economy. Ultimately, Hegel's *Philosophy of Right* reframes Smith's complex practical philosophy in terms of the morality distinctively proper to modern 'civil society', that is, to the sphere to which he assigns modern political economy. Bearing the full title: *Elements of the Philosophy of Right or Natural Law and Political Science in Outline*, Hegel's 1821 treatise marks the end of the natural right tradition in Germany. In this work, however, Hegel presents an idea of politics and society that is also very different from the one he formulated in his early years. The young Hegel had appealed to the model of harmonious political and social unity proper to the Greek *polis* as the highest philosophical ideal. Aristotle (but also Plato) was Hegel's main philosophical influence in this regard. The study of the political economy of the Scottish Enlightenment – of Smith in particular – is among the factors that awakened Hegel to the problems of modernity, and consequently to the fundamental and historically irretrievable distance that separates the ideal community of the ancients from the much more fragmented and disharmonious political reality of the modern world. Significantly, it is this same awareness of the contradictions of the modern world and of the role that material needs play in human action – the same needs accounted for by political economy – that prompts Hegel's early critique of the 'purity' of Kant's practical reason and of the formal morality based upon it. To reclaim the sensible, emotional and material aspects of humanity is, for Hegel, a task that must engage both moral and political philosophy.[13]

Manfred Riedel has stressed that the final systematic inclusion of political economy in Hegel's philosophy coincides with his definitive farewell to the ideal of Greek ethical life.[14] Expressed in terms of Hegel's dialectic, the ideal of the ancient community is now 'overcome' – taken up and radically transformed – within the framework of modern society. The latter is characterized by the emergence of an individualism that needs to be 'mediated' – justified, enriched, reined in, but also expanded at the same time – within the broader and higher political unity of the state. This is the complex dimension that Hegel calls 'ethical life'. Smith's political economy, crucial for Hegel's understanding of the social and political problems proper to modernity, is included in his mature political philosophy in the figure of 'civil society'. Placed between the 'Family' and the 'State', 'Civil Society' articulates the economic dimension of 'Ethical Life' and presents the interaction of equal individuals – family members and citizens – based on economic needs, the division of labour, membership in corporations, but also culture. This is the context that all interpreters discuss when Hegel's relation to Smith is at issue. However, as undeniably important this discussion is, if we limit ourselves to this picture we miss a fundamental dimension and a crucial problem of Hegel's 'ethical life' and consequently of his idea of civil society. This is the problem of the *specific morality* proper to this sphere. What are the moral ties that bind the individual agents of civil society? To understand that this was indeed a crucial question for Hegel – that is, that the morality proper to this sphere was, in fact, a fundamental problem not reducible to economic relations – we must clarify an often overlooked aspect of the systematic of the *Philosophy of Right*.

In Hegel's 1821 work the sphere of 'Ethical Life' (*Sittlichkeit*) is the culmination of a systematic progression that starts with 'Abstract Right' and moves on to 'Morality' (*Moralität*). Both abstract right and morality consider the human agent in abstraction from the social context in which action takes place and first becomes meaningful. Abstract right is approximately the sphere of jurisprudence, and encompasses the juridical relations among abstract individuals viewed as isolated property owners ('persons'). Morality instead addresses the issue of the moral personality of subjects taken in abstraction from intersubjective relations. Hegel's critique of Kant's moral philosophy takes place precisely at this level. As we gain the higher sphere of 'Ethical Life' juridical relations and morality are not left behind but are rather taken up, corrected, and rendered fundamentally concrete within the new social and political framework that Hegel articulates in the realms of family, civil society and the state. The general point of this systematic progression is that no theory of right and no doctrine of morality can claim any validity outside of – or in abstraction from – the concrete dimension of social life and its institutions. Right and morality are internal 'standpoints' within the articulated and complex sphere of ethical life. In this way, Hegel's idea of 'ethical life' functions as an immanent critique of traditional jurisprudence (abstract right) as well as Kantian morality. Both the idea of right and that of morality must be transformed – and indeed, differentiated – as internal 'standpoints' endorsed by individuals and communally realized within ethical life. In other words, notions such as duty, virtue, justice and equality are meaningful (descriptively as well as normatively) if and only if they presuppose and are based on the context of ethical life. In this case, however, those concepts are no longer the abstract and formalistic concepts of Kant's morality and traditional jurisprudence, as they no longer refer to a merely abstract rational subject. It is precisely at this point that Smith's 'moral sentiments' are embraced by Hegel as a viable alternative and a fruitful correction of Kant's morality.

As the youthful ideal of political unity proper to the ancient *polis* is abandoned under the influence of modern political economy, Hegel is well aware that economic relations alone do not constitute a sufficient bond of social unity. The ancient (Aristotelian) idea that man is a social being remains central for Hegel. Thus, at stake is the problem of finding a *modern* form of morality that can integrate virtues and duties within a complex social context – a morality that, unlike Kant's, is capable of giving an account of both the intersubjective connections in which the human being is placed and of the rich emotional, sensible and material life that characterizes the human being as moral agent (not as Kant's abstract 'person' or 'subject'). Duty, virtue and justice must be enacted and made concrete in light of specific human needs and feelings, and as part of a broader notion of culture. What is at stake, in other words, is a modern form of morality that working *from within the standpoint of the ethical world* shapes both the modern individual and the intersubjective context that gives different forms of individual action their meaning.

Impartial spectator, moral sentiments and the morality of civil society

In constructing the transition from 'Morality' to 'Ethical Life', Hegel offers a criticism of Kant's formalistic ethics in terms of the internal systematic of the *Philosophy of Right*. For Hegel, Kant's philosophy is the chief example of 'the merely moral standpoint that is unable to make the transition to ethical life' – that is, of a moral standpoint that, being unable to conceive of its subject as a concrete agent placed *within* the whole of society, is ultimately an ineffectual standpoint from nowhere and on nowhere.[15] On Hegel's view, this ineffectual moral standpoint is an 'empty formalism' (R §135 and Remark) in which neither the idea of duty nor that of virtue can display concrete meaning and hence cannot be endorsed by a real agent. Moral conscience is nothing more than an empty form that 'lacking objective content' cannot act. Action becomes possible only when subjective conscience is recognized and validated as an internal standpoint within the system of duties and principles that animates ethical life thereby becoming 'ethical disposition' (R §137). At the beginning of the sphere of 'Ethical Life' Hegel already announces this fundamental correction of the abstract idea of morality. Taking up the traditional terminology of practical philosophy embraced by Kant, Hegel claims that if the 'doctrine of duties' and the 'doctrine of virtues' (respectively R §148 Remark, §150 Remark) are to express the actual development of the idea of freedom in its articulation of real human relations, they must be rooted in ethical life and transformed accordingly. The correction of the shortcomings of the abstract concept of morality consists in recognizing that the 'moral standpoint' becomes effectual only as an *internal position within ethical life*. And yet, to conceive of morality *within* ethical life means to abandon once and for all the abstract tenet of Kantian ethics, namely, the idea that morality (and practical freedom) is a sort of absolute beginning not determined by any condition or context. On the other hand, it is clear that the need to supplement ethical life with the subjective requirement of a moral standpoint is a distinctively *modern* problem concerning the peculiar form proper to modern freedom. Greek ethical life displays an unquestioned identity of *Moralität* and *Sittlichkeit* – the individual being immediately one with the ethical substance. Hence the first question arises: What is the modern form of morality that for Hegel shapes from within ethical life? There is, however, an additional systematic problem outlined in the transition from 'Morality' to 'Ethical Life'. If morality is meaningful only within ethical life, given the complex articulation of this sphere (the more general being the division in 'Family', 'Civil Society' and the 'State') *where exactly* shall we expect to find Hegel's proposal of an 'ethical morality'? In response to these two questions, I shall argue that Hegel may have seen in Smith's morality the plausible modern alternative to Kant's formalistic ethics of duty, and that the peculiar systematic place of morality within ethical life is the sphere of 'Civil Society', precisely the same sphere in which Hegel places the reference to Smith's 'political economy'. With the help of the *Wealth of Nations*, Hegel places Smith's idea of morality at the heart of the ethical life of modern civil society.

I shall start from the latter, systematic problem and then outline the characters of the modern form of morality proper to ethical life. I propose to read some basic structures of civil society as Hegel's dialectical-speculative transformation or appropriation of crucial concepts of Smith's moral philosophy. Once again, what I am proposing here is an interpretive hypothesis, whose value consists, first, in answering the systematic problem of the place of morality in 'Ethical Life' in Hegel's 1821 work, and, second, in directly confirming a reading of Smith's moral theory as offering an idea of morality engaged from within with the concrete life of individuals (and not external to it). Ultimately, if we assume Hegel's perspective, the neutrality of the 'impartial spectator' can be seen as defining Kant's morality rather than Smith's.[16]

Civil society displays three different spheres: 'The System of Needs', 'The Administration of Justice', and 'Police and Corporation'. In the first, introductory section to the 'System of Needs' Hegel pays his famous tribute to Smith's (along with Say's and Ricardo's) idea of political economy. The 'System of Needs' develops the economic relations among individuals, discusses the division of labour, the membership in corporations, and the diverse interests of the estates. Significantly, however, at the end of this discussion, Hegel makes a crucial systematic point that reveals the necessary *subjective* condition that supports the economic life of the individuals and ultimately allows it to function. To present the mechanism of economic relations as one of the spheres of ethical life means precisely that economic relations, for Hegel, are neither self-sufficient nor self-regulating but are rather part of a broader organic unity that ultimately provides the condition for their actuality. Hegel explains that in the sphere of civil society the individual's 'ethical disposition [*sittliche Gesinnung*] is that of rectitude and the honour of one's own estate'. These are the moral feelings that are tied to the role that the individual plays within the broader context in which economic relations are specified – in the division of labour, corporations and estates. Accordingly, to be a citizen of civil society means to be motivated by such feelings as rectitude, honour and justice, to be active as a member of a certain corporation and estate, and 'to be recognized in one's own eyes and in the eyes of all others' as a subject that embodies such an ethical disposition. On this basis Hegel concludes, 'Morality [*die Moralität*] *has its proper place in this sphere*, where reflection on one's own action and the end of particular needs and welfare is dominant' (R §207 my emphasis) – for it is here that such reflection concretely generates appropriate virtues and duties. In this sphere the contingency that regulates economic transactions 'makes even contingent and individual help into a duty' (R §207).

This account of morality – of the morality within ethical life as morality of civil society – evokes Smith's in a number of ways. The idea that we seek recognition in our own eyes and the eyes of all others is central to the *Theory of Moral Sentiments*, as is the idea that justice is the basic virtue of civil society and amounts to an expression of mutual recognition (TMS II.ii.1–3). In TMS III, turning from our judgment regarding other people's motives to our judgment concerning our own, Smith underlines that we can judge of our own sentiments and motives only in a mediated or reflected way, only if we 'remove ourselves' from the immediacy of the relation to ourselves ('from our natural station'), thereby gaining distance from ourselves. Notably, this distance is neither abstract neutrality nor a flight from our entanglement with the social context that surrounds us. We gain an understanding of ourselves, rather, from a deeper connection and indeed a sympathetic identification with our context. Smith says that we can gain the necessary distance from ourselves that allows us to judge of our own motives 'in no other way than by *endeavouring to view them with the eyes of other people*, or as other people are likely to view them' (TMS III.1.2; my emphasis).[17] What brings Smith so close to Hegel in this claim is not only the mediated character of our access to ourselves or the notion that we have to see ourselves as others do (that we have to become, in Hegel's words, the other-of-ourselves) but also the assumption of a fundamental *visibility* of moral motives to the eye of society. This contrasts significantly with Kant's claim that even our own motives are 'invisible' to ourselves (and impenetrable to others: Kant 1910, vol. 4: 407).

The point, for Hegel as for Smith, is that only through society can we gain access to ourselves. For the social context is 'the only looking glass by which we can [...], with the eyes of other people, scrutinize the propriety of our own conduct' (TMS III.1.5). This is the starting point and the condition of morality for both Hegel and Smith – and the reason why, for Hegel, morality has its 'proper place' in the sphere of civil society.

Moreover, for Smith as for Hegel, the extension of our own perspective through the others' eyes is not simply instrumental in gaining a different, mediated access to merely natural passions and sentiments. The socially mediated character of our motives is disclosed by the crucial fact that in considering ourselves in the eyes of others our own 'passions will immediately become the causes of new passions' (TMS III.1.3). Personal sentiments are not just natural; they are socially produced and re-produced motives. In looking at our own motives with the eyes of others, new motives and a different type of satisfaction arises. For Hegel as for Smith, the satisfaction that we are after is not merely the satisfaction of a material need. It is, more fundamentally, the satisfaction of the 'opinion' that others have of us.[18] This is, for Smith, our 'love of praise' (or of 'just fame, of true glory': TMS III.2 in general; 2.3–9 in particular) and for Hegel the sense of 'honour' that we have as members of corporations and estates.

For Smith, justice and the connected feeling of resentment leading to punishment, is the fundamental virtue of civil society. As for Hegel, it is the virtue that differentiates the realm of family relations from civil society proper. Smith draws this distinction clearly:

> when a father fails in the ordinary degree of parental affection towards a son; [...] when brothers are without the usual degree of brotherly affection [...] though everybody blames the conduct, nobody imagines that those who might have reason, perhaps, to expect more kindness, have any right to extort it by force.
>
> (TMS II.ii.1.7)

As for Hegel, the morality in which justice is central has its proper place in the sphere of civil society. Justice and its administration are based on 'universal approbation' for Smith. For Hegel they hinge on the consciousness of the 'universal validity' of juridical norms (respectively, TMS II.ii.1.8 and R §210). And Hegel's related thought that only in a functioning society can 'contingent and individual help' turn into a 'duty' (R §207), is also present in the *Theory*: 'When one man attacks, or robs, or attempts to murder another, all the neighbours take the alarm, and think that they do right when they run, either to revenge the person who has been injured or to defend him who is in danger of being so' (TMS II.ii.1.7). No such intervention is deemed a duty in the example of family-related sentiments cited above (it would appear, on the contrary, 'the highest degree of insolence and presumption' TMS II.ii.1.7).

Thus, when Hegel says that morality has its proper place in civil society, the morality he seems to have in mind is Smith's. This morality is the texture that supports the contingency of economic life. Here we find the answer to the question raised in the transition from 'Morality' to 'Ethical Life'. It is precisely at the centre of civil society, within the 'System of Needs', that Hegel places the crucial correction of the abstract (Kantian) concept of morality developed in the second division of the *Philosophy of Right*. Systematically, the morality proper to the ethical world has its place within civil society – neither in the family, which is still dominated by the immediacy of natural relations such as love, nor in the state where the concrete universality of public ethical dispositions fully motivates the individuals. Within the economic life of civil society Hegel develops a model of subjective morality whose virtues and duties are rooted in individual feelings that have a fundamentally social nature (are not immediately natural),[19] are based on reciprocal recognition, and require that individuals take the perspective and the standpoint of others into account – indeed that they 'be recognized in one's own eyes and in the eyes of all others'. This is a Smithian conception of morality.

With the systematic claim that gives 'morality' its proper place in the 'System of Needs' Hegel draws a conclusion from his development of civil society, that is easily missed if we concentrate exclusively on his presentation of economic relations. In characterizing the agent at this point in his account, looking back at 'Abstract Right' and 'Morality' but also at the 'Family', Hegel claims that the 'citizen' of civil society, unlike the 'person' who is the subject of rights, the formal 'subject' of Kant's morality, and the 'family member', is a 'concrete' and not a merely abstract subject. It is here, Hegel explains emphatically, that we have for the very first time what 'we call *human being – Mensch*' (R §190). In other words, on Hegel's view, jurisprudence, moral philosophy, psychology, and even anthropology, as sciences that draw the concrete 'human being' to the centre, are meaningful only if they consider the *Mensch* as a 'citizen' of civil society; rather than, like Kant, in abstraction from it (Nuzzo 2008a: chs 4–6). This demand Hegel could find fulfilled in Smith's practical philosophy.

As 'human being', subject of social needs and feelings seeking their gratification, the citizen of civil society is set in relations of reciprocal dependence with all others. In this net of relations, the individual agent displays an aspect of 'universality as *being-recognized* [*Anerkanntsein*]' by the others. It is 'recognition' that confers a specifically 'social' character on the agent's needs, motivations and sentiments. That recognition is necessary to and constitutive of one's individual needs means, explains Hegel, that 'I have to orient myself according to the others': that in order to act on my motivations and to satisfy my needs 'I have to take the other's opinion' and indeed the other's standpoint into account (R §192 Addition). This means both that I have to view my own motives with the eyes of others, and that the others' opinion becomes for me a source of 'need': I seek the satisfaction of the opinion of others.

As argued above, Smith makes the same two points. We have to see 'ourselves in the light in which others see us' (TMS III.4.6); and we feel passions, such as the desire to be admired, whose satisfaction is the favourable opinion that others have of us: 'We must [...] believe ourselves to be admirable for what [other people] are admirable. But, in order to attain this satisfaction, we must become the impartial spectator of our own character and conduct' (TMS III.2.2). Moreover, for Hegel, the social character of recognition that mediates one's own individual action through the standpoint of all others implies equality among individuals as well as '*imitation* as the process whereby people make themselves like others' (R §193 my emphasis) – this imitation taking place both materially and psychologically. We find a similar point in Smith, who speaks about 'emulation' as the 'anxious desire that we ourselves should excel' – a sentiment that is 'originally founded in our admiration of the excellence of others' (TMS III.2.2), that is, in the recognition of the value of other people. The importance of this recognized equality even for justice can hardly be overestimated. It belongs to the culture and education of the individual in this sphere that 'a human being counts as such because he is a human being, not because he is a Jew, Catholic, Protestant, German, Italian, etc.' (R §209 Remark). This relation of mutual recognition – with its projection into the standpoint and opinions of others and with its inherent fundamental requisite of equality – can indeed be seen as Hegel's own appropriation and transformation, within civil society, of Smith's idea of 'the impartial spectator'. The latter is the perspective of 'man in general'[20] – a standpoint that, like Hegel's *Mensch*, is abstract and concrete at the same time: it is the concreteness of myself transfigured and transposed in the abstract universality of the other. Significantly, in both cases, moral motivation and judgment implies a process of reflective duplication in which the subject appears to herself as the other. As Smith puts it, 'When I endeavour to examine my own conduct [...] it is evident that [...] I divide myself, as it were, into two persons' (TMS 2nd edn, III.1.6). Since the *Phenomenology of Spirit*'s famous introduction of this concept, recognition marks for Hegel the achieved intersubjective context of the 'we'.[21] This is the same context in which Smith places his sentimentalist ethics.

Hegel introduces the sphere of 'Civil Society' by describing the action that takes place within it as the convergence of two principles. On the one hand, the agent is a particular, 'concrete person' characterized by a totality of needs, natural determinations and feelings, and arbitrary volitions. This person, observes Hegel, stands necessarily and essentially in relation to other particular individuals and it is only through these others that the agent is able to fulfil her volitions and satisfy her needs. This interaction is the basis of the second principle of civil society, namely, the 'universality' that characterizes the action mediated by the reciprocity in which the individuals are placed (R §182). Although individual ends are 'selfish', based on merely personal interests and motivations, they are also social and intersubjectively mediated for two reasons. First, individual ends are conditioned by the relations in which they stand within the universal context of reciprocal interaction because this context alone allows for those ends to be realized. Subsistence, welfare and rights of the individual are interwoven with and dependent on the subsistence, welfare and rights of all (R §183). An implicit principle of utility seems at work in this connection, which will be further developed as Hegel specifies the economic nature of some of those individual ends. This is the argument that makes political economy an accurate description of individual self-interested action within civil society.

However, Hegel offers a second reason for the social or 'universal' character of individual action and for the mutual dependence that binds individuals to each other in this sphere. At stake this time is not the issue of the realization or realizability of personal ends but the very nature of the volition or motivation on which individuals act. It is here, I submit, that Hegel's argument comes significantly close to Smith's peculiar 'impartial spectator' position.[22] Hegel's point is that within the sphere of civil society individual selfish motivations and practical feelings are acted upon (or do indeed motivate the agent to action) because they display a *reflective* character or universality that is due to their belonging to an individual *only through* their belonging to any other person. Although the individual is a 'concrete person', as citizen of civil society she is also an abstract universal; she is one of the many equal individuals with whom she is linked as in a *continuum* (R §187). Her motivations are *legitimate* motivations in their selfish character because they are selfish motivations of all other individuals. Disinterestedness is not the moral requirement here.[23] In order to act as a citizen of this sphere (and not, for example, simply as a family member or as a public person in the state), the individual is required to recognize this double character of her volitions – the *selfish* motivation must be recognized as a *shared selfish* motivation. Accordingly, individual ends require a person's projection into the standpoint of others: individuals 'can attain their ends only insofar as they themselves determine their knowledge, volition, and action' in connection with and from the standpoint of the others, hence 'in a universal way' (R §187).

Smith advocates a similar position: he does not claim the need for disinterested action but rather the need to view 'the selfish and original passions of human nature' from a standpoint that is more universal than the self-centred view of the abstract (and indeed a-social) individual (TMS III.3.3). This is the broader perspective of the 'impartial spectator'. Although the subject acts on selfish motives, she acts in the name of an intersubjective 'we'. As Hegel claims in the 'System of Needs', she must 'gain recognition in [her] own eyes and in the eyes of others' (R §207). In this way, the agent as citizen of civil society appears as a concrete person transfigured (or reflected, as it were) by the act of taking a position that is systematically similar to the abstract, universal standpoint of an 'impartial spectator' whereby a different – indeed mediated – standpoint on one's own volitions is gained. Smith used the image of the 'mirror' or the 'looking-glass' that society sets in front of us to see our own personal motives from a different standpoint (TMS III.1.3, III.1.5); and he spoke of the 'reflected passion' that we conceive when we look at ourselves as observed by others (TMS I.i.4.8). What Hegel presents here is the same kind of 'reflection' on one's own motivation for action. Conscience is a mirror of social feeling. 'Citizens' of civil society are 'private persons' who pursue individual ends and actions only by way of recognizing the shared character of their individual volitions and interests, that is, by projecting their motivations within the standpoint of every other member of this sphere – recognizing their own motives in the others' and the others' in their own. Although this projection does not change the selfish and private nature of individual action, it confers on it a shared universality. It is the latter that is a necessary requisite of civil society. Individual ends remain selfish and proper to the individual. They are not willed because of benevolence or because of the broader public good, as is the case within the higher unity of the state, nor are they required to renounce their particularity and interest-based nature to pass the universalizability test of Kant's categorical imperative. And yet those individual ends are *legitimately* proper to the individual as a citizen of civil society if and only if they can be viewed, recognized and endorsed from and by the standpoint of all others. Such projection implies the equality of all individuals as well as the reciprocity and reflexivity of our relations to them. This is the sense of the universality of individual action within civil society.

This, Hegel suggests, is the process in which 'subjectivity is *educated* in its particularity' (R §187). The universalization of the individual standpoint that Hegel calls '*Bildung*' (R §187 and Remark, §197, §209 Remark) – education and culture – begins precisely in this sphere with the capacity of taking the position of an impartial spectator quite in the sense defended by Smith. Although, on Hegel's view, the capacity of determining one's own action through the standpoint of others is not a merely natural disposition (or, indeed, a natural feeling) but is the product of education and culture, in civil society it is built to function as a 'second nature'. Significantly, education and culture along with 'work' are for Hegel the beginning of ethical freedom. In this way, Hegel's civil society brings together from the outset the two threads of Smith's practical philosophy – his idea of moral judgment and his economic thought.

In its first division, the 'System of Needs', civil society is presented as the sphere of the understanding. And yet, this sphere is also recognized as the 'appearance of rationality in the realm of finitude'. In Hegel's dialectic, while 'reason' indicates the highest, most complete and fully reconciled form of spirit's realization and actuality, the 'understanding' represents the phase of contradiction, negativity, conflict and finitude proper to all dialectical process (Nuzzo 2008b). In characterizing civil society as the realm of the understanding, Hegel places it between the immediate, still natural and relatively harmonious circle of family relations based on love, and the higher, fully reconciled realm of the public good proper to the state. From its intermediary position, we can expect individual activity in civil society to be characterized by contradiction in the motives of action, social tensions and deep dividing conflicts. Hence it should be of no little surprise that Hegel, instead, after having identified civil society with the realm of the understanding, indicates that the 'understanding' is '*the element of conciliation* [*das Versöhnende*] at work in this sphere' (R §189). The understanding, in Hegel's philosophy, is *never* a conciliatory force but rather its exact opposite. This passage stands as a quite unique occurrence in Hegel's thought.

Now I want to propose an explanation of this unique characterization of the understanding as the force that produces harmony and conciliation in a realm that is not yet the fully reconciled ethical state in terms of a hypothetical appropriation of Smith's idea of 'sympathy' within the dialectic of civil society. As mentioned above, my argument here is not historical but systematic. My basis is the discussion offered above, culminating in the claim that 'morality has its proper place' in the sphere of civil society. Assuming Hegel's further suggestion in the *Lectures on the History of Philosophy* that Smith develops a concrete idea of morality from the standpoint of the understanding and reflection (1986d: 285), I speculate that, appropriated in terms of the dialectic of civil society, Hegel is translating Smith's idea of 'sympathy' as a 'conciliatory understanding'.

Although the morality proper to civil society is a form of morality still proper only to the understanding and not to reason, it is already the 'appearance of reason' (R §189), the beginning of the conciliation between the individual and the universal that characterizes ethical life (the same conciliation at stake in culture). Having its proper place within civil society, Smith's sympathy would indicate the moral standpoint of the understanding within ethical life. It is the egoistic, individual morality that by being carried out from the perspective of all other equal individuals gains a universal dimension. Thereby, instead of being divisive it turns out to be an element of conciliation. Interestingly, on this model, sympathy does not display the immediacy of a natural feeling (which for Hegel is not an acceptable basis of morality) but the intellectual and reflective character of the understanding.[24] This, I submit, would not be an inaccurate rendition of the relationship that Smith himself establishes between 'sympathy' and the idea of an 'impartial spectator'. Sympathy, for Smith, is an intellectual disposition more than an original feeling – more precisely, it is a feeling intellectually produced; it has a mediating function and is not exhausted in the immediacy of natural feeling. The condition for sympathy – or the condition 'upon which […] sympathy is founded', is 'the imaginary change of situation' that leads one to assume the 'impartial spectator' standpoint.[25]

This reconstruction is further reflected in the argument that Hegel develops in the Remark to §189. Herein Hegel pays his famous tribute to the modern science of 'political economy' – to Smith, Say and Ricardo. He views political economy as the intellectual science that brings a lawful order into the apparently chaotic manifold of contingencies characterizing the economic life of society (also R §189 Addition). However, political economy itself does not properly produce any 'conciliation' within society. It accounts for one particular type of relationship among individuals in this sphere, namely, economic relations. These, in turn, are inscribed in a broader context held together by a specific form of morality – by the sympathetic morality of the understanding but also, significantly, by the idea of justice and moral resentment. Hegel argues that the manifestation of reason displayed in this realm by the activity of the understanding has two sides. On the one hand, we have the aspect of conciliation – sympathy and the sympathetic projection into the standpoint of others implying recognition, as I have suggested above. On the other hand, however, 'this is also the field in which the understanding with its subjective ends and moral opinions expresses its discontent and moral resentment' (R §189 Remark). The 'gratification' of needs at stake in this sphere is not only the gratification of material needs but also the gratification of moral feelings such as resentment and justice (TMS II.i.1–3).[26] It is no accident that the 'administration of justice' plays a fundamental role in civil society.

Thus we can now see that at the outset of the 'System of Needs' Hegel may be developing a full reference to Smith's philosophy, not only to the political economy of the *Wealth of Nations* but also to the ethics of *The Theory of Moral Sentiments*. What is relevant is that Hegel frames the dynamic of economic relations among individuals in terms of a morality in which the endorsement of the standpoint of others and their recognition along with the interaction between a 'sympathetic', conciliatory understanding, resentment and justice are essential. In contrast to the usual interpretations that view the sphere of civil society with its account of human needs and their gratification, the nature of labour, and resources exclusively in light of economic relations, I have argued that herein Hegel proposes the necessary interconnection between economics and a correspondent type of morality, which is, specifically, a morality very close to the one theorized by Smith. In other words, I contend that with his presentation of civil society Hegel proposes a reading – or better a dialectic adaptation – of the *Wealth of Nations* and *The Theory of Moral Sentiments* as constituting two aspects of the same social reality of the modern world.

Notes

1 See Brown (1991) and Teichgraeber (1981) for a history of the problem.
2 This is the position of Raphael and Macfie, editors of the Glasgow edition of the *Theory*, p. 20. For a critique of this position see Fricke (2005).
3 See Waszek (1988) for a thorough bibliography and discussion of Hegel's sources.
4 Which he owned in the English original. See Waszek (1988: 128–34).
5 Hegel's very first mention of Adam Smith is in the 1803/04 so-called *Jenaer Systementwürfe I*, Fragment 22 (Hegel 1968–, vol. 6: 323).
6 See Waszek (1988: 56–71) and its bibliographical appendix.
7 They are about aspects of civil society because these views are themselves parts of it.
8 Hegel's critique of Kant's morality is indeed in many ways questionable but this will not concern me here.

9 In introducing the concept of 'good will', Kant uses the expression 'rational and impartial spectator' in the *Groundwork* (1910, vol. 4: 393).

10 Darwall (1999: 153); also Darwall (1977). Fleischacker (1991; 1999: 42) who proposes to 'enrich' Kant's moral judgment by way of Adam Smith (and also of his view of reflective judgment) seems to go in a direction that is indeed close to Hegel.

11 My point is not to defend the accuracy of Hegel's interpretation of Smith's ethics. Indeed, Hegel's rendering of Smith's position is more an appropriation under the principles of Hegel's own philosophy than an interpretation. My point is to show that such appropriation amounts to Hegel's own rendering of the 'Adam Smith Problem'.

12 See Fleischacker (1999: 42ff.) for Smith's critique of casuistry.

13 This is the direction taken by the practical interests of the young Hegel.

14 Riedel (1969: 96–7) argues against Ilting's influential interpretation according to which Hegel reads political economy not in contrast to, but in the framework of, the categories of Aristotle's *Politics* (Ilting 1963); see also Waszek (1995: 43) who sides with Riedel.

15 At the beginning of the first chapter of the *Groundwork* (Kant 1910, vol. 4: 393), in presenting the idea of the 'good will' Kant refers to a 'rational and impartial spectator' who would declare the good will – and the good will only – worthy of happiness. If read in the framework of Hegel's critique of Kantian morality and of his endorsement of Smith's ethics within civil society, we can say that Kant appears as a proponent of an impartial spectator view similar to Hume's and Hutcheson's whereas Smith and Hegel favour a 'sympathetic' standpoint placed within ethical life itself (for this distinction see again Darwall 1999).

16 Thereby I confirm Darwall's suggestion in differentiating Smith's morality from Hume's and Hutcheson's (Darwall 1999: 141, 'the perspective of moral judgment […] is not strictly a spectator's standpoint at all').

17 See also III.2.3: we must endeavour to view our conduct 'with the eyes of other people, or as other people are likely to view them'.

18 Confront TMS III.2.3 with R §190 Addition: the needs that we aim at satisfying are not simply natural needs. We aim at satisfying the 'opinion' that those needs generate in ourselves and in others – and the opinion that others have of ourselves.

19 When Smith claims that 'Man naturally desires not only to be loved, but to be lovely' (TMS III.2.1) Hegel would agree, with the correction that the desire to be lovely is not a natural but a socially produced desire. Here is indeed a point in which both Smith's and Hegel's view intersects with Rousseau's (see extensively, Neuhouser 2008 for the notion of *amour propre*).

20 TMS 2nd edn for the 'impartial spectator' as 'man in general'; see the discussion of the passage in Raphael (1975: 91).

21 See Hegel (1986b: 145) for the role that the 'duplication' (*Verdoppelung*) of self-consciousness and the idea of 'recognition' play in the famous master–slave dialectic.

22 I endorse here Darwall's characterization of Smith's 'impartial spectator' standpoint (in contrast to Hutcheson's and Hume's) as a standpoint 'from within' the other's moral life (Darwall 1999: 141, 147). Notice, however, the transformation of the moral problem in Hegel: at stake is not moral judgment, but rather the issue of how determinate ends and feelings specifically and effectively motivate agents to action. Both for Smith and for Hegel at issue is the standpoint *on one's own* motivation for action.

23 As it was (albeit for very differently reasons) for Hume and Hutcheson as well as for Kant (see Raphael 1975: 86–7).

24 To appreciate the extent to which Smith offers Hegel with the alternative to Kant's morality, notice that Kant's practical reason is, for Hegel, still only understanding.

25 See for example, TMS I.i.4.6. Although Smith does speak of mankind as 'naturally sympathetic', the way in which sympathy actually works is not on 'natural' instinct but on the basis of an imaginative/intellectual projection. See also TMS I.i.3.2 for the intellectual character of 'approbation or disapprobation' of others' opinions.

26 A passage such as the following, for example, perfectly corresponds to Hegel's view of the moral standpoint of civil society, including the limits of this sphere (the arbitrariness of the moral opinion, the abstract character of its universality, the expression of mere 'moral opinions'): 'To us, surely, that action must appear to deserve reward, which every body who knows of it would wish to reward, and therefore delights to see rewarded: and that action must as surely appear to deserve punishment, which every body who hears of it is angry with, and upon that account rejoices to see punished' (TMS II.i.2.3).

Bibliography

Brown, V. (1991) 'Signifying voices: reading the "Adam Smith Problem"', *Economics and Philosophy*, 7: 187–220.

—— (1992/3) 'The dialogic experience of conscience: Adam Smith and the voices of Stoicism', *Eighteenth-Century Studies*, 26: 233–60.

Darwall, S. (1977) 'Two kinds of respect', *Ethics*, 88: 36–49.

—— (1999) 'Sympathetic liberalism: recent work on Adam Smith', *Philosophy & Public Affairs*, 28: 139–64.

Fitzgibbons, A. (1995) *Adam Smith's System of Liberty, Wealth, and Virtue*, Oxford: Clarendon Press.

Fleischacker, S. (1991) 'Philosophy and moral practice: Kant and Adam Smith', *Kant-Studien*, 82: 249–69.

—— (1999) *A Third Concept of Liberty: Judgment and Freedom in Kant and Adam Smith*, Princeton, NJ: Princeton University Press.

Fricke, C. (2005) 'Genesis und Geltungmoralischer Normen—Ein Gedankenexperiment von Adam Smith', in C. Fricke and H.P. Schütt (eds), *Adam Smith als Moralphilosoph*, Berlin: De Gruyter, pp. 33–63.

Griswold, C.L. (1999) *Adam Smith and the Virtues of Enlightenment*, Cambridge: Cambridge University Press.

Hegel, G.W.F. (1968–) *Gesammelte Werke*, in Verbindung mit der Deutschen Forschungsgemeinschaft, hrsg. Reinisch-Westfälischen Akademie der Wissenschaften, Hamburg: Meiner.

—— (1983) *Vorlesungen über Naturrecht und Staatswissenschaft. Heidelberg 1817/18 mit Nachtragen aus der Vorlesungen 1818/19*, Nachgeschrieben von P. Wannenmann, C. Becker (ed.), Hamburg: Meiner.

—— (1986a) *Werke in zwanzig Bände*, E. Moldenhauer and H.M. Michel (eds), Frankfurt a.M.: Surhkamp.

—— (1986b) *Phänomenologie des Geistes*, in Hegel (1986a), vol. 3.

—— (1986c [1821]) *Grundlinien der Philosophie des Rechts*, in Hegel (1986a), vol. 7.

—— (1986d) *Lectures on the History of Philosophy*, in Hegel (1986a), vol. 20.

Ilting, K.H. (1963) 'Hegels Auseinandersetzung mit der aristotelischen Politik', *Philosophisches Jahrbuch*, 71: 38–58.

Kant, I. (1910–) *Kants gesammelte Schriften*, hrsg. v. Der Preußischen Akademie der Wissenschaften, Berlin: De Gruyter.

Lukacs, G. (1948) *Der junge Hegel und die Probleme der kapitalistischen Gesellschaft*, Berlin: Aufbau.

Muller, J.Z. (1995) *Adam Smith in His Time and Ours: Designing the Decent Society*, Princeton, NJ: Princeton University Press.

Neuhouser, F. (2008) *Rousseau's Theodicy of Self-Love: Evil, Rationality and the Drive for Recognition*, Oxford: Oxford University Press.

Nuzzo, A. (2008a) *Ideal Embodiment: Kant's Theory of Sensibility*, Bloomington, IN: Indiana University Press.

—— (2008b) 'Dialectical reason and necessary conflict – understanding and the nature of terror', in P. Ashton, T. Nicolacopoulos and G. Vassilacopoulos (eds), *The Spirit of the Age: Hegel and the Fate of Thinking*, Melbourne: re.press, pp. 21–37.

Raphael, D.D. (1975) 'The impartial spectator', in A.S. Skinner and T. Wilson (eds), *Essays on Adam Smith*, Oxford: Clarendon Press, pp. 83–99.

Riedel, M. (1962) 'Hegels "bürgerliche Gesellschaft" und das Problem ihres geschichtlichen Ursprungs', *Archiv f. Recht und Sozialphilosophie*, 48: 539–67.

—— (1969) *Studien zu Hegels Rechtsphilosophie*, Frankfurt a.M.: Suhrkamp.

Smith, A. (1976) *The Theory of Moral Sentiments*, D.D. Raphael and A.L. Macfie (eds), Oxford: Clarendon Press.

Teichgraeber, R.F. (1981) 'Rethinking *Das Adam Smith Problem*', *Journal of British Studies*, 20: 106–23.

Waszek, N. (1988) *The Scottish Enlightenment and Hegel's Account of 'Civil Society'*, Dordrecht/Boston: Kluwer.

—— (1995) 'Hegels Lehre von der "bürgerlichen Gesellschaft" und die politische Ökonomie der schottischen Aufklärung', *Dialektik*, 3: 37–50.

Part II
Sympathy and moral judgment

Smith and Rousseau in dialogue

Sympathy, *pitié*, spectatorship and narrative

Charles L. Griswold

> There is a great deal of unmapped country within us which would have to be taken into account in an explanation of our gusts and storms.
> (George Eliot, *Daniel Deronda*, 2005: 244)

Some years ago Knud Haakonssen remarked to me during a break in David Gauthier's Benedict lectures at Boston University that Adam Smith seems to have spent a great deal of intellectual effort responding to the challenges he encountered in Rousseau's *Discourse on the Origin and the Foundations of Inequality among Men.*[1] This passing remark prompts one to speculate that Rousseau cost Smith more than a few sleepless nights, and indeed that if Smith was in a dogmatic slumber with respect to the moral and human problems of commercial society, Rousseau woke him from it. The evidence for any such thought is indirect, to be sure. Rousseau's *Second Discourse* appeared in 1755 and was immediately reviewed by Smith. His 1756 'Letter to the *Edinburgh Review*' contains significant commentary on the *Discourse* and his own translation of three passages.[2] Those passages are very well chosen, as they summarize some of Rousseau's most important criticisms of what one might call modernity. Published within a year of the appearance of the *Second Discourse*, this must be among the earliest reviews of Rousseau's hugely influential and controversial essay, and of course preceded by several years the first edition (1759) of *The Theory of Moral Sentiments* (henceforth abbreviated 'TMS'; Smith 1982a). Smith never refers to Rousseau by name in TMS, but there clearly are echoes; and in any case Smith refers to relatively few thinkers by name (Hume included). He does refer elsewhere to other of Rousseau's writings, and appears to have owned all of Rousseau's major and many of his minor works.[3] So far as we know, the two never met; Smith evidently decided to leave that delightful interaction to Hume. Hume certainly found Rousseau preoccupying personally and socially, but not (so far as I can tell) intellectually – the obverse of Smith's relation to Rousseau.

My aim in this essay is not to trace the ways in which Rousseau's thought finds echoes and responses in TMS. In their excellent work on Smith and

The Philosophy of Adam Smith, The Adam Smith Review, 5: 59–84 © 2010 The International Adam Smith Society, ISSN 1743–5285, ISBN 978-0-415-56256-0.

Rousseau, Dennis Rasmussen and Ryan Hanley have already made very helpful contributions to that project.[4] My aim is different: I shall reflect on two points Smith makes about Rousseau in his review, showing how they pose a challenge to Smith that would have warranted some sleepless nights on his part, whether or not Smith took them as such and whether or not Rousseau would have intended them as such. I am less concerned with tracing the historical transmission of ideas than with reconstructing several initial steps of a philosophical dialogue that might have taken place. It is a limitation of my essay that I attribute views to Rousseau that I do not sufficiently substantiate here. For now, let 'Rousseau' stand for both the letter and spirit of his views, backed by a promissory note for scholarly substantiation on another occasion. And sleepless nights can issue in decisive rebuttals: it may well be that Smith has the resources for persuasive replies to the Rousseauan criticisms I seek to articulate, and on another occasion I will pursue that further step. I do not here mean to endorse either side of the dialectic I am reconstructing.

My reflections amount to work in progress. In the background lies my even more speculative sense that Smith and Rousseau compose an unusually interesting pair. They share a similar set of concerns, themes, vocabulary, and even arguments; they are of course near contemporaries. In some sense, both espouse sentimentalist views of human nature. And yet what one might call their sensibilities or 'pictures' – to borrow a term from Wittgenstein – are deeply different. Rousseau is the great modern progenitor of notions of historicity, estrangement of self, social alienation, perspectivalism and narrative. He's a critic of philosophy (as an academic discipline) and a partisan of literature; indeed, as Peter Brooks notes, Rousseau's *Julie* is 'a novel that in so many ways announces the nineteenth-century tradition' of narrative writing (Brooks 1992: 21).[5] Rousseau's works are suffused with the themes of longing, fragmentation, reconciliation, redemption and forgiveness. While Smith is certainly attuned to problems of social and personal fragmentation, he is the great spokesman for the primacy of the social standpoint (crystallized in the 'impartial spectator'), a commitment not at all at odds with his supposed 'individualism' in the economic sphere (the impartial spectator endorses the individual's bettering his or her own condition, so long as rules of justice are not violated, and spectators admire wealth and greatness, as TMS explains). And while he is well aware of the pull of the Rousseauan vocabulary of loss and longing, and of the issue of paradoxical, unintended, and even ironical processes and outcomes, on the whole his outlook is more confidently reconciliationist, more trusting in the claims of philosophical theory (after all, he wrote a book containing the word 'theory' in its title, something Rousseau never did).

To return to the specifics to be discussed here: the first point has to do with what Rousseau calls '*pitié*', and the second with the rhetoric of the *Discourse*. I shall discuss these in turn, and hope to show that there is an unexpected connection between the two, between the 'content' and narrative 'form' of the text. From the Rousseauan perspective I reconstruct, they jointly amount to a sort of argument against Smithian 'sympathy' – one that Smith can rebut only with difficulty. At stake are the meanings of such terms as pity, commiseration, sympathy, sociability and self-love. The possibility of epistemic access to others, of something like spectatorial insight into the situation of another, is also at issue.

Pitié and sympathy

Towards the start of his discussion of Rousseau's *Discourse* Smith makes several intriguing comments, two of which I will mention. First, he claims that neither Rousseau nor Mandeville allows that human beings are social by nature. As Smith puts it, 'Both of them however suppose, that there is in man no powerful instinct which necessarily determines him to seek society for its own sake ...' ('Letter' 11, EPS: 250).[6] In Smith's special TMS sense of the word, neither allows that human beings are naturally *sympathetic*. Second, he notes that Rousseau agrees with Mandeville that pity is natural to us ('Letter' 11, EPS: 251). In Part VII of TMS (see VII.iii.1.1–4), Mandeville is cast as a 'self-love' theorist (even though he grants a place to pity). As glossed there, the proponent of the self-love theory holds that one is concerned for others only insofar as doing so is useful to oneself, that one approves or disapproves of others on similar grounds, and that one cannot fully enter into the situation of another (for this last point, see below). The last of these views would explain, for Smith, why there is no concern for 'society for its own sake'. Smith holds that concern for 'society for its own sake' is natural to us and that it is explained by a principle he also thinks undeniable, viz., 'sympathy'. He faults the self-love theorist for not understanding that and how we are sympathetic beings. Putting those passages together with the review, it would seem that from Smith's perspective – and here is an inference that Smith does not explicitly make – Rousseau is made a fellow traveller of Mandeville and so in some sense is a 'self-love' theorist. It is not that Rousseau's denial of natural sociability necessarily commits him, from Smith's perspective, to a crude version of the view that we are concerned for others just so far as we determine that doing so is useful to us, but that it is conceptually tied to the idea that our capacity to enter into the world of another is severely restricted. But how can that be – how can Rousseau reject the idea that we are naturally 'sociable', and thus implicitly reject the notion of 'sympathy' that Smith wants to defend against Mandeville (and Hobbes), all the while asserting that human beings naturally feel *pitié* (which itself seems able to restrain our self-interest)?[7]

The explanation of the consistency between *pitié* and (what Smith thinks of as) Mandevillean egoism has to do with the deep differences between *pitié* and Smithian sympathy. This is the first point that I would like to examine. In responding to Rousseau's thesis that we are naturally compassionate but not naturally sociable, Smith develops a notion of 'sympathy' that distances it from self-love theory at an epistemic level. The result (in TMS VII) is what from the Rousseauan perspective is a rather extreme and problematic view, and I shall attempt to explain how the objections to Smith's alternative might go.

As Rousseau describes *pitié* in the *Discourse*, it is one of two natural principles governing the residents of the state of nature; the other is the drive for self-preservation. Here is how Rousseau describes it in the passages to which Smith alludes: *pitié* having been given to humans (and some non-human animals) in the state of nature to

> soften the ferociousness of his amour propre or of the desire for self-preservation prior to the birth of amour propre, tempers his ardor for well-being with an innate repugnance to see his kind suffer. ... I speak of Pity, a disposition suited to beings as weak and as subject to so many ills as we are; ...
>
> (Rousseau 1997b: 152)

It is

> the pure movement of Nature prior to all reflection: such is the force of natural pity, which the most depraved morals still have difficulty destroying, since in our theaters one daily sees being moved and weeping at the miseries of some unfortunate person people who, if they were in the Tyrant's place, would only increase their enemy's torments; ...
>
> (Rousseau 1997b: 152)

And:

> Indeed, what are generosity, Clemency, Humanity, if not Pity applied to the weak, the guilty, or the species in general? ... Even if it were true that commiseration is nothing but a sentiment that puts us in the place of him who suffers, a sentiment that is obscure and lively in Savage man, developed but weak in Civil man, what difference could this idea make to the truth of what I say, except to give it additional force? Indeed commiseration will be all the more energetic in proportion as the Onlooking animal identifies more intimately with the suffering animal: Now this identification must, clearly, have been infinitely closer in the state of Nature than in the state of reasoning. It is reason that engenders amour propre, and reflection that reinforces it; reason that turns man back upon himself; reason that separates him from everything that troubles and afflicts him: It is Philosophy that isolates him; ...
>
> (Rousseau 1997b: 153)

Pity 'carries us without reflection to the assistance of those we see suffer', and is thus key to our 'natural goodness' (154). Rousseau goes on to paint a picture of the 'Savage' who lacks passions of (romantic) love, revenge, jealousy, and such; this creature seems to have no imagination or language (155–7, 165).

From this I think we can draw several conclusions about *pitié*. In its most primitive expression in the state of nature, it is minimally cognitive (it is pre-linguistic and spontaneous, but perhaps involves grasping what would be of help to the sufferer), and does not involve (in spite of some of Rousseau's formulations) putting oneself in the place of the agent if that means something like taking on the perspective of the agent.[8] Indeed, in the last passage from the *Second Discourse* just quoted, Rousseau seems to *oppose* commiseration understood as 'nothing but a sentiment that puts us in the place of him who suffers' and *pitié* understood as 'identification'. *Pitié* doesn't seem to require anything like perspective-shifting. It amounts to something like the disposition to respond to suffering by wishing to alleviate the cir-cumstances that create that condition – but all without plan, reflection, and comparison of self and other, at least in the pre-linguistic state of nature. Rousseau's remarks in the *Second Discourse* don't make *pitié* sound like a contagion of feeling, so much as spontaneous and ad hoc beneficence. Therein the source, in that text, of the moral virtues.[9]

Neither on Rousseau's account, nor on Smith's account of Rousseau, is *pitié* sufficient for natural sociability; so *pitié* still lies within the orbit of what Smith thinks of as Rousseau's Mandevillean orientation, that is, it is still compatible with self-love theory. And that is because there is no transposition of self involved, no viewing of the other from the other's perspective, and no viewing of self from the other's perspective. Without sympathy, there is no genuine interdependence. Indeed, for Smith, sympathy is constitutive of being a self (or, being an agential self); absent the 'mirror' in which one sees oneself, there is no self (recall TMS III.1.3–4). I note that unlike Smithian sympathy, *pitié* does not transmit the agent's joy or 'positive' feelings to the onlooker, feelings pleasurable to *both* their owner and the onlooker – another difference between the two.[10] It is hard not to read the first two sentences of TMS as referring to, or incorporating, Rousseau's remarks about *pitié* (of course, they may be read as responding to other thinkers as well). Smith begins as follows:

> How selfish soever man may be supposed, there are evidently some principles in his nature, which interest him in the fortune of others, and render their happiness necessary to him, though he derives nothing from it except the pleasure of seeing it. Of this kind is pity or compassion, the emotion which we feel for the misery of others, when we either see it, or are made to conceive it in a very lively manner. That we often derive sorrow from the sorrow of others, is a matter of fact too obvious to require any instances to prove it; for this sentiment, like all the other original passions of human nature, is by no means confined to the virtuous and humane, though they perhaps may feel it with the most

exquisite sensibility. The greatest ruffian, the most hardened violator of
the laws of society, is not altogether without it.

(TMS I.i.1.1)

I see little here that Rousseau would disagree with, indeed the multiple echoes
of the passages from the *Second Discourse* are striking. Yet it is also striking
that Smith is setting this up as a *response* to the supposition that man is
'selfish', given that he takes (or so I am arguing) Rousseauan *pitié* as compatible with that very view.

Smith's self-assigned task, in other words, could be put this way: to
articulate a conception of sympathy that incorporates Rousseauan *pitié* but
also something Rousseau's story rejects, viz. genuine interdependence from
the get-go. For then true sociality (such that, to quote again from Smith's
review of Rousseau, the human being possesses a 'powerful instinct which
necessarily determines him to seek society for its own sake') would be built
into the very fabric of the simplest moral exchanges of the sort Rousseau is
vividly depicting, and the supposition that we are naturally 'selfish' would be
refuted. Then the conceptual space for exploring the positive moral possibilities for sociality would open up – possibilities that scarcely seem to arise in
the *Second Discourse*.

Smith launches into that task in the second paragraph of TMS. And here
begins a series of formulations found throughout the book. They are not
equivalent to each other, and a hostile critic would no doubt argue that they
amount to a kind of equivocation. Smith starts off in the first sentence of
the second paragraph by glossing 'pity or compassion' as the spectator's
'conceiving what we ourselves should feel in the like situation'. Let us
observe, first, that as Smith sets up the discussion from the very first sentence
of the book, the axis is the relation between actor and spectator, not between
two actors or two spectators. Second, pity or compassion is extended by the
spectator. Smith does speak further on as though there could be agential
sympathy, but that seems to come to something like adopting a spectator's
point of view on self and other. So sympathy is spectatorial, and that seems
crucial for it already embodies the beginnings of the psychological – or better,
identity- and character-constituting – interdependence which Rousseau judges
to be at the heart of our loss of freedom, authenticity and happiness. I grant
that Rousseau too used, in talking about *pitié*, the metaphor of the 'onlooker',
a point Smith would no doubt drive home in a debate with Rousseau.

Third, to state the obvious, at least two people are written into the original
scene of Smithian commiseration; in that minimal sense it is already social.
Fourth, the controlling metaphor in Smith's articulation of the matter, from
the second sentence on, is visual.[11] By the fourth paragraph, he has deployed
the term 'spectator'. His is a spectator theory and not, say, an auditor theory,
a point to which I shall return. Fifth, Smith's use of the verb 'conceive' in the
first and second paragraphs already carries the un-Rousseauan suggestion
that the process is somehow, to some extent, intrinsically cognitive from the

get-go (in what Rousseau would think of as its natural state). It involves *understanding* the point of view and situation of the other, and thus perspective-shifting on the spectator's part. To be sure, he also uses the term in a way that suggests it is synonymous with 'imagine', as in 'to conceive or to imagine' (end of second paragraph); so the imagination must in some sense be cognitive (a point also evinced in Smith's lectures on the history of astronomy). That 'pity or compassion' will require imagination, for Smith, is explicitly asserted in the second paragraph.

Smith's first gloss on *sympathy* (our 'conceiving what we ourselves should feel in the like situation') doesn't seem to get us past the self-love theory, any more than do the others in TMS's second paragraph. He also says there such things as that '[b]y the imagination we place ourselves in his situation', and speaks of us as spectators who 'thus brought home to ourselves' the sufferer's sentiments and 'thus adopted and made them our own', and in the third paragraph of their 'changing places in fancy with the sufferer'. Versions of such formulations abound. In the fourth paragraph, when introducing the term 'spectator', Smith speaks of 'an analogous emotion' that 'springs up, at the thought of his [the agent's] situation', and he illustrates this with our response to tragedy or romance. In the sixth paragraph he acknowledges the possibility that on some occasions sympathy may spread emotions instantaneously (I.i.1.6); while this may allow for sympathy as contagion, the next three paragraphs seem to argue that even in such cases an exchange of places is taking place.[12]

If the 'imaginary change of situation' (I.i.4.7) that lies at the core of such formulations comes to feeling what I would feel were I in the agent's situation, Rousseauan *pitié* may have been modified but not in a way that decisively calls into question the self-love thesis Smith takes himself to be refuting. For that thesis seems primarily to be an epistemic one about our knowledge of others, and secondarily a moral one about motivation (expressed, say, in caring or endorsing attitudes and actions). Indeed, Smith seems to be assuming that one cannot rebut the second, moral sense of 'selfish' without rebutting the first, epistemic, sense. It is a crucial part of my argument that Smith's argument works in that way (I return to this contention below). But to borrow a thought Nagel offers in a not unrelated context, in asking ourselves 'what it is like' to be so and so, we are not asking ' "what (in our experience) it *resembles*" but rather "how it is for the subject himself" ' (Nagel 1974: 440, n. 6, and p. 439). We want to understand not what it would be like for us to be that other or in the other's situation, but what it is like for it to be what it is. Comprehension by analogy, or contagion of feeling, or simply bringing home the case by imagining myself in the other's situation, plainly won't do *that* job – even according to Smith, as I shall argue in a moment. Yet a tension is inherent in the matter. Since I can't actually *be* the 'person principally concerned' (as Smith insists at the start of the second paragraph), it would seem that there is going to have to be some sort of comparative work going on. I can't know what it is like for X to be itself without some relation of resemblance between it and me. So one pole of the imaginative relation will be the spectator, whose ego cannot therefore be subtracted out.

And that seems to me to be precisely the sort of point Rousseau might have driven home: the split between actor and spectator, and the demand that the former be accessible to the latter's sympathetic and supervisory gaze, already asks for the impossible and invites self-falsifying strategies on both sides – all the more so when the actor learns to need the spectator's review. Perhaps some such thought helps to explain why Rousseau distinguished between two kinds of self-love (*amour propre* and *amour de soi*) rather than simply opposing self-love and sympathy.

It seems that Smith was well aware of these sorts of considerations, and therefore that he needed to go beyond the formulations of sympathy that characterize the opening pages of TMS. When in Part VII he turns to the lengthy discussion of the 'self-love' theory of the sources of approbation, he wrote what I take to be the most extreme version of his anti-Rousseauan, non-egoistic doctrine of sympathy:

> Sympathy, however, cannot, in any sense, be regarded as a selfish principle. When I sympathize with your sorrow or your indignation, it may be pretended, indeed, that my emotion is founded in self-love, because it arises from bringing your case home to myself, from putting myself in your situation, and thence conceiving what I should feel in the like circumstances. But though sympathy is very properly said to arise from an imaginary change of situations with the person principally concerned, yet this imaginary change is not supposed to happen to me in my own person and character, but in that of the person with whom I sympathize. When I condole with you for the loss of your only son, in order to enter into your grief I do not consider what I, a person of such a character and profession, should suffer, if I had a son, and if that son was unfortunately to die: but I consider what I should suffer if I was really you, and I not only change circumstances with you, but I change persons and characters. My grief, therefore, is entirely upon your account, and not in the least upon my own. It is not, therefore, in the least selfish. How can that be regarded as a selfish passion, which does not arise even from the imagination of any thing that has befallen, or that relates to myself, in my own proper person and character, but which is entirely occupied about what relates to you? A man may sympathize with a woman in child-bed; though it is impossible that he should conceive himself as suffering her pains in his own proper person and character.
>
> (TMS VII.iii.1.4)

Smith concludes his proclamation by stating that the entire self-love theory of human nature seems to him 'to have arisen from some confused mis-apprehension of the system of sympathy' (VII.iii.1.4). Rousseau's theory of *pitié* is presumably one such misapprehension. Nothing in the remaining twenty-five or so pages of TMS modifies or dilutes this culminating passage; it is Smith's last, best stab at distinguishing his view from the self-love alternative, and it is noteworthy that it does not reduce to processes of analogizing or of finding resemblances between spectator and actor, and uses no phrases to suggest that the actor and his or her plight is in principle anything but fully perceptible, in its own terms, to the spectator.

This final formulation seems markedly different from most of the earlier ones in TMS. My bringing your case home now means my putting myself in your shoes, as you; not confusing myself with you, of course, but also not simply putting myself in your shoes. It entails my feeling not just with you, but feeling your feelings as you have them, and thus somehow sharing your perspective on your situation. This is quite far from the examples in the third paragraph of TMS, where the spectators' fellow-feeling 'arises from conceiving what they themselves would suffer, if they really were the wretches whom they are looking upon, and if that particular part in themselves was actually affected in the same miserable manner' (I.i.1.3). Now, by contrast, we have scenes of unambiguous and self-negating sympathy, epistemically speaking. As I read the Part VII passage, Smith thinks this is a necessary condition of adequate moral assessment, as already suggested. The repeated use of 'therefore' in the text just quoted at length makes best sense if Smith sees himself as making an inference from the affirmation of an epistemic possibility (viz., that the situation and perspective of another is accessible to the spectator) to the denial of the truth of the selfishness theory. Even at the start of the book, the references to changing places with the other seem clearly to be about epistemic access to another's self and world; but in Part VII we are given the most extreme statement of the thesis that the required epistemic access can be had. So a lot rides, for Smith himself, on whether or not he has got the epistemic issue right.

I should think that Rousseau would deny that he does, and would start by noting that Smith doesn't actually provide any *argument* in this key passage for the possibility of sympathy so understood. Smith is pounding the table and insisting, with the help of his two examples, that this is what is 'supposed' to go on when I sympathize with the sufferer. Smith had earlier said things to buttress his case, however, and I'd like briefly to examine one of them in particular.

I noted that Smith's controlling model for sympathetic spectatorship is visual (though other metaphors are deployed as well).[13] Recall several of the initial examples: we see the stroke about to land on another's body; the mob is 'gazing at a dancer on the slack rope'; 'persons of delicate fibres and a weak constitution' are 'looking on' the bodies of beggars (all from the third paragraph). When Smith introduces the term 'impartial', it is again in conjunction with the metaphor of sight (I.i.4.8, 'As their sympathy makes them look at it, in some measure, with his eyes …'). When discussing the possibility of a 'human creature' growing up outside of society, Smith uses metaphors of mirrors and looking-glasses to capture the sense in which self-spectatorship is there absent (III.1.3,4). And there are other such occurrences of visual metaphors scattered throughout the book.[14] The impartial spectator, who is the ideal sympathizer (VII.ii.1.49; VII.ii.3.21), has the keenest sight.

Why is the visual metaphor so useful for Smith? I speculate that he seized upon it for several reasons. First, as Smith wants to build an ethics on his doctrine of sympathy, ocular language is a natural way to talk about *perspective*, which of course is crucial to the effort. Second, the metaphor suggests detachment from the object seen, and that may be thought important for insulating the spectator from the agent's turbulence (in the form, say, of passions), and thus for correct perspective. Third, sight suggests a model of knowing that does seem, in the ideal case, to leave the spectator's ego behind. If I correctly see the tree outside my window, whatever else is true about me seems irrelevant: I really have grasped the object I am perceiving, and I have done so without altering the object of sight. The impartial spectator's own perspective-distorting turbulence is also left behind. Presumably this is one reason why the metaphor has been so attractive to philosophers back to Plato. It fits in with the sort of epistemic point about sympathy that Smith is trying to maintain, as I read him. Fourth, while Smith invokes examples that involve visual clues, he is also talking about the imagination; and it is natural to characterize the imagination as 'seeing' this or that. Imagining and visualizing seem connected.

Fifth, vision is correctable, as is intellectual vision. In discussing the authority of conscience, Smith talks about impartial sympathy as a process in which the spectator compensates for bias by learning to 'view them [the interests and passions of the agent], neither from our own place nor yet from his, neither with our own eyes nor yet with his, but from the place and with the eyes of a third person, who has no particular connexion with either, and who judges with impartiality between us' (III.3.3). This follows a paragraph in which Smith has described how the 'natural eye of the mind' learns to assess distances correctly, and he refers for support to the 'philosophy of vision', meaning Berkeley's *New Theory of Vision*, as the editors note.[15] Smith must have been attracted to the idea that sympathetic seeing could learn to assess impartially by correcting for subjective bias, that is, self-love.

But Rousseau would question the capacity of sympathy to 'see' the situation of the other in the sense required by Smith, and might do so by focusing on other features of Smith's account, some of which stand in tension with the thesis of transparency to the impartial spectator. Rousseau might start off by noting that for Smith, sympathizing is not really much like correctly seeing the object outside the window. All that is too external; what is at stake here is some process of getting 'inside' the agent and his situation, not simply a spectatorial appraisal of their features – aesthetic or other – from a third person standpoint.[16] The imaginative re-creation of 'the situation' is what interests us, whether in life or, Smith says, in literature or drama (I.i.1.10; I.ii.2.2, 3, 4; II.i.5.3). But this requires, Rousseau might insist, a discursive *description* of the situation, as well as a potentially complicated appraisal of what the *salient* features are. For Rousseau, the complications will be accentuated by what he takes to be the corruptions of our post-lapsarian state (one that includes, moreover, the weakening of *pitié*). 'The situation' does not consist simply in a set of facts; it will include, for any spectator however impartial, a judgment of what the relevant facts are, of their causal relations, of how they did or might have seemed to an actor at the time and why (not causally why, but why according to the actor). The salient features may lie in the (actor's) past, future, or both. The diachronic sequences of events will also have to be understood, as they are part of 'the situation'. The ocular metaphor tends to occlude the temporal dimension by suggesting a static, spatial model.[17]

There are a number of places where Smith brings out the interpretive complexity of grasping a situation, and yet without explicitly recognizing its tension with the visual model of impartial spectatorship. Consider for example his discussion of conscience, during the course of which he describes how the agent would review his conduct 'in the light in which the impartial spectator would view it', comparing it with how the misinformed public views it, and so forth (III.2.5). The interpretive and narrative manoeuvres required for the operation are quite complex. In another striking case, described in a passage leading up to one with a clear Rousseauan echo (duly noted ad loc. by the editors of TMS), Smith analyses the 'deception which rouses and keeps in continual motion the industry of mankind' (IV.1.10). The sympathetic and imaginative work of the spectator is amazingly complicated here, as it produces a story about the supposed happiness of the rich and the great, especially about their possessions. On account of their aesthetic qualities – 'the ingenious and artful adjustment of those means to the end for which they were intended' – these possessions strike the spectator as admirable. Smith follows all this with an account of how perspective on the whole scene changes as one enters old age, and with it the corresponding narrative: 'Power and riches appear then to be, what they are, enormous and operose machines contrived to produce a few trifling conveniences to the body ...' (IV.1.8).

The hermeneutic complexity of bringing the situation home to oneself was in fact implicit at the start of the book as well, perhaps most clearly in Smith's striking example of the 'illusion of the imagination' that enables our 'sympathy' with the dead (I.i.1.13). Smith vividly sketches a story about the situation of the dead, as recounted by us from their perspective as we imagine it. We should recall that his story is actually quite selective, as it effectively dismisses the notion that the souls of the dead are happily off in some other-worldly place (hence his use of the word 'illusion'). Humans have anciently told many a complex story about post-mortem life, sometimes spun in elaborate religious terms; perhaps this is one of the original subjects of story-telling.

Even the initial examples already mentioned are much more complex descriptively than they might appear. Your brother is upon the rack – is this judicial punishment? In a secular or religious frame? Is it torture? How you, *qua* spectator, answer such questions will surely affect your sympathetic understanding. The spectator draws back at the stroke aimed at the agent's leg or arm – is this observation of punishment? If so, an elaborate social context must be assumed. The mob gazes at the dancer on the slack rope – presumably this is at some public fair, a social scene whose character and very existence call for a complex narrative. Passersby squirm as they gaze upon the beggar – but beggars are, as Smith later points out, the object of a number of feelings in the spectator, such that he (the beggar) 'excites little compassion' but is nonetheless sufficiently 'pitied' as to be rescued from abject poverty. Our response is mingled with 'contempt', and depends in part on what story we tell about the role of the beggar in bringing about his own condition (III.3.18). A complex set of social norms as well as assumptions about the (un)fairness of the economic system also play into the sense in which we sympathize with the beggar.

And the plot thickens. The actor will often, Smith indicates, solicit the spectator's pity and compassion by telling his or her story, by advocating on his or her own behalf. Contrary to Smith's controlling formulations, it may well be not simply a question of the spectator looking at the scene, adjusting the eye of the mind, and sympathetically getting the full picture, so much as listening to the actor's suasive narrative, and then comparing it to his or her own interpretation. That may take place in the context of what Smith sometimes calls a 'conversation' (I.i.4.10). As I am picturing the exchange, it has a lot to do with competing stories and interpretations. There is not going to be, in many cases, a simple and decisive spectatorial grasping of the situation by bringing it home to oneself.

Consider once again the two key examples Smith provides in TMS VII. iii.1.4. The perspective one takes on what (one imagines) the bereft father is experiencing seems heavily dependent on the sort of story one tells about the particulars. Was the son killed fighting nobly in battle? Run over by a drunk driver? A suicide? Died in prison? While rebelling against the father's authority? How long ago was it and how old was the son? Obviously, different cultures will promote varying norms about what it is that one is to feel in the relevant context, which will inevitably affect the spectator's understanding of the matter. Smith himself brings up the very same example of the loss of an only son in Part V ('Of Custom') and makes just these sorts of points. As we 'bring home to ourselves' the situation of the sufferer, much will depend on our assumptions about his 'fixt habit and temper' derived from this or that way of life – Smith mentions that of a general as contrasted with that of a parent in private life (V.2.5).

And surely the narratively and socially embedded character of sympathy is all the more evident in the controversial example of the man sympathizing with the woman in child-birth. Introducing as it does interesting questions about the gendered character of sympathy, it problematizes still further the notion that impartial sympathizing can somehow see the other's situation from their standpoint fully and definitively. And yet Smith speaks in that

Part VII passage (VII.iii.1.4) as though the process weren't heavily mediated. As he there says, as spectator 'I change persons and characters' with you the agent and experience your situation as you, not as me – precisely in spite of the impossibility of my being in your situation.

Smith is right to emphasize that what he's calling 'sympathy' requires conception, that is, cognition, as well as imagination. But in TMS he doesn't seem to want to draw the consequence: viz. that there is no such thing as 'the' spectatorial perspective on the other's situation and experience, no 'imaginary change of situations' that gets the impartial spectator inside the agent or the agent's situation in the way Smithian sympathy requires. What there is instead, in all of the interesting cases, is an interpretive process expressed in part through narrative, or probably narratives whose competing claims must themselves be adjudicated somehow. And these will be socially mediated, reflective of custom and thus of a history of conventions. Not only will a multiplicity of narratively embedded perspectives present themselves, they will all be from some particular standpoint or other; the ego of the onlooker, itself socially embedded, is not simply left behind.[18] There is no such thing as '*the* impartial spectator', just this or that spectator who may be more or less impartial (in some sense of the term).

In sum, the Rousseau I have postulated would argue that Smith's account of sympathy contains an internal tension between its official claims, resoundingly asserted in the culminating Part VII passage I have examined, and much else that lies implicit in Smith's account of sympathy. From that deconstructive argument he would infer that Smith's rebuttal of the view that we are not by nature sociable (I am glossing this as the self-love theory, for the reasons mentioned) is undermined by the very terms in which it is, in good part, stated. The transparency of the agent to the impartial spectator, the definitiveness of the latter's knowledge and judgment, the hygienic separation of self-love from sympathy – these are among the views that Smith's reply to Rousseau seems to require according to Smith himself, and which Rousseau in turn would judge to be unsuccessfully defended. I also would argue that Rousseau thinks such extreme claims on behalf of sympathy to be unnecessary to understanding or feeling for another.

And this thought brings me to a second point Smith remarks upon in his review of Rousseau's *Second Discourse*.

Rhetoric and narrative

When not quoting from Rousseau, the point on which Smith perhaps remarks the most vividly in his review of the *Second Discourse* is Rousseau's rhetorical style. Before the three long quotations, he remarks:

Mr. Rousseau, intending to paint the savage life as the happiest of any, presents only the indolent side of it to view, which he exhibits indeed with the most beautiful and agreeable colours, in a style, which, tho' laboured and studiously elegant, is every where sufficiently nervous, and sometimes even sublime and pathetic. It is by the help of this style, together with a little philosophical chemistry, that the principles and ideas of the profligate Mandeville seem in him to have all the purity and sublimity of the morals of Plato, and to be only the true spirit of a republican carried a little too far.

('Letter' 12, EPS: p. 251)[19]

Smith goes on to remark that there is no point in analysing Rousseau's presentation of the state of nature or of its decline into civilization because the work 'consists almost entirely of rhetoric and description'. That is a rather harsh judgment but does point to something true: by and large Rousseau presents a narrative, not an argument. The *Second Discourse* is not fundamentally a theory, but a species of 'conjectural history', to borrow Dugald Stewart's description of some of Smith's work (Stewart 1966: 34).[20] It is a kind of genealogical narrative. Rousseau was, in fact, a narrator or storyteller *par excellence*. The autobiographical writings are obviously forms of genealogical narrative; but the stories about the genesis of the ideal state (the *Social Contract*) and ideal moral education (*Emile*) may also be seen as narratives. And of course, he is the author of the novel *Julie*, among other literary exercises. By contrast, TMS presents itself as a theory and analysis, not as a narrative, however much it deploys stories and other rhetorical or stylistic devices to make its argument.

Of course, Smith knew a lot about rhetoric, and in his lectures on the topic he explicitly made connections between the workings of sympathy and those of communication (e.g., Smith 1985, LRBL i.v.56 and i.133). He remarked on the different ways in which social status, as presented in literature, affects sympathy (LRBL ii.90–1), and in effect discusses how various forms of rhetoric – say, that of Thucydides – do or don't enable the spectator to sympathize with the actors (e.g., LRBL ii.28). He formulates the 'Generall rule that when we mean to affect the reader deeply we must have recourse to the indirect method of description, relating the effects the transaction produced both on the actors and Spectators' (LRBL ii.7).[21] If I am right that sympathetic spectating is often dependent on narrative, then the resources of the LRBL ought to have something to teach us about how the machinery set out in TMS is supposed to work.[22] To take a further example, historical narrative may, Smith states, retain its 'impartiality' while exciting emotions in the audience but only by narrating facts which excite those feelings. By contrast, the orator 'heightens every incident and pretends at least to be deeply affected by them himself' (LRBL ii.38). Applied to a complex scene of sympathy in which there is interchange between actor and spectator, we might think of the competing narratives as, in Smith's jargon, oratorical in the actor's case and historical in the spectator's. I earlier referred to this as a species of 'conversation'. The LRBL makes it clear that Smith considers language to be inherently persuasive (he 'makes rhetoric the genus to which all communication is species', to quote McKenna 2006: 1), and that the forms of communication relevant to explaining actions, sentiments and motives will include what we (not he) would call narrative. And this brings in some interesting problems of audience, the role of fiction, the question of perspective, and the role of social norms and political agendas, as the Smith of the LRBL well knew.[23]

Ironically, the notion that all communication – including narrative – is a form of rhetoric is affirmed by Smith himself in TMS. Some nineteen pages after the culminating passage on sympathy as the answer to self-love theory, and just a few paragraphs before the conclusion of TMS, Smith wrote these intriguing lines:

> The desire of being believed, the desire of persuading, of leading and directing other people, seems to be one of the strongest of all our natural desires. It is, perhaps, the instinct upon which is founded the faculty of speech, the characteristical faculty of human nature.
>
> (TMS VII.iv.25)

Framing the narrative of sympathy as part of an often bilateral process of discursive persuasion helps to underline the limitations of the ocular model embedded in the impartial spectator theory, which is the theory of sympathy. Sympathy now looks more and more like a communicative, rhetorical process.

I cannot here further work out how the rhetorical theory of LRBL might bear on TMS, as that would amount to a different inquiry. I am suggesting that there is such a connection; that, more specifically, there is a narrative dimension to sympathy as analysed in TMS; and that TMS tends to occlude that fact by advancing a non-narrativistic, ocular conception of sympathetic spectatorship with which the narrative dimension is in tension. All of that suggests a relatively neglected, second 'Adam-Smith Problem', viz. that of the relation between the moral theory and the theory of rhetoric. By contrast, Rousseau's writing trumpets its rhetorical or narrative frame, as Smith rightly if dismissively notes of the *Second Discourse*.

At this point, a definition of 'narrative' may be requested. Putting the technical complexities of the LRBL aside, including its definition of 'narrative', let me offer the briefest definition of the term, sufficient for the purposes of the present essay.[24] I am not claiming that Smith would agree with the following.

Let us begin by distinguishing between a 'chronicle' and a 'narrative'. I shall stipulate that the former refers to the bare facts: say, that X did Y in manner Z at time T. By referring to 'facts' I mean to keep the door open not just to events, but reactions to events. Notionally, a chronicle is content abstracted from viewpoint. Normally there will be different ways of trying to convey the chronicle, the content; but notionally, just one content to be conveyed. Narration does the conveying or the telling; it discursively organizes events into some sort of pattern – say, a temporal pattern, a causal one, or one that supplies insight into motivations (this is not a complete list, and these could hold concurrently) – *and* implies one or more perspectives.

Narrative does not aspire to be non-perspectival in the way that a mathematical treatise or logical proof or Smithian impartial spectatorship does. Narrative is necessarily diachronic in that it attempts to make an intelligible whole out of contingent events occurring through time.

The basic ideas of narrative include (i) the organization of events into a pattern or whole with beginning, middle and end – plot, in short; and (ii) the perspective of the narrator on events and on the perspectives of the agents or actors – a point of view implicit or explicit in the telling. A narrative is normally a unifying, and in that way meaning-making, discursive enterprise. The line between chronicle and narrative is not hygienic; how could one say what the chronicle is – how could one recount it – without narrating in any way whatsoever? Yet one cannot infer that a chronicle 'just is' a narrative, let alone that every narrative is a fiction.[25] The narrative *characterizes* what is happening or happened; in so doing it reshapes it, or remembers it, or re-imagines it, but does not necessarily fabricate it out of thin air. In the context relevant to the present discussion, narrative claims to represent, in some sense, how things are (or were), what happened, and why; not just causally 'why', but why from the perspective of the agent.

Now if some such view of narrative helps flesh out what the sympathetic spectator is doing, then we may perhaps draw the following conclusions. First, a narrative model should help articulate how the spectator understands what it is like to be the person in that situation without requiring full-blown Smithian sympathy (recall the examples of the woman in child-birth and of the man who loses his only son). As Goldie puts what is involved in such 'understanding' (whether in literature or life):

> our interpretive task involves what has been called the *hermeneutic circle* (see Gadamer, 1975, pp. 265ff.). Putting it as more paradoxical than it really is, we will not achieve an understanding of the episodes of thought and feeling involved in a person's emotional experience unless we have a prior understanding of his overall character (with that term taken in the broadest sense) and of his mood, and we will not achieve an understanding of a person's overall character and of his mood without some prior understanding of the episodes of emotional experience. It is not that paradoxical because, of course, it is possible to 'work one's way in to' the circle; one can and does on first acquaintance make certain assumptions about a person's thoughts, feelings, emotions, mood and character, and then one can revise those assumptions on the basis of further knowledge and acquaintance.
>
> (Goldie 1999: 398)[26]

A few pages further on in the article just quoted, Goldie notes:

> A further step in the interpretive project of piecing together a person's narrative structure will involve determining what is the object of his

emotion, and the way he is thinking of, and feeling towards, that object, as well as determining what are the emotional desires which he has about it.

(Goldie 1999: 401)

As Goldie emphasizes, this appraisal need not be (and usually is not) indifferent to the interpreter's mood, emotions, or character (p. 401). But *this* kind of understanding – one compatible with what we might call an 'informed narrator' rather than 'impartial spectator' theory – does not accomplish what Smith wanted to claim in TMS VII for his sympathy theory. This is so for several reasons.

First, if Smith's claim in that culminating passage really held, the narrative reconstruction of the other's situation would not be necessary, so far as understanding it goes. When any such perspective-laden reconstruction is required, it's because the transparency that Smith claimed for sympathy is impossible. It's not just a question of degree of transparency or clarity of perspective that is at stake, but the kind of imaginative procedure. Narrative understanding does not seem to require that 'I change persons and characters' (TMS VII.iii.1.4) with the agent, which is what Smith insisted is 'supposed to happen' in sympathizing.

Second, on this model, sympathetic understanding cannot uninvolve the ego of the spectator. And on the flip side, there is no reason to think that however well some aspect of the actor's experience is explained to the spectator, what that experience is like for the actor will be fully narratable to another. I would argue that this is more than a matter of the 'subjective' aspect of any experience. It also comprises – and here I assert merely – the sheer complexity of the relevant particulars, as well as the problem as to which particulars are relevant (these will include the actor's own perceptions, sentiments, memories, and so forth, many of them fleeting even to the actor) and why and to what degree. The 'identification' and complete sympathetic understanding of which Smith speaks is in that sense impossible.

Third, Smith's occasional appeal to literary narratives to illuminate how sympathy works (see the passages cited above) would now be seen not so much as mere examples or occasions for sympathy, but as expressing the type of understanding that goes on in sympathy. He can shift back and forth between literary models and real-life examples because they are fundamentally of a piece with respect to the narrative character of understanding others, in spite of the ocular, spectatorial model with which Smith leads. But interpreting literature need not be understood as Smithian sympathizing with the characters; one can enter into the fictional world, understand what it's like to be its characters, but not feel as they do. One might feel solidarity with them, wanting to encourage them along, as one does in watching a boxing match; or one might resonate with them; or identify with them. One might have the emotions appropriate to the other's joys or sufferings. But none of this seems to require Smithian sympathy, either when we interpret a work of literature, or a person in real life.[27]

Fourth, a narrative understanding of the other's situation does not, simply because it *is* narrative, reduce understanding to confabulating. But narrative understanding does introduce serious questions of perspective. Even in historical narrative it always seems possible to re-tell the events from a different perspective (hence we are on, for example, the nth book about the genesis of the French Revolution, and so forth).[28] It's not that anything goes, but that beyond basic threshold conditions of factual accuracy, establishing what does go seems perpetually open, with the result that claims to finality (the definitive account of X) seem insupportable. And the narrative view introduces problems as to where the line between understanding and fiction, or let us say more ambiguously, between understanding and imagining is to be drawn. I cannot literally put myself in the place of the woman in childbirth; as I try to give an account of what she's going through, I must in part posit or attribute what I cannot myself know. That is a far cry from the sort of imaginative transposition of self Smith ends up judging necessary if the self-love view is to be overcome.

Rousseau contra Smith: concluding thoughts

By way of conclusion, let me recast some of this dialectic between Smith and Rousseau. Rousseau understood, acutely and astutely, the problems of transparency of self, of getting inside someone else's experience, of the partiality and revisability of perspective, and of the pervasive role of narrative in rendering the human self intelligible. His novel *Julie*, for example, includes a great deal of discussion about the sense in which lovers can and cannot be known to and by each other (Rousseau 1997a: 45, 111, 270–1, 555, *inter alia*). Not surprisingly, Rousseau would see the impartial spectator as a character in a narrative. In *Julie*, one of the central characters (Monsieur de Wolmar, Julie's husband) is cast as an impartial observer.[29] I should think that Rousseau's deconstructive reaction to Smith's concluding insistence on the large sphere of sympathy would go something like this: Smith is telling a narrative throughout TMS in which a character, called 'the impartial spectator', is alleged to do such things as be a male who perfectly sympathizes with a woman in child-birth. The motivations for this story-line, he would continue, are ethical and in the broadest sense political: Smith wants to persuade his readers that we will be better off if we carry on *as though* it is true both that the impartial spectator can sympathize in this way and that we ought to take the impartial spectator as a role model, that is, subject ourselves to the social standard represented by the impartial spectator. The 'protreptic rhetoric' of the book, as I have elsewhere called it (Griswold 1999: 48–58), reflects the ethical and in a sense social agenda of Smith's story.

But Smith presents it all in the guise of a *theory* that plays down its narrative and rhetorical dimension. And this too, from the Rousseauan perspective, is part of the intent of Smith's story. The very idea of a non-narrative 'theory' of the moral sentiments reflects at the philosophical level an ideal represented by the impartial spectator as painted within that same theory: that of perfect perspective, of well-adjusted intellectual sight, of a timeless non-diachronic apprehension of how the matter stands. Such has always been the ambition of philosophical *theoria*. But for the Rousseau I am postulating, that is part of the philosopher's imaginative story about philosophy, and he questions just such claims to a-perspectival imagining. 'Theory' is itself a kind of gazing that conceals a tale about – in this case – the supreme value of social interdependence as regulated by an impartial spectator whose very character and existence are themselves postulated in the tale. My sense is that Rousseau doesn't share Smith's view that the story about impartial spectating, whether sympathetic and moral or merely intellectual, is in fact ethically and politically beneficial, and this perhaps for three reasons. I conclude with them.

First, it is built on what for Rousseau is a fiction: the alleged transparency of the actor to spectator. The most we can have is something like *pitié* or imaginative literary narrative accompanied by compassion, not full-fledged Smithian sympathy. For the individual, this may be a painful realization, to be sure; and it is a sort of headline of many of Rousseau's writings about the self, especially the autobiographical writings, that nobody ever *really* understands anyone else. Our mutual unnarratability at one level is lamented but not concealed by Rousseau. The recognition of that shared fate perhaps constitutes the deepest sense of commonality that narrative provides. And it is inscribed both into the state of nature, where we are each solitary, and into those socialized states of being in which we are still alone but pretend not to be. That pervasive social pretence is worse than the disease it might be thought to cure.

For, second, that pretence requires self-falsification as well as various oppressive mechanisms of social control, in particular the supervisory eye of Big Spectator armed with a big stick (the disbursement of social approval and other regulatory machinery). Rousseau's point here opens up, of course, a whole line of criticism that goes down through Marx and beyond. We would be better off figuring out a 'system of natural liberty' that is based on our natural separateness and equality, Rousseau would claim, rather than on our alleged sympathetic spectatorial reactions as well as subjection to the spectatorial point of view (think here one more time about the woman in child-birth subject to the man's assessing gaze). I suspect that he would push hard Smith's own admission that commercial society, especially when understood in terms of Smithian sympathy, leads to the 'corruption of our moral sentiments' (TMS I.iii.3.1), and would argue that we are better off dropping talk about sympathy (and for the most part, *pitié*, as already noted) when creating a just society.

Finally, for Rousseau it was a cardinal mistake of earlier state of nature theories to project the current traits of human beings onto original human nature (Rousseau 1997b: 132). Smith continually casts his theory as articulating the natural; for Rousseau, this is rationalizing rhetoric, something like 'ideology' in the sense later defined by Marx and Engels. Its fit with Smith's defence of the free market – a defence Rousseau did not share – would only amplify Rousseau's suspicions about Smith's agenda.

Acknowledgements

I am grateful to Vivienne Brown, Michael Davis, Remy Debes, Lucas Fain, Sam Fleischacker, Zina Giannopoulou, Peter Goldie, Knud Haakonssen, Ryan Hanley, Susan James, Dasha Polzik, David Raynor and Ian Ross for their comments on or discussion of this essay. Drafts were delivered at Oxford University (Balliol College), as a plenary address to a conference on the philosophy of Adam Smith (January 2009), at the University of Chicago (March 2009), at Harvard University (April 2009), and at the biennial colloquium of the Rousseau Association (UCLA, June 2009). I am indebted to audiences at all four venues for their helpful questions and comments. I gratefully acknowledge Fellowships from the American Council of Learned Societies and the Boston University Humanities Foundation, which supported my work on Rousseau and Smith during the 2009–10 academic year.

Notes

1 Gauthier's lectures were subsequently published as Gauthier (2006). A version of Haakonssen's thought (which I mention here with permission) has been noted in the secondary literature. For example, R. Wokler remarks that 'While it [the *Second Discourse*] attracted some praise and even more hostility from reviewers in France, its greatest impact was probably first felt in Scotland, where Adam Smith was to cast his *Theory of Moral Sentiments* in part as a reply to it … ' (Wokler 2001: 44). See also I. Hont and M. Ignatieff (1983: 10), as well as Ignatieff (1984, ch. 4).

2 Smith's 'Letter to the *Edinburgh Review*' is reprinted in his *Essays on Philosophical Subjects* (henceforth abbreviated 'EPS'; Smith 1982b: 242–56). Citations to this 'Letter' give paragraph number followed by page number.

3 On Smith's owning the works of Rousseau, see Leigh (1986: 11), Hanley (2006: 198, n. 9), and Rasmussen (2008: 57). I note that in the 'Considerations Concerning the First Formation of Languages', which he appended to editions 3–6 of TMS (it was there titled 'Dissertation on the Origin of Languages'), Smith refers to Rousseau by name (calling him 'ingenious and eloquent'), and specifically to the account of the origin of language in Part I of the *Second Discourse*. See Smith's *Lectures on Rhetoric and Belles Lettres* (henceforth abbreviated 'LRBL'; Smith 1985), p. 205.

4 See Rasmussen (2008) and Hanley (2006, 2008). Force (2003) is also a major contribution to the study of the relation between Smith and Rousseau. I regret that F. Neuhouser's *Rousseau's Theodicy of Self-Love* (Oxford: Oxford University Press, 2008) arrived on my desk too late to be taken into account in this essay.

5 Brooks adds: 'The question of identity, claims Rousseau – and this is what makes him at least symbolically the *incipit* of modern narrative – can be thought only in narrative terms, in the effort to tell a whole life, to plot its meaning by going back over it to record its perpetual flight forward, its slippage from the fixity of definition' (1992: 33). But the quest is unrealizable: 'Always out of place, never coincident with his inner self in the eyes of others – and thus in his behavior – he is always going back over the traces of conduct and interior disposition, not to reconcile them – which is impossible – but to confess their irreconcilability … ' (1992: 32).

Gauthier (2006: 50) usefully remarks that 'Rousseau is perhaps the first modern thinker to understand us as alienated from our true selves'. These comments are congenial to the contrasts between Rousseau and Smith I seek to draw out in this essay.

6 Smith's name was not attached to the review when it was published, but the editors of EPS clearly believe that it is by Smith (EPS: 230), as do most scholars. For some arguments in favour of Smith's authorship, see Ross (1995: 145), where he concludes that 'The phrasing of the letter itself and these points clinch the argument for Smith's authorship of the letter rather than Hume himself' (in private correspondence, which I mention with permission, Ross develops his case in even greater detail). In private correspondence, which I also mention with permission, David Raynor has expressed his scepticism concerning the widely-held view that Smith alone is the author of the 'Letter'.

7 In the *Second Discourse*, Rousseau is explicit that 'sociability' is not one of the two 'principles prior to reason' that define human nature (Rousseau 1997b: 127). The passages translated by Smith in his review are to be found at Rousseau (1997b: 167, 170, and 186–7). All these passages are from Part II of the *Second Discourse*, and the last quotation is from the second to last paragraph of Rousseau's text. In the last passage quoted by Smith, Rousseau refers to Stoic *ataraxia*; Smith's decision to quote that is suggestive, given the importance of Stoicism for his own thought.

8 My interpretation is thus at odds, so far as I can tell, with that of Force (2003: 31), who remarks that 'in Rousseau's theory, we experience pity by putting ourselves mentally in the position of the sufferer. Rousseau's key innovation consists in basing pity on identification'. Yet several pages later, Force notes that 'The ability to reflect has two decisive consequences: the rise of self-love, and the transformation of pity into a sentiment based on identification' (37). So pity cannot simply be based on identification. In any case, I would argue that once modulated by reflection, it still does not involve what *Smith* would think of as sympathy, that is, putting oneself in the place of the other in such a way as to adopt the other's perspective. Force remarks that '"Sympathy" in *The Theory of Moral Sentiments* corresponds to *identification* in the *Second Discourse*' (43; cf. 132–3); that may be true, but correspondence is very different from equivalence, in the particular ways I shall attempt to explain.

9 As he says in the text already quoted, 'what are generosity, Clemency, Humanity, if not Pity applied to the weak, the guilty, or the species in general?' (153). It would be interesting to compare Rousseauan *pitié* and Hutchesonian benevolence on this score. *Pitié* is not the same thing as moral virtue, though in the *Second Discourse* it is the origin thereof. From Smith's perspective, as I shall argue, Rousseau nonetheless fails to put enough daylight between other-regarding virtue and self-love, precisely since Rousseau did not found virtue in sympathy properly understood. I hasten to add that for Smith self-love *can* be compatible with virtue; when it is, though, it must be regulated by the impartial spectator, and that can take place only through (Smithian) 'sympathy'.

10 I would argue that Rousseau's comments on *pitié* in *Emile* book IV, and in his essay on the origin of languages, are consistent with the points I have just made, though the issue is contestable. The problematic status of spectatorial pleasure – mentioned by Smith in the passage I am about to quote – would provide another interesting point of comparison with *Emile*. Rousseau there remarks that 'Pity is sweet because, in putting ourselves in the place of the one who suffers, we nevertheless feel the pleasure of not suffering as he does' (Rousseau 1979: 221; also 229), a remark Smith would no doubt take as confirmation that Rousseau is at base a self-love theorist. In *Emile* Rousseau also speaks of *pitié* as extending to humanity as such, so that one learns to 'identify' with the species (233).

That is another indication that he cannot mean by the term what Smith means by 'sympathy', since one cannot put oneself in the position of humanity as such. All that said, *pitié* plays no role in the *Social Contract* (the general will and religion, *inter alia*, come to the fore) and only a limited role in *Emile's* moral education (cf. the importance of religion), and this pattern is repeated elsewhere in Rousseau's political writings. A more detailed reconstruction of the dialectic between Smith and Rousseau would take into account Rousseau's effort to understand political life not only without appealing to something like Smithian sympathy, but to a great extent without *pitié* as well.

11 Note also his use of 'seeing' in the first sentence of the book. Further instances are cited below.

12 I am indebted to S. Fleischacker for pointing this out. See Fleischacker (2004: 9–10).

13 The importance of the metaphor for Smith is also noted by Brown (1994: 59–62, 72). Brown notes that 'In TMS the activities of watching, seeing and observing all constitute forms of moral judgment, and the impartial spectator is simply the proper and most objective moral judge' (60). I do not mean to deny that Smith uses other metaphors too (for example, auditory ones at TMS I.i.4.7) when talking about sympathy.

14 For example, at III.4.4, where Smith refers to our being able to 'identify ourselves, as it were, with the ideal man within the breast, and, in our own character, view, as in the one case, our own situation, so in the other, our own conduct, with the severe eyes of the most impartial spectator'; cf. III.3.4, 'the eye of this impartial spectator'.

15 For Smith's comments on Berkeley's essay, see his 'Of the External Senses' (in EPS: 135-68), paragraphs 60–2, pp. 156–8 (citations to this essay give paragraph number followed by page number). The ways in which sight and reading or language are connected, in Smith's report of Berkeley, are fascinating, and pertinent to the sort of point I am about to make about narrative. For example, he remarks that 'The objects of sight, as Dr. Berkley finely observes, constitute a sort of language which the Author of Nature addresses to our eyes' ('Of the External Senses' 60, EPS: 156; cf. para 62, p. 158). There is much more to say about how Berkeley's theory of the relation between sight and conception might fit with Smith's appropriation of the metaphor to characterize the impartial spectator's sympathetic knowing.

16 Darwall notes that 'It is ironic, and not a little misleading, therefore, that the term "impartial spectator" originates with Smith (and not with either Hutcheson or Hume), since the perspective of moral judgment, according to Smith, is not strictly a *spectator's* standpoint at all' (Darwall 1999: 141). Smith's theory requires abandoning spectatorial detachment and sympathetically entering into the situation of the actor 'as any one of us' (Darwall 142, italicized in the original). That is accurate, but Smith *does* talk as though his is a spectator theory; and more importantly, from Rousseau's standpoint, talk about entering into the world of another 'as any one of us' imports the detachment and limitation of vision that characterizes spectatorship. Rousseau would strongly endorse Darwall's words 'ironic' and 'misleading', but would read their implications for Smith's theory rather more critically and deconstructively.

17 It would be very interesting to examine Rousseau's use of and comments about ocular metaphors for knowing. By way of preliminary observation, I note the superiority of touch to vision indicated in *Emile* (see Rousseau 1979: 138, 140, 143), though the context of those remarks – the early stage of Emile's education – would have to be taken into account. In addition, the metaphor of vision is used in the passages from the *Second Discourse* quoted above (but in a way that suggests that out of sight is out of mind!). Consider also Rousseau's comment in the *Essay on the Origin of Languages* (which Smith knew):

But when it is a question of moving the heart and enflaming the passions, it is an altogether different matter [than observing visually]. The successive impression of discourse, striking with repeated blows, gives you a very different emotion from the presence of the object itself, which you have seen completely with a single glance. Assume that someone is in a painful situation which you know perfectly well: you will not easily be moved to cry in seeing the afflicted person, but give him time to tell you everything he feels, and soon you will burst into tears. Only in this way do the scenes of a tragedy have their effect. ... The passions have their gestures, but they also have their accents, and these accents, which make us tremble, these accents, from which we cannot shield our organ, penetrate by it to the bottom of the heart, ... Let us conclude that visible signs convey a more precise imitation, but that interest is aroused more effectively by sounds.

(Rousseau 1998: 291–2)

Rousseau's views about the link between language and music (given the latter's deep connection to accent and rhythm) may also shed light on the power of narrative to affect and instruct (I am indebted to Julia Simon for pointing this out to me).

18 One could contend that the line of argument just presented is in fact Smith's own, as is suggested by his analogizing sympathy in life to sympathy in literature, his talk about spectators having emotions (I.i.2.6) and adjusting their sympathy in light of the actor's situation (I.i.4.8), and the seemingly contextualized character of sympathizing (I.i.4.7). Yet that defence of Smith would in turn underline a tension within Smith's thought, as I am about to suggest, given his insistence on the impartial spectator's sympathetic vision. For a humorous but pointed comment on the impossibility (for epistemic reasons) of a man pitying a woman in child-birth, see Diderot (1959: 17–19).

19 The striking phrase 'philosophical chemistry' is used by Hume in the second Appendix to *An Enquiry Concerning the Principles of Morals*, precisely in the context of objecting to the attempt by an 'Epicurean or a Hobbist' to 'explain every affection to be self-love', even one such as friendship. See Hume (1989: 296–7).

20 At the end of Part I of the *Second Discourse*, Rousseau refers to his account as based on 'conjectures' but adds:

> not only do such conjectures become reasons when they are the most probable that can be derived from the nature of things and the only means available to discover the truth, it also does not follow that the consequences I want to deduce from mine will therefore be conjectural since, on the principles I have just established, no other system could be formed that would not give me the same results and from which I could not draw the same conclusions.
>
> (Rousseau 1997b: 159)

21 At LRBL i.150–1 Smith is reported as saying that 'There are two different Sorts of facts, one externall, consisting of the transactions that pass without us, and the other internall, towit the thoughts sentiments or designs of men, which pass in their minds. The Design of History, compounded of both of th<ese> is to relate the remarkable transactions that pass in different nations, and the designs, motives and views of the most remarkable men in those times, so far as they are necessary to explain the great changes and revolutions of States which it is intended to relate'.

22 I am not claiming that this insight is original. See for example McKenna (2006). For a dissenting view, see Brown (1994, ch. 1).

23 For example, Smith comments that modern historians tend to be more 'didactic' than the ancient because there are 'now severall sects in Religion and politicall disputes which are greatly dependent on the truth of certain facts' (LRBL ii.40). In other words, historical narratives compete for political and social authority, and carry the corresponding agenda. As to the meaning of 'narrative' for Smith, he remarks at LRBL i.149: 'Every discourse proposes either barely to relate some fact, or to prove some proposition. In the first ... the discourse is called a narrative one. The latter is the foundation of two Sorts of Discourse: The Didactick and the Rhetoricall'.

24 The next two paragraphs are drawn from Griswold (2007, ch. 2.viii). The reader will find a much more detailed discussion of narrative in those pages. I have, however, departed from that version in the use of the terms 'story' and 'chronicle'.

25 For some helpful comments on both points, see Goldie (2003: 215–18).

26 Goldie's reference to Gadamer is to *Truth and Method*, trans. Weinsheimer and Marshall.

27 I owe the boxing match example to Peter Goldie. Elsewhere, he suggests the example of buying someone a birthday present; perhaps the worst way to make the right selection would be to put oneself in the shoes of the recipient (Goldie 2002: 202). I may come to know what you would want in all sorts of ways without entering your world through putting myself in your shoes and then attempting to adjust for perspective.

28 Rousseau asserts the ineluctable role of perspective in historiography in *Emile*, Book IV (Rousseau 1979: 238–40).

29 Wolmar remarks:

> My only active principle is a natural taste for order, and the right concurrence of the play of fortune and of men's acts pleases me exactly like a beautiful symmetry in a tableau, or like a well-contrived play in the theater. If I have any ruling passion it is that of observation. I like to read what is in men's hearts; as my own little deludes me, as I observe composedly and disinterestedly, and as long experience has given me some sagacity, I scarcely err in my judgments; and that is the whole compensation for self-love [*amour propre*] in my continual studies; for I do not like playing a role, but only seeing others perform. I enjoy observing society, not taking part in it. If I could change the nature of my being and become a living eye, I would gladly make that exchange. Thus my indifference for men does not make me independent of them; though I care not about being seen, I need to see them, and though I do not cherish them I find them necessary.
>
> (1997a: 403)

On p. 305, Julie refers to her husband as a person whose 'greatest predilection is for observation', which task he discharges with 'the most perfect impartiality'.

Bibliography

Brooks, P. (1992) *Reading for the Plot*, Cambridge, MA: Harvard University Press.

Brown, V. (1994) *Adam Smith's Discourse: Canonicity, Commerce and Conscience*, London: Routledge.

Darwall, S. (1999) 'Sympathetic liberalism: recent work on Adam Smith', *Philosophy and Public Affairs*, 28: 139–64.

Diderot, D. (1959) *Jacques the Fatalist and his Master*, trans. with Introduction and Notes by J.R. Loy, New York: New York University Press.

Eliot, G. (2005) *Daniel Deronda*, Introduction and Notes by E.L. Dachslager, New York: Barnes and Noble Classics.

Fleischacker, S. (2004) *On Adam Smith's* Wealth of Nations*: A Philosophical Companion*, Princeton, NJ: Princeton University Press.

Force, P. (2003) *Self-Interest before Adam Smith*, Cambridge: Cambridge University Press.

Gauthier, D. (2006) *Rousseau: The Sentiment of Existence*, Cambridge: Cambridge University Press.

Goldie, P. (1999) 'How we think of others' emotions', *Mind and Language*, 14: 394–423.

—— (2002) *The Emotions: A Philosophical Exploration*, Oxford: Oxford University Press.

—— (2003) 'Narrative and perspective; values and appropriate emotions', in A. Hatzimoysis (ed.), *Philosophy and the Emotions*, Cambridge: Cambridge University Press, pp. 201–20.

Griswold, C.L. (1999) *Adam Smith and the Virtues of Enlightenment*, Cambridge: Cambridge University Press.

—— (2007) *Forgiveness: A Philosophical Exploration*, Cambridge: Cambridge University Press.

Hanley, R. (2006) 'From Geneva to Glasgow: Rousseau and Adam Smith on the theatre and commercial society', *Studies in Eighteenth-Century Culture*, 35: 177–202.

—— (2008) 'Commerce and corruption: Rousseau's diagnosis and Adam Smith's cure', *European Journal of Political Theory*, 7: 137–58.

Hont, I. and Ignatieff, M. (1983) 'Needs and justice in the *Wealth of Nations*: an introductory essay', in I. Hont and M. Ignatieff (eds), *Wealth and Virtue: The Shaping of Political Economy in the Scottish Enlightenment*, Cambridge: Cambridge University Press, pp. 1–44.

Hume, D. (1989) *Enquiries concerning Human Understanding and concerning the Principles of Morals*, L.A. Selby-Bigge (ed.), 3rd edn rev. P.H. Nidditch, Oxford: Oxford University Press.

Ignatieff, M. (1984) *The Needs of Strangers*, New York: Picador.

Leigh, R.A. (1986) 'Rousseau and the Scottish enlightenment', *Contributions to Political Economy*, 5: 1–21.

McKenna, S.J. (2006) *Adam Smith: The Rhetoric of Propriety*, Albany, NY: State University of New York Press.

Nagel, T. (1974) 'What is it like to be a bat?', *Philosophical Review*, 83: 435–50.

Rasmussen, D. (2008) *The Problems and Promise of Commercial Society: Adam Smith's Response to Rousseau*, University Park, PA: Pennsylvania State University Press.

Ross, I.S. (1995) *The Life of Adam Smith*, Oxford: Oxford University Press.

Rousseau, J.–J. (1979) *Emile: or On Education*, trans. A. Bloom, New York: Basic Books.

—— (1997a) *Julie or the New Heloise*, trans. P. Stewart and J. Vaché, Hanover, NH and London: University Press of New England.

—— (1997b) *Rousseau: The Discourses and Other Early Political Writings*, ed. and trans. V. Gourevitch, Cambridge: Cambridge University Press.

—— (1998) *Essay on the Origin of Languages and Writings Related to Music*, ed. and trans. J.T. Scott, Hanover, NH and London: University Press of New England.

Smith, A. (1982a) *The Theory of Moral Sentiments*, D.D. Raphael and A.L. Macfie (eds), Indianapolis, IN: Liberty Press.

——— (1982b) *Essays on Philosophical Subjects*, W.P.D. Wightman and J.C. Bryce (eds), Indianapolis, IN: Liberty Press.

——— (1985) *Lectures on Rhetoric and Belles Lettres*, J.C. Bryce (ed.), Indianapolis, IN: Liberty Press.

Stewart, D. (1966) 'Account of the Life and Writings of Adam Smith, LL.D', in *Biographical Memoir of Adam Smith*, New York: A.M. Kelley.

Wokler, R. (2001) *Rousseau: A Very Short Introduction*, Oxford: Oxford University Press.

Adam Smith's concept of sympathy and its contemporary interpretations

Bence Nanay

Adam Smith's account of sympathy or 'fellow feeling' has recently become exceedingly popular. It has been used as an antecedent of the concept of simulation: understanding, or attributing mental states to, other people by means of simulating them (Gordon 1995a; Darwall 1998; Davies 1994). It has also been singled out as the first correct account of empathy (Goldie 1999, 2000, 2002; Neill 1996). Finally, to make things even more complicated, some of Smith's examples for sympathy or 'fellow feeling' have been used as the earliest expression of emotional contagion (M. Smith 1995, 1998).

The aim of the essay is to suggest a new interpretation of Smith's concept of sympathy and point out that on this interpretation some of the contemporary uses of this concept, as a precursor of simulation and empathy, are misleading. My main claim is that Smith's concept of sympathy, unlike simulation and empathy, does not imply any correspondence between the mental states of the sympathizer and of the person she is sympathizing with.

Introduction

Adam Smith's concept of sympathy is a form of imagining being in someone else's situation. When we sympathize with someone, what happens is the following:

> By the imagination we place ourselves in his situation, we conceive ourselves enduring all the same torments, we enter as it were into his body, and become in some measure the same person with him.
>
> (Smith 1976 [1759], TMS I.i.1.2)

This account has received special attention recently, partly as a result of its perceived similarity to some popular theories in contemporary philosophy of mind. It has been used as an antecedent of the concept of simulation: understanding, or attributing mental states to, other people by means of simulating them (Gordon 1995a; Darwall 1998; Davies 1994). It has also been singled out as the first correct account of empathy (Goldie 1999, 2000, 2002; Neill 1996). These contemporary uses of Adam Smith's concept of sympathy

The Philosophy of Adam Smith, The Adam Smith Review, 5: 85–105 © 2010 The International Adam Smith Society, ISSN 1743–5285, ISBN 978-0-415-56256-0.

converge into a neat and coherent picture whereby one important way of engaging with another person is simulation that is understood as a form of empathy and Adam Smith was the first philosopher who described this way of engaging with another person in a systematic manner.

The aim of this essay is to question this neat and coherent picture of the connection between simulation, empathy and Adam Smith's concept of sympathy and argue that while simulation and empathy presupposes a correspondence, or at least a certain degree of similarity, between the mental states of the simulator/empathizer and the person she is simulating/empathizing with, Adam Smith's concept of sympathy does not imply any such correspondence. Thus, if we want to understand what Adam Smith meant by sympathy, we have to resist its assimilation to simulation and empathy. Instead, we should focus on the simple, visceral, quasi-automatic imaginative reaction that is the common denominator between the cases Smith describes as sympathy.

The structure of the essay is the following. In the second section, I outline what I take to be the most important contemporary uses of Adam Smith's account of sympathy: as a precursor of the theory of simulation and as the first coherent formulation of what we mean by empathy. In the third and fourth sections, I analyze two important features of Smith's account of sympathy. Smith claims that sympathizing with another person is imagining myself in this person's situation. This account needs clarification at two points: (a) what is meant by 'myself' and (b) what is meant by 'the other person's situation'. I address these questions in the third and fourth sections, respectively. The conclusion of this analysis will be that Adam Smith's concept of sympathy covers a wide variety of importantly different cases. In the fifth section, I argue that we may be able to find a common denominator between these different cases of sympathy if we reject an important assumption about Adam Smith's concept of sympathy: namely, that it implies some kind of correspondence between the mental states of the sympathizer and of the person she is sympathizing with. But rejecting this assumption also breaks the similarity between Adam Smith's concept of sympathy on the one hand and that of simulation and empathy on the other. I consider two possible objections to these claims in the sixth section and point out that instead of jeopardizing my account, they provide further textual evidence in its favour.

Simulation, empathy, sympathy

An important question in the philosophy of mind is how we attribute mental states to other people (Davies 1994; Carruthers and Smith 1996). There seem to be two options. One possibility is that we are equipped with a theory whose domain of application is constituted by other agents' mental states. On this view, attributing a mental state to someone else is a case of applying a psychological theory. This is the *theory–theory* view. Another possibility is that we have the capacity to simulate other people's mental states; that is, we are able to put ourselves in other people's shoes, and go through in imagination the mental states we would go through were we really in the other person's circumstances. The end result of such a process, namely the mental state in which the simulator finds herself, can now serve as a guide to what mental state the simulated person is in. This is the *simulation* view (Gordon 1995a, b; Heal 1995; Stone and Davies 1996; Goldman 1992).

A standard way of characterizing simulation is the following: an agent A imagines herself in B's circumstances, gets a grip on what she, A, would do (see, feel, think, and so on) and concludes that this is what he, B, would also do (see, feel, think, and so on) in these circumstances. As Gregory Currie writes: 'I imagine myself to be in the other person's position, [...] I simply note that I formed, in imagination, a certain belief, desire or decision, then attribute it to the other' (Currie 1995: 144–5).

It is not difficult to spot the similarity between Smith's account of sympathy and the simulationist account of the attribution of mental states: both talk about imagining ourselves in someone else's position. And, unsurprisingly, both the advocates of the simulationist theory and its opponents quote Smith not only among the antecedents of the simulation view, but sometimes even as one of its most convincing instances (see esp. Gordon 1995a: 741 As Stephen Darwall says, 'several philosophers of mind [...] have recently argued that [...] simulation [...] is centrally involved in attributing mental states to others, *much as Smith had claimed*' (Darwall 1998: 267; my emphasis). Or, even more explicitly, 'contemporary work on imaginative simulation in mental-state attribution [...] derives directly from Smith' (Darwall 1999: 140).

The other important topic in contemporary philosophy of mind where Smith's account of sympathy is widely used is the empathy literature (as it is widely assumed that empathy is a form of simulation, these two lines of reasoning are often run together, see Adams 1998; Gordon 1995a, b; but cf. Currie and Ravenscroft 2002). Smith's account of sympathy is often taken to be *the correct way* of thinking not of sympathy, but of empathy.

A quick terminological note: the term 'empathy' did not exist in Smith's days. It was introduced to the English language as the translation of the German '*Einfühlung*' in 1909.[1] So Smith was not in the position to make a distinction between the two. The received wisdom is that if he had been, he would have talked about empathy and not about sympathy: the concept he really referred to was empathy – feeling *with X* – and not sympathy – feeling *for X* (see Neill 1996; Deonna 2007 for more on this distinction, but see also Sudgen 2002).

Empathy (or, as Smith would say, sympathy) has been argued to be a version of 'imagining from the inside' (Darwall 1998; Gordon 1995a; Walton 1990: 255, Currie 1995: 153; Wollheim 1974: 187; 1987: 103, 129; Neill 1996; Smith 1997; Gaut 1998; cf. Feagin 1996: 113–42). And Smith is taken to be the first person who put forward this view.

As empathy and simulation are widely held to have similar structure (Adams 2001; Gordon 1995a, b), these considerations give us a neat and coherent picture of one way of engaging with other people. Simulation theory describes something very similar to empathy and Adam Smith was the first philosopher who gave a coherent account of this way of engaging with other people. All these three concepts have a lot to do with imagination, more precisely, with imagining from the inside. Further, if we take this general simulation–empathy–sympathy picture seriously, we may even be able to clarify what Adam Smith meant by analyzing the details of simulation and empathy.

My aim is to revise this picture at least as far as Adam Smith's concept of sympathy is concerned. What contemporary philosophers of mind mean by simulation and empathy is not what Adam Smith's concept of sympathy is about. Importantly, I will argue that according to the most plausible interpretation, Adam Smith's concept of sympathy, unlike simulation and empathy, does not entail any correspondence between the mental states of the sympathizer and the person she is sympathizing with.

What does it mean to imagine *myself* in someone else's situation?

Adam Smith's concept of sympathy, whereby 'by the imagination, we place ourselves in [someone else's] situation' (TMS I.i.1.2) is a version of imagining someone else from the inside. But what does imagining from the inside mean?

Imagining X from the inside is a way of imagining X. But there are two different views about what this entails:

(1) Imagining having X's experiences: X occurs in the content my imaginative episode, I myself may not.
(2) Imagining being in X's situation: X herself does not even occur in the content of my imaginative episode.[2]

(1) has been the dominant view of 'imagining from the inside' (Currie 1995: 153; Neill 1996). To quote just one example, Kendall Walton's account is a clear example of (1): when I imagine X from the inside, I imagine experiencing what I think X experiences (Walton 1990: 255, 344).

Smith was perhaps the first philosopher who held a version of (2) (a detailed contemporary formulation of (2) is in Gaut 1999). The crucial difference from (1) is that X is not part of the content of this imaginative episode. Only I myself and X's situation are.[3] Hence, if we want to explicate what this concept entails, we need to explicate what is meant by 'I myself' and what is meant by 'X's situation.' I analyse the former in this section. The latter will come in the next section.

The question of what (or who) is being imagined in the other person's situation could be thought to be a problematic feature of Smith's account. Robert Gordon argues that Smith's account of sympathy 'misses the distinction' between imagining myself being in X's situation and imagining being X in X's situation – he conflates these two very different concepts

(Gordon 1995a: 741; also Gordon 1995b: 55). Gordon says that this is the reason why Smith's concept of sympathy cannot give rise to a valid criterion for assessing the 'propriety' of other people's actions. Whether Smith's concept of sympathy can give rise to a valid criterion for assessing the 'propriety' of other people's actions is a question I will return to in the penultimate section. But at this point it is enough to point out that Gordon's charge against Smith can be supported by some discrepancies in *The Theory of Moral Sentiments*. Although Smith's initial characterization of sympathy is imagining being in someone else's situation, at the end of the book, he writes:

> When I console with you for the loss of your only son, in order to enter into your grief I do not consider what I, a person of such a character and profession, should suffer, if I had a son, and if that son were unfortunately to die: but I consider what I should suffer if I was really you, and I not only change circumstances with you, but I change persons and characters.
>
> (TMS VII.iii.1.4)

This passage sounds very much as if sympathy were imagining being X in X's situation. And this seems to support Gordon's point about the lack of clarity in *The Theory of Moral Sentiments* with regards to the distinction between imagining being in X's situation and imagining being X in X's situation.

The distinction between imagining being in X's situation and imagining being X in X's situation is not new (Williams 1973; Wollheim 1973, 1974; Reynolds 1989; Velleman 1996) and this distinction is not as straightforward as it may seem (see, for example Recanati 2007: 22–3). One way of drawing this distinction that is prevalent in the contemporary literature is the following (see esp. Walton 1990). Imagining being in X's situation is a form of self-imagining, whereas imagining being X in X's situation is not. In other words, the former, but not the latter is imagining *de se*.

The concept of imagining *de se* was introduced by Kendall Walton (see Recanati 2007 for a thorough analysis):

> 'Imagining *de se*' [is] a form of self-imagining characteristically described as imagining *doing* or *experiencing* something (or *being* a certain way), as opposed to imagining merely *that* one does or experiences something or possesses a certain property.
>
> (Walton 1990: 29; original emphasis)

Imagining *de se* is a form of self-imagining: a form of imagining whereby the self, represented from a first person point of view, is part of the content of what is imagined. Walton makes it clear that the self is not imagined from a first person point of view if I imagine *that* I am on the beach. If I imagine *being* on the beach, then I do indeed imagine myself from the first person point of view (Walton 1990: 29–30). The latter episode of imagining is imagining *de se*, whereas the former is not.

This, in itself, will not keep imagining being in X's situation and imagining being X in X's situation apart, as neither of these two descriptions use that-clauses: both can be 'characteristically described as imagining doing or experiencing something (or being a certain way)'. But Walton makes it clear that although that-clauses may be good indicators of imaginings that are not *de se*, this is not what *defines* imagining *de se*. What defines imagining *de se* is the following: to imagine something *de se* is 'to imagine about oneself in such a way that one cannot be unaware that it is oneself about whom one imagines' (Walton 1990: 29). Does this help with the distinction we are trying to draw? Not really. When I imagine being X in X's situation, do I imagine myself in such a way that I cannot be unaware that it is myself about whom I imagine? That depends on how rich a conception of 'myself' we are presupposing. As imagining being X in X's situation is imagining *myself* being X in X's situation (not imagining Bill being X in X's situation), there is a sense in which I indeed imagine myself in such a way that I cannot be unaware that it is myself about whom I imagine. So imagining being X in X's situation may turn out to be as genuine a form of imagining *de se* as imagining being in X's situation. But then what is the difference between the two?

Imagining being X in X's situation is a special case of imagining being X. And there is no agreement about what imagining being X entails (for some of the most important papers on this question, see Williams 1973; Wollheim 1973, 1974; Reynolds 1989; Velleman 1996). It has been argued that it does not entail an imagined identity between X and the imaginer, as identity is transitive, whereas imagining being X is supposedly different from imagining X being me (Wollheim 1973, 1974; Velleman 1996; for a dissenting view, see Walton 1990).

The crucial question from our perspective is whether there is a difference between imagining being X and imagining being in X's situation. If there is no difference between these two imaginative episodes, then Gordon's distinction collapses. And David Velleman argued at length that imagining being Napoleon is just imagining being in a Napoleonic situation, for example seeing the battlefield of Austerlitz, hearing the cannons, and so on (Velleman 1996; see also Williams 1973 for similar claims). In other words, for Velleman, imagining being Napoleon in Napoleon's situation would just be imagining Austerlitz in a 'Napoleonic first person'. Is Napoleon part of the content of this imaginative episode? In a way, he is, but our imagination is not directed at him.

A natural way of extending Velleman's analysis is that imagining Napoleon at Austerlitz is just imagining being in Napoleon's situation, where Napoleon's situation includes important elements of Napoleon's psychological and maybe emotional situation. Thus, the difference between imagining being in X's situation and imagining being X in X's situation is really a difference of the way we individuate the situation we imagine ourselves in.

In other words, another, maybe more charitable interpretation of Smith's passage about the dead son would be to say that Smith argues that when we sympathize with someone, that is, when we imagine ourselves in her situation, her situation must (sometimes) include some psychological factors. And this takes us to our second point of clarification about Smith's account of sympathy.

It is worth recapitulating where we are in our analysis of Adam Smith's concept of sympathy. We have seen that this concept needs clarification at two points: he talks about imagining oneself in someone else's situation, but what does he mean (a) by 'myself' and (b) by 'the other person's situation'? In this section, I analyzed what could be meant by 'myself' and this question has boiled down to the question about what is meant by 'the other person's situation': clarifying (a) presupposes the clarification of (b). In other words, we now have all the more reason to examine how 'X's situation' is to be individuated when we talk about imagining oneself in X's situation.

What does it mean to imagine myself *in the other person's situation*?

Another crucial question to ask about Smith's account of sympathy is what we should mean by 'X's situation' when talking about imagining oneself in someone else's situation. Depending on the way we interpret this notion, we end up with very different accounts of imagining from the inside and of sympathy.

It is important that we should not restrict X's situation to X's physical situation. X's situation should also include facts about what X knows. Suppose X is attacked by someone. The experience of imagining myself in X's situation will depend on whether X has a gun in her pocket, as this is an important element of X's physical situation. Similarly, the experience of imagining myself in X's situation will also depend on whether X knows something about the attacker that could be a means of defending herself (say, by blackmailing). And this is not an element in X's physical, but psychological/epistemic situation.

The upshot is that Smith should be interpreted as using the term 'situation' in a way that allows for psychological/epistemic elements in the other person's situation. This seems to be the standard interpretation of what Smith means by 'the other person's situation': 'the other person's situation as presented to her'. As Stephen Darwall says, 'Smithian sympathy [...] implicitly recognizes the other as having an independent perspective' (Darwall 2004: 131). Or, more precisely:

> For Smith, when we judge an agent's motive, we do so from the agent's own perspective, viewing the practical situation *as we imagine it to confront her* in deliberation. And when we judge someone's feeling or reaction, we do so from her patient's perspective, viewing the situation

as we imagine it to confront her as someone responding to it. Both judgments involve an implicit identification with, and thus respect for, the other as having an independent point of view.

(Darwall 2004: 132; my emphasis. See also Fleischacker 2006: 4)

In short, for Smith, sympathizing with someone entails imagining oneself in someone else's *psychological* situation. Smith's example about the grieving father should be interpreted accordingly. When 'I change persons and characters' with you (TMS VII.iii.1.4), this means that I imagine myself in your *psychological* situation: when I imagine being in your situation, I include facts about your person and character in the content of my imaginative episode.

The problem with this way of interpreting Smith is that he talks a lot about instances of sympathy where this is not so. In an often-quoted paragraph, Smith talks about emotional contagion:

> Persons of delicate fibres and a weak constitution of body complain, that in looking on the sores and ulcers which are exposed by beggars in the streets, they are apt to feel an itching or uneasy sensation in the correspondent part of their own bodies. The horror which they conceive at the misery of those wretches affects that particular part in themselves more than any other; because that horror arises from conceiving what they themselves would suffer, if they really were the wretches whom they are looking upon, and if that particular part in themselves was actually affected in the same miserable manner.
>
> (TMS I.i.1.3)

In the case of emotional contagion, the other person's psychological situation is irrelevant. So if we imagine ourselves in the other person's situation, this situation is unlikely to involve the other person's psychology (see Gaut 1999; M. Smith 1995).

To make things worse, some of Smith's examples seem to entail that we ignore the psychological elements of the other person's situation. When we sympathize with the lunatic or with the dead, we need to ignore the psychological elements in their situation. As he says:

> The poor wretch [...] laughs and sings perhaps, and is altogether insensible of his own misery. The anguish which humanity feels, therefore, at the sight of such an object, cannot be the reflection of any sentiment of the sufferer. The compassion of the spectator must arise altogether from the consideration of what he himself would feel if he was reduced to the same unhappy situation.
>
> (TMS I.i.1.11)

The important consideration here is not that the 'sentiment of the sufferer' is different from ours – I will return to this point shortly. But if it is possible at all to feel sympathy towards the 'poor wretch', one must imagine oneself in her situation, not as actually presented to her, but as presented to her, were she to know that she is in this state. Thus, when one imagines oneself in her situation, then one needs to abstract away from the psychological elements in her situation.[4] In other words, we can sympathize with people even if we know significantly more (or significantly less) about their situation than they themselves do.

If we take examples of all three kinds in consideration, we get a very complicated picture. The situation in which we imagine ourselves is such that it (a) sometimes necessarily contains elements of the other person's psychology, (b) sometimes necessarily excludes elements of the other person's psychology and (c) sometimes is noncommittal about the other person's psychology.

Thus, the answer to our original question about how to individuate the situations we imagine ourselves in when sympathizing depends on the act of sympathizing. Smith's concept of sympathy allows for psychological/epistemic elements in the other person's situation, but it also allows for the lack of any such elements.

This heterogeneity of the situations we imagine ourselves in when sympathizing could be taken to be indicative of the fact that Smith's concept of sympathy is not a monolithic concept. It has been argued that he does not use the concept of sympathy consistently in *The Theory of Moral Sentiments*. James Otteson distinguishes three distinct senses in which he uses 'sympathy': 'natural fellow feeling for others, pity for others, and correspondence of sentiments between two or more people' (Otteson 2002: 17). Philippe Fontaine made further distinctions (Fontaine 1997; see also Levy and Peart 2004) and Charles Griswold even talks about the 'spectrum of sympathy' (Griswold 1999: 87–8; 2006: 27).

I will argue that we can find a common denominator between these seemingly diverging uses of the concept of sympathy, but in order to do so, we need to get rid of some connotations of the concept of sympathy that are mainly due to contemporary interpretations.

The structure of my argument is the following. In order to understand what Adam Smith meant by sympathy, we need to clarify how 'myself' and 'X's situation' are to be interpreted in 'imagining myself in X's situation'. And if we flesh out what is meant by these concepts, then Adam Smith's concept of sympathy covers cases of the kinds (a), (b) and (c). Now, if we want to find a common denominator between these three very different kinds of cases, we have to revise Adam Smith's concept of sympathy. More precisely, I will argue that if we reject a premise that has been taken for granted in analyzing Adam Smith's concept of sympathy, then we may be able to do justice to Adam Smith's intention to use sympathy in the very different cases of the kind (a), (b) and (c). This premise is that sympathy implies some kind of correspondence between the mental states of the sympathizer and the person she is sympathizing with. Rejecting this premise will break the neat and coherent contemporary simulation–empathy–sympathy picture I outlined in the second section. But if it gives us a better guide to what Adam Smith in fact meant by this concept, this is a sacrifice worth making.

Sympathy without correspondence

It is widely assumed about Smith's concept of sympathy that it gives us reliable access to the other person's mental states. This assumption is in the background of considering Smith to be an antecedent of the simulationist view of the attribution of mental states to others and this is also in the background of taking him to be the first philosopher who talked about what we now refer to as empathy.

If sympathizing with someone is the same as, or at least can give rise to simulating that person, then sympathy must be a correct guide to the other person's mental states. Simulating another person, as we have seen, is a way of attributing mental states to her. If sympathy were an unreliable guide to what mental state the other person has, it would be of no use in the attribution of mental states to others.

The same applies in the case of considering Smith's account of sympathy to be similar to what we mean by empathy these days. There is no consensus about what exactly the concept of empathy entails, but one point of agreement is that it entails that the empathizer is feeling with the other person: there is some kind of (not necessarily complete) symmetry between the two people's mental states (Deonna 2007; M. Smith 1995; Neill 1996; Goldie 1999, 2002). But this can only be so if feeling empathy guarantees that we get into a state that is similar to that of the person we are empathizing with.

I will argue against the assumption that sympathy, as Adam Smith uses the concept, gives us access to the other person's mental states. Right after introducing the concept of sympathy, Smith gives a number of examples where sympathy does not give us access to the other person's mental states. We sympathize with lunatics and what we feel when we do so is very different from what they feel. We sympathize with the dead and what we feel when we do so is clearly very different from what the dead feel, as they do not feel anything. And the mother who is worried for her child has some complex feeling that the child herself is incapable of.

Smith sums up the moral of these examples in a very explicit manner:

> We sometimes feel for another, a passion of which he himself seems to be altogether incapable; because, when we put ourselves in his case, that passion arises in our breast from the imagination, though it does not in his from the reality.
>
> (TMS I.i.1.10)

In the examples above, there is an asymmetry between the mental states of the sympathizer and the person she is sympathizing with. If she were to take her imaginative episode as a reason to attribute the mental state she finds herself in to the other person, as the simulationists would suggest, she would be wrong. And as there is no symmetry between the two agents, we can't talk about empathy either. Thus, if the assumption that sympathy gives us a reliable access to other people's mental states is rejected, Adam Smith's concept of sympathy turns out to be very different from its contemporary uses. It turns out to be very different from simulation and from empathy as both of these two concepts presuppose some kind of similarity between the mental states of the simulator/empathizer and the other person.

Smith uses the expression 'illusive sympathy' to describe our sympathy for the dead (TMS II.i.2.5). But the very idea of illusive sympathy could be thought to be problematic (Griswold 1999: 89–90). If our sympathy for the dead and the lunatic is illusive, how can we know that not all instances of sympathy are illusive? As Charles Griswold puts it:

> Is every sympathetic identification of spectator with actor an illusion, in that the spectator simply projects his or her own feelings into the situation and then attributes them to the actor?
>
> (Griswold 1999: 90)

This is a crucial puzzle about Smith's concept of sympathy and all interpretations of this concept need to provide some kind of answer. One possible response would be to say that illusive sympathy is somehow importantly different from 'genuine' or 'non-illusive' sympathy, that is, sympathy where there is correspondence between the feelings of the sympathizer and the person she is sympathizing with. I take it that this is what motivates the distinction Otteson makes between different senses of sympathy. Only one of the three senses he differentiates (and the most important one) is 'correspondence of sentiments between two or more people' (Otteson 2002: 17). As he says:

> What happens is this. We see the misery or happiness of another, we imagine ourselves in the same situation, and a real or imagined feeling wells up in us as a result of this imaginative changing of place. We then compare what our own feelings would be if we were in the other's situation with what his actual feelings are in his situation. If our respective feelings are commensurate, Smith says that we sympathize with that other; if they are not, we do not. Thus sympathy is correspondence between the imagined feelings of the spectator and the actual sentiments of the person primarily concerned.
>
> (Otteson 2002: 19; also Otteson 2000: 64)

So the strategy would be to take this notion of sympathy and use it as the genuine notion and demote 'illusive sympathy', sympathy without such correspondence, to a secondary status. We can draw a clear distinction between 'illusive' and 'genuine' cases of sympathy as the 'correspondence between the imagined feelings of the spectator and the actual sentiments of the person primarily concerned' is absent in the former and necessarily present in the latter. A helpful analogy would be true and false beliefs. Not all instances of sympathy are 'illusive': some are, some are not. Just like not all beliefs are false. Some are, some are not. Those instances of sympathy where there is no correspondence between the feelings of the sympathizer and the person she is sympathizing with are illusive. Those where there is such correspondence are 'genuine'. Similarly, those instances of beliefs where there is correspondence between the content of the belief and the state of affairs in the world are true. The ones where there is no such correspondence are false.

I think that this strategy is neither independently plausible nor consistent with Smith's text. Why should we accept that sympathy where I feel what the other person feels is more genuine than sympathy where this is not the case? Why should we suppose that correspondence between the feelings of the sympathizer and the person she is sympathizing with is a necessary or even an important feature of sympathy?

The analogy with beliefs breaks down at this point. Beliefs have correctness conditions: if these conditions are satisfied, the belief is true, if they are not, it is false. Sympathy does not have correctness conditions. Feeling sympathy for the dead or for the lunatic is not incorrect or false or in any way defective. It is as genuine an instance of sympathy as those cases where there is perfect symmetry between the feelings of the sympathizer and the person she is sympathizing with. Illusive sympathy is not 'defective' sympathy in the same way as a false belief could be construed as 'defective' belief. Illusive sympathy is a paradigmatic case of sympathy and illusive sympathy may be stronger/more salient than the non-illusive one.[5]

Importantly, Smith clearly does not want to make a distinction between the two kinds of sympathy ('illusive' and 'genuine'): that is why, right after introducing the concept, he reminds us with no fewer than four examples that sympathy does not guarantee that there is correspondence between the feelings of the sympathizer and the person she is sympathizing with (see also Ashraf et al. 2005: 436).

Thus, excluding 'illusive' instances of sympathy and restricting sympathy to those cases where there is correspondence between the mental states of the sympathizer and the person she is sympathizing with leads to an account that is both arbitrary and, more importantly, also flatly contradicts Adam Smith's explicit intention to use this concept more broadly.

Hence, we have good reason to suppose that Adam Smith's concept of sympathy does not guarantee that there would be correspondence between the mental states of the sympathizer and the person she is sympathizing with. If this is so, then the two recent popular uses of Smith's concept are unjustified. Smithian sympathy cannot be considered to be similar to what happens to us when we attribute mental states to other people by simulating them, as nothing would guarantee that we attribute the correct mental state to others.

And Smith's concept of sympathy cannot be considered to be an early expression of the idea of empathy either, as empathy entails some kind of similarity between the empathizer's emotions and those of the person she empathizes with and this condition will not be met in many instances of what Smith would describe as sympathy.

A helpful way of bringing out this point is Berys Gaut's distinction between empathy and identification (Gaut 1999, see also Gaut 1998; and see Neill 1996 for a dissenting view on the relation between empathy and identification). In the case of empathy we *actually* feel what the other person feels, whereas in the case of identification we *imagine* feeling what the other person feels. Smith's concept of sympathy is closer to what Gaut refers to as identification than it is to empathy (see also Sugden 2002).

The argument I presented in this section focuses on what Adam Smith's concept of sympathy is not: it is not a mental state that requires correspondence between the sympathizer and the person she is sympathizing with. But this argument also gives us at least the sketch of a positive account of what Adam Smith meant when he talked about sympathy.

If we encounter genuine instances of sympathy in cases (a), (b) and (c), then sympathy must be a very basic, quasi-automatic process that happens to us without any concern about whether we are 'getting it right' what mental state the other person is in. It is a simple imaginative process: imagining ourselves in a certain situation – the situation we take the other person to be in, which may or may not be the situation she takes herself to be in.

Smith's examples right after having introduced the concept of sympathy make it clear that sympathy is a visceral reaction. Here are a few examples:

> When we see a stroke aimed and just ready to fall upon the leg or arm of another person, we naturally shrink and draw back our own leg or our own arm [...]
>
> (TMS I.i.1.3)

> Persons of delicate fibres and a weak constitution of body complain, that in looking on the sores and ulcers which are exposed by beggars in the streets, they are apt to feel an itching or uneasy sensation in the correspondent part of their own bodies.
>
> (TMS I.i.1.3)

> The mob, when they are gazing at a dancer on the slack rope, naturally writhe and twist and balance their own bodies, as they see him do, and as they feel that they themselves must do if in his situation.
>
> (TMS I.i.1.3)

For Smith, these reactions all count as sympathy. But if they do, then sympathy can only be a visceral, quasi-automatic[6] reaction of imagining ourselves in a certain situation – the situation we perceive or believe someone else to be in. But why should we call simple visceral reactions of this kind 'sympathy' at all? It may be true that when Adam Smith talked about sympathy, what he meant was this simple quasi-automatic imaginative reaction. But what does this concept have to do with our concept of sympathy?[7]

The short answer is that what Adam Smith calls 'sympathy' is a necessary component of what we call 'sympathy'. The visceral imaginative reaction sometimes (but not always) gives rise to what we call sympathy: a mental state that involves some kind of correspondence between the sympathizer and the person she is sympathizing with. In other words, 'sympathy' in our sense presupposes 'sympathy' in Smith's sense: the latter is a more basic state that the former is based on.

And, as a result, 'sympathy' in Smith's sense shares some important features with 'sympathy' in our sense. Most importantly, they have similar emotive undertone and phenomenal character. There is an important phenomenal similarity between the visceral imaginative reaction Smith describe in the paragraphs quoted above and standard examples of sympathy: they feel similar. If it is true that sympathy in Smith's sense is a necessary constituent of sympathy in our sense, this phenomenal similarity should not come as a surprise.

Two objections

There are two passages in *The Theory of Moral Sentiments* that seem to be inconsistent with the interpretation of sympathy I outlined above. I will argue that the inconsistency is only apparent and under closer scrutiny it turns out that these passages not only fail to jeopardize my interpretation of sympathy, they in fact provide further textual evidence in its favour.

First objection

One may object that this interpretation of sympathy, according to which sympathy has no correctness conditions and is not to be taken to guarantee any correspondence between the feelings of the sympathizer and the person she is sympathizing with, seems to flatly contradict a famous and often-quoted claim Smith makes. At the very beginning of *The Theory of Moral Sentiments*, he writes: 'As we have no immediate experience of what other men feel, we can form no idea of the manner in which they are affected, but by conceiving what we ourselves should feel in the like situation' (TMS I.i.1.2). Although this sentence seems to suggest that sympathy is a reliable way of tracking other people's emotions, it is important to note that Smith here makes a negative claim only, namely, that there is no other way of getting information about what other people feel but by sympathy. He does not make the stronger claim that sympathy (always, or even normally) gives us a reliable representation of other people's emotions. All he says is that nothing other than sympathy could acquaint us with other people's emotions. He does not say how reliable this acquaintance can be, but his repeated dismissal of the reliability of imagining (TMS I.iii.2.2, 8; IV.1.9) makes it even more likely that he did not think of sympathy as a reliable guide to others' mental states.[8]

But if this is so, then sympathy is not an infallible, and not even a very reliable, way of tracking other people's mental states. It does not guarantee any similarity, let alone correspondence between the state the sympathizer finds herself in and the state of the person she sympathizes with. Those instances of sympathy where there is such correspondence are as genuine as those where there isn't. Sympathy does not have correctness conditions.

The second objection

Finally, the following possible objection to the interpretation I outlined above needs to be addressed. One may worry that the most important use of Smith's concept of sympathy, namely, its use in characterizing moral judgments, would be threatened by the interpretation given above. The worry, in short, is the following. If sympathy has no correctness conditions, how could our moral judgments, which should be correct or incorrect, be based on it?

The first thing to note is that this is an immediate worry only if we assume, as many scholars do (for example, Tugendhat 2004: 90), that sympathy *entails* judgment of propriety. But Smith explicitly denies this. Judgment of propriety is a two-step process, only the first step of which is sympathy: 'The approbation of propriety therefore requires, not only that we should entirely sympathize with the person who acts, but that we should perceive this perfect concord between his sentiments and our own' (TMS II.i.5.11). In short, sympathy does not entail judgment of propriety. Judgment of propriety is a two-step process: (a) we sympathize with the other person and (b) we 'perceive this perfect concord between his sentiments and our own'. Step (a) does not presuppose correspondence between the mental states of the sympathizer and those of the person she is sympathizing with. The correspondence comes with step (b).

We can have (a), that is, sympathy, without (b), that is, the perception of perfect concord between his sentiments and our own'. The perception of 'perfect concord between his sentiments and our own' supposedly implies there actually being 'perfect concord between his sentiments and our own'. But sympathy itself (step (a)) does not imply such 'perfect concord'.

This essay is not about Smith's account of moral judgment. The reason why I need to focus on his account of moral judgment is to show that the interpretation of sympathy I outlined above is consistent with his account of 'judgments of propriety'. Thus, I will not elaborate on what constitutes the second step of the two-step process of our judgment of propriety: I will not say much about what 'perceiving this perfect concord between his sentiments and our own' (TMS II.i.5.11) consists in (Smith says a lot about what step (b) consists of at TMS I.i.3.1–4.10).

For the purposes of this essay it suffices to point out that whatever the exact structure of moral judgment is, sympathy is a necessary but not sufficient constituent of it. In other words, sympathy, that is, step (a), is necessary for judgments of propriety – with the caveat Smith talks about at TMS I.i.3.3–4, namely that the sympathy in question is sometimes conditional sympathy. But it is not sufficient: we also need step (b) to form judgments of propriety. And as step (b) is the one of the two steps that requires 'perfect concord between his sentiments and our own', sympathy (step (a) does not necessarily imply such 'perfect concord'.

Here is another consideration in favour of this claim. Smith contrasts judgments of propriety with judgments of 'merit or beneficence' (TMS II. i.5.11). The latter can be based on 'illusive' as well as 'non-illusive' instances of sympathy. In other words, it does not presuppose that there is a correspondence between the mental states of the sympathizer and those of the person she is sympathizing with: '[O]ur sense of merit is often founded upon one of those illusive sympathies, by which, when we bring home to ourselves the case of another, we are often affected in a manner in which the person principally concerned is incapable of being affected' (TMS II.i.5.11). In other words, both judgments of propriety and our 'sense of merit' are based on sympathy. But it is only the former, not the latter, that requires correspondence between the mental states of the sympathizer and those of the person she is sympathizing with. When it comes to our 'appropriation of merit or beneficence', in contrast, as Smith explicitly states, 'no actual correspondence of sentiments, therefore, is here required' (TMS II.i.5.11).

To sum up, our 'sense of merit' is based on sympathy and it does not require that there is 'actual correspondence of sentiments' between the two agents. In other words, sympathy itself requires no such correspondence. Our judgment of propriety is also based on sympathy, but it does require that there is correspondence between the mental states of the two agents. Hence, the difference in terms of correspondence between the mental states of the two agents must be external to sympathy itself – what both 'sense of merit' and 'judgment of propriety' are based on. And this makes it clear that the correspondence between the mental states of the two agents is not a necessary attribute of sympathy.[9] In short, under closer scrutiny, the role sympathy plays in Adam Smith's moral philosophy not only fails to constitute an objection to my proposal, but it also provides some further textual evidence in its favour.

I proposed an interpretation of Smith's concept of sympathy according to which if we sympathize with someone else, there does not need to be 'harmony and correspondence of the sentiments between him and ourselves' (TMS II.i.5.11). This interpretation is consistent with Smith's claim that moral judgment is based on sympathy.

Conclusion

The aim of this essay has been to suggest a new interpretation of Smith's concept of sympathy and point out that on this interpretation some of the contemporary uses of this concept are misleading. I argued that sympathy should be interpreted as not necessarily involving 'harmony and correspondence of the sentiments' between the sympathizer and the other person, and that this interpretation could be made consistent with Smith's account of moral judgment.

In other words, we cannot use Adam Smith's concept of sympathy to support the empathy/simulation picture of our engagement with other people. The concept of sympathy, as Adam Smith used it, denotes a much simpler mental phenomenon: a visceral imaginative reaction, which is very different from both empathy and simulation (but which may be a necessary constituent thereof).[10]

I criticized the contemporary uses of Smith's concept of sympathy. But does this mean that Smith's concept of sympathy has no use for our contemporary thinking? Not at all. In fact, we can learn something much more surprising if we take Adam Smith's account of sympathy seriously: that our emotional engagement with other people is based on a very simple visceral, quasi-automatic imaginative process, which is at the centre of Smith's analysis. And maybe the reinterpretation of Smith's account of sympathy should help us to question the empathy/simulation framework for talking about our engagement with other people and to replace it with the analysis of the much simpler imaginative process that Smith talks about.

Acknowledgements

I am grateful for comments by Sam Fleischacker, Margaret Schabas, Eric Schliesser, Vivienne Brown and two anonymous referees.

Notes

1 The term was apparently introduced by none other than the psychologist Edward Titchener. See Darwall (1998: 262) for details.
2 This imagining episode is about myself, not about X. As a result, I will use the phrases 'imagining being in X's situation' and 'imagining myself being in X's situation' interchangeably in what follows.
3 Not all accounts of imagining from the inside fall clearly into one of the two categories I differentiated above. Gregory Currie's account, for example, is ambiguous between (1) and (2). It is important to note that he does not talk about imagining from the inside, but about what he calls 'secondary imagining'. Sometimes he characterizes secondary imagining in ways that correspond to (1): as imagining 'the experience of the character' or 'in imagination, feeling what the character feels' (Currie 1995: 153). Sometimes, however, he gives formulations of secondary imagining that is very similar to (2): 'as a result of putting myself, in imagination, in the character's position, I come to have imaginary versions of the thoughts, feelings and attitudes I would have in that situation' (Currie 1995: 153). As these two different conceptions of secondary imagination occur on the very same page, we have good reason to suppose that he takes 'X's situation' to be so broad that (2) would collapse into (1). See also Currie (1998) and Currie and Ravenscroft (2002).
4 It is important that in these cases of sympathy, we need to be aware of the other person's situation as it is presented to her and nonetheless abstract away from it.

If we are not aware of the other person's situation at all, then we tend not to be able to sympathize with her, as Smith's example of the lack of sympathy for the angry man shows. See TMS I.i.1.8.

5 Interestingly Alfred Hitchcock made the same point:

> A curious person goes into somebody else's room and begins to search through the drawers. Now, you show the person who lives in that room coming up the stairs. Then you go back to the person who is searching, and the public feels like warning him, 'Be careful, watch out. Someone's coming up the stairs'. Therefore, even if the snooper is not a likeable character, the audience will still feel anxiety for him. Of course, when the character is attractive, as for instance Grace Kelly in *Rear Window*, the public's emotion is greatly intensified.
>
> (Truffaut 1967: 21)

Here the 'sympathy' the audience feels is 'illusive' as there is an important asymmetry between the mental states of the 'snooper' and the members of the audience: the 'snooper' does not know that someone is coming up the stairs, but we do. Yet, our 'sympathy' with her is very strong, arguably stronger than it would be if there were more correspondence between her mental states and ours (that is, if she were to know that someone is coming up the stairs or if we were to be ignorant of this fact).

6 This interpretation of Adam Smith's concept of sympathy is consistent with those recent suggestions according to which Adam Smith conceived of sympathy as a physiological reaction (see, for example Schabas, 2003, esp. section 4).

7 I am grateful to Sam Fleischacker for raising this question.

8 Further, denying that sympathy *in itself* is a reliable indicator of other people's emotions is consistent with the claim that sympathy can be a component of a mental process that reliably tracks other people's emotions – as we shall see in the next sub-section. An analogy would be the following. Perception is a reliable process, but one's retinal image, a necessary component of the perceptual process, is not: the shape of our retinal image when we are looking at a circular object is very rarely (only in those cases when we are looking at it head on) a reliable indicator of the actual shape of the object we are looking at.

9 This conclusion may have significant implications for one of the most important questions in the background of the infamous Das Adam Smith Problem (the problem about the apparent conflict between the claims of *The Theory of Moral Sentiments* and of the *Wealth of Nations*; see Montes 2003): the question about whether sympathy is a 'motive to action' (Broadie 2006: 164–5; see also Werhane 1991: 97; Otteson 2000: 64; Ashraf *et al.* 2005: 435; Raphael and Macfie 1976: 21–2; Montes 2004: 45–55; Khalil 1990; Raphael 2007: 117ff.). A crucial question about sympathy is what role it plays in our moral psychology: whether it is a 'motive to action'. Of course this depends on what we mean by 'motive to action', whether we interpret Smith as holding that motives must be causes and if so, what kind of causes (see Fleischacker 2004, Brown 2009 and Otteson 2002 for overview). It is clearly beyond the scope of this essay to engage with this debate. But it is important to note that if we accept the interpretation of sympathy I proposed above, the debate may look different.

On the picture I outlined here, sympathy is the first step in a two-step mental process that constitutes judgments of propriety. We may or may not consider judgments of propriety to be 'motives to action', but even if we do, it is still debatable whether we should consider a proper part of a 'motive to action' (the judgment of propriety) to be a 'motive to action' itself – as sympathy is a proper part of the judgment of propriety. If it is true that sympathy for someone does not imply 'harmony and correspondence of the sentiments between him and ourselves' (TMS II.i.5.11), then a number of assumptions behind the debate about whether sympathy is a 'motive to action' need to be reevaluated (see also Fleischacker 2004: 67).

10 This change in the interpretation of Smith's concept of sympathy may also help us to put in perspective some other key concepts of *The Theory of Moral Sentiments*, such as that of deception (see esp. TMS IV.1.10) and Smith's emphasis on the importance of self-approbation/disapprobation (as opposed to the approbation/disapprobation of others, see esp. TMS IV.1.8). I am grateful to Margaret Schabas for drawing my attention to some of these implications of my argument.

Bibliography

Adams, F. (2001) 'Empathy, neural imaging and the theory versus simulation debate', *Mind & Language*, 16: 368–92.

Ashraf, N., Camerer, C.F. and Loewenstein, G. (2005) 'Adam Smith, behavioral economist', *Journal of Economic Perspectives*, 19: 131–45.

Berry, C.J. (2006) 'Adam Smith and science', in K. Haakonssen (ed.), *The Cambridge Companion to Adam Smith*, Cambridge: Cambridge University Press, pp. 112–35.

Brown, V. (2009) 'Agency and discourse: revisiting the Adam Smith problem', in J.T. Young (ed.), *Elgar Companion to Adam Smith*, Cheltenham: Edward Elgar, pp. 52–72.

Broadie, A. (2006) 'Sympathy and the impartial spectator', in K. Haakonssen (ed.), *The Cambridge Companion to Adam Smith*, Cambridge: Cambridge University Press, pp. 158–88.

Carruthers, P. and Smith, P.K. (eds) (1996) *Theories of Theories of Mind*, Cambridge: Cambridge University Press.

Currie, G. (1993) 'Impersonal imagining, a reply to Jerrold Levinson', *Philosophical Quarterly*, 43: 79–82.

—— (1995) *Image and Mind: Film, Philosophy, and Cognitive Science*, Cambridge: Cambridge University Press.

—— (1998) 'Pretence, pretending and metarepresentation', *Mind & Language*, 13: 35–55.

Currie, G. and Ravenscroft, I. (2002) *Recreative Minds: Imagination in Philosophy and Psychology*, Oxford: Clarendon Press.

Darwall, S. (1998) 'Empathy, sympathy, care', *Philosophical Studies*, 89: 261–82.

—— (1999) 'Sympathetic liberalism: recent work on Adam Smith', *Philosophy & Public Affairs*, 28: 139–64.

—— (2004) 'Equal dignity in Adam Smith', *The Adam Smith Review*, 1: 129–34, V. Brown (ed.), London and New York: Routledge.

Davies, M. (1994) 'The mental simulation debate', in C. Peacocke (ed.), *Objectivity, Simulation and the Unity of Consciousness: Current Issues in the Philosophy of Mind*, Oxford: Oxford University Press, pp. 99–127.

Deonna, J. (2007) 'The structure of empathy', *Journal of Moral Philosophy*, 4: 99–116.

Feagin, S.L. (1996) *Reading with Feeling: The Aesthetics of Appreciation*, Ithaca, NY: Cornell University Press.

Fleischacker, S. (2004) *On Adam Smith's* Wealth of Nations*: A Philosophical Companion*, Princeton, NJ: Princeton University Press.

—— (2006) 'Adam Smith and equality', *Estudios Públicos*, 104: 1–23.

Fontaine, P. (1997) 'Identification and economic behaviour: sympathy and empathy in historical perspective', *Economics and Philosophy*, 13: 261–80.

Gaut, B. (1998) 'Imagination, interpretation, and film', *Philosophical Studies*, 89: 331–41.
—— (1999) Identification and emotion in narrative film', in C. Plantinga and G.M. Smith (eds), *Passionate Views: Thinking about Film and Emotion*, Baltimore, MD: Johns Hopkins University Press, pp. 200–16.

Goldie, P. (1999) 'Understanding other people's emotions', *Mind & Language*, 14: 394–423.
—— (2000) *The Emotions: A Philosophical Exploration*, Oxford: Oxford University Press.
—— (2002) 'Emotion, personality and simulation', in P. Goldie (ed.), *Understanding Emotions: Mind and Morals*, Aldershot: Ashgate Publishing, pp. 97–109.

Goldman, A. (1992) 'In defense of the simulation theory', *Mind & Language*, 7: 104–19.

Gordon, R.M. (1995a) 'Sympathy, simulation, and the impartial spectator', *Ethics*, 105: 727–42.
—— (1995b) 'Simulation without introspection or inference from me to you', in M. Davies and T. Stone (eds), *Mental Simulation*, Oxford: Blackwell, pp. 53–67.

Griswold, C.L. (1999) *Adam Smith and the Virtues of Enlightenment*, Cambridge: Cambridge University Press.
—— (2006) 'Imagination: morals, science and arts', in K. Haakonssen (ed.), *The Cambridge Companion to Adam Smith*, Cambridge: Cambridge University Press, pp. 22–56.

Heal, J. (1995) 'How to think about thinking', in M. Davies and T. Stone (eds), *Mental Simulation*, Oxford: Blackwell, pp. 33–52.

Khalil, E.L. (1990) 'Beyond self-interest and altruism', *Economics and Philosophy*, 6: 255–73.

Levy, D.M. and Peart, S.J. (2004) 'Sympathy and approbation in Hume and Adam Smith: a solution to the other rational species problem', *Economics and Philosophy*, 20: 331–49.

Montes, L. (2003) '*Das Adam Smith Problem*: its origins, the stages of the current debate, and one implication for our understanding of sympathy', *Journal of the History of Economic Thought*, 25: 63–90.
—— (2004) *Adam Smith in Context*, London: Palgrave Macmillan.

Neill, A. (1996) 'Empathy and (film) fiction', in D. Bordwell and N. Carroll (eds), *Post Theory: Reconstructing Film Studies*, Madison, WI: Wisconsin University Press, pp. 175–94.

Otteson, J.R. (2000) 'The recurring "Adam Smith Problem"', *History of Philosophy Quarterly*, 17: 51–74.
—— (2002) *Adam Smith's Marketplace of Life*, Cambridge: Cambridge University Press.

Raphael, D.D. (2007) *The Impartial Spectator: Adam Smith's Moral Philosophy*, Oxford: Oxford University Press.

Raphael, D.D. and Macfie, A.L. (1976) Introduction to Adam Smith, *The Theory of Moral Sentiments*, Oxford: Clarendon Press.

Recanati, F. (2007) 'Imagining *de se*', unpublished ms.

Reynolds, S.L. (1989) 'Imagining oneself to be another', *Nous*, 23: 615–33.

Schabas, M. (2003) 'Smith's debts to nature', *History of Political Economy*, 35 (Suppl. 1): 262–81.

Smith, A. (1976 [1759]) *The Theory of Moral Sentiments*, D.D. Raphael and A.L Macfie (eds), Oxford: Clarendon Press.

Smith, M. (1995) *Engaging Characters*, Oxford: Oxford University Press.

—— (1997) 'Imagining from the inside', in R. Allen and M. Smith (eds), *Film Theory and Philosophy*, Oxford: Oxford University Press, pp. 412–30.

Stone, T. and Davies, M. (1996) 'The mental simulation debate: a progress report', in P. Carruthers and K.P. Smith (eds), *Theories of Theories of Mind*, Cambridge: Cambridge University Press, pp. 119–37.

Sudgen, R. (2002) 'Beyond sympathy and empathy: Adam Smith's concept of fellow-feeling', *Economics and Philosophy*, 18: 63–87.

Truffaut, F. (1967) *Hitchcock*, New York: Simon and Schuster.

Tugendhat, E. (2004) 'Universalistically approved intersubjective attitudes: Adam Smith', *The Adam Smith Review*, 1: 88–104, V. Brown (ed.), London and New York: Routledge.

Velleman, D. (1996) 'Self to self', *Philosophical Review*, 105: 39–76.

Walton, K. (1990) *Mimesis and Make-Believe: On the Foundations of the Representational Arts*, Cambridge, MA: Harvard University Press.

Werhane, P.H. (1991) *Adam Smith and His Legacy for Modern Capitalism*, Oxford: Oxford University Press.

Williams, B. (1973) 'Imagination and the self', in B. Williams, *Problems of the Self*, Cambridge: Cambridge University Press, pp. 26–45.

Wollheim, R. (1973) 'Imagination and identification', in R. Wollheim, *On Art and the Mind: Essays and Lectures*, London: Allen Lane, pp. 54–83.

—— (1974) 'Identification and imagination', in R. Wollheim (ed.), *Freud: A Collection of Critical Essays*, New York: Anchor Press, pp. 172–95.

—— (1984) *The Thread of Life*, Cambridge, MA: Harvard University Press.

—— (1987) *Painting as an Art*, Princeton, NJ: Princeton University Press.

Smith's ambivalence about honour

Stephen Darwall

Honour, Montesquieu tells us, is the 'principle of monarchy' (1989: 27). Monarchy 'assumes ... preeminences' and 'ranks', and it is 'the nature of honour ... to demand preferences and distinctions' (27). In monarchies (and honour cultures more generally), 'ambition', the desire for honour, is a source of social order. 'Honour makes all parts of the body politic move' (27). People seek honour, as it were, from below, and honour is bestowed from above, ultimately, by the king. Or to use Montesquieu's preferred metaphor, honour is conferred from the 'centre' and pursued from the periphery (27).

Elsewhere I have argued that honour and the form of respect of which it is the distinctive object (and through which hierarchies of honour are them-selves constituted), form a dyad that opposes the dyad characteristic of liberal moral and political order, namely, the equal dignity of persons along with its distinctive form of respect (as I argue, respect for one another as mutually accountable equals) (Darwall 2008). Both *honour respect* and *second-personal respect* (as I call respect for our equal authority to hold one another answer-able) are forms of *recognition* for *persons*, but persons conceived in two fun-damentally different ways.[1] We can appreciate this difference by reflecting on a phrase that is sometimes used to signify equality under law, namely, that the law is no 'respecter of persons'. Familiar as this phrase may be, it can sound odd to contemporary ears. What can it mean to say that the law does not respect persons? Isn't the very idea of equal legal dignity that the law respects all persons equally? What this phrase means, of course, is that the law does not respect differences or 'distinctions' between persons, specifically, that it pays no heed to differences of social status – Montesquieu's 'rank' and 'preeminence' – that it is the nature of honour respect to constitute. Honour respect is in this sense quite precisely a respecter of persons. It respects, and thereby constructs, the *persona* in its classic sense of social role or 'mask', the 'face' of social self-presentation. It is possible to occupy any given social status, rank, or role only if the attempt to do so is appropriately recognized or honoured by others.

Honour respect and respect for equal dignity thus define two opposing conceptions of social and moral order. The most obvious difference between them, of course, is between the hierarchy and equality they respectively

The Philosophy of Adam Smith, The Adam Smith Review, 5: 106–123 © 2010 The International Adam Smith Society, ISSN 1743–5285, ISBN 978-0-415-56256-0.

recognize and support. No less significant, however, are different forms of *relationship* they respectively mediate. We treat one another as equals by engaging and relating to them on equal terms 'upon ordinary occasions', as Adam Smith puts it (Smith 1976a, TMS I.iii.2.3, p. 53), by holding ourselves answerable to one another, whereas honour respect and contempt manifest themselves in very different forms of treatment – deference or disdain, for example, or by just playing social roles that support or undermine the roles that others attempt to play. This puts mutual accountability at the heart of a society of equals and makes it an anathema to cultures of honour. In the former, holding someone accountable is itself a form of respect for their equal authority as persons. In the latter, it is often most naturally taken as an insult: 'You talkin' to me?'.

A number of recent writers, most prominently Emma Rothschild, but also others, including Samuel Fleischacker, Charles Griswold and myself, have stressed strong egalitarian themes in Adam Smith's writings (Rothschild 2002, Fleischacker 2005, Griswold 1999, Darwall 2004, 2006). For my part, I have argued that we can find in Smith an early form of the idea I develop in Darwall (2006), namely, that we share a common basic standing (second-personal authority, as I call it) to make claims of others and hold ourselves accountable to one another. But this is only part of the story. Although Smith had a detailed appreciation of the conflicts between an order of honour and one based on equal respect, he was nonetheless drawn to certain aspects of honour culture. In what follows, I wish to explore what we might call Smith's 'ambivalence' about honour. On the one hand, Smith calls the disposition to admire those of rank and wealth 'the great and most universal cause of the corruption of our moral sentiments', and he notes that it is almost impossible to treat those of exalted rank 'as men' and 'reason and dispute with them upon ordinary occasions' (TMS I.iii.3.1, p. 61; I.iii.2.3, p. 53). On the other, there are many passages in which Smith praises a concern with rank and criticizes those who are oblivious to it and prepared to suffer insults to their honour and station as 'mean-spirited' (TMS VI.iii.16, p. 244). 'Magnanimity, or a regard to maintain our own rank and dignity in society', he writes, 'must characterize our whole stile and deportment' (TMS I.ii.3.8, p. 38).

It is not surprising that Smith's thought displays these complexities and tensions. In addition to the fact that Smith was an enormously subtle philosopher and moral psychologist, we should also bear in mind his social and political context. Smith was not the only acute moral philosopher of his time to show ambivalence about honour. Kant was another who played an important role in shaping liberal egalitarian moral and political ideas while also having one foot in an earlier ethic of honour.[2] In mid- to late-eighteenth-century Europe, a fundamentally hierarchical order along with its traditional status notions of rank and honour were just beginning to shift towards a conception of moral and political relations grounded in equal dignity and equal respect.

Dominance, honour, authority and esteem

Before we begin, we should note some analytical distinctions that will prove useful in coming to terms with Smith's views; first, a distinction between two fundamentally different kinds of respect (Darwall 1977). One thing 'respect' can mean is an attitude of *appraisal* or esteem, specifically, esteem for someone or her conduct or character as a person (moral esteem) or for how she conducts herself in some more specific area or pursuit (for example, as a philosopher). Respect of this kind (*appraisal respect*) is a response to *merit*, and though it may be expressed or show itself in our conduct towards someone, it is not constituted by that. That someone is worthy of respect in this sense is one thing, and how we should conduct ourselves towards her in virtue of that is another. The latter, however, is precisely what is involved in *recognition respect*. Recognition respect consists in *treatment*, more specifically, in how we regulate our conduct towards someone or something by virtue of what we take to be its authority or standing. Thus whereas appraisal respect responds to (putative) merit, recognition respect responds to (presumed) dignity, authority or status. Whether we have appraisal respect for someone is manifested in appraising attitudes that leave open the question of how to conduct ourselves in relation to our respect's object. But the latter is precisely what recognition respect concerns. Whether (and how) to respect someone in the recognition sense just is the question of how to treat him, that is, how whatever constraints his status, authority or dignity place upon us should regulate our conduct towards him.[3]

We can bring out the difference between appraisal and recognition respect by noting that we can simultaneously believe that all persons are equally entitled to respect simply by virtue of being persons *and* that whether a person deserves respect, and how much respect he deserves, depends on how he conducts himself as a person. These beliefs do not conflict since they concern two different kinds of respect: recognition and appraisal respect. What someone deserves or earns by virtue of his conduct and character is appraisal respect or moral esteem. What someone is entitled to or has authority to claim or demand simply because he is a person (and so, it is worth noting, a being who can deserve more or less appraisal respect) is recognition respect for his equal dignity as a person. The former is an attitude of esteem towards the person that may or may not show itself in any particular choices or actions regarding him. The latter consists in the way we regulate our choices or conduct towards him by virtue of constraints we take to be placed on us by his being a person just like us.

In Darwall (2006) I argue that our equal dignity as persons includes a shared basic *authority* to make claims and demands of and hold ourselves accountable to one another. Partly this point concerns a conceptual connection between authority and recognition respect in general. We recognize authority by how we regulate our conduct towards or take account of it in our deliberative reasoning. This is true of authority of any kind, whether epistemic, moral, political, or of any sort whatever. Consider the difference, for example, between esteem for someone on account of his knowledge, on the one hand, and recognition respect for his epistemic authority, on the other. The latter is realized in an esteeming attitude towards him, whereas the latter is manifested in how we treat him, whether epistemically, by giving weight to his opinion in deciding what to believe ourselves, or by other forms of deference or recognition.

In addition, I argue that our fundamental authority (dignity) as persons is *second personal*: it is a standing to make claims on and demands of one another and hold each other accountable. We show (recognition) respect for practical authority of any kind by taking it appropriately into account in our practical reasoning. Thus we respect a speeding law, and the state's authority to impose it, when we take the law to give us a reason not to speed that is additional to any deriving from extra-legal considerations, say, from potential harm to others. But this is only part of what respect for practical authority involves, whether our equal basic authority as persons or the kind of authority the state has to make demands of our driving behaviour. If someone makes a legitimate demand of me, then I am *accountable* for complying with it, and accountability is, in its nature, a second-personal relation; it is always *to* someone, either as an individual or as having a representative authority of some kind (say, as a public official or even just as an equal person or representative member of the moral community). The way one respects practical authority is thus itself second personal not just in the sense that the authority one recognizes is a standing to make demands of one, but that adequately respecting that authority involves making oneself accountable to the authority second-personally – holding oneself answerable *to* her and so, in that way, putting oneself in her hands. Unlike non-second-personal forms of authority like epistemic authority, practical authority cannot be fully respected by recognition that does not involve acknowledgement, at least implicitly.

We will return to this aspect of second-personal respect when we consider Smith on respect and justice below. At this point, I want to consolidate the distinction between honour and second-personal respect I drew above and contrast it both with appraisal respect, and with another form of deference, namely, submission, that is akin to honour respect but nonetheless importantly different from it. Both honour respect and second-personal respect are forms of recognition that concern how we treat or regulate our conduct towards something rather than any appraising, non-choice-regulating attitude we may have towards it like esteem. So both are forms of recognition respect rather than appraisal respect. Moreover, for this reason, both are essentially implicated in forms of social organization and governance. Nevertheless, there is, again, a basic difference between the way honour respect mediates hierarchy and the way second-personal respect as an equal mediates mutual accountability.

Rank as a place of honour is respected by treating it and the person who occupies it with *deference* of a sort that helps constitute its status.

One occupies a given status or rank just in case others treat one as having it. Status is socially constituted or constructed through honour respect. This means that status or honour is not itself a normative idea. Whether someone or something occupies a place of honour or status is a social fact, which differs from any normative fact, say, whether she or it deserves or merits honour or is *honourable*. Honour or status differs in this way from dignity, which is the object of second-personal respect, and as well from virtue or merit, which is the object of appraisal respect. Although something has dignity or authority *de jure* only if it warrants or demands second-personal respect, something has status or rank only if it is in fact the object of honour respect. Dignity and authority, as I shall understand them, are inherently normative, whereas status or rank is a matter of 'positive' social fact.

Although it need not, rank can include powers to direct or order others to do things. Obviously, the king has this power in a monarchy. But whereas it is part of the very idea of authority that one is accountable or answerable for recognizing it in ways that constitute second-personal respect, answerability need be no part of an order of honour.[4] One respects honour by deference, not by holding oneself answerable for compliance. The king's subjects defer to his wishes, and even if they may be imprisoned if they do not, this need not be thought of as their being held accountable for non-compliance. Deferring to the king's standing to issue orders is not the same thing as acknowledging any legitimate authority he might claim to do so. (In an order of honour, it's deference all the way down, including when the king orders those who violate his orders to undergo certain sanctions.) The idea of legitimate authority, on the other hand, is connected to accountability conceptually and so is second personal in its nature. It requires the assumption that subjects are capable of accepting the authority and regulating themselves by it. Evidently, this need be no part of the thought that it is the king's place to rule his subjects.

Thus honour respect differs from second-personal respect in two fundamental ways. First, honour respect's object is not, though second-personal respect's object is, an essentially normative idea. The dignity of persons we acknowledge in second-personal respect is their being warranted objects of respect – as I analyse it, their having the authority to demand this respect, or as Rawls puts it, their being 'self-originating sources of valid claims' (Rawls 1980: 546). Whether someone has status or rank, however, is simply a matter of whether he or she is in fact the recipient of the relevant honour respect. The second basic difference between honour and second-personal respect is, again, that the latter is, though the former is not, conceptually connected to accountability. We recognize status by deferring to it, whereas we acknowledge dignity or practical authority by holding ourselves answerable to it (Darwall 2009).

Finally, though honour respect differs from recognition respect in lacking an inherently normative object, it nonetheless differs also from mere submission of the sort involved in pure domination and control, whether in a group of elephant seals or a human gang. Even if honour respect need not express any normative judgment (or even emotional appearance) that its object deserves honour, it nonetheless enacts a role in which such normative expressions are among the things one's character, or *persona, says,* 'lines' in the drama that takes place on an honour culture's 'stage'. Even if the individuals playing the roles need not think, feel, or do anything normative in actuality (though they of course may), the drama they enact is essentially normative – the characters they play have various normative relations of superiority and inferiority to one another.[5] In the enacted drama the characters are more or less honourable, though the statuses occupied by the people actually playing them are not. The latter depend entirely on other individuals continuing to play their roles in the appropriate way.

The form that taking someone down a peg assumes in an honour culture, whether or not it involves any physical or psychic attack, is the insult. To be sure, retaliating against or avenging injuries or insults may be as mandatory in an order of honour as repelling attacks is in a pure power hierarchy. Unavenged insults lower status as much as unopposed attacks lower their victims in a hierarchy of domination and control. But humiliation differs from mere submission to greater power. The former is an acknowledgement of lower status within a socially enacted, putatively normative hierarchy whereas the latter simply signals that one will no longer contest another's dominating power.

Perhaps there is a kind of recognition or respect that we can speak of even in a dominance hierarchy. Less powerful elephant seals might be said to recognize an alpha male by acting in ways that signify their willingness to accept his domination. We might think of this as a kind of respect (call it *submission respect*), at least by analogy. This would give us three different forms of recognition respect that can mediate social order. Submission respect constructs relations of power; honour respect constitutes relations of status or rank; and second-personal respect mediates relations of legitimate authority. Only the first lacks even an appearance of the normative. In the second, though the standing that honour respect constitutes, rank and status, is not normative in actuality, it is in the social drama of the *dramatis personae* whose roles social individuals actually play. And in the third, it is part of the very idea of a moral order of mutually accountable equals that every person has, and conceives one another as having, a common basic dignity that warrants second-personal respect, even when this is taken to ground relations of hierarchical authority.

Rank, honour and the moral sentiments

We turn now to considering Smith's ambivalence towards honour. I.iii.2 of *The Theory of Moral Sentiments* concerns 'the origin of Ambition, and of the distinction of Ranks' (TMS I.iii.2.1). Even if rank and honour are constituted by public social treatment,[6] Smith argues in this and the next chapter (I.iii.3) that what underlies the desire for rank (ambition), the respect that constitutes it (honour respect), and distinctions of rank themselves, are subtle and complex psychic mechanisms whose ultimate objects are substantially deeper and more interesting than mere 'external honours' (TMS III.5.8, p. 166). 'To deserve, to acquire, and to enjoy the respect and admiration of mankind', Smith writes, 'are the great objects of ambition and emulation' (TMS I.iii.3.2, p. 62). What the ambitious are ultimately after in Smith's view is not simply social status, that is, honour *de facto*, but to be deserving of honour. The problem is that the ambitious have a distorted sense of the honourable, which they tend to conflate with being honoured in fact. They are not, however, unusual in confusing being honourable with being honoured. Smith argues that the mechanisms of sympathy work to lead human beings quite generally to esteem those of higher rank: 'Upon this disposition of mankind, to go along with ['sympathize with'] all the passions of the rich and powerful, is founded the distinction of ranks, and the order of society' (TMS I.iii.2.3, p. 52).

Smith argues, however, that the human 'disposition' to sympathize with and so admire 'and almost to worship' those of higher rank disfigures moral judgment in a fundamental way. Sympathy with the higher ranked is not only 'necessary to establish and maintain the distinction of ranks', but 'at the same time, the great and most universal cause of the corruption of our moral sentiments' (TMS I.iii.3.1, p. 61). In this section, we shall consider these aspects of Smith's ambivalence towards honour. On the one hand, honour hierarchies result from and sustain human desires whose objects are not simply riches, power or status, but a moralized aim, being deserving of honour and esteem. On the other, the sympathetic mechanisms that explain why this is so also explain why status hierarchies distort moral judgment and corrupt moral sentiment.

Rank of course brings consequential benefits such as wealth and power, but Smith is clear that this is not what ambition most distinctively seeks, even superficially: 'It is not ease or pleasure, but always honour, of one kind or another, though frequently an honour very ill understood, that the ambitious man really pursues' (TMS I.iii.3.8, p. 65). Ambition seeks rank at least partly for its own sake and so pursues the honour respect that constitutes it. But this raises a puzzle. How could rank be seen as valuable in itself, even partly? There is no problem understanding rank's instrumental value, but how could anyone see social status as having intrinsic value? As I have been emphasizing, status or being the object of honour respect is simply a social fact with no intrinsic normative relevance. Even if an honour hierarchy involves a kind of social drama or pretence that one's *persona* or character has greater worth and occupies a normatively superior position when one has a high position in a social hierarchy, why should playing that role be *actually* desirable *intrinsically*?

Here we should note that Smith adds that the honour ambition seeks is but 'very ill understood'. What the ambitious fail to appreciate, according to Smith, is that the desire for honour is actually just an instance of the normal human desire for fellow-feeling, that is, to be in sympathy with others. It is just that the fellow-feeling the ambitious seek is not so much that of their fellow man but of those of higher rank. Actually, even this diagnosis is superficial, according to Smith. The ambitious desire the sympathy and approbation of the highly ranked not just for itself, but as evidence of their *deserving* honour and esteem, that they are *honourable*. And this mistake infects their moral judgment and 'corrupts [their] moral sentiments'. Although the highly ranked have standing to confer honour and rank, in taking their sympathy as a standard of what deserves honour and esteem, the ambitious mistake their social status for epistemic moral authority. Instead of enshrining the 'impartial spectator' as the 'man within', the ambitious regulate their judgment by that of their social superiors. Of course, this is a source of error. When it comes to morality, even a king is a usurper.

In deferring to the sympathy of the highly ranked, moreover, the ambitious abdicate their standing to make their own impartial judgments and so threaten their own self-respect. They are like the puppy that Smith describes in the *Wealth of Nations* who 'fawns upon its dam', or comparable men who 'endavou[r] by every servile and fawning attention to obtain their [betters'] good will' (Smith 1976b, WN I.ii.2, p. 26). Smith contrasts such self-abasing servility with the way individuals relate to one another when they 'truck, barter, and exchange', and, in so doing, show respect for themselves and one another (WN I.ii.1–2, pp. 25–7). In putting even their own self-judgment at the mercy of their social superiors, the ambitious relinquish their fundamental dignity to claim their own worth.

Here we see in stark terms the contrast between honour cultures and cultures of mutual accountability to which I referred at the outset. Honour cultures give the highly ranked a unique standing to determine social worth and inferiors no standing to challenge the ranking or call their betters to account. The most those below can do is to seek their betters' favour, thereby debasing themselves before them. 'By your leave.' 'As you please.' By contrast, as Smith sees it, when individuals engage in free exchange, each simultaneously expresses respect for himself and holds himself accountable to the other.

Guiding their judgment by that of their social superiors is not, however, unique to the ambitious. There is a general 'disposition of mankind, to go along with all the passions of the rich and powerful'; this, moreover, provides the psychic basis for the existence of rank and status itself (TMS I.iii.2.3, p. 52). Though status is a socially constituted non-normative fact, it nonetheless depends in Smith's view on individuals actually seeing, better *feeling*, it to have a legitimating normative dimension and not just on their pretending to do so when they play their social roles. Honour hierarchies wouldn't get the purchase they have on their participants unless they penetrated beneath social appearances to their participants' inner lives. In doing this, however, they corrupt moral sentiments and distort moral judgment.

We should examine in more detail how Smith believes these phenomena operate. The key components are the human desire for fellow-feeling, the role of sympathy in moral judgment, and a natural deference to status in which these are both implicated, but which also ultimately threatens both.

First and foremost in the depth psychology of the ambitious is the natural human desire to be recognized, even just in the minimal sense of being attended to or noticed. In a famous and moving passage about the obscurity of poverty, Smith writes:

> to feel that we are taken no notice of, necessarily damps the most agreeable hope, and disappoints the most ardent desire, of human nature. The poor man goes out and comes in unheeded, and when in the midst of a crowd is in the same obscurity as if shut up in his own hovel.
>
> (TMS I.iii.2.1, p. 51)

What the poor lack and the ambitious seek, however, is not just being noticed, but being attended to *with sympathy*. When the poor are noticed, Smith remarks, it is without 'fellow-feeling' (TMS I.iii.2.1, p. 51). This is what the ambitious are really after: 'to be observed, to be attended to, to be taken notice of with sympathy' (TMS I.iii.2.1, p. 50).

Of course, Smith means sympathy in his sense, that is, not benevolent concern but the sharing or 'fellow-feeling with any passion' upon imaginatively putting ourselves in someone's shoes, which Smith believes underwrites moral judgments of propriety (TMS I.i.1.5, p. 10). When we are 'taken notice of with sympathy' in this sense, we don't just feel connected to our fellows, we feel ourselves objects of their approval or 'approbation' (TMS I.iii.2.1, p. 50). According to Smith, it is by imaginatively placing ourselves in others' perspectives and seeing whether we can 'go along with' or share their motives, feelings, and actions that we judge these proper and approve of them.

So the ambitious are like everyone else in seeking approval. But even this is apparently just another social fact. If it is mysterious why being honoured can be intrinsically valuable, it should also be mysterious why being esteemed (or being an object of appraisal respect) can be. Smith's point, however, is that the ambitious are also like us in not just noticing *that* others esteem them, but in *accepting* others' esteem at face value and through sympathy esteeming themselves as well. When others esteem us, it is *to them* as if we are *worthy* of esteem, and so when we accept their esteem through sympathy, it is to us also as if we are indeed thus worthy.

In this way, Smith follows Aristotle's claim in the *Nicomachean Ethics* that what those seeking honour really want is to be assured of their own virtue, that they deserve honour, as is shown by the fact that they value more the honour of those whose judgment they trust (I.5). Smith often argues that people desire praise-worthiness no less than praise, in fact, like Aristotle, that the desire for praise often derives from the desire for praise-worthiness (see esp. TMS III.2.1–2, p. 114).

But if what the ambitious seek is to be worthy of respect and esteem, why then do they seek status and rank? Smith is the first to insist on a distinction between being honoured and being honourable. So why does he think that the desire to be warrantedly respected leads to the desire for rank? The explanation is to be found in Smith's view that human sympathy functions to create admiration and almost 'worship' of the 'rich and powerful'. When human beings project themselves into the shoes of the rich and famous, they frequently share the same attitudes towards themselves and their standing that the rich and famous have. Despite the 'doctrine of reason and philosophy' that 'kings are the servants of the people', this is not, Smith says, the 'doctrine of Nature'. Human sympathy works to create a natural esteem and respect for status and rank. And because this is so, occupying positions of status can provide the ambitious what they seek, a sense of not just being honoured but also of deserving their position of honour, of being honourable.

Since it works through human sympathy, the natural esteem for rank and status tends to corrupt moral judgment. Smithian judgments of propriety are appropriately regulated by the standard of the 'impartial spectator'. To judge the propriety of any act or motive is not to judge that one would in fact share the agent's intention or motive were one to project as oneself into her circumstances. It is to judge that one would share the act or motive were one to project *impartially*, that is, as *anyone*, into the agent's circumstances.[7] However, the natural esteem for those of higher rank leads us to substitute their attitudes for those of an 'impartial spectator'.

Thus even if the ambitious are able to distinguish in principle between what is honoured in fact and what is genuinely honourable, the widespread human 'disposition to go along with all the passions of the rich and powerful' upon which the 'distinction of ranks' is itself 'founded', makes it all too easy for them to suppose that what they themselves sympathize with and so approve, they do so impartially – that is, that, in practice anyway, being honoured and being honourable come to much the same thing.

Rank, insult and retaliation

Smith's ambivalence about honour shows itself also in what he says about *defending* status and rank. On the one hand, Smith maintains that indifference towards insults is the vice of mean-spiritedness and that magnanimity or a 'regard to maintain our own rank' should 'characterize our whole stile and deportment' (TMS I.ii.3.8, p. 38). On the other, Smith holds that since it is difficult for human beings to sympathize with retaliatory impulses, when we resent injuries, we should do so more from a sense 'that mankind expect and require it of us' than from resentment itself (TMS I.ii.3.8, p. 38). Still, Smith is in no doubt that defending rank is both virtuous and necessary, and that the failure to do so is a vice:

> The man, however, who, in matters of consequence, tamely suffers other people, who are entitled to no such superiority, to rise above him or get before him, is justly condemned as mean-spirited. ... Such weakness,

however, is commonly followed by much regret and repentance; and ... frequently gives place to a most malignant envy in the end, and to a hatred of that superiority, which those who have once attained it, may often become really entitled to, by the very circumstance of having attained it. In order to live comfortably in the world, it is, upon all occasions, as necessary to defend our dignity and rank, as to defend our life or our fortune.

(TMS VI.iii.16, p. 244)

Partly, Smith's ambivalence is about the *emotion* of resentment. 'Many things', he says, 'are requisite to render [resentment's] gratification completely agreeable':

There is no passion, of which the human mind is capable, concerning whose justness we ought to be so doubtful, concerning whose indulgence we ought so carefully to consult our natural sense of propriety, or so diligently to consider what will be the sentiments of the cool and impartial spectator.

(TMS I.ii.3.8, p. 38)

Nevertheless, Smith also praises resentment as 'the safeguard of justice and the security of innocence' (TMS II.ii.1, 4, p. 79). Indeed, since Smith *defines* justice in terms of proper resentment, he is committed to thinking that there would be no such thing as justice without warranted resentment.[8] A 'violation of justice' he says, is simply whatever is 'the proper object of resentment' (TMS II.ii.1.5, p. 79).

When Smith expresses concerns about resentment, he seems to identify it with a desire for retaliation. But there are other places where he appears to have something different in mind, namely, a response that expresses equal respect and mutual accountability. The difference is between a reaction, retaliation or revenge, that seeks to return contemptuous insult for contemptuous insult, and a form of resentment that seeks not to demean or degrade its object, but simply to give an aggressor a sense of one's own dignity and respectfully to demand respect of it. Whereas retaliation attempts to lower its object's status and thereby raise its own through a form of honour contempt that aspires to elicit others' honour respect, what we might call 'second-personal resentment' functions, as Smith sometimes discusses it, within a framework of mutual accountability, demanding respect from but also expressing respect for its object.

In this section, however, I wish first to focus on retaliatory defence, that is, on the response to dishonouring insult within a framework of honour respect and contempt and so ranks and statuses. When one person insults another and shows him contempt, the latter's status or honour is thereby challenged. But insults do not simply challenge status epistemically; their point is not to question the *proposition* that someone has a certain standing. Rather they attempt directly to bring lower standing about, to *dishonour*. They attempt to 'take' the insulted person 'down a peg'. In this way, honour cultures are like hierarchies of power. Just as the failure to resist domination amounts to submission, so also do unchallenged dishonourings stand. Other things being equal, the insulted person who simply takes it is thereby dishonoured and acquires lower status.

So far, this is just a point about how honour cultures function as a matter of social fact. I have been arguing in addition, however, that honour respect and contempt construct a kind of social drama or fiction and that within the fictional world of the characters whose roles actual individuals occupy there will be normative facts that correspond to these social facts, for example, that someone who suffers contempt is contemptible, that he is genuinely of lower worth and so worthy of contempt.

And we can say more. Just as honour cultures could not have the hold on participants they do if everything stayed at the level of public pretence in respect of the honourable character of those of higher rank who are honoured in fact, so also is it with those who are made objects of contempt. As those of high status are likely to feel proud, so also are the low likely to feel *contemptible*, that is, to feel shame: as if they were warranted objects of contempt and disdain. And just as, in Smithian fashion, sympathy for the high leads us to share in their self-admiration, so also are we likely to share their contempt for the low, as are the latter likely to feel the contempt of the highly ranked for them by sympathy, and to feel shame or contemptible themselves. And no more so, perhaps, than when someone of rank issues a lowering insult: 'A person becomes contemptible who tamely sits still, and submits to insults, without attempting either to repel or to revenge them. We ... call his behaviour mean-spiritedness ...' (TMS I.ii.3.3, pp. 34–5). Thus Smith the moral philosopher, no less than Smith the society member, has little sympathy for those who will not defend their rank. But though he thinks a rank-defending response of some kind is called for, Smith is also clear that it should be regulated by propriety:

> How many things are requisite to render the gratification of resentment completely agreeable, and to make the spectator thoroughly sympathize with our revenge? The provocation must first of all be such that we should become contemptible, and be exposed to perpetual insults, if we did not, in some measure, resent it. Smaller offences are always better neglected; nor is there any thing more despicable than that froward and captious humour which takes fire upon every slight occasion of quarrel. We should resent more from a sense of the propriety of resentment, from a sense that mankind expect and require it of us, than because we feel in ourselves the furies of that disagreeable passion. There is no passion, of which the human mind is capable, concerning whose justness we ought to be so doubtful, concerning whose indulgence we ought so carefully to consult our natural sense of propriety, or so

diligently to consider what will be the sentiments of the cool and impartial spectator.

(TMS I.ii.3.8, p. 38)

So difficult is it to go along with excessive resentment, Smith thinks, that even observing third parties are apt to feel imposed upon, to the point indeed of feeling insulted themselves:

> The expression of anger towards any body present, if it exceeds a bare intimation that we are sensible of his ill usage, is regarded not only as an insult to that particular person, but as a rudeness to the whole company. Respect for them ought to have restrained us from giving way to so boisterous and offensive an emotion.
>
> (TMS I.ii.3.4, p. 35)

Putting these remarks together, we can conclude that though we should not let insults and other forms of contempt pass without some form of self-defence, we should nonetheless be careful to regulate our resentment by what an impartial observer can sympathize with and take care that any expression of our resentment involve 'proper regards' for uninvolved bystanders and 'even for the person who has offended us' (TMS I.ii.3.8, p. 38).

Resentment, revenge and accountability

In this penultimate section, I want to consider a Smithian ambivalence about what the emotion of resentment actually is and what it seeks. As I see it, Smith conflates two somewhat different psychic states. One is essentially retaliatory along the lines we have just been discussing.[9] The other, what we might call second-personal resentment, seeks not to get back, but to hold its object answerable within a framework of mutual respect and accountability. We can already see movement in the latter direction in Smith's remark that we should only resent injuries in ways that show 'proper regards even for the person who has offended us'. First, however, let us consider some remarks about resentment and revenge that take Smith's thought in a very different direction.

Although Smith says that 'resentment seems to have been given us by nature for defence, and for defence only' (TMS II.ii.1.4, p. 79), he clearly thinks this includes 'retaliation' and 'vengeance' as resentment's 'natural consequence' (TMS II.i.5.6, p. 76). We 'are rejoiced to see' a victim of an attack 'attack his adversary in his turn', and are happy not just to assist in his defence but also in his gaining 'vengeance', albeit 'within a certain degree' (TMS II.i.2.5, pp.70–1). In a particularly striking passage about sympathy for a murder victim, Smith writes:

> We feel that resentment which we imagine he ought to feel ... if in his cold and lifeless body there remained any consciousness of what passes

upon earth. His blood, we think, calls aloud for vengeance. The very ashes of the dead seem to be disturbed at the thought that his injuries are to pass unrevenged.

(TMS II.i.2.5, p. 71)

'Nature', Smith adds, 'antecedent to all reflection upon the utility of punishment, has in this manner stamped upon the human heart, in the strongest and most indelible characters, an immediate and instinctive approbation of the sacred and necessary law of retaliation' (TMS II.i.2.5, p. 71).

Consider now how Smith believes 'the sacred and necessary law of retaliation' (TMS II.i.2.5, p. 71), operates from the perspective of the perpetrator. Retaliation makes him 'feel himself that evil which he has done to another' (TMS II.ii.1.10, p. 82). 'And since', Smith continues, 'no regard to the sufferings of his brethren is capable of restraining him, he ought be over-awed by the fear of his own' (TMS II.ii.1.10, p. 82). Like the ancient Furies, the human desire for retaliation and vengeance ultimately turns evil back on itself and 'the insolence of … injustice is broken and humbled by the terror of … approaching punishment' (TMS II.ii.3.7, p. 88). The way retaliation 'humbles the arrogance of [the victimizer's] self-love' is by humiliating it (TMS II.ii.2.1, p. 83).[10] Retaliation forces a submission in which it is the victimizer rather than the victim who ends up dishonoured.[11]

As Mill would point out a century later, however, 'the natural feeling of retaliation or vengeance, … in itself, has nothing moral in it' (*Utilitarianism*, V.§22). And even if we feel that a victim is warranted in retaliating, that feeling seems impotent to produce by sympathy anything like contrition or guilt in the victimizer. But Smith is clear that part of the function of resentment is to make the victimizer feel something of this sort:

> As the greater and more irreparable the evil that is done, the resentment of the sufferer runs naturally the higher; so does likewise the sympathetic indignation of the spectator, as well as the sense of guilt in the agent.
>
> (TMS II.ii.2.2, pp. 83–4)

There is nothing, however, in the thought that another person is justified in responding to one's action in kind that can ground the thought that one should feel guilty for having treated him or her unjustly. The fact that one 'has it coming' *from that person* cannot warrant the thought that one should *hold oneself* responsible, as one does in feeling guilt.

(Second-personal) Respect, dignity and mutual accountability

This brings us, in this final section, to a rather different psychic state that Smith sometimes uses 'resentment' to refer to, namely, a Strawsonian 'reactive attitude' of the sort that, according to Strawson, holds its object responsible in a way that simultaneously expresses respect for him. Resentment of this sort is implicitly second personal in a way I have discussed in Darwall (2006). It respectfully calls for respect. It demands respect but simultaneously expresses it, since it presupposes that both parties share a common basic dignity or authority to make demands of each other and so are accountable to one another.

That Smith is committed to thinking that resentment (in one guise, at least) differs from the desire to retaliate, avenge, or get back (even justifiably) simply follows from the connection to guilt noted in the passage just quoted, for the reason we mentioned. What guilt and resentment of the requisite kind must share is the sense that the victimizer violated a legitimate demand that, though it emanates from the victim's point of view, does not come simply from there but as well from a perspective that victim and victimizer share as mutually accountable beings. This is what I call 'Pufendorf's Point' in Darwall (2006). A victim can intelligibly hold a victimizer responsible in resenting her treatment of him in this sense only if he sees her as capable of holding herself responsible, for example, by feeling guilt. He must think that she can see not only why some kind of resistance, retaliation or complaint would be warranted from his point of view, but that she is also capable of accepting *blame*, that is, an expectation or implicit demand issued from a standpoint that victimizer and victim share as mutually accountable beings. In other words, the victimizer must be supposed capable of accepting that she is *to blame*, which she does by blaming herself (and so making a demand of herself) in feeling guilt.

We have seen the strictures that Smith places on resenting others' bad treatment that move his thought in this direction. Any expression of anger that 'exceeds a bare intimation of ... ill usage' will offend impartial observers and 'insult' the victimizer herself (TMS I.ii.3.4, p. 35). Proper resenting of injury must be 'full of all proper regards, even for the person who has offended us' (TMS I.ii.3.8, p. 38). Moreover, there is a striking passage in which Smith explicitly says that what resentment itself aims at is to communicate vividly to the victimizer that she has violated the victim's dignity:

> The object ... which resentment is chiefly intent upon, is not so much to make our enemy feel pain in his turn, as to make him ... repent of [his] conduct, and to make him sensible, that the person whom he injured did not deserve to be treated in that manner.
>
> (TMS II.iii.1.5, pp. 95–6)

Smith then continues in a vein that strongly suggests that he is supposing that the victim's dignity is a common human one, one that victim and victimizer share:

> What chiefly enrages us against the man who injures or insults us, is the little account he seems to make of us, the unreasonable preference which he gives to himself above us, and that absurd self-love, by which he seems

to imagine, that other people may be sacrificed at any time, to his conveniency or his humour.

(TMS II.iii.1.5, p. 96)

What is particularly striking in this last remark is that it is, as it were, 'no
respecter of persons' in the sense we noted at the outset. It presupposes that
human beings share a basic common standing or authority to demand that
others not 'sacrifice' them to their convenience regardless of their rank or
social status. Each of us, Smith says, is 'but one of the multitude in no respect
better than any other in it' (TMS II.ii.2.1, p. 83).

But if such a common basic standing exists, then the victimizer will of
course share it. It will be the standing we presuppose when, as Smith says, we
'reason and dispute' with people 'upon ordinary occasions' (TMS I.iii.2.3,
p. 53). It follows that in holding the victimizer accountable one must simultaneously be prepared to hold oneself accountable to her as well. And if that
is true, then one is subject to a shared legitimate demand to hold her
answerable in a way that is 'full of proper regards, even' for her.

In the first edition of *The Theory of Moral Sentiments* makes this implicit
assumption explicit:

> A moral being is an accountable being. An accountable being, as the
> word expresses, is a being that must give an account of its actions to some
> other ... But tho' [man] is principally accountable to God, he must
> necessarily conceive himself as accountable to his fellow creatures, before
> he can form any idea of the Deity, or of the rules by which that Divine
> Being will judge of his conduct.
>
> (TMS: 111)

Smith dropped this language in later editions, but regardless of any reason he
might have had to do so owing to seeming irreligion, there is no reason
whatsoever to think that he changed his mind about the mutual accountability of all persons.

All in all, therefore, it seems that Smith had reasons for genuine ambivalence about honour. Whatever its real attractions for people still in its grip
in the middle of the eighteenth century, a culture of honour is deeply at
odds with the doctrine of equal human dignity. To be a 'respecter of persons'
in the traditional sense of honouring distinctions of status and rank is
decidedly not to respect persons in the sense that Smith would help to
bequeath to the tradition of liberal moral and political thought that would
follow him.

Notes

1 So both are forms of 'recognition respect' and so different from the kind of esteem
I call 'appraisal respect' in Darwall (1977).

2 Anderson (2008) and LaVaque-Manty (2006) discuss Kant's complex attitude towards honour. Anderson argues that Kant holds that respect for the moral law and the dignity of persons is actually a development, and not simply repudiation, of an ethic of honour.

3 Not just persons, but also norms, authorities, principles, and even, in an extended sense, an opponent's left hook can be objects of recognition respect.

4 Thus, as I am using terms, status is to be distinguished from authority. The latter differs from the former in two ways: (a) it is inherently normative, and (b) it is conceptually related to answerability.

5 I am indebted here to discussion with Patrick Frierson.

6 See Smith's use of 'honours' in TMS I.iii.2.7, p. 57; II.ii.2.1, p. 83; II.iii.3.3, p. 106; III.5.8, p. 166; III.5.9, p. 167; VII.ii.1.16, p. 272.

7 I discuss this further in Darwall (2004).

8 On this point, see Darwall (2004).

9 Cf. Mill in *Utilitarianism*: 'the sentiment of justice appears to me to be, the animal desire to repel or retaliate a hurt or damage to oneself, or to those with whom one sympathizes, widened so as to include all persons, by the human capacity of enlarged sympathy, and the human conception of intelligent self-interest. From the latter elements, the feeling derives its morality; from the former, its peculiar impressiveness, and energy of self-assertion' (V.§23).

10 Cf. Kant on respect for the dignity of persons 'strik[ing] down self-conceit [*arrogantia*]' (1996: 199).

11 Cf. Hampton and Murphy on punishment: 'The lord must be humbled to show that he isn't the lord of the victim' (1988: 125). Perhaps needless to say, I take the conception of punishment as an exercise of mutual accountability, which is sketched in the final section, to be a significant improvement.

Bibliography

Anderson, E. (2008) 'Emotions in Kant's later moral philosophy: honour and the phenomenology of moral value', in M. Betzler (ed.), *Kant's Virtue Ethics*, New York and Berlin: de Gruyter.

Darwall, S. (1977) 'Two kinds of respect', *Ethics*, 88: 36–49.

—— (2004) 'Equal dignity in Adam Smith', *The Adam Smith Review* 1: 129–34, V. Brown (ed.), London and New York: Routledge.

—— (2006) *The Second-Person Standpoint: Morality, Respect, and Accountability*, Cambridge, MA: Harvard University Press.

—— (2008) 'Two kinds of recognition respect for persons', (trans. into Italian as 'Due tipi di rispetto come riconoscimento per le persone'), in *Eguale Rispetto*, I. Carter (ed.), Milan: Mondadori.

—— (2009) 'Authority and second-personal reasons for acting', in D. Sobel and S. Wall (eds), *Reasons for Action*, Cambridge: Cambridge University Press, pp. 134–54.

Fleischacker, S. (2005) *A Short History of Distributive Justice*, Cambridge, MA: Harvard University Press.

Griswold, C.L. (1999) *Adam Smith and the Virtues of Enlightenment*, New York: Cambridge University Press.

Hampton, J. and Murphy, J.G. (1988) *Forgiveness and Mercy*, Cambridge: Cambridge University Press.

Kant, I. (1996) *Critique of Practical Reason*, in M.J. Gregor and A. Wood (eds), *Practical Philosophy*, Cambridge: Cambridge University Press.

LaVaque-Manty, M. (2006) 'Dueling for equality: masculine honour and the modern politics of dignity', *Political Theory*, 34: 715–40.

Montesquieu, Charles du Secondat, Baron de (1989) *The Spirit of the Laws*, A.M. Cohler, B.C. Miller and H.M. Stone (trans), Cambridge: Cambridge University Press.

Rawls, J. (1980) 'Kantian constructivism in moral theory', *Journal of Philosophy*, 77: 515–72.

Rothschild, E. (2002) *Economic Sentiments: Adam Smith, Condorcet, and the Enlightenment*, Cambridge, MA: Harvard University Press.

Smith, A. (1976a) *The Theory of Moral Sentiments*, D.D. Raphael and A.L. Macfie (eds) Oxford: Clarendon Press; Liberty Press imprint, 1982.

—— (1976b) *An Inquiry into the Nature and Causes of the Wealth of Nations*, R.H. Campbell and A.S. Skinner (eds), Oxford: Clarendon Press.

Sentiments and spectators

Adam Smith's theory of moral judgment

Geoffrey Sayre-McCord

Introduction

Often, those who know something of Adam Smith are tempted by the follow-ing three claims: first, that in the *Wealth of Nations* Adam Smith argues that in a well structured market economy the private pursuit of interest works – as if guided by an invisible hand – to promote the public interest. Second, that in *The Theory of Moral Sentiments* (1976) Smith introduces the notion of an Impartial Spectator and appeals to the reactions of such a spectator as setting the standard for our moral judgments. And, third, the Impartial Spectator, properly understood, sets a standard that endorses actions and institutions in proportion as they contribute to the public good or overall happiness.[1]

In obvious and satisfying ways, these three claims fit together well, attri-buting to Smith a systematic, coherent, and many think independently attractive, theory. Most notably, the three claims work to make clear how an appeal to the invisible hand would count, for Smith, as a specifically moral vindication of a (properly structured) market economy. In any case, I think it is fair to say that many have thought that Smith embraced some version of utilitarianism and that he saw the principle of utility as vindicated by his account of moral judgment and as vindicating a market economy.[2]

Strikingly, however, when one turns to the *Theory of Moral Sentiments*, the Impartial Spectator that emerges neither endorses, nor approves in a pattern that conforms to, the principle of utility. In fact, Smith goes out of his way to reject the idea that utility either explains or sets the standard for our moral judgments. To complicate matters, Smith's Impartial Spectator suffers a number of 'irregularities of sentiment' – irregularities the impact of which Smith then defends by appeal to their utility. These irregularities play an important role in explaining why the Impartial Spectator neither endorses, nor approves in conformity with, the principle of utility. At the same time, though, the irregularities seem to undermine the Impartial Spectator's quali-fications as a standard for our moral judgments, while Smith's defence of them apparently presupposes utility as the fundamental standard of morality.

These complications, in particular, are my concern in this essay. Specifically, I argue that Smith has a sophisticated account of moral judgment that allows

The Philosophy of Adam Smith, The Adam Smith Review, 5: 124–144 © 2010 The International Adam Smith Society, ISSN 1743–5285, ISBN 978-0-415-56256-0.

him (1) to embrace the Impartial Spectator, irregularities and all, as setting the standard for our moral judgments, (2) to then appeal to utility in defending that standard as the correct one, and yet (3) to reject utility as a fundamental standard of morality.

As a first step, let me offer a very brief summary of the view Smith defends in *The Theory of Moral Sentiments*.[3]

Smith's theory in brief

Smith sets out to explain the principles humans actually, as a matter of fact, use in making moral judgments. This is, he insists, a matter of fact, not of right. He is not concerned to identify, he says, how it would be good for us to judge if we were not so 'weak and imperfect' as we are, but were instead, say, gods. Nor does he mean to recommend a new standard for us. He is concerned, rather, to identify – and explain the emergence of – the standard we actually use (TMS II.i.5.10 note, p. 77).

Of course the standard in question is a standard we use in judging how things – people, actions, institutions – *should* be, not how they happen to be. So part of Smith's burden is to articulate a standard that we can recognize as being for judgments of that distinctive kind. As a result, Smith needs to make sense of the difference between our thinking something happens to be a certain way and our thinking that it ought to be that way (or different). We'll come back to this point, but it is worth noting here that one of the worries about the Impartial Spectator being less than ideal is that in falling short of the ideal the Impartial Spectator may seem unqualified to set a standard for judging how things ought to be.

In *The Theory of Moral Sentiments* Smith starts where he thinks we all start: evaluating other people. Early on, he thinks, we find ourselves approving or disapproving of what others do and why they do it. In judging others, he thinks, we focus in particular on why they are doing what they do – on the 'sentiment or affection of the heart from which any action proceeds'. And, he argues, we look at the sentiment or affection in the light of two distinct considerations – its 'relation to the cause that excites it, or the motive which gives occasion to it' and its 'relation to the end which it proposes, or the effect which it tends to produce' (TMS II.i.3.5, p. 18).

Judgments that focus on the first relation, in effect on the circumstances of the agent and, thus, on the grounds she might have for performing the actions in question, are what Smith calls judgments of 'propriety' (and 'impropriety'). Those that focus on the second relation, in effect on what the (intended) outcome of the action is, or would be, are what Smith calls judgments of 'merit' (and 'demerit'). As Smith puts it:

> The sentiment or affection of the heart from which any action proceeds, and upon which its whole virtue or vice must ultimately depend, may be considered under two different aspects, or in two different relations;

first, in relation to the cause which excites it, or the motive which gives occasion to it; and secondly, in relation to the end which it proposes, or the effect which it tends to produce.

In the suitableness or unsuitableness, in the proportion or disproportion which the affection seems to bear to the cause or object which excites it, consists the propriety or impropriety, the decency or ungracefulness of the consequent action.

In the beneficial or hurtful nature of the effects which the affection aims at, or tends to produce, consists the merit or demerit of the action, the qualities by which it is entitled to reward, or is deserving of punishment.

(TMS I.i.3.5–7, p. 18)

While the terms Smith uses to describe the judgments may seem a little stilted to our ears, the judgments he has in mind are, I think, familiar and, indeed, ubiquitous. For instance, in thinking someone's action proper, in Smith's sense, we are thinking that her reactions, and consequent actions, are (as we might put it) appropriate and called for, in the circumstances. And in thinking someone's action as having merit, in Smith's sense, we are thinking that what she did was (as we might put it) praiseworthy, in the circumstances.

On Smith's account, we judge the *propriety* of someone's reaction to her situation by, in effect, putting ourselves in her place and seeing whether we would respond as she does. If we would, then (on noticing this) we approve of her reaction and take it to be proper; if we wouldn't, then (on noticing this) we disapprove of her reaction and think of it as, in some respect, improper. Smith distinguishes here cases in which doing what is appropriate or called for is neither difficult nor unusual, from cases in which it is difficult or unusual or both, arguing that this difference shows up, within our judgments of propriety, in the distinctions we draw between what is not, and what is, admirable. Often, he notes, doing what is proper is no special accomplishment.

On Smith's account, we judge the *merit* of someone's reaction to her situation by, in effect, putting ourselves in the place of those who are, or would be, affected by her action and seeing whether we feel either gratitude or resentment towards her in their place. If we feel gratitude, then (on noticing this) we approve of their being grateful and see the action that prompts our gratitude as being worthy of praise and reward. If, alternatively, we feel resentment, then (on noticing this) we approve of their being resentful and see the action that prompts our resentment as being worthy of blame and punishment.[4]

When it comes to judgments of merit, Smith emphasizes that our approval of either gratitude or resentment depends in large part on whether we see as proper the original action that might prompt either gratitude or resentment. So, for instance, he argues that we will not approve of the resentment of one man against another, merely because this other has been the cause of his misfortune, unless he has been the cause of it from motives which we cannot enter into. Before we can adopt the resentment of the sufferer, we must disapprove of the motives of the agent, and feel that our heart renounces all sympathy with the affections which influenced his conduct. If there appears to have been no impropriety in these, how fatal soever the tendency of the action which proceeds from them to those against whom it is directed, it does not seem to deserve any punishment, or to be the proper object of any resentment.

(TMS II.i.4.3, pp. 73–4)

Similarly, he argues that our judgments of gratitude are sensitive to what we think of the original action towards which someone might feel gratitude. He maintains that we are able fully to approve of the gratitude, and thus able to see the action as meritorious, only if we think the action was itself proper.[5]

Underwriting Smith's account of when and why we approve of various sentiments and actions are (1) our capacity for sympathy – our feeling certain ways as a result of imagining ourselves in other people's situation[6] – and (2) our capacity for approbation (and disapprobation) – our approving on noticing that our reactions coincide (and disapproving on noticing that they do not) of the people in question.[7] For our vicarious reactions to coincide with someone else's is for us to sympathize with them. And noticing this sympathy, Smith argues, gives rise to approval of what we sympathize with (while noticing a failure of sympathy gives rise to disapproval).

In the course of articulating this account of approval, and its dependence on our capacity for, and discoveries of, sympathy, Smith emphasizes the ways in which our judgments of other people's beliefs are paralleled by our judgments of their sentiments. He maintains that our approval of what others think or feel, of their beliefs as well as their sentiments, rests on whether we share those beliefs and sentiments:

To approve of another man's opinions is to adopt those opinions, and to adopt them is to approve of them. If the same arguments which convince you convince me likewise, I necessarily approve of your conviction; and if they do not, I necessarily disapprove of it; neither can I possibly conceive that I should do the one without the others. To approve or disapprove, therefore, of the opinions of others is acknowledged, by every body, to mean no more than to observe their agreement or disagreement with our own. But it is equally the case with regard to our approbation or disapprobation of the sentiments or passions of others.

(TMS I.i.3.2, p. 17)[8]

There are, not surprisingly, all sorts of nice complexities here, when it comes to distinguishing between thinking someone's beliefs are true or her sentiments fitting and thinking that they are understandable or even justified under the (perhaps misleading) circumstances in which they are held or felt. Thus we might recognize that we would share someone's belief, if we were in her situation, without thinking her belief is true, and we might similarly recognize that we would have the very same sentiments, if we were in her situation, without thinking her sentiments are actually fitting.

Yet Smith's view, importantly, is not that approval reflects what one believes one would think or feel were one in another person's situation. Rather, on his account, approval reflects the thoughts and feelings one actually has, having put oneself, in imagination, in her place. This restricts which beliefs might be endorsed by us as true to those we actually end up sharing and similarly restricts the feelings we approve of to those we actually end up sharing. As a result, to think of someone's belief or feeling that it is understandable – perhaps exactly the belief or feeling one would actually have, without fault, were one in her position – is compatible with thinking the belief false and the feeling improper, since it is compatible with not actually believing or feeling that way, having put oneself, in imagination, in her place.

Needless to say, working out this sort of view requires making good sense of how one might successfully imagine oneself in another's situation, and might as a result think or feel a certain way, without believing that were one actually in that person's situation one would think or feel that way. Smith speaks to this a bit, discussing the ways in which we might imagine ourselves in the situation of someone who is dead and vicariously feel sadness or resentment, even as we recognize fully that a cadaver feels nothing. For example, if we consider the case of someone who has been killed in a fight

> ... we put ourselves in his situation, as we enter, as it were, into his body, and in our imaginations, in some measure, animate anew the deformed and mangled carcass of the slain, when we bring home in this manner his case to our own bosoms, we feel upon this, as upon many other occasions, an emotion which the person principally concerned is incapable of feeling, and which yet we feel by an illusive sympathy with him. The sympathetic tears which we shed for that immense and irretrievable loss, which in our fancy he appears to have sustained, seem to be but a small part of the duty which we owe him. The injury which he has suffered demands, we think, a principal part of our attention. We feel that resentment which we imagine he ought to feel, and which he would feel, if in his cold and lifeless body there remained any consciousness of what passes upon earth.
>
> (TMS II.i.2.5, p. 71)

How this all works is nicely puzzling, and what counts as having successfully put oneself in another's place, in imagination, needs to be worked out. But the phenomena Smith is relying on here look familiar and the basic outlines of his explanation of when and why we might approve of what others think and feel is at least on to something.

Approving vs. seeing as approvable

As Smith recognizes, our natural disposition to approve and disapprove of others is quickly turned on ourselves, as we come to recognize that others are regarding what we do sometimes with approval and sometime not. Smith argues that we naturally hope to secure the approval of others in a way that gives rise to a problem. For we learn that, no matter what we do, not everyone will always actually approve, and even in cases where people do approve, it is not always (we know) for how we have actually responded to our circumstances in feeling or action.

This problem forces us to figure out whose approvals to try to secure and, in the process, generates for us a distinction between doing what will, as a matter of fact, garner approval, and doing what is approv*able* (that is, approval-worthy). As Smith notes, man

> ... naturally dreads, not only to be hated, but to be hateful; or to be that thing which is the natural and proper object of hatred. He desires, not only praise, but praise-worthiness; or to be that thing which, though it should be praised by nobody, is, however, the natural and proper object of praise. He dreads, not only blame, but blame-worthiness; or to be that thing which, though it should be blamed by nobody, is, however, the natural and proper object of blame.
>
> (TMS III.2.1, pp. 113–14)

On Smith's view, our need to distinguish among those whose approval we might seek, and the attendant distinction between what is merely approved and what is approvable, go hand in hand with privileging the approval of certain actual or imaginable people in preference to others.

In particular, Smith maintains, we rule out the reactions of those who misunderstand either our circumstances or our reactions to those circumstances (as we take them to be),[9] and we rule out too those who have a personal stake in what is happening that would influence their reactions.[10] That is, we restrict our concern for the approval of others, at least to the extent that we are interested in whether we have acted with propriety and merit, to the reactions of one who is appropriately informed and impartial.[11] The Impartial Spectator thus comes on the scene, constituting our conscience and setting a standard for what is worthy of approval.

At the same time, and crucially, we acquire the resources to review our own pattern of approvals, directed at others, asking of them whether they are of what is, in fact, approvable. Our reliance on what we happen to approve of, in judging of others, is thus augmented in ways that allow us to evaluate the standards we actually rely on asking both whether they pick out what is in fact approvable and whether they themselves are approvable.[12]

We thus begin to be able to ask not simply whether we do approve of some sentiment or action, but whether that sentiment or action is, in fact, approvable.

Now, and not really earlier, Smith has on hand not simply an account of what we might approve of, an account grounded in the discovery of a sympathy with the feelings of others, but an account of our thinking of others, and of ourselves, as not merely approved but as approvable.

How ideal is the Impartial Spectator?

It is worth noting that, at this point, the distinction between approving of some sentiment or action, and thinking it approvable, is a matter of thinking it would secure the approval of an Impartial Spectator. And it is worth noting too, that at this point, the pressure on spectators, for them to count as setting the standard for what is approvable, goes only so far as is necessary for them to have an accurate understanding of the people's particular situations, sentiments and intentions, and have no personal stake in the situation.

Significantly, Smith spends no time whatsoever suggesting that Impartial Spectators have still more information – about the long-term effects of one's actions, or the alternatives available to, but not appreciated by, the agent, or about the full range of non-moral facts. Nor are Impartial Spectators characterized by Smith as being equally concerned about all who might be affected or moved to approve in proportion as people are benefited. Nor does Smith elaborate the characteristics of the Impartial Spectator in any other way that might underwrite thinking the approvals of such spectators would either support or correspond to anything like the principle of utility.

Still, in places Smith does speak of the Impartial Spectator as an 'ideal spectator' (TMS III.3.38, p. 153) and 'the ideal man within the breast' (TMS III.3.26, p. 147; III.3.28, p. 148; III.3.29, p. 148; III.4.4, p. 158) and he clearly sees the Impartial Spectator, in standing as the voice of conscience, as being free of defects that would undermine his role as setting the standard for our judgments of propriety and merit. This all might reasonably recommend thinking that a fuller specification of the Impartial Spectator – fuller than the one actually offered by Smith – would naturally extend the list of his attributes to include omniscience and an equal concern for all who might be affected. The result would be a standard for our judgments of propriety and merit that would make them, properly understood, answerable to the expected or actual effects, on everyone, of the sentiments, actions and reactions in question.

Yet Smith explicitly rejects such a standard, arguing specifically that our judgments of propriety and merit are both focused much more narrowly, on the people 'principally concerned' (the agent and his or her circumstances, for questions of propriety and the intended or usually affected others, for questions of merit) always with an eye primarily looking to the circumstances that prompted the behaviour, and the impact on those who might be directly affected in ways that would prompt gratitude or resentment, and not to the general and long-term effects of the action (or reaction).

Smith does of course make important room for the relevance of particular effects. And he clearly thinks that intentionally acting to help others, depending on who one would be helping, and how, can be both proper and meritorious. So he acknowledges that the effects of people's sentiments, actions and reactions, can all matter morally.

But he thinks their moral significance is not properly seen as depending primarily – let alone exclusively – on their contribution to overall happiness or welfare.[13] In fact, he argues that our concern for overall happiness makes sense only against a background concern, on other grounds, for the happiness of particular people.[14] Moreover, he thinks that the moral importance of the happiness of particular people itself turns on consideration of how and why they might be made happy. Improper happiness and happiness that is properly resented are not, according to Smith, of moral value. At the same time, he argues that even where the value of the outcome is not in question, our actual interest is not so much in securing the outcomes (in utility, that is) but in good design. The suitability of things to certain ends recommends them to our approval, often more than what they might actually produce:

> If we examine ... why the spectator distinguishes with such admiration the condition of the rich and the great, we shall find that it is not so much upon account of the superior ease or pleasure which they are supposed to enjoy, as of the numberless artificial and elegant contrivances for promoting this ease or pleasure. He does not even imagine that they are really happier than other people: but he imagines that they possess more means of happiness. And it is the ingenious and artful adjustment of those means to the end for which they were intended, that is the principal source of his admiration.
>
> (TMS IV.1.8, p. 182)[15]

It is not simply that Smith thinks that our judgments happen to be influenced by considerations other than, and sometimes at odds with, utility. Smith's own sincere judgments run counter to what an exclusive concern for utility would countenance. This means he is committed to thinking not merely that people's judgments happen to be sensitive to things other than utility, but that their correctness turns on their being sensitive in this way – that the standard for the judgments in question is not set by someone who approves in proportion as sentiments, actions, or reactions either do or are expected to contribute to overall utility.

Irregularities of sentiment

Smith's characterization of the Impartial Spectator does go beyond crediting him with understanding the circumstances and sentiments of those principally concerned and with not having any personal stake in the situation. In particular,

Smith notes that our sympathetic responses are consistently more moderate than the feelings had by those in the situations we are (merely) imagining ourselves in, with the result that the feelings spectators (impartial or not) sympathize with, and so approve of, are regularly milder than those people tend to experience directly (TMS I.i.4.7, pp. 21–2). The upshot is that morality recommends and approves self-control and moderation. Specifically, morality valorizes limitations on the expression of grief at the loss of a loved one, calmness in the face of danger, as well as restraint when in the grip of love and controlled enthusiasm in the face of good fortune.[16]

Moreover, Smith identifies a number of 'irregularities of sentiment' that shape an Impartial Spectator's approvals no less than anyone else's, all of which then have an impact on what counts as proper or meritorious. Thus, for instance, Smith notes that precisely because sympathy relies on the imagination, we end up being better able to sympathize with passions 'which take their origin from the imagination' than with pleasures and pains of the body. The former are simply more accessible to the imagination, and so to sympathy.[17]

Along the same lines, he maintains that 'It is because mankind are disposed to sympathize more entirely with our joy than with our sorrow, that we make parade of our riches, and conceal our poverty' (TMS I.iii.2.1, p. 50).

Similarly, Smith maintains, our judgments of both propriety and merit are heavily influenced by fortune, with our approvals being sensitive not merely to how people reacted to their circumstances in feeling and action, but to what the effects of their reactions turned out to be, even where they had no control over those effects. We are more grateful, Smith notes, to those who have actually helped us, than to those who have tried just as hard, but not succeeded. And we blame, and punish more severely, those who have actually committed murder than those who have attempted and failed. These are not merely differences in how *we* happen to react. They are differences reflected as well in the responses of Impartial Spectators, and they then make a difference to what counts as meritorious or not.[18]

In the same spirit, Smith goes on to note the extent to which the workings of sympathy make spectators, impartial and otherwise, subject to the influence of fashion, custom and rank, all in ways that shape dramatically what secures approval.

Smith's attitude towards these influences is complex. On the one hand, he is manifestly unwilling to countenance everything that is a matter of good fortune, is fashionable, or customary, or done by those in power. In each case, he mentions examples that would, he maintains, properly secure the disapproval of an Impartial Spectator. On the other hand, Smith just as clearly thinks that differences in fortune, fashion, custom and rank do make a difference to what is proper or meritorious, and do so in a way that is reflected in, and vindicated by, the reactions of an Impartial Spectator.

So when, why, and to what degree should we see imaginative accessibility, fortune, fashion, custom and rank, as having an impact on an appropriately specified Impartial Spectator? The answer to this question will, of course, make a substantive difference to the standard the Impartial Spectator then sets. Yet Smith's answer is less than clear, to say the least.

Explaining vs. justifying our judgments

One natural thought is that Smith neither has, nor owes, an answer. After all, one might argue, Smith's aim is simply to describe our moral judgments, not justify them. As long as he is right that, as a matter of fact, our judgments of propriety and merit are influenced in the ways he describes, which seems plausible enough, he will have accomplished his goal. Going beyond that to argue that the standard we rely on in making our judgments is the right one may seem to be no part of his project.

But this is too quick. Consider the parallel project of explaining our judgments of size and shape, which Smith sees as analogous.[19] No doubt a catalogue of the various things (light, perspective, attention) that might influence such judgments would be important. Equally important, however, would be an account of what the difference is between thinking, say, that something is circular and thinking that it is square. Having some account of that difference is crucial and is accomplished by articulating the standard in the light of which some things count as circular and others as square. Only against this background will we be in a position to explain people's judgments that things are circular. Of course, providing such an account does not involve justifying particular judgments of shape, nor does it require justifying thinking in terms of shape at all. Explaining what it is to make a shape judgment (the judgment, for instance, that something is circular) is not the same as justifying such judgments. Nonetheless, the explanation will barely be started unless it has on hand a standard of shape to rely on in sorting the judgments as being of one shape rather than another (or none at all).

Similarly, any attempt to explain our judgments that things are appropriate or inappropriate, right or wrong, praiseworthy or blameworthy, has to provide an account of what the differences are among these various thoughts and what distinguishes them from thoughts of other kinds. Discovering what might influence such judgments plays out against an at least implicit understanding of what one is doing in thinking (mistakenly or not) that something is appropriate, or right, or praiseworthy. Of course, again, providing such an account does not involve justifying particular moral judgments, nor does it require justifying thinking in moral terms at all. Explaining what it is to make a moral judgment is not the same as justifying such judgments. Nonetheless, the explanation will barely be started unless it has on hand a moral standard to rely on in sorting the judgments as being of one moral sort rather than another (or none at all).[20]

So, even giving due attention to the difference between explaining moral judgments and justifying them, Smith's project calls for some account of the standard(s) in the light of which things count as proper or meritorious.

Smith's official answer, of course, seems to appeal directly to the Impartial Spectator. But his perceptive description of the irregularities of the sympathetic responses of even Impartial Spectators (influenced as they are by imaginative accessibility, fortune, fashion, rank, and so on) threatens to discredit the view. It is worth noting why. The problem is that the various irregularities all look as if they constitute *defects* that disqualify those who suffer them as setting a standard for our moral judgments.

One might, at this point, think that Smith's apparent comfort with allowing the influences he describes is due to his failure to keep a clear eye on the difference between explaining our making the judgments we do (accurate and inaccurate alike) and identifying the standard in the light of which accurate judgments are to be distinguished from inaccurate ones. We may well be influenced, in the ways Smith catalogues, by failures of imagination, by fortune, fashion, custom and rank. The same is probably true of the real spectators we might actually turn to in checking our reactions against those of others. Yet granting that is compatible with holding that all the resulting judgments are distorted and that the standard for our judgments is set by someone not subject to such influences.

A defective standard?

If the irregularities do render defective a putative standard for our moral judgments, we will have reason, whatever Smith thinks, for holding that he has got the standard for our moral judgments wrong. This thought recommends a familiar proposal. Wouldn't an improved version of Smith's theory, one that retains his appeal to a suitably described spectator as setting the standard of moral judgment, be one that idealizes away these defects, and any others, so as to have a defect-free standard? Isn't the right standard constituted by an appropriately characterized Ideal Observer?

One suggestion might be that the right standard is set by a spectator (1) who knows not merely the circumstances of, and effects on, those principally involved, but all the facts as they relate to all who might be affected, (2) who is not merely impartial in Smith's sense, but who is equally concerned for the welfare of all who might be affected, and (3) who is not subject to the irregular influences Smith catalogues but instead consistently responds proportionately to the actual feelings of the people involved. But other suggestions of course will be in the offing, depending on which characteristics one regards as defects and on what one might think would eliminate or correct for them.[21]

Smith, though, seems not to think of the Impartial Spectator, as he describes him, as suffering defects at all, despite the irregularities of sentiment Smith highlights. It is true that Smith does, in one place, refer to the influence of fortune as a reflection of 'a great disorder in our sentiments'; but he immediately comments, in the same sentence, that it is by 'no means, however, without its utility; and we may on this, as well as on many other occasions, admire the wisdom of God even in the weakness and folly of man' (TMS VI. iii.30, p. 253). And Smith does begin his discussion of the influence of fortune with a principled argument for thinking that fortune is irrelevant to virtue. Yet, without criticizing the argument, he goes on directly not merely to argue that fortune does have an influence but to defend that influence. In the course of doing so, he appears to attribute the argument's apparent force to our considering things only in abstract and general terms without regard to particular cases.[22]

In fact, Smith consistently follows up his discussion of the ways in which fortune, fashion, custom and rank, influence sympathy, with arguments meant to show that the influences are salutary and so should be welcomed, not rejected.

Rather than lamenting the influence of fortune, for instance, Smith argues that our disposition to judge people by the effects of their actions, and not merely by their intentions, both introduces a welcome incentive that would otherwise be lacking and removes what would otherwise be a strong temptation to probe invasively into people's intentions. And he defends our liability to the influence of fashion, custom and rank as all being crucial to establishing social order and rending political authority stable. In short, he defends the irregularities of sentiment on the grounds that their influence is useful.

Of course, one might think that Smith is simply defending the utility of making false judgments or of being subject to the illusions caused by the various irregularities he recognizes. If so, then the defence would be compatible with seeing the irregularities as defects of the Impartial Spectator, considered as a standard for our judgments, even if not as defects in our making judgments that meet the defective standard. Smith himself, however, seems to think the judgments, while surprising until one moves to particular cases, are neither false nor illusions. The standard he articulates is one he embraces.

Alternatively, one might see Smith's defence of the Impartial Spectator, sentimental irregularities and all, on the model of his 'invisible hand' defence of a market economy.[23] In the case of the market, Smith emphasizes that people perfectly properly pursue their private interest, without regard to public welfare or the happiness of mankind, even though it is the resulting contribution to welfare and happiness that justifies the workings of the market. Analogously, one might suggest, Smith may be supposing that people perfectly properly regulate their moral judgments by appeal to the standard set by the Impartial Spectator, having no further end in view, even though it is the resulting contribution to public welfare and the happiness of mankind that justifies our judging in this way.

Just as our political economy is vindicated by its contribution to overall happiness, one might argue, so too is our moral economy vindicated by its similar contribution. While this view does not have Smith embracing an Impartial Spectator who, in turn, endorses utility as the standard of judgment, it has the virtue of stressing an appealing structural parallel within Smith's views, and makes sense of Smith's explicit appeals to utility in defending both markets and the Impartial Spectator.

Nonetheless, the proposal quickly runs into problems if we take seriously Smith's criticisms of utility as an over-arching or fundamental principle of morality. Most significantly, Smith rejects the idea that happiness, no matter whose, no matter how secured, is valuable. That someone might take pleasure in some activity is no defence of the activity, if the pleasure is improper, nor does the fact that some action might promote happiness work to justify the action, if the happiness depended on doing something wrong. On Smith's view, happiness is not unconditionally valuable. Its value depends on it meeting, or at least not running contrary to, another standard.[24] This means that any appeal to a system's contribution to happiness or public welfare will itself presuppose some independent standard, an independent standard which it was manifestly Smith's hope to identify.

Smith has no problem with such appeals to happiness or public welfare, of course. Still, on his view, they play out *within* a context set by some other standard which cannot itself initially and primarily be justified by its contribution to happiness or to the public welfare.

Standards for standards: a puzzle

Smith's aim, recall, is to account for the nature of moral judgment, and doing this involves successfully identifying the standard for such judgments. So Smith cannot appeal to an independent and prior standard – especially one that his standard rejects (when in the unqualified form it would be, were it fundamental) – in defending the Impartial Spectator as being defect-free. But that leaves us with a puzzle.

How is Smith thinking of the standard he has identified such that it makes sense to defend it, as he does, against worries that it is defective, without presupposing (for its defence) some other standard?

The place to look for an answer is Smith's discussion of Hutcheson's moral sense theory. As Smith highlights, Hutcheson, in pressing the analogy between the moral sense (as he conceived of it) and our other senses, notes that the qualities 'which belong to the objects of any sense, cannot, without the greatest absurdity, be ascribed to the sense itself. Who ever thought of calling the sense of seeing black or white, the sense of hearing loud or low, or the sense of tasting sweet or bitter?' Similarly, Hutcheson claims, 'it is equally absurd to call our moral faculties virtuous or vicious, morally good or evil. These qualities belong to the objects of those faculties, not to the faculties themselves' (TMS VII.iii.3.8, p. 323).[25] On the contrary, Smith argues:

> surely if we saw any man shouting with admiration and applause at a
> barbarous and unmerited execution, which some insolent tyrant had

ordered, we should not think we were guilty of any great absurdity in denominating this behaviour vicious and morally evil in the highest degree, though it expressed nothing but depraved moral faculties, or an absurd approbation of this horrid action, as of what was noble, magnanimous, and great.

(TMS VII.iii.3.9, p. 323)

And this highlights a crucial resource unavailable to Hutcheson which is important for solving our puzzle.

As Smith points out, we can and do morally evaluate people's sense of morals, our own and others'. In doing so we are not pulling our standards out of thin air, nor are we relying on standards that have been established *ex ante* and *a priori*, independent of the standards we currently embrace. Rather, inevitably, our judgments of others, and our judgments concerning the standards we rely on in making those judgments, implicate and rely on the standards we currently have. But they also reflect the resources we have to take seriously and, potentially, respond to, worries that the standards we use are problematic.

That we rely on the standards we have in thinking about whether our standards are justified doesn't mean that the standards end up vindicated. There is a real possibility that once we uncover and examine our standards, we'll discover that, by our own lights, they don't stand up to scrutiny. In those cases, we will then have found reason to change them. Alternatively, though, we might discover that our standards, once examined and understood, actually withstand the test well and emerge as not subject, after all, to the worries we might otherwise have had. How things turn out can't be settled ahead of time, nor can they be settled for all time, given that new grounds for worry, and new discoveries about the standards themselves, might come into view. But when our standards do survive reflective scrutiny they are appropriately seen as having been shown to be, at least in the respects explored, defect free, so far as we can tell.[26]

Smith's discussion and defence of, as well as his comfort with, the irregularities of sentiment, as well as all the other features of the Impartial Spectator, should be understood against this background. Having, as he thinks, successfully articulated the standard that we do rely on in making moral judgments, Smith explores the concerns we might have about it, relying, in the process, on the only criteria we have for determining whether the concerns are well founded (those set by the Impartial Spectator). Thus, when Smith highlights the benefits of a standard that lets fortune have its effect, he is not reaching back to a different and independent standard set by the principle of utility. He is relying (if he is right) on our standard, the standard we do in fact embrace – the standard set by the Impartial Spectator – which countenances an appeal to utility, not as an unrestricted or fundamental principle, but as a consideration that, when sensitive to propriety and merit, carries real weight (with an Impartial Spectator).[27]

It is worth noting, though, that Smith's main concern, in his discussion of Hutcheson, is not to respond to the puzzle I have been pressing, though it provides the resources he needs. Smith's main concern it to take issue with Hutcheson's view that moral judgments are properly seen as strictly analogous to the other sorts of judgments we make. Smith thinks this fails to get right the distinctive nature of moral judgment and so mistakes the principle of approbation that underwrites those judgments.[28] In the process, Smith gestures towards an account of the distinctive nature of moral judgments that has a great deal of promise, I think, though Smith himself doesn't pursue the issue.

According to this account, what is distinctive about our moral judgments is that the standard(s) we rely on in making them are liable to challenge as unjustified and such challenges are, as we might put it, probative with respect to whether we have the standard(s) right. If, by our own lights, a standard we have been relying on in making our moral judgments fails to meet our standards, then we have reason to think the standard itself is wrong as a standard for what is morally proper or meritorious. 'Correct moral sentiments', Smith maintains ' … naturally appear in some degree laudable and morally good'. And this means that if we discover of some sentiments that they do not appear laudable and morally good, we have grounds for thinking they are not correct (TMS VII.iii.3.10, p. 323).

It is worth stressing that Smith is neither advancing nor presupposing a view according to which any imaginable standard of moral judgment is vindicated, if only it manages to secure its own approval. Reflexive endorsement is no evidence of truth, just a reflection of the fact that in the light of the standard one has, it measures up. We might well be in a position to think of some standard that it is defective even if, by its lights, no defect emerges.

The idea, rather, is that our standards for moral judgments are themselves liable to moral evaluation in the light of which we may find reason not merely to think that the standards are morally wrong but that, because of that, the judgments they inform are not correct. In contrast, to the extent our perceptual and other non-moral judgments might be liable to moral evaluation, the result may call into question whether we are morally justified in making the judgments, but they won't thereby show that the judgments are incorrect. (Moreover, if somehow (contra Hutcheson and seemingly Smith too) our perceptual faculties came within their own purview, the fact that our faculty of vision, say, had one or another visible quality would be irrelevant to whether the judgments to which it gives rise are correct.)

What marks moral judgments as distinctive is that in making them we are committing ourselves, at least implicitly, to thinking of the standards we are using as morally justifiable. To discover they aren't, which is what happens when we discover they don't live up to their own standards, is to discover that the standards need to be changed and that the judgments they underwrote are not correct.[29]

Conclusion

At the beginning, I sketched three claims that, taken together, characterized Smith as having a systematic view, in the light of which (1) the Impartial Spectator sets the standard of moral judgment, (2) that standard is one of utility, and (3) that explains and underwrites the moral significance of Smith's appeal to utility in defending market economies.

I have argued that, indeed, the theory that Smith develops in *The Theory of Moral Sentiments* explains and underwrites the moral significance of Smith's appeal to utility in defending market economies. But the explanation comes via appeal to an Impartial Spectator who differs significantly from any that would endorse, wholesale, anything like the principle of utility.

I have also argued that it would be a mistake to see Smith's work as playing out in a way that relies on the principle of utility as an independent standard of morality in defending a (perhaps admittedly non-utilitarian) Impartial Spectator or in defending a market economy.

Yet my main concern has not been to defend Adam Smith's non-utilitarian credentials, but to highlight a sophisticated and attractive account of moral judgment available to Smith that would fit well with his specific substantive judgments and the standards he defends. It is an account that explains the emergence of our capacity to think in moral terms, mobilizing standards that distinguish between accurate and inaccurate moral judgments. It does this without supposing that there are *a priori* or otherwise independently available principles we might use for evaluating those standards. And it makes sense of how the standards we actually use are liable to challenge or criticism even as they might, at least in principle, also be defensible.

Acknowledgements

Versions of this essay were given in Balliol College, Oxford, at a conference sponsored by the Adam Smith Society and *The Adam Smith Review*, on 7 January 2009; at the Australian National University, as the John Passmore Lecture, on 11 August 2009; and at a conference on The Human Nature Tradition in Anglo-Scottish Philosophy, in Jerusalem, sponsored by the Shalem Center, on 15 December 2009. On each occasion I received very helpful questions and comments. I am especially grateful for comments from Geoffrey Brennan and Samuel Fleischacker.

Notes

1 For just one suggestive passage concerning the approval of the Impartial Spectator, consider Smith's reflections on those who sacrifice themselves for society:

> The patriot who lays down his life for ... this society, appears to act with the most exact propriety. He appears to view himself in the light in which the impartial spectator naturally and necessarily views him, as but one of the multitude ... bound at all times to sacrifice and devote himself to the safety, to

the service, and even to the glory of the greater number. But though this sacrifice appears to be perfectly just and proper, we know how difficult it is ... and how few people are capable of making it.

(TMS VI.ii.2.2, p. 228)

Roderick Firth is largely responsible for the idea that Smith's Impartial Spectator is best viewed as, specifically, an ideal observer (Firth 1952). But John Rawls has contributed significantly to the sense that Smith's use of the Impartial Spectator was in the service of utilitarianism, even as Rawls recognized that the connection between impartial spectator theory and utilitarianism turns crucially on the supposed attributes of the impartial spectator (Rawls 1971: 184–8).

2 Needless to say, this view is far from universal. Perhaps as influential is the suggestion that Smith shouldn't be seen as holding a single systematic view at all, but as developing in intriguing ways a collection of insights into human nature and political economy that don't add up to a single coherent position, despite their evident value.

3 For an extended exploration of the Impartial Spectator in Smith's moral theory, see Raphael (2007), Campbell (1971), Broadie (2006) and Shaver (2006).

4 In the course of setting out this account, Smith offers some wonderfully subtle observations about the nature of gratitude and resentment. Among other things, he stresses the ways in which these sentiments are intimately bound up with wanting to be the agent of, and the recognized grounds for, the object of the gratitude (or resentment) enjoying some benefit (or suffering some loss).

5 Interestingly, Smith recognizes an asymmetry between gratitude and resentment, in that while our capacity to sympathize with resentment depends entirely on our not seeing the original action as proper, he seems to see that we might sympathize with gratitude for actions even when we don't see the original action as proper. Thus while he thinks we 'cannot at all sympathize' with resentment directed towards an action we deem proper, we simply can't sympathize 'thoroughly and heartily' with gratitude directed towards an action we deem improper, though it seems we might sympathize a bit (TMS II.i.4.3–4, pp. 73–4).

6 'By the imagination we place ourselves in his situation, ... we enter as it were into his body, and become in some measure the same person with him, and thence form some idea of his sensations, and even feel something which, though weaker in degree, is not altogether unlike them' (TMS I.i.1.2, p. 9).

7 Smith's account of sympathy shifted under pressure from Hume. Smith originally identified approval of some sentiment with sympathizing with it. But he agrees with Hume that approval was always pleasant while also agreeing with Hume that some sympathetic feelings were themselves unpleasant, as when, for instance, we sympathize with someone else's suffering. To reconcile these views, Smith ends up identifying approval not with the sympathetic feelings (which after all might be painful) but with recognizing the coincidence, that is, the sympathy, in feelings – which he thinks our social nature makes always pleasant. According to Smith:

> in the sentiment of approbation there are two things to be taken notice of; first, the sympathetic passion of the spectator; and, secondly, the emotion which arises from his observing the perfect coincidence between this sympathetic passion in himself, and the original passion in the person principally concerned. This last emotion, in which the sentiment of approbation properly consists, is always agreeable and delightful. The other may either be agreeable or disagreeable, according to the nature of the original passion, whose features it must always, in some measure, retain.
>
> (TMS I.iii.1.9 note, p. 46)

8 Similarly, he argues, 'To approve of the passions of another ... as suitable to their objects, is the same thing as to observe that we entirely sympathize with them; and not to approve of them as such, is the same thing as to observe that we do not entirely sympathize with them. The man who resents the injuries that have been done to me, and observes that I resent them precisely as he does, necessarily approves of my resentment. The man whose sympathy keeps time to my grief, cannot but admit the reasonableness of my sorrow' (TMS I.i.3.1, p. 16).

9 'The most sincere praise can give little pleasure when it cannot be considered as some sort of proof of praise-worthiness. It is by no means sufficient that, from ignorance or mistake, esteem and admiration should, in some way or other, be bestowed upon us. If we are conscious that we do not deserve to be so favourably thought of, that if the truth were known, we should be regarded with very different sentiments, our satisfaction is far from being complete. The man who applauds us either for actions which we did not perform, or for motives which had no sort of influence upon our conduct, applauds not us, but another person. We can derive no sort of satisfaction from his praises' (TMS III.2.5, pp. 115–16).

10 In places Smith describes the relevant sort of impartiality as a matter of the spectator being 'indifferent'. But the indifference at stake here needs to be compatible with being engaged, when imagining being in the positions of the people 'principally concerned'. Being indifferent is being unbiased, not being insensitive.

11 As Smith notes, 'The love and admiration which we naturally conceive for those whose character and conduct we approve of, necessarily dispose us to desire to become ourselves the objects of the like agreeable sentiments, and to be as amiable and as admirable as those whom we love and admire the most. Emulation, the anxious desire that we ourselves should excel, is originally founded in our admiration of the excellence of others. Neither can we be satisfied with being merely admired for what other people are admired. We must at least believe ourselves to be admirable for what they are admirable. But, in order to attain this satisfaction, we must become the impartial spectators of our own character and conduct' (TMS III.2.3, p. 114).

12 These resources, which play, I think, a crucial role in giving Smith a plausible theory of moral judgment, are regularly ignored or underplayed. I will be relying on them towards the end of the essay when I contrast Smith's account of the standard of moral judgment with the standards that might be set by Ideal Observers.

13 'The utility of those qualities, it may be thought, is what first recommends them to us; and, no doubt, the consideration of this, when we come to attend to it, gives them a new value. Originally, however, we approve of another man's judgment, not as something useful, but as right, as accurate, as agreeable to truth and reality: and it is evident we attribute those qualities to it for no other reason but because we find that it agrees with our own. Taste, in the same manner, is originally approved of, not as useful, but as just, as delicate, and as precisely suited to its object. The idea of the utility of all qualities of this kind, is plainly an after-thought, and not what first recommends them to our approbation' (TMS I.i.4.4, p. 20). Also: 'Nature, indeed, seems to have so happily adjusted our sentiments of approbation and disapprobation, to the conveniency both of the individual and of the society, that after the strictest examination it will be found, I believe, that this is universally the case. But still I affirm, that it is not the view of this utility or hurtfulness which is either the first or principal source of our approbation and disapprobation. These sentiments are no doubt enhanced and enlivened by the perception of the beauty or deformity which results from this utility or hurtfulness. But still, I say, they are originally and essentially different from this perception' (TMS IV.2.3, p. 188).

14 'The concern which we take in the fortune and happiness of individuals does not, in common cases, arise from that which we take in the fortune and happiness of

society. We are no more concerned for the destruction or loss of a single man, because this man is a member or part of society, and because we should be concerned for the destruction of society, than we are concerned for the loss of a single guinea, because this guinea is a part of a thousand guineas, and because we should be concerned for the loss of the whole sum. In neither case does our regard for the individuals arise from our regard for the multitude: but in both cases our regard for the multitude is compounded and made up of the particular regards which we feel for the different individuals of which it is composed' (TMS II.ii.3.10, pp. 89–90).

15 What causes admiration, he notes, 'is not so much the utility, as the aptness ... to promote it' (TMS IV.1.6, p. 180).

16 In general, Smith's focus is on the expression of sentiments, rather than the sentiments themselves, with the sympathetic responses of the Impartial Spectator setting a standard not so much for how one is to feel as for how one should express the feelings one has. In some places, in fact, Smith's account of what counts as a virtue plays out taking for granted a certain feeling, of grief, or fear, or hunger, as given and focusing simply on the manner and degree such feelings might properly be expressed. See Shaver (2006) for a very nice description of the ways in which Smith's theory regularly focuses more on the expression of passions than on the passions themselves.

17 'The loss of a leg may generally be regarded as a more real calamity than the loss of a mistress. It would be a ridiculous tragedy, however, of which the catastrophe was to turn upon a loss of that kind. A misfortune of the other kind, how frivolous soever it may appear to be, has given occasion to many a fine one' (TMS I.ii.1.7, p. 29). And this is because we are able to engage sympathetically with the suffering felt on losing a mistress, but not with the pain felt on the loss of a limb.

18 Smith is intriguingly ambivalent about how to think of the Impartial Spectator's liability to the influence of fortune. On the one hand, at one point he argues that the Impartial Spectator's reaction, being 'just and well-founded' will also be 'a steady and permanent one, and altogether independent of ... good or bad fortune'. Yet he immediately follows that claim with the observation that, in fact, Impartial Spectators are influenced by fortune, approving 'with the most enthusiastic admiration' what he would condemn as imprudence and injustice in the absence of success (TMS VI.iii.30, p. 252). Moreover, having catalogued the various influences of fortune, he proceeds to defend the impact of fortune. Smith's ambivalence finds an echo, I think, in most people's thoughts about what has come to be called 'moral luck'. See Williams (1976) and Nagel (1976).

19 'As to the eye of the body, objects appear great or small, not so much according to their real dimensions, as according to the nearness or distance of their situation; so do they likewise to what may be called the natural eye of the mind: and we remedy the defects of both these organs pretty much in the same manner. In my present situation an immense landscape of lawns, and woods, and distant mountains, seems to do no more than cover the little window which I write by and to be out of all proportion less than the chamber in which I am sitting. I can form a just comparison between those great objects and the little objects around me, in no other way, than by transporting myself, at least in fancy, to a different station, from whence I can survey both at nearly equal distances, and thereby form some judgment of their real proportions. Habit and experience have taught me to do this so easily and so readily, that I am scarce sensible that I do it; and a man must be, in some measure, acquainted with the philosophy of vision, before he can be thoroughly convinced, how little those distant objects would appear to the eye, if the imagination, from a knowledge of their real magnitudes, did not swell and dilate them' (TMS III.3.2, pp. 134–5).

20 One could avoid this argument by embracing a version of non-cognitivism according to which (i) the 'judgments' in question are not judgments at all and

(ii) what distinguishes judgments of, for instance, merit from others has nothing to do with their content. In that case the contrast between thinking something meritorious and thinking it otherwise will not presume a standard of merit. But this is pretty clearly neither what Smith has in mind nor what he is hoping for. His project would be especially frustrated, I think, if he ended up being unable to draw the distinction between something securing approval and it meriting that approval. That distinction plays a key role in Smith's story of the nature of moral motivation and conscience. This means, I think, that the non-cognitivist alternative would stand as, at best, a fall-back interpretation if Smith turns out not to have available any plausible account of the standard for moral judgments.

21 The description I have just offered corresponds fairly closely to the one defended by Firth (1952), and would work to vindicate a version of utilitarianism. But variations on the same theme, with different substantive implications, have been offered by others. See, for instance, Brandt (1979) and M. Smith (1994).

22 Although, this discussion is intriguingly ambiguous. Smith clearly thinks that we 'seem to be persuaded of the truth of this equitable maxim [that fortune is irrelevant merit and demerit]' only if we consider things in the abstract. Attention shows that 'when we come to particular cases, the actual consequences which happen to proceed from any action, have a very great effect upon our sentiments concerning its merit or demerit', which shows that we are not really persuaded of the principle. Still, Smith remarks that 'we all acknowledge' that the principle 'ought entirely to regulate' our sentiments. Whether he is simply registering that we all find the argument for the principle, considered in the abstract, convincing, or he is holding that the particular cases are misleading, is unclear. What is clear is that he thinks allowing fortune its influence serves a purpose 'which the Author of nature seems to have intended by it' (TMS II.iii.intro.5–6, p. 93).

23 Smith in fact mentions the invisible hand explicitly in *The Theory of Moral Sentiments*, in arguing that social and economic inequalities work to 'advance the interest of the society' (IV.1.10, pp. 184–5).

24 This view of Smith's is nicely echoed by Kant, in Section I of the *Groundwork of the Metaphysics of Morals*, where he notes that 'The sight of a being who is not graced by any touch of a pure and good will but who yet enjoys an uninterrupted prosperity can never delight a rational and impartial spectator. Thus a good will seems to constitute the indispensable condition of being even worthy of happiness' (Kant 1993: [393] p. 7).

25 As Hutcheson puts it no one 'can apply *moral Attributes* to the very *Faculty* of perceiving *moral Qualities*; or call his *moral Sense morally Good* or *Evil*, any more than he calls the *Power of Tasting*, *sweet*, or *bitter*; or of *Seeing*, *strait* or *crooked*, *white* or *black*' (Hutcheson 2002, p. 149).

26 Smith's view here is reminiscent of Hume's vindication of the 'General Point of View' as a standard for moral judgment. In particular, they both recognize that the standards we do in fact embrace (whether set by the Impartial Spectator, or how things would appear from the General Point of View, or in some other way) will inevitably play a role in any attempt we make to respond to substantive worries about those very standards. See Sayre-McCord (1994).

27 This whole structure is built on the account Smith offers of how we move, first, from approving or disapproving others, through discovering that they likewise are responding to us, to distinguishing what is approved from what merits approval, to subjecting our own patterns of approval to the standard of merit, on, finally, to asking whether the standard of merit itself merits approval.

28 Smith thinks making a mistake about this principle is 'of the greatest importance in speculation', though he thinks it 'is of none in practice' (TMS VII.iii.intro.2, p. 315).

29 Smith is concerned exclusively with moral judgments and what distinguishes them from judgments that depend on ideas derived from our various senses.

However, I think he has hit upon a principled contrast that lines up almost perfectly with what has come to be thought of as the difference between normative and non-normative judgments, where the former include, in addition to moral judgments, judgments of rationality (in action and belief) and others that carry the implication that we have reason to do or feel something, on the one hand, and non-normative judgments, that have no direct implications, considered in themselves, for what there is reason to do or feel. I explore and work to defend this more general account in 'Rational agency and the nature of normative concepts' (manuscript).

Bibliography

Brandt, R. (1979) *A Theory of the Good and the Right*, Oxford: Oxford University Press.

Broadie, A. (2006) 'Sympathy and the impartial spectator', in K. Haakonssen (ed.), *The Cambridge Companion to Adam Smith*, Cambridge: Cambridge University Press, pp. 158–88.

Campbell, T.D. (1971) *Adam Smith's Science of Morals*, Lanham, MD: Rowman and Littlefield.

Firth, R. (1952) 'Ethical absolutism and the ideal observer', *Philosophy and Phenomenological Research*, 12: 317–45.

Hutcheson, F. (2002) *An Essay on the Nature and Conduct of the Passions and Affections, with Illustrations on the Moral Sense*, A. Garrett (ed.), Indianapolis, IN: Liberty Fund.

Kant, I. (1993) *Groundwork of the Metaphysics of Morals*, J. Ellington (trans.), Indianapolis, IN: Hackett.

Nagel, T. (1976) 'Moral luck', *Proceedings of the Aristotelian Society*, Supplementary Volume, 50: 137–51.

Rawls, J. (1971) *A Theory of Justice*, Cambridge, MA: Harvard University Press.

Raphael, D.D. (2007) *The Impartial Spectator*, Oxford: Oxford University Press.

Sayre-McCord, G. (1994) 'On why Hume's "General Point of View" isn't ideal – and shouldn't be', *Social Philosophy & Policy*, 11: 202–28.

Shaver, R. (2006) 'Virtue, utility, and rules', in K. Haakonssen (ed.), *The Cambridge Companion to Adam Smith*, Cambridge: Cambridge University Press, pp. 189–213.

Smith, A. (1976) *The Theory of Moral Sentiments*, D.D. Raphael and A.L. Macfie (eds), Oxford: Clarendon Press; Liberty Press imprint, 1982.

Smith, M. (1994) *The Moral Problem*, Oxford: Blackwell.

Williams, B. (1976) 'Moral luck', *Proceedings of the Aristotelian Society*, Supplementary Volume, 50: 115–35.

Smith's anti-cosmopolitanism

Fonna Forman-Barzilai

> Cosmopolitanism is the shedding of all that makes one most human, most oneself.
>
> (Berlin 2000: 255)

Smith's idea of 'sympathy' in *The Theory of Moral Sentiments* [1759] is often invoked in literatures seeking to assert humanitarian duties towards distant strangers, and is often mis-characterized as compassion or care, rather than the 'fellow-feeling' Smith meant by it. Smith also had something to say about the scope of our beneficence – he spent an entire section of Part VI in the *Moral Sentiments* reflecting on the 'foundation of that order which nature seems to have traced out for the distribution of our good offices' – but what he does say there rubs hard against lay cosmopolitan interpretations of his thought (Smith 1976, TMS VI.ii, 218–37). On the whole, Smith's orientation to the proper scope of moral concern was remarkably narrow from a cosmopolitan perspective. Indeed, he seemed to agree with Isaiah Berlin's assertion above when he claimed that the cosmopolitan project, as it was articulated by the ancient Stoics, 'endeavours to render us altogether indifferent and unconcerned in the success or miscarriage of every thing which Nature has prescribed to us as the proper business and occupation of our lives' (TMS VII.ii.1.46, 292–93).

Smith once refers with trepidation to 'the very suspicion of a fatherless world' (TMS VI.ii.3.2, 235) but I argue here that Smith's moral universe ultimately looked like something very close to this. This may seem a provocative claim on its face, given the ubiquity of providentialism in Smith's thought, and given his emphasis on sympathy and its unifying role in human experience. Nevertheless, I argue that Smith's *Theory of Moral Sentiments* is systematically *anti-cosmopolitan* – and I piece together his view of the *world*, what we might think of as the 'international realm', as (1) deeply conflictual (without law or oversight); (2) remarkably lacking in beneficence (literally, without sympathy, in the generic sense of that term), and (3) fundamentally pluralistic morally (without a grounding in universal truths, without a *summum bonum*).[1]

The Philosophy of Adam Smith, The Adam Smith Review, 5: 145–160 © 2010 The International Adam Smith Society, ISSN 1743–5285, ISBN 978-0-415-56256-0.

Demonstrating Smith's anti-cosmopolitanism involves integrating various dimensions of his thought, scattered throughout his texts. Here I emphasize three, largely contained in *The Theory of Moral Sentiments*: his thoughts about international relations, his moral psychology, and his cultural anthropology. First, I explore Smith's 'realist' orientation to international relations. Without an effective scheme of international law, or settled authorities to enforce compliance, Smith argued that international relations in the eighteenth century were highly unstable. Further compounding the problem, Smith was keenly attuned to the social psychology of nationalism, which served to undermine loftier hopes of cultivating a genuine cosmopolitan sensibility.

Second, I develop Smith's claim, drawn from Stoic moral psychology, that human affection and beneficence tend to weaken as their object becomes further removed from the spectatorial centre. From this natural tendency, Smith concluded that both Stoic cosmopolitan apathy, and Christian aspirations to brotherly love, were out of touch with human nature, and that our duties should be limited therefore to caring for those closest to home, to what Smith referred to as the 'humbler departments'. I refer here to Smith's concentric view of our ethical duties, the narrow scope of beneficence in his thought, as his 'localism'.

I will devote the bulk of my space to the third dimension of Smith's anti-cosmopolitanism, for I believe it is the most interesting and provocative of the three for contemporary debate. I characterize Smith's moral psychology as an anthropological description of the processes through which moral communities arise and perpetuate themselves. What emerges from his description, I argue, are practices of moral judgment that are remarkably parochial and particularist in scope, and which look a lot more like Humean conventionalism than Smith himself wanted them to. Probing the old question of conventionalism in Smith's account of moral judgment is essential to understanding his ultimate relation to cosmopolitanism, for most interpreters today who draw cosmopolitan inspiration from him tend to focus on his model of the Impartial Spectator, its potential for transcending local prejudice and judging distant and unfamiliar people and practices from an impartial standpoint. My essential claim here is that the Impartial Spectator founders as a cosmopolitan device for transcending local prejudice. Understanding why will require that we differentiate two sorts of bias, and two corresponding sorts of self-distancing that are involved in making impartial judgments. The first we might call 'affective bias', which I believe Smith's moral psychology successfully confronts. Smith described a process through which we learn over time to regulate our passions and become proper members of a particular society. The second sort of bias is what we might call 'cultural bias', reflexivity about and overcoming of which is essential to any cosmopolitan project. Here, I argue that Smith's moral psychology does not get us very far. And we shall see that there is good evidence in the revisions to the *Moral Sentiments* that Smith himself recognized this. After the first edition, Smith struggled to overcome charges that his spectator theory provided no real escape from convention.[2] Many of the revisions that resulted demonstrate that Smith understood the extent that a sociological account of morality that explicitly resists theism and casuistry will have trouble transcending local bias – what Smith sometimes called 'the general contagion', or 'custom' or 'the way of the world' (TMS III.3.43, 155; V.2.3, 201). I argue that in these passages in which Smith struggled with localism and conventionalism, he richly described the cultural barriers that any cosmopolitan theory must consider.

So, three themes: first, Smith's realist view of international relations; second, his Stoic view of the concentric structure of human beneficence and duty; and finally, his description of moral culture and the resulting insularity of moral judgment. When taken together, we get a fairly robust picture of Smith's world-view, and why he believed that cosmopolitan imperatives were implausible, best suited to saints and sages and not to the ordinary people – the 'tolerably good soldiers' (TMS III.3.6, 138) – he always preferred to write about.

Considering Smith's view of the world as I present it here, one might wonder about the fate of global ethics in his thought. How did he address the problems of cross-cultural understanding, humanitarian care and international peace given the various constraints that his realist orientation to international relations, his localist moral psychology, and his particularist anthropology revealed to him? In the end, I argue that despite his anti-cosmopolitanism – or perhaps because of it – Smith is remarkably relevant to current debates in global ethics discourse. Unlike contemporary critics of the cosmopolitan agenda who too often surrender to a troubling parochialist relativism, I argue that Smith understood and struggled with the implications of his moral philosophy by attempting to locate alternative resources for a distinctively modern cosmopolitanism in the realms of commerce and jurisprudence. I will conclude the essay with a brief discussion of this.

Realism

I begin exploring Smith's anti-cosmopolitanism with his 'realist' orientation to international relations.[3] Smith was a notorious lover of harmony and equilibrium who detested war and all things that contributed to it. Anything that smacked of nationalism, or political faction or fanaticism of any kind was a poison for him (see for example TMS III.3.39–45, 154–6; VI.ii, 227–34). He never suggested that nations were continually at war with each other. But he seems fully to have embraced the Hobbesian view that conflict exists when there is 'no assurance to the contrary'. In *Leviathan* Hobbes famously wrote: 'For as the nature of Foul weather, lyeth not in a showre or two of rain, but in an intention thereto of many dayes together: So the nature of War, consisteth not in actual fighting; but in the known disposition thereto, during all the time there is no assurance to the contrary' (Hobbes 1991: 88–9). Smith agreed fully with this.

Although realists today insist on the predictability of state action under conditions of anarchy (most famously Waltz 1959) Smith emphasizes the 'uncertainty and irregularity' of international relations in the absence of a 'supreme legislative power' with the power to 'settle differences' and to enforce 'international law' (TMS III.3.42, 154–5; VI.ii.2.3–15, 228–33). As such, national self-interest guides every treaty, every project, and the norms of fair play are regularly violated. Smith's moral philosophic reflections on national self-preference are rich and largely under-explored (TMS VI.ii.2, 227–34). An excellent example of Smith's ingenuity and salience in this regard is his discussion of nationalism. He characterizes national 'prejudice' and 'partiality' as a 'noble love of country' that has become distorted and ugly through an insular process of socialization. Surely this is a form of corruption tragically familiar to us today. Citizenship galvanizes around the vilification of the outsider, generating suspicion, hatred and violence. Isolationism further intensifies the problem, according to Smith, for the insular victim of national prejudice pays little attention to what is or might be 'the sentiments which foreign nations might entertain' concerning his country's conduct (TMS III.3.42, 154). He simply continues on, self-justified, certain that his country does no wrong. For reasons confirmed every day in the morning paper, national prejudice poses serious barriers to generating a cosmopolitan sensibility.

Stoic *oikeiosis*

I turn next to Smith's localism, which finds its intellectual roots, I believe, in the ancient Stoic idea of *oikeiosis*, which I suspect Smith may have first encountered in Cicero's *De Officiis*. The influence of Stoicism on Smith's moral thought is generally well acknowledged; there has been much work done for example on the Stoic implications of Smith's providentialism and his appropriation of Stoic 'self-command'.[4] But I will focus here on Smith's engagement with the Stoic idea of *oikeiosis*, which has received comparatively less attention.[5]

Stoic *oikeiosis*, drawn from the root *oikos*, the Greek household, referred to the familiarity that develops over time among those who live in close proximity with one another – those who literally share physical space. The Stoics mapped our affections concentrically, arguing that our affections are strongest at the centre, closest and most familiar to the self, and that they weaken progressively as an object radiates further and further away.

My essential claim here is that Smith's appropriation of Stoic *oikeiosis* was partial and conflicted. On the one hand, he wholly embraced *oikeiosis* as an empirical fact, an accurate description of the concentric structure of human affection and care. Significantly, he organizes his entire discussion of beneficence in *Moral Sentiments* VI.ii in concentric terms, mirroring the Stoic argument in faithful detail. He begins in VI.ii.1 at the centre with man 'himself' and his natural beneficence towards his most intimate relations. Beneficence weakens as Smith radiates outward in VI.ii.2 to consider various 'societies' of which man is a part. In VI.ii.3 beneficence fades away altogether in the outermost reaches of human comprehension – all those 'innocent and sensible beings' that reside somewhere in 'the immensity of the universe'. Surely our 'good-will is circumscribed by no boundary', Smith asserts. 'We cannot form the idea of an innocent and sensible being, whose happiness we should not desire.' But genuine affection is something very different for Smith, and is closely related to beneficence, which is an active principle (TMS VI.ii.3.1, 235). Affection is the emotional product of 'association' and 'connexion' with others over time, which commonly evolve through our physical proximity and shared experiences with them. This is captured nicely in his claim that 'affection, is in reality nothing but habitual sympathy' (TMS VI.ii.1.7, 220). It is not an abstract entity like benevolence or compassion, which moralists traditionally attempted to teach and to shift about from object to object. For Smith, the Stoic circles were firmly grounded in human nature, solidified through experience, and therefore highly resistant to manipulation. As Jacob Viner once described the spatial arrangement of affective connection in Smith's thought:

> spatial distance operates to intensify psychological distance … the sentiments weaken progressively as one moves from one's immediate family to one's intimate friends, to one's neighbors in a small community, to fellow-citizens in a great city, to members in general of one's own country, to foreigners, to mankind taken in the large, to the inhabitants, if any, of distant planets.
>
> (Viner 1972: 80–1)

So Smith resisted the Stoic cosmopolitan imperative that rational agents cultivate 'apathy' towards the centre, collapse the circles inwards like a telescope and become 'citizens of the world' (TMS III.3.11, 140–1; VI.ii.3.3–6, 235–7). He refused to make the leap 'from primary impulse to virtue', to borrow A.A. Long's particularly apt formulation of the Stoic agenda (1986: 184–9). Smith's focus was always on the capacities of ordinary people; he didn't accept that our highest human end is a revolt against nature. Indeed, he insisted that Stoic apathy 'endeavours to render us altogether indifferent and unconcerned in the success or miscarriage of every thing which Nature has prescribed to us as the proper business and occupation of our lives' (TMS VII.ii.1.46, 292–3).

Like his friend Edmund Burke who directed us to the little platoons to which we belong, Smith directed us to the 'humbler departments', insisting that cosmopolitan apathy was too rigouristic and perfectionist, too high-minded and unrealistic, suited perhaps to saints and sages, but inconsistent with the inclinations and capacities of ordinary people who were preoccupied with and best situated to engage local, 'humbler' concerns (TMS VI.ii.3, 235–7).[6] Ought was ultimately limited for Smith by can. While he praised acts of great beneficence he doubted that most of us should aspire to live that way. While mankind would focus on the humbler departments, each tending to his own business, God (or the great *œconomy* of nature) would tend to the business of universal happiness.

One is struck sometimes by Smith's rather cool attitude towards the suffering of distant strangers. For example:

> All men, even those at the greatest distance, are no doubt entitled to our good wishes, and our good wishes we naturally give them. But if, notwithstanding, they should be unfortunate, to give ourselves any anxiety upon that account, seems to be no part of our duty.
>
> (TMS III.3.9, 140)

Even Clifford Geertz, perhaps the twentieth century's most influential proponent of localism, would have characterized Smith's position here as 'parochialism without tears' (cited in Hollinger 1993: 328). But considering Smith's orientation in context, think how vastly different his world was from our own: the slowness, the difficulty of travel and communication, the paucity of information about the condition of distant peoples, the comparative insularity of state and corporate activity, the impotence of international law, the absence of international and transnational dialogue, as well as international and non-governmental agencies that might assist distant spectators in their desire to act, and so on. Obviously we cannot know whether Smith might have paid his Oxfam dues today; but we should consider how our global condition, and its vast networks of knowing and assisting, might have changed Smith's mind about the proper scope of our duties. Surely our tiny planet is not the world described in the *Moral Sentiments*, where 'knowing' about distant suffering was unlikely or where assisting was beyond our capacity.

Anthropology of the moral life: insular moral judgment

I turn next to Smith's distinctive moral psychology and the theory of moral judgment that it produced. It is generally acknowledged that Smith developed a social theory of the self in *The Theory of Moral Sentiments*. But I would like to suggest here that the self is not the only unit of analysis in Smith's thought. Smith's moral psychology is not merely an account of how selves are socialized. It is also a highly original anthropological description of moral culture. In other words, sympathy is the process through which the self learns the tastes and values of the people with whom it lives and interacts, and becomes a member of that particular moral culture. When compounded over time, sympathetic experiences progressively constrain the agent's understanding of herself, of others, and of the world, and serve to condition the criteria that she will come to use when judging others. We might characterize this as the transmission of moral culture, passed from each generation to the next through the repetition of sympathetic contacts. In this sense Smith's 'social theory of the self' is also a cultural anthropology – thicker, more textured and psychologically complex than perhaps any other in the eighteenth century. In the

Moral Sentiments Smith described in rich detail how moral culture is shaped and sustained by its own participants, without a value-giver, without traditional forms of authority. For him, it served as proof for critics of progress and modernity that free men could avoid moral chaos and order themselves.

A key implication of my interpretation here is that the Impartial Spectator is very much a cultural artefact, and not an independent, transcendent faculty likely to generate unbiased cosmopolitan judgments.[7] Smith's description of the moral life confirms that the standards people use when they judge themselves and others tend to derive from their own social experiences and are thus largely indexed to those experiences. Recall Smith's account of the criteria we use when we judge others:

> I judge of your sight by my sight, of your ear by my ear, of your reason by my reason, of your resentment by my resentment, of your love by my love. I neither have, nor can have, any other way of judging about them.
>
> (TMS I.i.3.10, 19)

And again:

> When we judge ... of any affection ... it is scarce possible that we should make use of any other rule or canon but the correspondent affection in ourselves.
>
> (TMS I.i.3.9, 18)

On Smith's description, spectators judge from a *self-referential* standpoint, which means that we judge the actions and opinions of others 'as right, as accurate, as agreeable to truth and reality ... for no other reason but because we find that [they] agree with our own' (TMS I.i.4.4, 20). Smith couldn't be clearer about this. But the issue of where *our own* perspectives come from is not addressed overtly by Smith in this context. However, the source should be obvious to anyone familiar with his central account of the sympathy process. In a particularly well known passage Smith speculated that a person who grew up in solitude 'could no more think of his own character, of the propriety or demerit of his own sentiments and conduct, of the beauty or deformity of his own mind than of the beauty or deformity of his own face' (TMS III.1.3, 110). Along these lines, a spectator in Smith's theory comes to know who she is, what she believes, and the standards by which she will judge herself and others through a lifetime gazing into the 'mirror of society', participating repetitively in sympathetic exchanges over time with those around her. Sympathy thus is the process through which we learn and teach others what it means to be 'us'; and what emerges is a moral culture that is particular to those who participate in it. I agree with Samuel Fleischacker when he observes that Smith's 'procedure of moral judgment' makes 'the standards of one's society largely determinative of one's moral judgments'

(2005: 4; also 2004: 52–4). And because this anthropology is a universal one for Smith, a description of how all moral cultures unfold, we are left with a picture of deep moral diversity; moral cultures particular to their participants, overlapping and communicable in some ways *perhaps*, but profoundly and deeply pluralistic.

I am not arguing here that moral cultures cannot overlap and coincide with one another and therefore become in varying degrees intelligible to one another on Smith's model. But there is nothing in his anthropology to suggest that they must or will. Smith's moral psychology thickly describes how deeply entrenched our perspectives really are, how difficult it is to cultivate a critical distance from ourselves, and to approach others who are culturally remote without assimilating them to ourselves. It is for this reason, I submit, and not for his alleged cosmopolitanism, that Smith speaks most insightfully to moral and political theory today.

Most claims about the transcultural or cosmopolitan potential of Smith's moral psychology focus on the impartial spectator, for obvious reasons. Smith argued that this ideal 'third person', whom he sometimes called 'reason', 'principle', 'conscience', 'the man within' (TMS III.3.5, 137), helps us to rise above the natural consequences of having private desires and interests, of living in families and communities and thus feeling more affection and concern for some people than others. As such, the Impartial Spectator would seem to be the perfect cosmopolitan device for getting us beyond ourselves, permitting access into the worlds of others and generating an impartial perspective from which to condemn or condone their practices. So let's consider it further.

There has been much relevant debate over the years. Sheldon Wolin, T.D. Campbell, Vincent Hope, Samuel Fleischacker and many others have insisted on Smith's underlying conventionalism, which would seem to undercut its cosmopolitan potential (Wolin 1960: 343–51; Campbell 1971; Hope 1984: 157–67, and 1989: 1–11, 83–117; Fleischacker 2004, 2005). If the impartial spectator merely absorbs the norms of social propriety; if the logic of Smith's account of ordinary morality merely recapitulates and protects conventional wisdom, then Smith's idea of conscience will look far more like a Humean habit or a Freudian superego, as many have described it, than a mature, independent foundation for moral judgment (Campbell 1971: 149, 165; Raphael 1975: 97–8, 1985: 41–4, and 2007: 48–9; Fleischacker 1991: 259). Others have strongly disagreed, drawing parallels between the impartial spectator and John Rawls' device of the 'original position'. Martha Nussbaum, for example, observes that the spectator's position in Smith's theory 'is designed to model the rational moral point of view by ensuring that he will have those, and only those, thoughts, sentiments, and fantasies that are part of a rational outlook on the world' (Nussbaum 1995: 134 n. 23).[8] Similarly Luc Boltanski suggests that Smith's impartial spectator is 'aperspectival' (1999: 49). Knud Haakonssen, Charles Griswold, Emma Rothschild and most recently Jennifer Pitts find themselves somewhere mid-way – recognizing that conscience is sociologically embedded for Smith, but emphasizing its distinctive ability to mature, to 'detach' itself through reflection from social morality. Moral maturity for Smith has been described variously as 'an ongoing process of adjustment', a 'refinement', a 'continual search for equilibrium', an 'oscillation … from the world to the mind, and from the mind to the world', and so forth (Griswold 1999: 102; Haakonssen 1981: 58–9; Rothschild 2004: 154; Pitts 2005: 43; also Hope 1989: 87; Valihora 2000).

But how do spectators come to do this on Smith's account? How, within the terms of Smith's thick description of the sociological process through which spectators come to be proper members and gatekeepers of a moral culture, do they now detach themselves, become critical of and able to transcend their own histories when they imaginatively enter into the world of others with potentially very different histories? How do Smithian spectators overcome cultural bias? Jennifer Pitts and Amartya Sen have made perhaps the most progress here, by giving the process of reflective refinement a multicultural twist. In her book on empire in eighteenth- and nineteenth-century thought, *A Turn to Empire*, which includes a sensitive essay on Smith, Pitts argues that the impartial spectator can judge unfamiliar practices morally from within a particular moral context since moral judgment is a 'process by which we continually revise our opinions in response to new experiences and new opportunities for comparison with the views of others' (Pitts 2005: 45). She includes in her depiction of these 'new experiences and new opportunities' broader interaction with unfamiliar others, larger circles, less partial spectators, and concludes that Smith's theory encourages 'openness towards unfamiliar values and practices' (Pitts 2005: 45). Similarly Amartya Sen argues that the Smithian spectator refines his judgments as he comes into contact with 'broader circles', with 'people who are far as well as those who are near' and thus can generate a 'forceful scrutiny of local values', an 'adequately objective scrutiny of social conventions and parochial sentiments' (Sen 2002: 457–59).

But this sort of claim that the spectator refines his/her judgments by 'broadening' his/her 'circle of comparison' to cultural strangers strikes me as a wishful addendum to Smith's thought, resonant with contemporary multicultural theory, but really quite alien to what Smith was doing given his preoccupation with *local* order and stability, harmonizing differences among people who already tended to share much in common.[9] Moreover, I'm not convinced that mere exposure to difference – without something more – will necessarily facilitate the sort of openness Pitts and Sen describe, at least among adults. Coming upon something strange without a disposition of openness and humility, without some suspension of certitude, without a willingness to learn and to broaden oneself, may actually reinforce one's biases and smug presumptions, and stimulate a desire to mock or assimilate or transform or destroy what one encounters. Think of European encounters in the 'New World' – but this is beyond my scope here.

Ultimately I doubt that the process of reflective refinement turns Smithian spectators into cosmopolitans. In fact, I suspect that in Smithian terms, the 'progress' implied in reflective refinement and self-correction involves becoming better and better interpreters of our *own* cultural signals, becoming more disciplined, more in 'command' of ourselves, proper, sociable, polite, whatever these things might mean in our *own* particular social world. In short, we enlarge our affective scope beyond our little selves by attuning ourselves more closely to our society's particular expectations of us. Haakonssen observes that the 'process' of refining our judgments for Smith 'is a continual weeding out of behaviour which is incompatible with social life' (Haakonssen 1981: 58). This reinforces my argument that Smith was concerned primarily with social coordination. But how does this process of becoming a more mature, proper and congenial member of my society help me to know myself better, or better understand someone who has learned (through the same process as I have, for sympathy is a universal process) what it means *in her world* to be 'in command' of herself, proper, sociable, polite, and so on? In fact, it seems that as my capacity for sympathetic judgment 'progresses' and 'matures' in Smith's theory, I become *more* deeply entrenched culturally, more tractable and docile, less critical, less inclined to understand myself and others. Fleischacker put it well when he observed that Smith's 'focus is on self-correction and not on the reform of social standards of morality' (2005: 20, n. 16). Moral maturity for Smith seems to function without the reflective space which is necessary for critical self-awareness and cross-cultural judgment. Surely some might find ways beyond, but as Fleischacker notes, 'this will be fortuitous, not built into the very nature of Smith's moral method' (2005: 20, n. 15).

At various points, no doubt, Smith argued that a mature spectator will learn to distinguish what is inherently 'praise-worthy' from that which is conventionally praised. This distinction would seem to provide the spectator with some measure of critical distance from his own history, and a capacity for cultivating a more impartial, less insular view of the world. Since it is easy to see why one might wish to hang one's cosmopolitan hat on such moments in Smith's thought, let's explore this further.

Smith sought to advance on the conventionalism of Humean common sense when he proposed an impartial spectator that could improve itself by learning to distinguish praiseworthiness from mere praise (TMS III.2.7, 117; III.2.32, 130–31). From the second edition of the *Moral Sentiments* until the last, Smith ached over the problem of conventionalism. Humean efficiency was not reason enough to surrender our moral judgments to convention, to what is merely praised. What if convention happened to be corrupt? Corrupt societies might be successful in their socializing missions – deeply consensual and harmonious – but this does not entail that the judgments they cultivate are necessarily good ones. This phenomenon was not lost on Smith, who speaks at length in *Moral Sentiments* V about those 'who have had the misfortune to be brought up amidst violence, licentiousness, falsehood, and injustice'. He says they 'have been familiarized with it from their infancy, custom has rendered it habitual to them, and they are very apt to regard it as, what is called, the way of the world' (TMS V.2.2, 201). Corrupt moral cultures, like all moral cultures, function through habits, and most often carry on without reflection or analysis by participants of their assumptions, beliefs and practices. That Smith was troubled by the relativity of Hume's conventionalist approach to coordinating our sentiments seems to be a key reason why he attempted to locate a more stable foundation for moral judgment in the 'impartial spectator' and its ability to identify corruption within itself.

However, the problem with believing that Smith succeeds in achieving cultural reflexivity and unbiased cross-cultural judgments by positing an impartial spectator capable of identifying its own corruption, is that Smith asserted the distinction between praise and praise-worthiness without saying a word – not a single word – about how ordinary people within his empirical description come to know the difference, and where this new knowledge about the world might come from. Certainly he argued that the distinction exists, but it seems to be an epiphenomenal assertion, divorced from Smith's anthropological description of the process by which our standards of judgment are formed. Understanding when common sense is perverted, understanding the difference between what is praiseworthy and what is merely praised, requires a critical distance that Smith's moral psychology, on its face, fails to supply.

Smith tries to finesse the problem by crafting a deistic argument about the divinity of praiseworthiness – recall the 1790 argument that conscience is best understood as a 'demigod' residing in the breast (TMS III.2.32, 131) – but he never explains to a secular audience where this knowledge comes from. Surely some people find a way beyond, as Smith himself did with regard to British prejudices that favoured slavery and empire. The sober point is that most people simply do not. Most people conform; they capitulate to the 'way of the world' without critique or resistance. Smith confronted the problem by temporarily suspending the thick empiricism which generated his sociological account of moral life and shrouding the impartial spectator in theological garb – which may have settled the matter for some. But I believe we learn more about the depth of the problem through Smith's struggles than about resolving it through his solutions.

Conclusion

After examining Smith's worldview we seem to be left with a strikingly parochial ethics. But did Smith ultimately believe that our moral horizon fades out at the edges of familiarity? Did his *oikeiosis* remain intact 'all the way down', so to speak? Was Smith's notorious belief in a divine *œconomy* his final word about the cosmopolis – a system in which God minds the happiness of the universe, leaving each of us free to indulge ourselves, blind to the world we harm though our greed? Such assertions would make his thought seriously uninteresting, isolationist and relativist at its core, and of no help in thinking through the most salient issues today in ethical and political thought.

The interesting concern for contemporary thought is how Smith ultimately addressed larger and broader circles in light of his moral psychology.

I have argued elsewhere that unlike many localist and particularist reactions to cosmopolitan and universalist thinking today, Smith did not abandon his international political thought to anarchy nor his moral philosophy to relativism. Smith's thought resonates with dilemmas faced by those of us today who are drawn to the virtues of a global humanity and repelled by the dangers of localism, and yet who also resist the ways that universalist impulses can devalue local affiliations and identities. I believe there are at least two distinctive 'strands' of cosmopolitanism in Smith's thought, each largely independent of his moral psychology, that cogently navigate the twin dangers of realism and particularism. For closure here I'd like to signal these cosmopolitan directions.

First, there is Smith's commercial cosmopolitanism, his belief that commercial intercourse among self-interested nations can emulate beneficence on a global scale, balancing national wealth and international peace without a coercive apparatus to enforce compliance with international law. Smith conceived of a new cosmopolis that could replicate the harmony born of familiarity and habitual fellow feeling in the *oikos*, without stifling modern commercial aspirations. We might say that for Smith sympathy followed money in the society of nations; commerce produces cosmopolitan ends without cosmopolitan intentions.

Second, there are the cosmopolitan dimensions of Smith's jurisprudence. As we have seen, an implication of Smith's moral psychology and the conventionalism it produces is that people tend to employ partial, biased, criteria when judging the practices of others, which becomes problematic from a cosmopolitan perspective when judging distant, unfamiliar strangers. What I find most compelling about Smith is that he refused to surrender to relativity. The horrors around him – slavery, imperial conquest – demanded something more robust. I believe Smith speaks most perceptively to political theory and international ethics today when he seeks to navigate his way jurisprudentially out of this corner.

This jurisprudential cosmopolitan strand in Smith's thought is most clearly identified in his idea of 'negative justice'; frequently marginalized by interpreters since he said comparatively little about it, what he did say was scattered, unsystematic and incomplete, and it is overshadowed by other more prominent themes in his work. Smith notoriously left his jurisprudence unfinished, and there has been much debate on how to interpret this.[10] Nevertheless one might profitably gather Smith's reflections on the subject of justice scattered throughout the *Moral Sentiments*, the *Wealth of Nations* and *Lectures on Jurisprudence*, unfinished and aspirational though they were, and weave them together into a coherent, universalist narrative. Smith asserted that justice is a 'negative virtue', grounded not in an abstract moral good, a *summum bonum*, which is inevitably arbitrary, particular and subject to great cultural variation and contestation, but in the human aversion to cruelty, a *summum malum* which struck Smith as 'natural', 'instinctive' and thus 'universal' among people. This foreshadows Judith Shklar's late essay 'Liberalism of Fear' (Shklar 1998). Smith's idea of justice conceived 'negatively' as the prohibition against inflicting cruelty was *insulated from* and *prior to* the particularity of the moral sentiments. While Smith resisted slavery and the horrors of imperial conquest, and Shklar Nazism in every guise, they shared a basic intuition that cruelty was universally recognizable across moral cultures and provided a language for a genuinely global ethics – a natural jurisprudence, Smith called it – 'independent of all positive institution' (TMS VII.iv.37, 341–2). Shklar called this jurisprudence 'cosmopolitan' (1998: 11).

In the end, my focus on Smith's anti-cosmopolitanism should not be taken as a suggestion that cosmopolitans today cast Smith aside. What makes Smith so important an interlocutor for us is that he didn't surrender to the parochial implications of his moral psychology. He appreciated the rich local texture of human identity and affiliation – moreso, indeed, than he has been given credit for. But he also struggled with the difficulties of surmounting the barriers that localism created for broader human understanding and care. He continued to aim high, ever seeking to address larger and broader spaces *in the face* of his particularism and realism. Cosmopolitans today can learn from Smith's attempts to build commercial and jurisprudential bridges across cultural and spatial divides and to achieve international harmony without relying on moral imperatives which inevitably vary from context to context, and which tend to wither in the face of baser motives.

Acknowledgements

Sincere thanks to Sam Fleischacker and Vivienne Brown for organizing an excellent conference and a fitting tribute to Smith's *Moral Sentiments*, as well as the conference volume that now follows. For stimulating questions and good advice (which I usually took), my thanks to Sam Fleischacker, Jacob Levy, Jonathan Rick, Eric Schliesser, Tracy Strong and audiences at the 'TMS and Politics' panel at Oxford, and at the conference on 'Civil and Religious Liberty, 1640–1800' at Yale, July 2008.

Notes

1 This scheme is a refinement of several arguments in my *Adam Smith and the Circles of Sympathy: Cosmopolitanism and Moral Theory* (2010). The current essay presents a more synthetic view of Smith's *Theory of Moral Sentiments* as an 'anti-cosmopolitan' text.
2 On the circumstances surrounding Sir Gilbert Elliot's letter to Smith, see Raphael and Macfie (1976: 16–17).
3 For further discussion see Forman-Barzilai (2002, 2010).
4 The literature is rich. See notably the editors' 'Introduction' to Smith (1976); Waszek (1984); Brown (1994); Heise (1991, 1995); Griswold (1999: 217–27, 317–24); Clarke (2000); Forman-Barzilai (2002, 2010); Vivenza (2002: ch. 2 and 191–212); Montes (2004, 2008).

5 The notable exception here is Brown (1994: 95–7). See also Heise (1991, 1995) and Montes (2008).
6 'To be attached to the subdivision, to love the little platoon we belong to in society, is the first principle (the germ as it were) of public affections. It is the first link in the series by which we proceed towards a love to our country and to mankind' (Burke 1981: 97–8).
7 I am indebted here to Charles Griswold's account of Smith's 'ordinary morality' (1999) – though I am less optimistic that Smith managed to transcend ordinary morality with the device of the impartial spectator. I tend to agree here with Samuel Fleischacker who characterized Smith's description of ordinary morality as an 'anthropology' which is highly determinative of a person's moral outlook. See Fleischacker (2004: 52–4; elaborated in 2005). Thanks to Samuel Fleischacker for sharing the English version with me.
8 For an excellent recent discussion of Smith and Rawls that addresses the issue of Smith's 'contextualism' see von Villiez (2006).
9 For more on this theme, see Forman-Barzilai (2007), and more generally (2010).
10 See, for example, the debate between Charles Griswold and Ian Simpson Ross: Ross (2004, 2006) and Griswold (2006).

Bibliography

Berlin, I. (2000) 'Counter-Enlightenment', in H. Hardy, R. Hausheer and N. Annan (eds), *The Proper Study of Mankind: an Anthology of Essays*, New York: Farrar, Straus & Giroux.

Boltanski, L. (1999) *Distant Suffering: Morality, Media and Politics*, Cambridge: Cambridge University Press.

Brown, V. (1994) *Adam Smith's Discourse: Canonicity, Commerce and Conscience*, London: Routledge.

Burke, E. (1981) *Reflections on the Revolution in France*, in *The Writings and Speeches of Edmund Burke*, Oxford: Clarendon Press, vol. VIII.

Campbell, T.D. (1971) *Adam Smith's Science of Morals*, London: Allen & Unwin.

Clarke, P.H. (2000) 'Adam Smith, Stoicism and religion in the 18th century', *History of the Human Sciences*, 13: 49–72.

Fleischacker, S. (1991) 'Philosophy in moral practice: Kant and Adam Smith', *Kant-Studien*, 82: 249–69.

—— (2004) *On Adam Smith's* Wealth of Nations*: A Philosophical Companion*, Princeton, NJ: Princeton University Press.

—— (2005) 'Smith und der Kulturrelativismus', in C. Fricke and H.-P. Schütt (eds), *Adam Smith als Moralphilosoph*, Berlin: de Gruyter. Translated 'Smith and cultural relativism'.

Forman-Barzilai, F. (2002) 'Adam Smith as globalization theorist', *Critical Review*, 14: 391–419.

—— (2007) 'Book review' of J. Pitts, *A Turn to Empire: The Rise of Imperial Liberalism in Britain and France*, Princeton, NJ: Princeton University Press, 2005; in *Ethics & International Affairs*, 21: 265–67.

—— (2010) *Adam Smith and the Circles of Sympathy: Cosmopolitanism and Moral Theory*, Cambridge: Cambridge University Press.

Griswold, C.L. (1999) *Adam Smith and the Virtues of Enlightenment*, Cambridge: Cambridge University Press.

—— (2006) 'On the incompleteness of Adam Smith's system', *The Adam Smith Review*, 2: 181–6, V. Brown (ed.), London and New York: Routledge.

Haakonssen, K. (1981) *The Science of a Legislator: The Natural Jurisprudence of David Hume and Adam Smith*, Cambridge: Cambridge University Press.

Heise, P.A. (1991) 'Stoicism in Adam Smith's model of human behaviour: the philosophical foundations of self-betterment and the invisible hand', *Oekonomie und Gesellschaft: Adam Smith's Beitrag zur Gesellschaftswissenshaft*, Jarbruch 9: 64–78.

—— (1995) 'Stoicism in the *EPS*: the foundations of Adam Smith's moral philosophy', *Perspectives in the History of Economic Thought*, XI: 17–30.

Hobbes, T. (1991) *Leviathan*, ed. and introd. R. Tuck, Cambridge: Cambridge University Press.

Hollinger, D. (1993) 'How wide the circle of the "we"?', *American Historical Review*, 98: 317–37.

Hope, V. (1984) 'Smith's demigod', in V. Hope (ed.), *Philosophers of the Scottish Enlightenment*, Edinburgh: Edinburgh University Press.

—— (1989) *Virtue by Consensus: The Moral Philosophy of Hutcheson, Hume and Adam Smith*, Oxford: Clarendon Press.

Long, A.A. (1986) *Hellenistic Philosophy: Stoics, Epicureans, Sceptics*, Berkeley, CA: University of California Press.

Montes, L. (2004) *Adam Smith in Context: A Critical Reassessment of Some Central Components of His Thought*, London: Palgrave Macmillan.

—— (2008) 'Adam Smith as an *ecelctic* Stoic', *The Adam Smith Review*, 4: 30–56, V. Brown (ed.), London and New York: Routledge.

Nussbaum, M.C. (1995) *Poetic Justice: The Literary Imagination and Public Life*, Boston, MA: Beacon.

Pitts, J. (2005) *A Turn to Empire: The Rise of Imperial Liberalism in Britain and France*, Princeton, NJ: Princeton University Press.

Raphael, D.D. (1975) 'The impartial spectator', in A.S. Skinner and T. Wilson (eds), *Essays on Adam Smith*, Oxford: Clarendon Press.

—— (1985) *Adam Smith*, Oxford: Oxford University Press.

—— (2007) *The Impartial Spectator: Adam Smith's Moral Philosophy*, New York: Oxford University Press.

Raphael, D.D. and Macfie, A.L. (1976) Introduction to A. Smith, *The Theory of Moral Sentiments*, Oxford: Clarendon Press; Liberty Press Imprint, 1982.

Ross, I.S. (2004) '"Great works upon the anvil" in 1785: Adam Smith's projected corpus of philosophy', *The Adam Smith Review*, 1: 40–59, V. Brown (ed.), London and New York: Routledge.

—— (2006) 'Reply to Charles Griswold: "On the incompleteness of Adam Smith's system"', *The Adam Smith Review*, 2: 187–91, V. Brown (ed.), London and New York: Routledge.

Rothschild, E. (2004) 'Dignity or meanness', *The Adam Smith Review*, 1: 150–64, V. Brown (ed.), London and New York: Routledge.

Sen, A. (2002) 'Open and closed impartiality', *Journal of Philosophy*, 99: 445–69.

Shklar, J.N. (1998) 'Liberalism of fear', in S. Hoffman (ed.), *Political Thought and Political Thinkers*, Chicago: University of Chicago Press.

Smith, A. (1976) *The Theory of Moral Sentiments*, D.D. Raphael and A.L. Macfie (eds), vol. I of The Glasgow Edition of the Works and Correspondence of Adam Smith, Oxford: Clarendon Press; Liberty Press Imprint, 1982.

Valihora, K. (2000) 'The judgment of judgment: Adam Smith's *Theory of Moral Sentiments*', *British Journal of Aesthetics*, 41: 138–59.

Viner, J. (1972) *The Role of Providence in the Social Order: An Essay in Intellectual History*, Princeton, NJ: Princeton University Press.

Vivenza, G. (2002) *Adam Smith and the Classics: The Classical Heritage in Adam Smith's Thought*, Oxford: Oxford University Press.

von Villiez, C. (2006) 'Double standard naturally! Smith and Rawls: a comparison of methods', in L. Montes and E. Schliesser (eds), *New Voices on Adam Smith*, London and New York: Routledge.

Waltz, K. (1959) *Man, the State and War*, New York: Columbia University Press.

Waszek, N. (1984) 'Two concepts of morality: a distinction of Adam Smith's ethics and its Stoic origin', *Journal of the History of Ideas*, 45: 591–604.

Wolin, S. (1960) *Politics and Vision: Continuity and Innovation in Western Political Thought*, Boston, MA: Little, Brown and Company.

Resentment and moral judgment in Smith and Butler

Alice MacLachlan

> How many things are requisite to render the gratification of resentment completely agreeable … ?
>
> (TMS I.ii.3.8)

Introduction

Adam Smith expresses a fair amount of ambivalence towards the passion of resentment. In the opening pages of *The Theory of Moral Sentiments*, he cites it as a passion whose expression initially 'excites no sort of sympathy, but … serve[s] rather to disgust and provoke us' (Smith 1976, TMS I.i.1.6). Even more than in other cases, we must 'bring home' the particularities of the resentful person's circumstances and provocation to ourselves – and, in particular, we must figure out whether we sympathize with his antagonist's motives – before we can possibly 'enter into' his emotional state. Our sympathy with resentment is always indirect and secondary. Indeed, resentment belongs to the class of 'unsocial' passions, alongside hatred and spite: those emotions whose immediate effects are most disagreeable to the spectator (I.ii.3.5). There is thus almost no foreshadowing, in the opening pages of TMS, of the role resentment will come to play in Part II: Of Merit and Demerit. Resentment reappears there as a fully-fledged moral sentiment, whose natural attributes are such that they successfully ground our moral judgments of demerit or blame, just as our natural sentiments of gratitude ground our judgments of merit or praise. Resentment – it would appear – has become *moralized*.

This essay is a discussion of the 'moralization' of resentment. By moralization, I do not refer to the complex process by which resentment is transformed by the machinations of sympathy, but a prior change in how the 'raw material' of the emotion itself is presented. In just over fifty pages, not only Smith's attitude towards the passion of resentment, but also his very conception of the term, appears to shift dramatically. What is an unpleasant, unsocial and relatively amoral passion of anger in general metamorphoses into a morally and psychologically rich account of a cognitively sharpened,

The Philosophy of Adam Smith, The Adam Smith Review, 5: 161–177 © 2010 The International Adam Smith Society, ISSN 1743–5285, ISBN 978-0-415-56256-0.

normatively laden attitude, an attitude that contains both the judgment that the injury done to me was unjust and wrongful, and the demand that the offender acknowledge its wrongfulness.[1] Two very different readings of 'Smithian resentment' are thus available from the text. Indeed, the notion of two distinct forms of resentment – an instinctive, amoral version and a rich, rationally appraising attitude – would bring Smith into line with an earlier account of resentment, found in Bishop Joseph Butler's *Fifteen Sermons Preached at Rolls Chapel*, first published in 1726. Ultimately, I argue, the differences in their theories are to Smith's credit. It is precisely because the 'thin' or generic retaliatory passion described in Part I can be reconciled with the rich, normative attitude in Part II, that Smith is able to accomplish his meta-ethical goal of grounding moral judgments in naturally occurring emotions.

Resentment in *The Theory of Moral Sentiments* Part I

When resentment makes its first appearance in TMS, it does so as a completely disagreeable emotion, belonging to a class of 'unsocial passions' whose occurrences are unlikely to elicit sympathy from a spectator. Smith offers a couple of reasons for our lack of sympathy with resentment. In the first place, situations of resentment always present two individual interests in conflict: 'our sympathy is divided between the person who feels [it], and the person who is the object of [it]' (I.ii.3.1). As spectators, we therefore necessarily lose a little of our potential passion to an opposing sympathy, at least until we are convinced that the resentment is appropriate given its occasion (provocation) and its intensity is moderate. We can accomplish this only by attempting and failing to sympathize with the motives of the object of resentment (the original offender). Sympathy with resentment always requires some reflection. But not even justified resentment can wholly capture our sympathy; its 'immediate effects are so disagreeable, that even when [it is] most justly provoked, there is still something about [it] which disgusts us' (I.ii.3.5).

Smith concludes in Part I that even warranted, moderate resentment presents something of a challenge to our capacities for imaginative sympathy, and its naturally unsympathetic nature should give us great pause before we endorse any expression of it: 'there is no passion, of which the human mind is capable, concerning whose justness we ought to be so doubtful, concerning whose indulgence we ought so carefully to consult our natural sense of propriety, or so diligently to consult what will be the sentiments of the cool and impartial spectator'. In fact, the passion of resentment is best *simulated*: we should resent more from a 'sense of the propriety of resentment, from a sense that mankind expect and require it of us' than because we *actually experience* the emotion (I.ii.3.8). Appropriate resentment is alienated resentment; rather than a naturally occurring emotion, it is in fact the barest simulacrum of one. Only once resentment has been lowered in pitch, tested in reflection and expressed more from guarded duty than anything else, can we render it agreeable to a sympathetic spectator.

Resentment in *The Theory of Moral Sentiments* Part II

Given the vivid picture Smith paints of resentment's disagreeable and fundamentally anti-social nature in Part I, it is surprising that in Part II of TMS, resentment takes on a much more significant role in our moral psychology, and that our sympathy with resentment now becomes absolutely crucial to our ability to form judgments of moral demerit. In Part II Smith adopts a generally more balanced view of resentment, presenting it as potentially sociable in nature, and capable of appearing sympathetic to onlookers. Under the right conditions, we may 'heartily and entirely sympathize with the resentment of the sufferer' (II.i.4.4) so that our 'own animosity entirely corresponds' with her own (II.i.5.8). Smith now acknowledges that a deficiency of resentment may be censured as well as its excess: 'we sometimes complain that a particular person shows too little spirit, and has too little sense of the injuries that have been done to him; and we are as ready to despise him for the defect, as to hate him for the excess of this passion' (II.i.5.8).

Smith is not unaware of the apparent incongruence of these two pictures of resentment, or the common hesitation to grant resentment the status of a moral sentiment. He remarks:

> To ascribe in this manner our natural sense of the ill desert of human actions to a sympathy with the resentment of the sufferer, may seem, to the greater part of people, to be a degradation of that sentiment. Resentment is commonly regarded as so odious a passion, that they will be apt to think it impossible that so laudable a principle, as the sense of the ill desert of vice, should in any respect be founded upon it.
>
> (TMS II.i.5.7 note)

Wary of his audience's natural suspicion of resentment, Smith takes great care to develop his account of resentment as a moral sentiment, capable of grounding judgments of demerit, in a series of small steps, and always in parallel with claim that judgments of merit are grounded in natural feelings of gratitude, 'because gratitude ... is regarded as an amiable principle, which can take nothing from the worth of whatever is founded upon it' (II.i.5.7). He accomplishes this task in several stages.

Smith's first step is to note that demerit is the quality of *deserving* punishment. But determining that something deserves punishment is to say no more or less than that we do (or would) approve of its punishment, or rather: that it is an approved or proper object of whatever it is that motivates us to punish. At this point in the text, Smith defines punishment as a kind of 'recompense': 'to return evil for evil that has been done' (II.i.1.4). Punishment is not necessarily a moral reaction to wrongdoing (and it includes revenge), but approved or deserved punishment is. So the second step is to move from the object of deserved punishment to the object of a motive to punish which we can approve – or, drawing on the materials of Part I – with which we can sympathize.

Here Smith re-introduces resentment. Resentment, he argues, is the only passion that directly motivates us to be the instrument of another's misery (i.e. to render evil) (II.i.1.5). Hatred and dislike might lead us to *wish* misery on someone else, but unless we are exceptionally vicious, we do not also want to be the cause of that misfortune: the 'very thought of voluntarily contributing' to such misery will shock us beyond all measure. Resentment is the only passion to contain, necessarily, the desire that the object of our resentment suffer 'by our means, and upon account of that particular injury which he had done to us' (II.i.1.7). The passion of resentment is what motivates us to punish others, and so the third step of Smith's argument is to conclude that the object of deserved punishment, that is, the object of an approved motive to punish, is also the proper object and thus the appropriate target of our naturally occurring resentment. For this to carry explanatory weight, Smith must presumably draw on the picture of this naturally occurring passion already familiar to the reader from Part I. In the final step of his argument, Smith notes that the proper object of resentment is the object, or target, of proper resentment: that is, of resentment with which 'the heart of every impartial spectator sympathizes ... and every indifferent by-stander entirely enters into, and goes along with' (II.i.2.2).

Thus for Smith, our judgments of demerit are ultimately grounded in our naturally occurring sympathies with resentment: both our own and other people's. This is not a counter-intuitive account of retributive judgments, but it is perhaps a little surprising, given Smith's conclusion in TMS Part I: namely, that resentment is all but utterly unsympathetic and whatever sympathy we do achieve is an indirect consequence *of not* sympathizing.[2] In fact, he remarks, our judgments of demerit are compound sentiments, composed both of our direct *antipathy* to the motives of the perpetrator, and our resulting indirect sympathy with the resentment of the sufferer. One might think that Smith could skip over the problem of sympathizing with resentment altogether, and develop an account of demerit from the impropriety of the perpetrator's motives, deduced by our failure to sympathize with those motives, and an objective assessment of the resultant harm to the victim. Indeed, were Smith to account for judgments of demerit in the manner just sketched, he would have emerged as far more of a proto-utilitarian than he does. But Smith expressly avoids grounding our sense of demerit and injustice in general assessments of social harm or utility in II.ii.3.4–5, focusing instead on 'that consciousness of ill-desert' which 'nature has implanted in the human breast': namely, resentment (II.ii.3.4).

Smith takes resentment to be crucially important to moral judgment – and indeed, to political and legal institutions of punishment. At first, resentment's importance appears to be a matter of utility: 'the natural gratification of this passion tends, of its own accord, to produce all the political ends of punishment; the correction of the criminal, and the example to the population' (II.i.1.6), but Smith paints a much more vivid picture of the *immediate* propriety of punitive resentment, prior to any considerations of utility, when describing a murder victim:

> His blood, we think, calls aloud for vengeance. The very ashes of the dead seem to be disturbed at the thought that his injuries are to pass unrevenged. ... Nature, antecedent to all reflections upon the utility of punishment, has in this manner stamped upon the human heart, in the strongest and most indelible characters, an immediate and instinctive approbation of the sacred and necessary law of retaliation.
>
> (II.i.2.5)

In tying judgments of demerit so closely to our desire to punish, expressed by the naturally occurring passion of resentment, Smith argues that moral judgments of demerit contain a motivational element, necessarily shared by those who make the judgment. Judgments of blame have action-guiding properties, and these explain how we come to have a sense of justice, necessary for social mechanisms of retributive justice.

Furthermore, resentments of any kind, whether proper or improper, contain a desire for *accountability* and *acknowledgement* from the wrongdoer: that she be made to grieve on account of her behaviour towards me, the resenter: 'not only that he should be punished, but that he should be punished by our means, and upon account of that particular injury which he had done to us' (II.i.1.6). Sympathy with that resentment is, at the same time, approval of that demand for acknowledgement. Our judgments of demerit, as implicit gestures of such sympathy, are thus also judgments of respect towards the victim of wrongdoing, as they acknowledge her claims in ways that an alternative, utilitarian route to demerit would not.

Two Resentments in *The Theory of Moral Sentiments*?

The account of moral judgments presented in Part II of the TMS describes us as experiencing, when we resent, a normatively laden, moralized retributive emotion. Smith's description will be familiar to those acquainted with contemporary philosophical discussions of resentment, for example Peter Strawson's description of resentment as a participant reactive attitude (2003), Jeffrie Murphy (2003) and Jeffrie Murphy and Jean Hampton's (1988) defence of resentment as a virtue, and recent treatments by Charles Griswold (2007) and Thomas Brudholm (2008) among others. Not everything we ordinarily describe as resentment, for example, can meet this account: a more technical, rarefied definition is required.[3] Does Smith provide such an appropriately technical definition in his initial description of the passion? The answer is both yes and no. In fact, it's possible to read the TMS as presenting two entirely separate accounts of resentment, only one of which meets the standard demanded by contemporary philosophical treatments of resentment. This is, for example, the reading offered by Stephen Darwall.[4] On this reading, we can understand Smith to use 'resentment' loosely at first, as nothing more than a rough synonym for anger. Later in Part II, when it becomes necessary to explain how certain kinds of angry reactions are capable of grounding fully-fledged moral judgments, he focuses on a richer, more sympathetic, cognitively sharpened, attitude. The second alternative is to argue that Smith uses resentment consistently to describe a single psychological state, but that his discussion in Part II draws out aspects or implications of that state left dormant in Part I. This interpretation requires that we square the rich, normatively laden properties of what I have called Smith's moralized resentment and what Darwall calls 'second-personal resentment' with the thinner, unmoralized account of naturally occurring resentment Smith provides in Part II. While eventually I intend to defend the second alternative, and to argue that a full understanding of the moralized resentment of Part II recognizes it as the culmination of Smith's earlier, non-moral resentment and not as a separate if related psychological state, it is important to establish just how much Smith's presentation of resentment changes.

In the opening sections of the TMS, Smith uses 'resentment' interchangeably with 'anger', 'fury', 'outrage' and 'indignation' (I.i.1.7, I.i.4.6, I.i.5.4). He does not consistently reserve one term for moderate instances of the others, or those instances which an independent third party could recognize as having been justified by (appropriate to) the act that provoked them. Smith notes these are passions we share with children and with 'brutes' (I.ii.1.3), and that they are passions apt to seize hold of and distort our reason, rather than remaining sensitive to it. Sometimes, 'resentment' contains the expressed desire for revenge or retaliation (though the desired act does not appear to be a fully-fledged retributive response, as warranted punishment might be), and at other times it is little more than an instinctive angry reaction. Neither is one anger-term the genus of which others are the species. Much later in the TMS, when criticizing Hutcheson's moral system, Smith alludes in passing to 'emotions of particular *kinds*' whose general features are consistent even while subject to variation, and he mentions anger/resentment as one such generic kind (VII.iii.3.13). The term thus seems to refer to a family of retaliative states.

Clearly, Smith's description of resentment in Part II is much more elaborate. While he continues occasionally to swap the terms 'resentment', 'anger' and 'indignation' (II.ii.2.3, II.iii.1.1), resentment is now that sentiment which not only directly prompts us to punish, but also wishes evil (punishment) to the wrongdoer by our means, on account of our injury, and in such a way that he be made to suffer grief, repentance and regret for that injury (and not simply regret at having experienced the punishment). In other words, the passion of resentment now contains the wish that the perpetrator come to feel towards the original injury in just the same way that we do, that he now share our attitude. The sufficient conditions for resenting someone have risen dramatically.

We cannot make sense of this textual shift by insisting that resentment in Part II is simply what Smith intended by 'proper' resentment in Part I; what I have called 'moralized' resentment is not a moderate, appropriately occurring version of 'thin' or generic resentment. In the initial passages on resentment, Smith speaks of proper or sympathetic resentment, not as a moralized version of the general passion, containing an explicitly moral claim about wrongful injury, but rather as a verbally and behaviourally moderate instance of it. Proper resentment is fury held in check (I.ii.3.8). There is little or no allusion to the kind of desire for accountability described in Part II, where to resent someone is, at the same time, to wish to 'bring him back to a more just sense of what is due to other people, to make him sensible of what he owes us, and of the wrong he has done us' (II.iii.1.6). In Part II, the criteria for what qualifies as resentment have not only risen but have also *changed* in nature: to resent is to wish specific things regarding the wrongdoer's attitudes and not simply his (mis)fortunes. Proper resentment, in Part I, is that resentment which is justified and moderate. Resentment in Part II can be both justified and unjustified; we can be wrong about what transpired or who is responsible for our wrongdoing; we can wish a change of attitude on the wrong person, or under the wrong circumstances. Darwall's claim – that Smith appears to be discussing a new psychological state altogether – is far from implausible. Furthermore, in Part II, resentment has been recast as a sociable attitude, in at least two senses: first, we can resent sympathetically with others, or on their behalf, as well as our own. Second, in resenting, we demand something from the perpetrator – a change in her attitudes. Resentment thus represents an ongoing emotional engagement with her: again, a more sociable attitude than is presented in Part I.

Resentment in Butler's *Fifteen Sermons*

Were Smith to identify resentment as a broad emotional category, containing both moralized and non-moralized versions, he would not be the first. That is exactly the account of resentment offered in Bishop Joseph Butler's *Fifteen Sermons Preached at the Rolls Chapel* (1949 [1726]). There is not an extensive literature exploring Butler's influence on Smith's understanding of resentment, although Griswold notes that 'several of the points Smith makes about anger or resentment' including a crucial distinction between moral and non-moral resentment, are anticipated in Butler's *Sermons* (Griswold 1999: 117).[5] D.D. Raphael and A.L Macfie limit Butler's influence on Smith to the 'unconscious repetition of phrases' in their introduction to TMS (1976: 11), while a recent paper by James Harris suggests that Smith's affinity and debt to Butler has been generally under-appreciated (Harris 2008: 15).

Resentment presents a slightly different puzzle for Butler than it does for Smith. He opens his sermon on resentment by asking: 'Why had man implanted in him a principle, which appears the direct contrary to bene-volence?' (Butler 1949: 121). On the one hand, resentment can't be written off, since 'no passion God hath endued us with can be in itself evil' (122), but at the same time resentment does not appear to be good, either: its object (the misery of another person) appears directly contrary to the duty of bene-volence, and to the Christian precept 'love thine enemies'. He is even prepared to allow that resentment 'is in every instance absolutely an evil in itself, because it implies producing misery' (139). Yet, resentment is a natural passion, and 'natural' for Butler carries normative force, as it implies God-given.[6] Ultimately, Butler argues for the compatibility of moderate resentment with both benevolence and his admittedly minimalist reading of Christian forgiveness, but it remains in his text a 'painful remedy' to the fact of injury and violence, and is subject to excess and abuse.[7] We need the passion of resentment to correct for what would otherwise be motivational deficiencies: namely, our ability to punish and deter wrongdoing – but it would be better if offenders were brought to justice through the cool considerations of reason and reflection alone (131).

What, according to Butler, do we mean by resentment? According to his sermon on the topic, 'resentment' represents both a genus and a species of emotion – and again, his distinctions are complicated by the fact that he occasionally exchanges the word 'anger' for 'resentment'. He divides generic resentment (generic anger) into two kinds: (1) 'hasty and sudden' anger, also known as passion, and (2) 'settled, deliberate' resentment. Hasty anger is morally indifferent, instinctive and often irrational; Butler compares it to blinking something out of one's eye. It is experienced by infants and animals as well as adults and from this Butler concludes it cannot be the effect of reason, but is excited by 'mere sensation and feeling' (124).[8]

Butler spends a great deal more time tackling the problematic phenomenon of settled, deliberate resentment. Because even rational, reflective people can experience resentment, it must be the effect of reason, he argues, but the only way reason could raise any anger is to represent not just harm, but injustice or injury of some kind. The object of resentment is thus not suffering or harm *per se*, but moral evil (126). The very emotion of (settled, deliberate) resent-ment always contains the belief that the object of my resentment has behaved unjustly, and has caused an injury of some kind. This is evident, Butler suggests, from the considerations likely to raise or lower our resentment: whether the act was performed by design or was inadvertent, whether the offender yielded to strong temptation or acted without provocation, whether a prior friendship offers evidence of the offender's other redeeming qualities, and so on – that is, moral considerations concerning the wrongdoer's motives and her character (126). Butler concludes that settled resentment is 'plainly connected with a sense of virtue and vice, of moral good and evil' (125): that is, it is always already moralized. In fact, he uses the moralized nature of resentment as evidence against psychological egoism: 'why should men dis-pute concerning the reality of virtue, and whether it be founded in the nature of things ... when every man carries about him this passion, which affords him demonstration, that the rules of justice and equity are to be the guide of his actions?' (131).

Settled resentment is certainly not morally infallible; Butler provides a long and rather wonderful discussion of its various excesses and abuses, including malice and revenge. In fact, while raised by reason and nominally sensitive to reason's claims, resentment also has 'a certain determination and resolute bent of mind, not to be convinced or set right' (129). We should thus be wary of resentment's ability to latch on and take hold. Butler's cautions regarding resentment resonate with Smith's admonition that we resent more from a distanced sense of its propriety than because we have actually succumbed to its charms (TMS I.ii.3.8). Luckily, though, the abuses of resentment are primarily limited to our own, personal grudges: those resentments arising from injuries to ourselves, or those whom we consider as ourselves (Butler 1949: 126). Impartial resentment or indignation – in other words, a spectator's resentment – is thus an appropriate standard for measuring partial resentment: the victim ought 'to be affected towards the injurious person in the same way any good men, uninterested in the case would be, if they had the same just sense, which we supposed the injured person to have, of the fault' (Butler 1949: 143) – that is, if they are impartial and well-informed.

Smith vs. Butler on moralizing resentment

Butler outlines two distinct forms of resentment or anger: a thin, instinctive reaction to harm of any kind and a rich, moralized attitude that targets only our perceptions of injustice and injury. The latter is expressly identified as the origin of our motive to punish, and is 'plainly connected' with our 'sense of virtue and vice'. Furthermore, we evaluate the latter emotion with reference to the standard of an impartial bystander.[9] Can we make sense of the apparent inconsistency in Smithian resentment by reading Butler's two kinds of resentment into the text of TMS? If so, the discussion of resentment in Part I could be understood as a discussion of sudden, hasty anger, or, more plausibly, of anger/resentment in general, containing – for the time being – both hasty, sudden anger and settled, deliberate resentment, so that we can better understand our judgments of propriety towards *both* kinds as they naturally occur in everyday life. Part II, on the other hand, focuses on the salient kind, namely settled, deliberate resentment, because it is a discussion of moral judgments of demerit and these judgments are concerned with the proper objects of deliberate resentment: injustice and wrongful injury.

This Butlerian account is a tempting interpretation of Smith, but in the end it is not convincing; moreover, adopting it does not do Smith's moral psychology any favours. There are both textual and philosophical reasons to resist a reading that sharply separates the 'resentments' discussed in Parts I and II. First of all, Butler simply asserts what Smith attempts to demonstrate: that we can trace a path from resentment as we ordinarily experience it to our cognitively sophisticated judgments of good and evil, merit and demerit. Butler starts out by announcing, 'resentment is of two kinds' (Butler 1949: 123). In doing so, he has both differentiated and connected sudden and deliberate anger. His claim is that among our natural experiences of angry feelings, there is a particular kind that always already contains claims of *moral* wrong. In helping himself to an already moralized attitude, Butler makes the connection between natural resentment and a sense of justice far easier to prove, but perhaps less interesting to contemporary audiences unconvinced that the moral and the natural are so easily reconciled, as a result. If the goal is to demonstrate our essentially moral nature by demonstrating how moral claims are grounded in our natural emotional reactions to the world, then surely the interesting question is whether we can pick out a 'natural' (in the sense of non-moral) sub-class of angry feelings that are also easily distinguished by an overtly moral claim. Picking out just those reactions that can be developed into moral judgments, for no other reason that these are the reactions that can be developed into moral judgments, appears – at least to the observer not already convinced of the thesis – to be worryingly circular.

Furthermore, it seems fairly obvious that we experience more kinds of anger/resentment than instinctive, irrational episodes of lashing out and overtly moralized resentment; we resent individual acts of moral injury, yes, but we may also resent other threats to and burdens on our wellbeing, at least according to everyday understandings of the word. We can resent the demands of a difficult and unrewarding job or a demanding, draining relationship; we can resent feelings of disappointment or vulnerability. We may resent others for failing to live up to our expectations, or for their expectations of us. Griswold gives the example of a painful, persistent disease; over time my reaction to it might at least feel like resentment (2007: 22). Margaret Walker notes that we resent disruptions to a wide variety of social and political norms as well as the overtly moral, and our resentment is sometimes inflected with fear, envy and a variety of anxiety (2006).[10] If Butler meant his distinction to be exhaustive, his taxonomy is startlingly incomplete, and his psychology less compelling as a result. If he is singling out only those instances that are independently, recognizably moral and those that are most obviously *not* moral (an instinctive reaction to harm), then his use of resentment as a passion that comes in moral and non-moral form, as evidence of our moral nature, is suspect.

Finally, Butler leaves us with little sense of how our rational 'deliberate' resentment is related to instinctive anger. He certainly doesn't provide a genetic or developmental account of how the moralized passion emerges from the non-moral; rather, it is divinely 'implanted' in us. In contrast, one of the great strengths of TMS is how carefully the moral distinctions and categories of its subsequent parts are built using only the materials of Part I: our natural impulses and emotions, social and unsocial, and the capacity for imaginative sympathy that links us to one another. It is uncharacteristic for Smith to develop the conditions of propriety for one psychological state in Part I, then switch terms to an entirely different state – and indeed, a normatively laden one – in Part II, without explaining how these states are related, or how the emotion in Part II came to be so readily laden with appropriate normative claims.

Thus, a Butlerian account of resentment is a pitfall that Smith would do well to avoid – and indeed, one that he does avoid. The discussion of resentment in Part II is not just a story of how to derive moral judgments of demerit from a moralized version of natural resentment; it is a story of how resentment lends itself to moralization. In Part II, Section III, when Smith discusses the 'irregularity' of our resentments and our gratitude, he simultaneously takes us through the stages of resentment's shift from initial, instinctive emotional retaliation to cognitively sharpened demands for accountability. This is not only a story of propriety; it reveals how the raw emotion of resentment develops, apart from and prior to any interventions of sympathy,

First, Smith notes that all animals resent any cause of pain, whether the cause is animate or inanimate: 'we are angry, for a moment, even at the stone that hurts us. A child beats it, a dog barks at it, a choleric man is apt to curse it' (TMS II.iii.1.1). For rational creatures, a little reflection corrects this general response, at least in most cases. We realize, Smith notes, that 'before anything can be the proper object of gratitude or resentment, it must not only be the cause of pleasure or pain, it must likewise be capable of feeling them'; and his use of 'before' rather than 'in order' is absolutely crucial, here. This is not a statement about attitudinal propriety grounded in sympathy, but rather a 'precondition' of sorts. The proper objects of resentment must be capable of feeling pain, *so that our resentment can be fully satisfied*, not so others can sympathize with it. The latter is a separate, later question. And so Smith continues. Animals are better, but not perfect or 'complete' objects of resentment, as there is something missing – or wanting – in our resentment of animals: we cannot demand recognition from them; we cannot bring their attitudes to the original harm in line with our own. In other words, we can't get satisfaction. To be a truly satisfactory object of resentment, our antagonist must have caused our pain, be capable of feeling pain herself, and have caused our pain *from design*: that is, from the kinds of mental faculties required for us to *change her mind* about her actions (II.iii.1.4). Only then will we attain what is, Smith argues, the real aim of our resentment: to have the object of our resentment, the offender, experience the same painful attitude towards the injury that we currently feel – and, in so feeling, acknowledge its status as a wrongful injury. The vengeful aspect of resentment desires a particular *kind* of misery for its object: 'resentment cannot be fully gratified, unless the offender is not only made to grieve in his turn, but to grieve for that particular wrong which we have suffered from him' (II.i.1.7).[11] Smith is able to claim, in Part II, that resentment contains a demand for acknowledgement because that acknowledgement emerges as part of the retributive desire, sketched in Part I.

What strikes me in this developmental story is that Smith is concerned to identify the shift, not simply from instinctive to *proper* resentment, but also from instinctive to *satisfying* resentment. He is identifying the 'complete' or 'perfect' objects of our resentment – complete *from the standpoint of that resentment*: its internal logic, as it were. In doing so, he paints a picture of how resentment moralizes itself on its own terms – what Griswold calls its propensity to tell a justifying story about itself (2007: 30), rather than merely introducing a moralized version of a naturally amoral sentiment. This developmental story makes Smith's account psychologically more insightful than Butler's, and ultimately allows him to ground genuinely moral claims of merit and demerit into what first seemed to be a decidedly non-moral aspect of our psychologies.

Conclusions

At first glance, Smith's account of resentment in *The Theory of Moral Sentiments* seems to suffer from an unfortunate inconsistency, perhaps even an ambiguity, in the referent of the central term. He appears to conflate several emotions under a single heading, failing to appropriately distinguish them, as done in an earlier treatment of resentment by Joseph Butler. In fact, this apparent inconsistency is evidence of a much richer and more nuanced moral psychology of retributive attitudes, which pays significant and much-needed attention to the phenomenology and satisfaction of our resentments, both instinctive and 'moralized'. It is because, and not in spite of, the variation in Smith's description of resentment, that he is able to employ it as the grounding for judgments of demerit and injustice.

I have focused on a key difference in the accounts of resentment provided by Adam Smith and Joseph Butler. While it is tempting to read both philosophers as using a single term 'resentment' to describe two distinct, if related, emotional states, this temptation would be an unfortunate misrepresentation of Smith on resentment. It may appear that Smith presents two entirely different versions of resentment in Parts I and II of the TMS; in fact, the narrower, more overtly normative attitude described in Part II develops naturally out the natural reactive instinct presented in Part I, according to what I have called resentment's 'internal logic'.

There is a great deal more to be said about the affinities between Smith and Butler on resentment than is covered in this essay. Certainly, in praising Smith's developmental story of resentment at Butler's expense, I have not done justice to some of the remarkable strengths of Butler's account. These strengths include Butler's emphasis on the sociability of resentment, that is, our ability to experience vicarious resentment (indignation) on behalf of others and the moral expectations we place on offenders in resenting them. Butler also illustrates how we exercise our capacity for sympathetic, imaginative engagement with the emotional lives of others in navigating our own; we learn to curb our resentment to appropriate levels (and indeed, even to forgive) by training ourselves to 'be affected towards the injurious person in the same way any good men, uninterested in the case, would be' (Butler 1949: 143). Impartial third parties play a key role in assessing 'proper' resentment in Butler's sermons, as they do in Smith; the wide moral community is thus invoked, even in interpersonal instances of wrongdoing. In fact, Butler anticipates Smith by drawing key connections among resentment, on the one hand, and moral judgment, retributive justice and the defence of moral norms, on the other. And Butler's analysis of resentment extends beyond Smith's in his elaborate discussion of forgiveness alongside resentment. In this manner, Butler indicates how resentment plays a role, not only in retribution, but also in reconciliation.

Furthermore, it might appear that in focusing on the 'raw material' of resentment, I have missed the import of Smith's account. For Smith, the true 'moralization' of any emotion, social or unsocial, takes place through the complex psychological mechanism of sympathy. It is in sympathizing or failing to sympathize with the motives and reactions of others that we develop a sense of their propriety or impropriety. Ultimately, any experience of resentment, whether instinctive or cognitively laden, is judged appropriate or inappropriate according to whether or not an impartial and well-informed spectator would sympathize with it.

Yet Smith is not interested in resentment for matters of emotional propriety alone. In Part II, proper resentment is the natural, affective ground for our moral judgments of demerit. Resentment is one of 'the great safe-guards of the association of mankind, to protect the weak, to curb the violent and to chastise the guilty' (TMS II.ii.3.4). It also represents our 'natural sense of the propriety and fitness of punishment' (II.ii.3.7). Smith is reluctant to grant that justice is a matter of mere utility; rather, our sense of justice is *natural*, grounded in that natural sentiment which animates us to abhor 'fraud, perfidy, and injustice, and to delight to see them punished' (II.ii.3.9). It therefore matters significantly to Smith's project that the normatively laden reactive attitude capable of grounding our retributive judgments and motivations in Part II can be found among the natural passions and emotions described in Part II. The text of TMS reveals a consistent, sophisticated account of the passion of resentment.

Moreover, Smith's analysis is significant for contemporary discussions of resentment. In contemporary philosophical literature on retribution and reconciliation, resentment has come to stand as the retributive reactive attitude *par excellence*.[12] As a result, the story philosophers tell about resentment – its distinctive features, aims, rationality and gratification – will affect the conclusions we draw about which actual angry experiences to take seriously as *resentments*. Contemporary philosophers have typically argued for a narrow, technical account of resentment, in order that this moral attitude can be distinguished from the wide range of angry feelings we may experience in everyday life, few of which can be articulated as anything close to a moral demand. Resentment, they argue, is moralized anger; or just that anger which ought, at least *prima facie*, to be taken seriously.

Yet it is quite possible that limiting the scope of morally significant angers does a further injustice to those with the most reason to feel rage. As feminist scholars like Alison Jaggar have noted, under hierarchical conditions of social inequality in which dominant values will tend to service the interest of dominant groups, those most burdened by the status quo may find themselves experiencing 'outlaw emotions': emotional reactions that are dismissed by others precisely because they cannot be reconstructed as recognizable moral claims, at least according to the framework operating in a particular moral community (2008: 31). The example Jaggar offers of an outlaw emotion is resentment (in this case, resentment at 'kindnesses' which are actually subtle expressions of oppressive power-relationships). In distinguishing sharply between 'moralized' and non-moralized angers, philosophers may hamper themselves from focusing on morally significant angers – in this case, resistance to oppression – that cannot currently be articulated as moral claims.

Smith, on the other hand, is prepared not only to connect our moral judgments of injustice and wrongdoing to our natural emotional reactions of resentment, but also, to allow for the possibility that the moral attitudes grounding these judgments are not so different from many other kinds of anger we typically experience. According to the Smithian 'story' of resentment, our natural passions are subject to the influence of fortune (both individual and social) and are vulnerable to the sympathy – or lack of sympathy – we receive from others around us. These contingent features of our social context may well influence how even our best reflection is able to correct and curb our immediate and instinctive angry reactions to the world. Smith gives us more room, and more reason, to take seriously angers that contemporary philosophical accounts cannot. In refusing to distinguish absolutely between narrow, 'moralized' resentment and a wider range of our instinctive angry reactions – indeed, by illustrating how beautifully the former arises out of the distinctive aims and features of the latter – Adam Smith may well be an important ally for critical scholars wishing to broaden the range of social angers we ought to take seriously.

Acknowledgements

I am grateful to James Harris and to Eric Schliesser for their help in putting together this essay, and especially to Samuel Fleischacker and Vivienne Brown, for their insightful editorial assistance.

Notes

1 I borrow the term 'cognitively sharpened' from D'Arms and Jacobson (1993).
2 The idea that judgments of demerit (or blame) are grounded in our natural attitudes of resentment has been taken up by a number of contemporary philosophers, most notably in Peter Strawson's 'Freedom and resentment' (2003).
3 In everyday life, 'resentment' may describe many different kinds of anger or envy, and may be used interchangeably with indignation, irritation, frustration, begrudgement,

distress, contempt, hatred, malice, *schadenfreude*, vengefulness, vindication and rage, among others.

4 In Stephen Darwall's plenary session at 'The Philosophy of Adam Smith' (Darwall 2009), he describes Smith as 'conflating two psychic states': retaliatory resentment and second-personal resentment. Retaliatory resentment seeks revenge or reciprocal harm only, while second-personal resentment seeks not to get back at the offender but to hold her *answerable*, and thus contains a kind of proper regard for the person who has injured me. Retaliatory resentment is presumably described in Part I of TMS, while second-personal resentment emerges in the discussion of Part II. As I argue in this essay, I am not convinced that the 'resentments' of Parts I and II are as separable as Darwall allows, but I take his point that the focus of Part I is retaliation, while the focus of Part II is recognition, or acknowledgement (Darwall 2006: 178–80).

5 Griswold also alludes to Smith, several times, in his discussion of Butler on resentment and forgiveness (Griswold 2007: 22–8).

6 Austin Duncan-Jones refers to this normative force as Butler's theological teleology (1952: 148).

7 According to Butler, to forgive is to perceive one's wrongdoer and her actions without the distorting effects of partiality and self-love and, as a result, to experience a moderate resentment, no more than what 'any good man, uninterested in the case' would feel (143). We must forswear revenge, but not all our angry feelings, in order to forgive. Forgiveness *is* compatible with some enduring level of resentment. This definition of forgiveness is at odds with most contemporary philosophical accounts, including those who claim to take Butler as their historical inspiration (Murphy and Hampton 1988; Murphy 2003; Haber 1991; Holmgren 1993; Hieronymi 2001).

8 Griswold notes that Butler divides resentment both by duration, whether sudden or settled, and by its object, that is harm or injury (2007: 22). So, we can experience sudden anger that is instinctive and non-moral, and is occasioned by harm, but we can also experience sudden *moral* anger, that is occasioned by injury. Butler's text does suggest he thinks moral anger (or resentment) can be sudden as well as slow, or deliberate, but it appears that the crucial distinction for him is not duration, but the object and origin of anger (Butler 1949: 124). He wants to distinguish between the kind of anger that comes from instinct and is occasioned by any harm at all, from the kind of anger that comes from reason and understanding, and is occasioned by the idea of injustice or injury: 'I am speaking of the former only so far as it is to be distinguished from the latter. The only way in which our reason and understanding can raise anger is by representing to our mind injustice or injury of some kind or other' (124). Thus, I focus on the distinction that Butler himself takes to be crucial.

9 There is a certain affinity between Smith's image of a mirror, and Butler's suggestion that 'we are in such a peculiar situation, with respect to injuries done to ourselves, that we can scarce any more see them as they really are, than our eye can see itself' (Butler 1949: 144).

10 Walker gives an impressive list of resentments not provoked by personal moral injury: true, she acknowledges, we resent harms and losses, but some people also resent cheaters and free riders (even when we do not suffer as a result), those who engage in exploitation. We resent certain improprieties, as when someone gives themselves 'airs' or authority to which we don't think they are entitled (again, even if we do not suffer), and – in contrast – we resent unjustified demotions or slights to our own status. Finally, resentment is often prompted by victim-less cases of 'rule-breaking, norm-violating, or simply behavior seen as "out of bounds"': all seen as unacceptable offences (2006: 123–4). People can prickle, react or seethe with resentment when provoked by any of these. Her examples include foreign

accents, urban development and – in an amusing reference borrowed from Alan Gibbard – peculiar haircuts.

11 There is a ringing familiarity to any student of philosophy in this description of resentment, of course. It is reminiscent of Nietzsche's famous treatment of existential resentment, or *ressentiment* in Section I of *The Genealogy of Morals* (1967).

12 See, for example, Murphy and Hampton (1988), D'Arms and Jacobson (1993), Walker (2006), Griswold (2007), Brudholm (2008).

Bibliography

Brudholm, T. (2008) *Resentment's Virtue: Jean Amery and the Refusal to Forgive*, Philadelphia, PA: Temple University Press.

Butler, J. (1949 [1726]) *Fifiteen Sermons Preached at the Rolls Chapter and a Dissertation Upon the Nature of Virtue*, W.R. Matthews (ed.), London: G. Bell and Sons Ltd.

D'Arms, J. and Jacobson, D. (1993) 'The significance of recalcitrant emotion (or, anti-quasijudgmentalism)', in A. Hatzimoysis (ed.), *Philosophy and the Emotions*, Cambridge: Cambridge University Press.

Darwall, S. (2006) *The Second-Person Standpoint: Morality, Respect and Accountability*, Cambridge, MA: Harvard University Press.

—— (2009) 'Smith on honour and self-respect', plenary address to 'The Philosophy of Adam Smith', a conference to commemorate the 250th anniversary of *The Theory of Moral Sentiments*, Oxford, January 2009; reprinted in this volume as 'Smith's ambivalence about honour', pp. 106–23.

Duncan-Jones, A. (1952) *Butler's Moral Philosophy*, London: Pelican Books.

Griswold, C.L. (1999) *Adam Smith and the Virtues of Enlightenment*, Cambridge: Cambridge University Press.

—— (2007) *Forgiveness: A Philosophical Exploration*, Cambridge: Cambridge University Press.

Haber, J.G. (1991) *Forgiveness: A Philosophical Study*, Lanham, MD: Rowman and Littlefield.

Harris, J. (2008) 'Early reception of Hume's theory of justice', unpublished.

Hieronymi, P. (2001) 'Articulating an uncompromising forgiveness', *Philosophy and Phenomenological Research*, 62: 529–55.

Holmgren, M. (1993) 'Forgiveness and the intrinsic value of persons', *American Philosophical Quarterly*, 30: 341–52.

Jaggar, A. (2008) 'Love and knowledge: emotion in feminist epistemology', in A. Bailey and C. Cuomo (eds), *The Feminist Philosophy Reader*, New York: McGraw-Hill.

McCloskey, D. (2008) 'Adam Smith, the last of the former virtue ethicists', *History of Political Economy*, 40: 43–71.

Murphy, J.G. (2003) *Getting Even: Forgiveness and its Limits*, Oxford: Oxford University Press.

Murphy, J.G. and Hampton, J. (1988) *Forgiveness and Mercy*, Cambridge: Cambridge University Press.

Nietzsche, F. (1967) *The Genealogy of Morals*, trans. Walter Kaufmann, New York: Vintage Books.

Raphael, D.D. and Macfie, A.L. (1976) Introduction to Adam Smith, *The Theory of Moral Sentiments*, Oxford: Clarendon Press; Liberty Press imprint, 1982.

Smith, A. (1976) *The Theory of Moral Sentiments*, D.D. Raphael and A.L Macfie (eds), Oxford: Clarendon Press; Liberty Press imprint, 1982.

Strawson, P. (2003) 'Freedom and resentment', in G. Watson (ed.), *Free Will*, Oxford: Oxford University Press.

Walker, M.U. (2006) *Moral Repair: Reconstructing Moral Relations after Wrongdoing*, Cambridge: Cambridge University Press.

Wallace, R.J. (1994) *Responsibility and the Moral Sentiments*, Cambridge, MA: Harvard University Press.

Part III
Economics, religion, aesthetics and value theory

Adam Smith's problems

Individuality and the paradox of sympathy

Robert Urquhart

Introduction

For a quite broad consensus in contemporary Adam Smith scholarship the Adam Smith Problem is just a mistake. The *Wealth of Nations* and *The Theory of Moral Sentiments* are compatible elements of an overall system that, regrettably, Smith left unfinished at his death: but we have his word for it that the system existed as a coherent project in his own mind.[1] I am not at all sure that the Problem can be got rid of quite so easily – there is too much of a tendency to take the wish for the deed. However, I am not going to take that up here. Rather, I want to think about some oppositions and tensions within *The Theory of Moral Sentiments*, and then see how they help us understand its relation to the *Wealth of Nations*.

The great feature of these oppositions and tensions is that they are never resolved: Smith stands between them; and it is a serious question to ask whether he ever made a decisive move in one direction or the other.[2] But far from this being a weakness of Smith's thought, it is a sign of his willingness to follow what Hegel calls 'the strenuousness of the concept' (Hegel 1977: 35, translation modified), that is, to follow where the thought leads. He is thinking about the character of a society that is still in the process of formation. Smith's problems, at the beginning of the modern era, are also our problems.

Smith's work contains many oppositions and tensions. It also contains responses to these that may be called silences. He says nothing about how to resolve the tensions that we will see in *The Theory of Moral Sentiments*. Nor does he say anything, for example, about how to resolve the contradiction between the account of the benefits of the division of labour for workers in Book I of the *Wealth of Nations* with the account of the damage it does to them in Book V: a process founded on human nature causing a terrible deformation of human nature (Smith 1976b, WN I.i.10–11, V.i.f.50–61).[3] He is also strangely silent when it comes to naming writers to whose work he is quite obviously referring. He rarely mentions the names of other philosophers in *The Theory of Moral Sentiments*;[4] and we know that he deliberately did not name Steuart once in the whole of the *Wealth of Nations*.[5] Moreover, he never gives a name to what he is doing in the *Wealth of Nations*, other than

The Philosophy of Adam Smith, The Adam Smith Review, 5: 181–197 © 2010 The International Adam Smith Society, ISSN 1743–5285, ISBN 978-0-415-56256-0.

that contained in the title.[6] Finally, Smith conceived of a general system of quite breathtaking extent. But in neither of the main texts of the two works that he actually published, and which he claimed to be parts of this system, is there a single word referring to the other, nor to the system itself, for that matter.[7]

The best way to think about this situation, it seems to me, is to try to follow Smith, without preconceptions, as he follows where his thought leads him: and this requires considering not only divergences of meaning but also variations in tone.[8] So although I am sympathetic to Charles Griswold's claims for authorial intention and the principle of charity in his magnificent *Adam Smith and the Virtues of Enlightenment* (1999), I do not think that his approach, with its initial presumption of coherence in Smith's project, does justice to the simple *oddness* of what happens within and between Smith's two books. There are good reasons for thinking that Smith's intentions were not all of a piece. I will just mention three. First, each of the books is self-contained, and written on its own terms without reference to the other or to the system. Smith's announcement of the system, external to the two books, seems very much of an afterthought. Moreover, the goals of the books are very different in kind, in a way in which Smith's point of view might shift from one to the other without his being fully aware of the shift. Second, the line of argument of *The Theory of Moral Sentiments* is notably complex. As Griswold points out, views are substantially refined over the course of the book, 'so that later on the reader confronts unexpected questions about points advanced earlier' (Griswold 1999: 61).[9] The overall point of the book cannot be grasped until we have read the whole thing.[10] Third, in *The Theory of Moral Sentiments* Smith is consciously attempting to synthesize, as Griswold puts it, 'an ancient view about the nature of virtue with a modern approach to the problem of the source of moral value' (Griswold 1999: 181). This attempt to combine ancient and modern is one of the most important features of the book, and one of its chief claims to enduring value – indicating again why Smith's problems are our own.

None of these points would lead us to deny the significance of Smith's intentions, but they do indicate a way of thinking about them that would lead through the works rather than beginning from an external order within which they are presumed to fit. The first suggests that the relation between the two books may be problematic. The second and third, referring specifically to *The Theory of Moral Sentiments*, suggest why we would expect to find oppositions and tensions within it.

Oppositions are precisely what we find in *The Theory of Moral Sentiments*. In the next section, I am going to concentrate on that between moral sentiments and general moral rules, because it is the focal one: all the others arrange themselves around it. I will argue that this opposition produces a paradox of sympathy, and that this paradox points to two divergent concepts of individuality, one based on necessary relations among individuals, the other tending towards a view of the individual alone. In the final section,

I will consider the relationship between *The Theory of Moral Sentiments* and the *Wealth of Nations* in the light of this divergence.

Moral sentiments, general rules and the paradox of sympathy

The distinction between *moral sentiments* and *general moral rules*, and the movement from one to the other, are central to the argument of *The Theory of Moral Sentiments*. A parallel distinction and movement is to be found in the original situation of sympathy, imagination and spectatorship, on the one hand, and the impartial spectator on the other. Together, these distinctions and movements embody the paradox of sympathy. Moral sentiments and general rules are principally distinguished in that the former are always already there, naturally, in individual human beings; while the latter are the result of a complex process that involves society as a whole.

Since moral sentiments are constitutive elements of human nature prior to any reflection or to the formation of any moral principle, it is only through them that we are able to form general moral rules. But such rules are necessary, and necessarily the foremost guarantors of morality because, in the end, Smith does not trust moral sentiment. He insists on the priority of the moral sentiments.[11] He thinks that the general rules come in time to be 'universally acknowledged and established, by the concurring sentiments of mankind' (Smith 1976a, TMS III.4.11) just because of the universality of natural moral sentiments. Nonetheless, it is the general rules that must serve as the actual guide: 'Without this sacred regard to general rules, there is no man whose conduct can be much depended on' (TMS III.5.2).[12] As immediate feelings of the individual, moral sentiments are untrustworthy because they are bound up with what distinguishes him from others, making him likely to regard himself as more significant than they.[13] This is the natural state for the individual at birth and in childhood (TMS III.3.22). Even for an adult, 'the natural view of his own situation' (TMS III.3.28) is the one that puts him first. 'The great school of self-command' (TMS III.3.22) is always difficult. Thus we may say that the individual's sense of self, along with the natural sentiments themselves, is bound up with the partial standpoint, and the necessary dividing of the self required for moral conduct (TMS III.1.6) must be an act of violence against our original natural state. At this point then, the nature of individuality is brought into question.

Moral sentiments, with sympathy as their inter-subjective transmitter, are, in a sense, always already there, naturally, in individual human beings. *The Theory of Moral Sentiments* begins with the account of the working of sympathy and imagination in terms of a spectator observing an actor or agent. But it later becomes clear that something crucial has been left out of this account. For Smith, to understand what it is to approve or disapprove, to see beauty or deformity, to know what propriety is, are things I can only do through others, not alone. 'A human creature' (TMS III.1.3) that somehow grew up in isolation could not have these things: such a creature could not function morally.

Even this isolated creature has moral capacities: he is *potentially* moral. But the capacities can only become actual under certain conditions, their mere existence in the individual is not enough. These conditions are provided by society, which serves as a 'mirror ... placed in the countenance and behavior of those [the individual] lives with, which always mark when they enter into, and when they disapprove of his sentiments' (TMS III.1.3).[14] The individual learns morality through spectatorship: through others seeing him and responding to him, and through his own looking at others, modelled on their looking at him. Not simply a means for moral judgment, spectatorship is foundational to the very existence of morality. But it is also the necessary foundation for our sense of ourselves. Smith makes the capacity for individuality and the conditions for its realization identical to the capacity and conditions for morality. We can neither be moral, nor individuals, alone. For there to be an 'I' there must be a 'we'. An isolated individual's attention would be directed entirely outwards to external objects, the objects of his passions, not to the passions themselves (see TMS III.1.3). He could have no inner life.

This is Smith's most important and characteristic contribution, and one of his best attempts to combine ancient and modern: an Aristotelian view of relations as partly constitutive of individuality, and a modern sense of subjectivity and perception. But the view of perceptual reciprocity joining internal and external, rooted in his championing of ordinary experience against philosophical rarefication, is distinctive.[15] This account of individuality was submerged in the flood tide of atomic individualism (and if the *Wealth of Nations* helped prepare for the flood, *The Theory of Moral Sentiments* contains one of the most unanswerable refutations of methodological individualism). It played no role at all in the main line of economic thought, nor in the Anglo-American tradition of philosophy. But strikingly similar accounts, formulated independently, became crucial elements of twentieth-century thought: phenomenology, especially the works of Merleau-Ponty and Arendt, emphasizing embodiment of consciousness, reciprocity of perception, and the necessary plurality of human life;[16] and the post-Freudian ideas of internal objects and introjection, are two examples.[17] These mid-twentieth-century views have been strikingly confirmed by contemporary developments in neuroscience, especially in the discovery and study of so-called *mirror neurons* by Giacomo Rizzolatti and others.[18] But anyone who has read *The Theory of Moral Sentiments* will feel a thrill of recognition reading Rizzolatti's account of an experiment in which the same neurons in a monkey's brain fired when it grasped an object, as when, a spectator, it watched another grasp the object.[19] The independent rediscovery of this view of individuality demonstrates the living significance of Smith's moral philosophy. But it is also true that this is where his (and our) problems start.

The nascent individual, Smith says, responds to the responses of those around him, learning what it is to approve and disapprove, and so on. But there was already something in him, potentially: natural moral sentiment.

So, while we can only gain a sense of ourselves through others (the mirror of society), we can only recognize others through something that was already in us potentially (moral sentiments, imagination). This necessarily double character of human life rests on the double fact that we *are* separate from one another, but we can partially overcome that separation.[20] The working out of moral principles and moral action depends on the *partial* character of our sympathy. Only because I am a separate being with my own sentiments can I place myself in your situation. But because we are separate we can never fully feel what the other feels. *Fully* sympathetic beings would inhabit an entirely different moral world; and beings wholly lacking the capacity for sympathy could neither be moral nor individuals. Morality then requires both that I have a strong sense of myself as an individual, and that I divide myself, displacing myself as a moral agent, looking at myself as I can only look at you – from outside (see TMS III.1.6). This is the ground of the opposition between moral sentiments and general rules, and also of the paradox of sympathy.

General rules take on social legitimacy as the primary guide to moral behaviour through a process of agreement founded on the universality of moral sentiment. They must overcome the self-regard of the individual. In this, the rules are linked to the impartial spectator. Smith does not explain the relation between them, and usually speaks of them separately. But there are many passages where a connection can be inferred,[21] and some where they are clearly brought together. In one such place, an individual unfamiliar with the general rules would be mistaken about what 'every impartial spectator would approve of' (TMS III.4.12). So the rules may be seen here as part of what creates an impartial spectator in the individual.[22] This allows us to see the impartial spectator as something like an agent of the general rules within each individual; and it is indeed the case that both insist on self-division and self-distancing.[23] When I acknowledge the impartial spectator[24] as arbiter, I look at myself as at another to whom I am indifferent, practising a deliberate self-estrangement. With 'a sacred regard to general rules' I must not follow where the voice of my own sentiments leads, just because they are my own.

And yet this does not quite do justice to Smith's idea. The impartial spectator is much more than a set of rules, however sacred. He is 'the man within the breast', 'the great inmate', sometimes even the 'demigod within the breast', a person within who *speaks* to me. He must have all the *moral* attributes, and in the greatest perfection, so that in him moral sentiments and general rules are one.[25] He will *feel* the rules, and not simply *know* them, with the most perfect sympathy. Smith enhances this view by dramatic metaphors of light and darkness, colour, touch and sound. Nature and the spectator do not merely speak, they cry aloud; individuals must tune their passions so as to make them harmonize with those of others; those in adversity are exhorted to come out of the 'darkness of solitude' and into 'the day-light of the world and of society'.[26]

And yet in this way too we are brought to a halt. For even amidst this wealth of imagery we cannot fail to see the impersonalism of the impartial spectator. If he is to be like a person, he must not be any particular person, and his mission is to make me see myself as though I were no particular person, as though I were just anyone. If the impartial spectator has no feeling for himself it is hard to see how he can have feelings for others: after all, my sympathy with others depends on my feelings for myself. Smith insists that there cannot be just one rule, there are many, and the general rules cannot be laid down in advance, definitively. But in the face of the entirely individual charm of his voice in so much of this work, we must remember that for Smith those particular features by which one person is irreducibly different from another have no relevance at all for morality (see, for example, TMS I.ii.2.1).

This pulling backwards and forwards as we try to describe what Smith is saying shows us the paradox of sympathy. In order to feel with another, I must be able to feel for myself: for it is only by imagining what the other feels as a feeling of my own that I can sympathize with him. Sympathy seems to require a strong sense of self. Yet this is just what Smith tells us we must avoid, seeking instead to see ourselves with indifference, from the standpoint of the impartial spectator, and in this way, find it in ourselves to sympathize with others. Not fellow feeling, beginning from my own sense of self-identity, but common feeling, where I see how interchangeable I am with the other, is the ground of sympathy. At least, it is so when Smith has the impartial spectator and the general rules firmly in view. For all that, the very possibility of general rules, and their personification in the spectator, rest on the existence of moral sentiments, and if it is true that these are common to all mankind, it is also true that they only operate self by self, and in the immediacy of feeling.

Smith casts his moral theory in the theatrical terms of spectator and actor. To consider the images of spectator and actor in the light of the paradox of sympathy will illuminate the play in which Smith invites us all to take a role, the theatre in which it is to be performed, and, especially, the method in which he would instruct his actors.[27] The relation between spectator and actor (someone, for instance, who is suffering from some cause or another) is a reciprocal one. Not only does the spectator attempt to sympathize with the sufferer, but the sufferer, who so strongly desires sympathy, must also sympathize with the spectator, and so adjust his performance as to elicit sympathy.[28] But the spectator can never sympathize with the full measure of the sufferer's suffering, and the sufferer knows this from his own experience as spectator on other occasions. To gain sympathy at all, he must settle for less, and play the part accordingly. The drama is going to be quite a muted one, almost, one might say, rather dull. But this is only the beginning, for the real audience for whom we should all play in the end is not some other person, but the impartial spectator within each of us. The turn to the impartial spectator does two things: first, it is a move from the social stage to an inner, subjective drama. Second, it eliminates the element of reciprocity. For however complete his sympathy 'the man within the breast' is always *spectator*, never actor or sufferer.[29] Thus the interchange of roles, which had enacted the principle of sympathy, is superseded, and the inner drama returns to the conventional division between actor and audience.

The absoluteness of the impartial spectator's judgment overrides the judgments of actual spectators; and the logic of sympathy, which is the heart of social order for Smith,[30] has the paradoxical result of leading the individual away from society. Or, rather, it will do so for those who have most fully adopted the standpoint of the impartial spectator. The murderer is forced back into society to seek respite from the implacable rulings of the man within the breast in the milder judgments of his fellow men. But the good man wronged by society retires into himself, to seek in the impartial spectator the approbation that society denies him.[31] The complete impartiality of the impartial spectator undermines the foundation of morality in sympathy and spectatorship. But this must also mean that something has happened to individuality.

Individuality, for Smith, depends on innate moral capacities and on conditions given by society. My individuality depends on others. But something happens in the move from immediate moral sentiments, sympathy, and spectatorship to the impartial spectator and the general rules: the necessity of relations among individuals is brought into question. So the paradox of sympathy is worked out by a paradoxical situation in which the moral capacities within one individual push out towards others, while the social development of general rules can isolate individuals within themselves. But we must be careful to describe this clearly.

For a start, we must recognize a difference between the position of the impartial spectator and that of the general rules. As Smith describes him, the impartial spectator is in some sense *within* the individual, a part, though an odd part, of his subjectivity. The general rules, by contrast, seem to have something like an objective existence. What they have in common is that both are impersonal in demanding that we view all individuals, ourselves included, as interchangeable and replaceable. Both demand that I divide myself, and look at myself from the outside, as I would look at anyone else. Moreover, heeding the voice of the impartial spectator, paying a sacred regard to the general rules, must take me away from the particulars of any situation. This indifference to situation pushes me back into subjectivity, away from the world. But as soon as we put it this way, we are pulled back to the other side: concern for situation is precisely the ground of sympathy. So the opposition between centrality of situation and indifference to situation is a specific manifestation of the paradox of sympathy; and it leads us to consider the relation between the opposing sides.

The impartial spectator and the general rules push towards the individual alone. But they are still a part of the movement that begins with natural moral sentiments, sympathy and imagination. So we may say that the paradox of sympathy is within them. But then the same is true for our sentiments, sympathy, imagination: however much they push me out towards others, they too contain potentially the indifference and self-estrangement of the one wholly guided by the impartial spectator and the general rules. Thus the paradox of sympathy is not between two separate things that happen to come into conflict. It is within each, and operates as a dynamic tension linking them.

Individuality in *The Theory of Moral Sentiments* and in the *Wealth of Nations*

So far, I have considered the paradox of sympathy in the terms of Smith's own argument. I want now to consider, very briefly, how different traditions of thought influence the two sides of that argument. This will lead us to the question of the relation between *The Theory of Moral Sentiments* and the *Wealth of Nations*.

The paradox of sympathy turns on the problem of individuality. It is fair to say that not merely the concept, but the condition of having individuality is inherently problematic: it is indeed a central problem of the modern world. In Smith's account, its problematic character is displayed in a tension between what may be described somewhat loosely as Aristotelian and Stoic elements of his thought. The former pushes towards an idea of individuality as partly constituted by relations, the latter towards an idea of the individual alone. Thus we see the ground of the opposition between general rules and moral sentiments.

Smith's relation to Stoicism is complex; he was both highly critical of and strongly influenced by it. The criticism is directed against the absoluteness of Stoic principles themselves. The influence can be seen in a sort of moderate Stoical *tone* that is one of the most typical elements of *The Theory of Moral Sentiments*. Thus Smith rejects the Stoic *apatheia* as an absolute principle, but a moderate form of Stoic indifference is central to much of his argument. It extends to his claim that whereas the Stoics were wrong to say that all situations (including those of unremitting pain) should be alike to the good man, it remains true that '[t]he great source of both the misery and disorders of human life, seems to arise from over-rating the difference between one permanent situation and another' (TMS III.3.31). Further, it is important in his acceptance of the Stoic view of happiness as tranquillity; and also in his very strong endorsement of the Stoic claim '[t]hat every man is first and principally recommended to his own care' (TMS VI.ii.1.1). More broadly, Smith's view of the overall harmony of the universe draws on Stoic cosmology, though, once again, in a quite critical manner.[32] All of these views point to an idea of the individual in which the individual is alone, or in which relations among individuals are largely formal, emptied of substantial psychological content.[33] This singularity is related to the Stoic view that the world is ordered by a single principle, a single good.

But this is only one side of things. We already know that Smith has an extraordinary sense of the foundational importance of sympathy, imagination and relation for individuality. On this other side, the influence of Aristotle is clear. For Aristotle, good is to be found in action. But good is not singular and there are many virtues. There is no pre-determined law to be followed, every action is something new, and we must find, or fail to find, virtue ever anew, hence the importance of situation. The virtuous man will desire the good, and will act from this desire, and not simply because there is a pre-established rule telling him what the good is and to which he must submit in order to be good. Thus the virtuous man is engaged with others in the world, valuing them for themselves in their particularity. When Smith has the moral sentiments clearly in view, he comes close in all these ways to Aristotle. But when he goes over to the general rules and the impartial spectator, then the Stoical indifference takes command, distancing him from the world, flattening out the virtues into a unified good, denying action in favour of the state of goodness, and insisting that goodness is a submission and a renunciation of self and of desire – even of the desire for good.

There are other terms for thinking through the oppositions in Smith's thought – ancient and modern, pagan and Christian, providence and fortune – but they will have to wait. The point here is that in *The Theory of Moral Sentiments* the opposing sides go along together. The argument depends on the dynamic tension between them, and this is worked out in a sort of principle of compensation, so that each view is almost immediately followed by its contrary.[34] Smith never gets too far from either side. The paradox of sympathy remains, and individuality is pulled back and forth between isolation and relations.

In the *Wealth of Nations* something very different happens. Oppositions remain, but they function in another way. First, one view predominates far more than in *The Theory of Moral Sentiments*. Second, this view changes and becomes more extreme, in part because of the lessened opposition, in part because of Smith's goal here. The goal of the later book is much simpler than that of the earlier, and he follows where the goal leads him. It is also true that the goal of the *Wealth of Nations* is more technical than that of *The Theory of Moral Sentiments*, and so there is what could be called a shift from the ethical to the scientific. In the dominant view of the *Wealth of Nations* individuals typically appear as isolated, motivated by interests defined for themselves alone, without reference to others.[35] Relations with others are indeed necessary, but they are the instrumental relations of the division of labour and exchange. Very occasional mention is made of some notion of approbation.[36] But what has vanished without trace is the fundamental insight into the necessity of others for the development of individuality and a sense of self.

I think that it is important to see the shift here as part of a wider movement of thought. A simple way to put it is to place Utilitarianism as a stage in this movement that comes after Smith. However, we may add two further claims. First, the *Wealth of Nations* is closer to Utilitarianism than is *The Theory of*

Moral Sentiments. Second, the *Wealth of Nations* is indeed importantly linked to a line of thought in *The Theory of Moral Sentiments*. This is the line most influenced by Stoicism, and most tending towards an idea of the individual alone.[37] The *Wealth of Nations* then appears as a sort of bridge between a moderate Stoicizing line and Utilitarianism.

Stoicism and Utilitarianism are distinguished by the ethical character of the former, and the claim to science of the latter; answering to the objective order of Stoicism, as opposed to the subjective order of Utilitarianism. Nevertheless, they are strikingly similar in form, both at the level of the whole and that of the individual. Stoical and Utilitarian individuals have in common a withdrawal from the world around them, though for different reasons. The Stoic withdraws with (dreary) disdain from the entrapments of the world; the Utilitarian withdraws because things in the world (including other individuals) are never valued for themselves, but only for the subjective satisfaction (utility) they afford. For both, a single principle orders the whole, working through individuals automatically, and without any requirement that the order be understood by them. Here, the bridging character of the *Wealth of Nations* is very clear. For the image of individuals in the market directed by an invisible hand looks back to the one, and forward to the other; and Smith claims that the order of the market is beyond human wisdom (see WN IV.ix.51).[38]

Smith is drawn by the study of wealth to push the Stoic side of his conception of individuality in what turns out to be the direction of the Utilitarian isolated individual. I want to translate this claim into terms used by Max Horkheimer to describe a fundamental movement in modern thought towards what he calls *subjectivization* and *formalization*. The move towards the individual alone is a move towards subjectivity, for, to be alone, the individual must be separated from all that is outside itself. (So, in the end, it must be cut off even from its own body: a result implied by Utilitarianism at least in its Benthamite form, and pretty much fully realized in neoclassical economics.) Since this move must also make relations external, and so never necessary for the individual, and must empty relations of substantial content (since content can only be subjective), it is also a move towards formalization, the adequate form of which is quantification (see Horkheimer 2004: 5–7). Utilitarianism, with its double and exclusive focus on subjectivity and quantity, is a defining stage of this movement.

The movement towards subjectivization and formalization helps us to understand the complex relationship between Smith's two books, in which the later is indeed very importantly influenced by at least an element of the earlier; but in which this element is transformed by the requirements of the later work. The difference may be felt in the different way in which oppositions appear. As I have already said, in the later work, one view predominates, although the other is never completely eliminated. It is also true that there is very little dynamic tension between the different views – they simply exist side by side. The overall line of the book is laid down by the dominant position.

In *The Theory of Moral Sentiments*, by contrast, the tension is what carries the book along.

The difference in the treatment of oppositions is related to the difference in content, and Smith's approach to the content of the two books. The subject of *The Theory of Moral Sentiments* is complex, and Smith approaches it correspondingly. It is only possible to understand how the book works by reading it all the way through: and even then, it is an enormous help to have someone like Charles Griswold explaining to us why it had to be like this. In particular, he shows us how it begins, without any introductory material, in the middle of a longstanding argument (see Griswold 1999: 78–81). The content of *An Inquiry into the Nature and Causes of the Wealth of Nations* is fully conveyed by its title. It is about just one thing, and Smith carefully explains in the Introduction and Plan of the work how he is going to proceed: he will consider topics in the order of their importance to the question of the nature and causes of wealth. We might almost say, crudely, that oppositions exist in *The Theory of Moral Sentiments* because Smith is trying to do several things at once; they exist in the *Wealth of Nations* because he occasionally forgets that he is doing only one.[39]

Economists have for the most part simply accepted that the *Wealth of Nations* prefigures the main atomic individualist line of nineteenth- and twentieth-century economic thought. And this is no accident; Steuart, for example, would never have been interpreted in this way. Since the interpretation clearly is at odds with the argument of *The Theory of Moral Sentiments*, a tension between the two books is suggested. But the interpretation is plausible because of Smith's silence on just how the books are related. Since so little in the *Wealth of Nations* reflects the complex and profound view of individuality in *The Theory of Moral Sentiments*; and since Smith does portray the market as a natural self-regulating order – even if he also expresses reservations about this view – economists can hardly be blamed for placing him as founder of free-market, atomic individualist economic theory.

However, one of Smith's most careful readers took a different view. Hegel's depiction of civil society in the third part of *The Philosophy of Right* may be seen as an extensive gloss on the *Wealth of Nations* (though he mentions Say and Ricardo as well as Smith). He is sympathetic to political economy, saying of it that it 'is a credit to thought because it finds laws for a mass of accidents' (Hegel 1952: 268). Nonetheless, he thinks that it is inadequate just because it has not seen beyond these accidents and their regularity to the order that makes them possible. This is not the place to work through Hegel's argument, but two points will give a sense of its relevance here. First, Hegel places what we would call the economy within the sphere of civil society. In this sphere individuals confront each other as isolated beings pursuing their own ends. So far, this corresponds to the account of 'political economy'. But he also claims that if there were nothing but this random pursuit, civil society would break apart. Even within it, some more inclusive order is necessary: he calls this order the *corporation*, and it points towards the all-inclusive order of the state (see Hegel 1952: 152–5).

Second, civil society itself is only one of the spheres, along with the family and the state, that together make up what Hegel calls Ethical Life (*Sittlichkeit*). These are the objective structures necessary for the existence of modern society, each with its own proper ethical content. Hegel is drawing here on much eighteenth-century thought – including that of the pioneers of what came to be called political economy – with its emerging sense of a new social domain opening up between the household and the state. But he is the first to formulate a complete theory of modern society; and he insists that it is only in virtue of the overall order that the individual parts can be adequately understood.

It would be too much to expect Smith to have anticipated Hegel's view of modern society. Nonetheless, a serious issue arises here. For Smith does claim to think in terms of an entire system, and yet he never tells us how its parts are to fit together: he never says how anything in one part is systematically related to the others. I spoke in the Introduction of the oddness of Smith's silences. But here, his silence appears as a major structural flaw, because we need to know how the economy fits into the rest of society, and he does not tell us. Hegel does take up this question, and though he is clearly sympathetic to Smith, he shows what Smith is lacking. He shows convincingly, I think, that the economy cannot be a self-contained system independent of everything around it, and also that it is historically determined: it belongs to modern society. The issue of how the economy fits into society is largely lost in later economic thought because of the image of a self-contained economic system, and this has meant that no satisfactory account can be given of the limits of economic activity. Smith both prepares for this by his account of the market in the *Wealth of Nations*, and questions it by his unargued assertion that the *Wealth of Nations* is nonetheless a part of a larger whole. The issue remains as a largely unanswerable question in neoclassical economics, because it can make no theoretical distinction between exchange and use, between the economic sphere and the sphere of private life.[40]

Hegel, in a way, does for us what Smith himself does not do. He pulls the *Wealth of Nations* back towards *The Theory of Moral Sentiments* by claiming that it would be impossible for anything like the order described in the former to exist without something like what is described in the latter. But this should not be taken as demonstrating that the two books fit together as parts of a larger whole. Hegel is right, I think, in seeing that there is something lacking in the *Wealth of Nations*. Or, we might put this in another way: Smith should have placed his economics explicitly in the framework of his ethics. But if he had done this, his economics would have had to be different, and different in such a way that no one could have interpreted it as describing a natural self-regulating system operating through the self-interested pursuits of isolated individuals with only instrumental relations among them.

Acknowledgements

I would like to thank David M. Levy for comments on a much earlier version of this essay. I would also like to thank Vivienne Brown and Samuel Fleischacker for their comments on the essay at 'The Philosophy of Adam Smith' conference.

Notes

1 For representative instances of this view from the large literature, see Macfie (1967), Winch (1978), D.D. Raphael and A.L. Macfie (1976), R.H. Campbell and A.S. Skinner (1976) and C.L. Griswold (1999). For a recent dissenting opinion, see Brown (1994). For an earlier, but still challenging, claim for an Adam Smith Problem, see Viner (1958).

2 Macfie notices 'the convenient, but often agonizing spread of meaning, at times almost amounting to self-contradiction, in some of the strategic ideas' of *The Theory of Moral Sentiments*, but he shrugs it off rather lightly (Macfie 1967: 58).

3 The opposition between these two passages has received considerable attention. Marx noticed it (Marx 1976: 483–4, n. 47). E.G. West sees it as contradictory (West 1964); though he argues that outrage caused the Book V view to be wildly overstated, and that this is the cause of the contradiction. I do not think that this does justice to the Book V view (and I am rather suspicious of the implication that moral engagement, and its attendant outrage, *must* lead to analytical failure). Nathan Rosenberg attempts to show that there is no contradiction (Rosenberg 1965). But although he offers a valuable framework for understanding the issue, I do not think that he succeeds in explaining away the simple shock of the contrast between the division of labour of Book I, that focusses labourers on their labour in such a way as to allow them wide opportunity to conceive of means to abridge it through the introduction of machinery, and that of Book V, that makes labourers 'as stupid and ignorant as it is possible for a human creature to become'.

4 See Griswold's interesting discussion of this point as expressing Smith's desire to appeal 'to our everyday experience and reflection' (Griswold 1999: 47).

5 Smith explains this in the letter to William Pulteney, 3 September 1772 (Smith 1987, *Corr.* Letter 132).

6 He clearly regards 'political economy' as precisely what he is *not* doing: the distinctive feature of 'systems of political economy' as Smith describes them in Book IV is that they lead to *actions* by the state ('extraordinary encouragements or restraints').

7 The Advertisement added to the sixth edition of *The Theory of Moral Sentiments* mentions the *Wealth of Nations* as partly fulfilling the task of the never completed jurisprudential component of the system, 'in what concerns police, revenue, and arms' (TMS Advertisement), but this is the only reference to one of the books in the other. In the last paragraph of *The Theory of Moral Sentiments*, Smith does say that he plans 'another discourse' on the subject of jurisprudence. But he does not say anything about the system as a whole (though he uses the word 'system' earlier in the paragraph to refer, somewhat disparagingly, to Grotius).

8 Heilbroner (1982) and Evensky (1987) have eloquently employed the image of different 'voices' in Smith's work, while defending the claim for the non-existence of the Adam Smith Problem. Vivienne Brown analyses differences in Smith's discourse. Griswold discusses the complexity of Smith's rhetoric. But I am not sure that they are sufficiently sensitive simply to what happens in the sentences themselves as one succeeds the other.

9 On occasion, Griswold uses the term 'dialectical' to describe Smith's thought (for example 1999: 74), and it is not unreasonable to see *The Theory of Moral Sentiments* as a relatively simple precursor of the Hegelian mode of argument.

10 By contrast, the overall line of argument of the *Wealth of Nations* is very straightforward, and its aim is clearly announced in the Introduction and Plan of the Work.

11 Thus, Smith criticizes 'several very eminent authors' for taking the general rules to be the 'the ultimate foundations of what is just and unjust in human conduct' (TMS III.4.11).

12 In TMS III.6, however, he does enumerate cases in which we should be guided by moral sentiments rather than by the general rules.

13 Smith, as was usual for his time, always used masculine pronouns to refer to an unspecified individual, and he always treated the impartial spectator as male. He also seems to have conceived of the abstract individual, in theory, as male. Virtually all pronouns in the present text are used in writing directly of Smith's views and I will follow his usage in these cases. The issue of gender in Smith's work, and throughout eighteenth-century political economy, is an important one, but I am not going to take it up here. For interesting discussions, see Justman (1993) and Poovey (1994).

14 Smith uses an Aristotelian view of capacities and their realization in other places, and it is reasonable to impute it to him here.

15 For Smith's championing of the ordinary against the pretensions of philosophy, see Griswold (1999: 141–2). The image of the mirror itself is not new. Hume, for example, had used it in the *Treatise on Human Nature* (1888: II.ii.5), but in a quite offhand way, and without the socially constitutive emphasis given by Smith here. Smith's mirror is not just an optical mechanism, it reflects *expression*; and the individual does not merely passively adopt the standards of society, but responds to them through his own innate faculties. For Smith's concern with this issue, and its elaboration over successive editions of the book, see Raphael (1975: 90 ff.)

16 See, for example, Merleau-Ponty (1962: Two, ch. 4); Arendt (1977: One, 19–30).

17 See, for example, Klein (1977) and Winnicott (1986: chap. 5).

18 Rizzolatti introduces a general account of his work by speaking of 'how bizarre it would be to conceive of an *I* without an *us*' (Rizzolatti and Sinigaglia 2008: xii–xiii).

19 See Rizzolatti (2004: 6). Rizzolatti acknowledges the importance of Merleau-Ponty as a precursor of his research (Rizzolatti 2004: 5).

20 See Griswold's excellent discussion of this (Griswold 1999: 83–7).

21 For example TMS III.5.6, where violations of the general rules are punished by '[t]hose viceregents of God within us', which are, presumably, the impartial spectators in each of us.

22 Although the use of the term 'impartial spectator' here suggests simply other individuals who happen to be impartial in this case, rather than 'the man within the breast'.

23 But this is an interpretation, and there is much more to say on the issue; and since Smith does not explain the relation between them, the possibility arises that one or the other is redundant. However, I am not going to take that up here.

24 Smith almost always refers to the impartial spectator in the singular. This is presumably because he is 'the man within the breast' of a single individual: thus the singularity of the impartial spectator underlines the singularity of each of us in relation to all others, even though sympathy is possible. But see Griswold's account of this singularity on different grounds (1999: 142, including n. 25).

25 D.D. Raphael writes that the impartial spectator 'has the normal feelings of a normal human being', and 'simply *is* any normal observer who is not personally affected' (1975: 95). Apart from the oddness of thinking of any normal observer as

a demigod, I think that this misses the importance of the spectator's absolute impartiality: he is *never* personally affected, and so cannot be a *normal* human being.

26 Light, darkness, colour, harmony, and voices crying aloud all appear together, for example, at TMS II.ii.2.1–4. Darkness and daylight are at TMS III.3.39.

27 For Smith's use of the theatrical metaphor, see Marshall (1986).

28 For the importance of reciprocity in sympathy, see Marshall (1986: 173–5), and Haakonssen (1981: 52–4).

29 See above, n. 25.

30 For the centrality of sympathy in social order, see Haakonssen (1981: 136–9).

31 For the murderer, see TMS II.ii.2.3; for the good man wronged, see TMS III.2.32–3.

32 Though this is a tremendous over-simplification. See Griswold's important discussions of Smith's views both of Stoicism and of natural harmony (1999: 317–30).

33 Though the Stoic goal is the good of all, it nonetheless pushes individuals into themselves, distancing them from the world, hence, from each other. In this, it has striking similarities to Utilitarianism (see below, p. 190).

34 We have seen this generally in the movement back and forth between moral sentiments and general rules. It can also be seen in the sequence from the necessary acknowledgement of pain, to the danger of over-rating differences in permanent situations, to praise for the admirable man, whose admirableness is demonstrated in action (TMS III.3.28–36). In another place, Smith has hardly finished mocking the strivings after wealth by a poor boy who wastes his life in its pursuit, and is too exhausted to enjoy it once he achieves his goal (TMS IV.1.8), when he tells us of 'that eminent esteem with which men naturally regard a steady perseverance in the practice of frugality, industry, and application, though directed to no other purpose than the acquisition of fortune' (TMS IV.2.6–8).

35 The idea of self-betterment offers a good contrast here: in *The Theory of Moral Sentiments*, the drive to self-betterment arises from our desire for the approbation of others, and Smith regards it as an irregularity of sentiment, though one that is socially useful (TMS I.iii.2.1). In the *Wealth of Nations*, the desire for self-betterment is something each individual is born with, so it is natural and purely self-regarding, and in no way depends on relations with others. Moreover, it leads to parsimony, and so is understood to be reasonable, and of service to the individual as well as to society (WN II.iii.28). I cannot understand Griswold's assertion that the two passages give the same account of self-betterment (Griswold 1999: 262–3).

36 See, for example, Smith WN I.xi.c.31, where 'the parade of riches' is what the rich are most concerned with. But even here, what in *The Theory of Moral Sentiments* was true of everyone, and was of fundamental importance to the order of society, is now offhandedly said to be true of the rich alone.

37 Luigino Bruni (2006) notes that the Stoic influence leads Smith away from civil virtues towards individual virtues. His statement that Smith's 'theory is more Stoic than Aristotelian' (Bruni 2006: 84) is more applicable to the *Wealth of Nations* than to *The Theory of Moral Sentiments*.

38 The idea of the market as beyond human wisdom is at least implicit in neoclassical economics. But Hayek is one of the few later economists to think in an interesting way about what this means. And as in other places, he is consciously developing Smith's position. See, for example, Hayek (1960: ch. 2).

39 Compare Vivienne Brown's application of the terms 'dialogism' and 'monologism' to *The Theory of Moral Sentiments* and the *Wealth of Nations* respectively (Brown 1994: 31, 43–6).

40 But for an important account of the place of the economy and of its limits, that draws on Hegel's view of Ethical Life, see Levine (1988: 1–4).

Bibliography

Arendt, H. (1977) *The Life of the Mind*, New York and London: Harcourt Brace & Co.

Brown, V. (1994) *Adam Smith's Discourse: Canonicity, Commerce, and Conscience*, London and New York: Routledge.

Bruni, L. (2006) *Civil Happiness: Economics and Human Flourishing in Historical Perspective*, London: Routledge.

Campbell, R.H. and Skinner, A.S. (1976) Introduction to Adam Smith, *An Inquiry into the Nature and Causes of the Wealth of Nations*, Oxford: Clarendon Press; Liberty Press imprint, 1981.

Evensky, J. (1987) 'The two voices of Adam Smith: moral philosopher and social critic', *History of Political Economy*, 19: 447–68.

Griswold, C.L. (1999) *Adam Smith and the Virtues of Enlightenment*, Cambridge: Cambridge University Press.

Haakonssen, K. (1981) *The Science of a Legislator: The Natural Jurisprudence of David Hume and Adam Smith*, Cambridge: Cambridge University Press.

Hayek, F. (1960) *The Constitution of Liberty*, Chicago, IL: University of Chicago Press.

Hegel, G.W.F. (1952) *The Philosophy of Right*, trans. T.M. Knox, Oxford: Oxford University Press.

—— (1977) *Phenomenology of Spirit*, trans. A.V. Miller, Oxford: Oxford University Press.

Heilbroner, R.L. (1982) 'The socialization of the individual in Adam Smith', *History of Political Economy*, 14: 421–31.

Horkheimer, M. (2004) 'Means and ends', in *Eclipse of Reason*, London and New York: Continuum.

Hume, D. (1888) *A Treatise of Human Nature*, L.A. Selby-Bigge (ed.), Oxford: Oxford University Press.

Justman, S. (1993) *The Autonomous Male of Adam Smith*, Norman, OK: University of Oklahoma Press.

Klein, M. (1977) 'A contribution to the psychogenesis of manic-depressive states', in *Love, Guilt and Reparation and Other Works, 1921–1945*, New York: Delta Books.

Levine, D. (1988) *Needs, Rights, and the Market*, Boulder, CO: Lynne Rienner.

Macfie, A.L. (1967) *The Individual in Society: Papers on Adam Smith*, London: George Allen & Unwin.

Marshall, D. (1986) *The Figure of Theater: Shaftesbury, Defoe, Adam Smith, and George Eliot*, New York: Columbia University Press.

Marx, K. (1976) *Capital*, vol. I, trans. B. Fowkes, Harmondsworth: Penguin Books.

Merleau-Ponty, M. (1962) *Phenomenology of Perception*, trans. C. Smith, London: Routledge.

Poovey, M. (1994) 'Aesthetics and political economy in the eighteenth century: the place of gender in the social constitution of knowledge', in G. Levine (ed.), *Aesthetics and Ideology*, Piscataway, NJ: Rutgers University Press.

Raphael, D.D. (1975) 'The impartial spectator', in A.S. Skinner and T. Wilson (eds), *Essays on Adam Smith*, Oxford: Oxford University Press.

Raphael, D.D. and Macfie, A.L. (1976) Introduction to A. Smith, *The Theory of Moral Sentiments*, Oxford: Clarendon Press; Liberty Press imprint, 1982.

Rizzolatti, G. (2004) 'Understanding the actions of others', in N. Kanwisher and J. Duncan (eds), *Functional Neuroimaging of Visual Cognition, Attention and Performance XX*, Oxford: Oxford University Press.

Rizzolatti, G. and Sinigaglia, C. (2008) *Mirrors in the Brain – How Our Minds Share Actions and Emotions*, Oxford: Oxford University Press.

Rosenberg, N. (1965) 'Adam Smith on the division of labour: two views or one?', *Economica*, 32: 127–39.

Smith, A. (1976a) *The Theory of Moral Sentiments*, D.D. Raphael and A.L. Macfie (eds), Oxford: Clarendon Press; Liberty Press imprint, 1982.

—— (1976b) *An Inquiry into the Nature and Causes of the Wealth of Nations*, R.H. Campbell, A.S. Skinner, and W.B. Todd (eds), Oxford: Clarendon Press; Liberty Press imprint, 1981.

—— (1987) *The Correspondence of Adam Smith*, E.C. Mossner and I.S. Ross (eds), Oxford: Clarendon Press.

Viner, J. (1958) 'Adam Smith and laissez faire', in *The Long View and the Short: Studies in Economic Theory and Policy*, New York: The Free Press.

West, E.G. (1964) 'Adam Smith's two views on the division of labour', *Economica*, 31: 23–32.

Winch, D. (1978) *Adam Smith's Politics*, Cambridge: Cambridge University Press.

Winnicott, D.W. (1986) *Playing and Reality*, London and New York: Routledge.

Scepticism and naturalism in Adam Smith

Ryan Patrick Hanley

Is Adam Smith a sceptic? It's difficult to imagine a question more funda-mental to our understanding of his project. Yet it's also difficult to imagine a question that has received more varying answers from Smith scholars. Thus we find Charles Griswold on the one hand arguing that Smith is best under-stood as a 'nondogmatic sceptic' whose epistemology 'unquestionably repre-sents an appropriation of Hume' (Griswold 1999: esp. 164–6, 171, 336–44; 2006: 22, 40, 50, 53–4, 56 n. 27; cf. Haakonssen and Winch 2006).[1] On the other hand we find D.D. Raphael arguing with equal directedness that 'Adam Smith was not a sceptic', but a 'theist' (Raphael 2007: 104).[2] My aim in what follows is to reconsider the evidence for each of these claims. In so doing, I want to argue that Smith's epistemology is indeed indebted to Hume's – but for reasons in fact quite different from those often insisted upon. Smith's chief debt to Hume is not to Hume's scepticism but his naturalism. This is most evident in the specific concern on which I want to focus: namely Smith's embrace of Hume's conception of natural belief.

The advantages of this approach are threefold. First, it illuminates a neglected aspect of Smith's debts to Hume, debts that extend well beyond the familiar ones to Hume's scepticism and his conception of the imagination.[3] Second, such an approach clarifies Smith's intention in some of the most enigmatic and frequently misunderstood passages in his writings. Third, and perhaps most importantly, appreciation of the role of natural belief in Smith's project offers a persuasive alternative to the sceptical and the theistic conceptions alluded to at the outset. Each position of course has considerable merit, at least in its moderate form. But in their strong forms – tending to anti-realism on the one hand and personal theism on the other – they're less satisfying insofar as they aspire to ascribe to Smith an authoritative position on the nature of external reality or on God's existence.[4] Such ascriptions will strike many as incongruent with Smith's own intentions – intentions in some respects more modest and in others more daring than such labels suggest. In an effort to illuminate certain of these intentions, this essay sug-gests an interpretation focusing on naturalism and natural belief as an alternative to both strong sceptical and strong theistic interpretations of Smith's project.

The Philosophy of Adam Smith, The Adam Smith Review, 5: 198–212 © 2010 The International Adam Smith Society, ISSN 1743–5285, ISBN 978-0-415-56256-0.

What then is natural belief? Natural belief has yet to become a topic of analysis among Smith scholars,[5] yet it's long been a crucial category of Hume scholarship. This scholarship has itself been immersed for some time in a debate over the nature of Hume's scepticism and the place of natural belief in it. Dubbed the 'New Hume' debate, it pits defenders of the traditional view of Hume's scepticism as a negative or deflationary project against those emphasizing his naturalism and its positive and productive intentions (Read and Richman 2007).[6] Thus where defenders of the 'old Hume' understand him to be chiefly concerned to demonstrate our necessary uncertainty regarding the existence of the external world and the nature of causal powers, many champions of the 'new Hume' aim to explain how his sceptical statements can be reconciled with his commitments to naturalism. By displacing the traditional centrality of Hume's 'copy principle' – the principle that all ideas are mere copies of impressions derived from sensory experience, and all imaginings extending beyond such ideas are necessarily arbitrary – advocates of the 'new Hume' tend instead to call attention to those instances in which Hume focuses on the principles of the mind that we employ in common life in order to make sense of the world around us.[7] That said, the 'new Humeans' hardly deny the obvious scepticism that Hume elsewhere espouses; most agree that Hume thinks that our epistemological limits forbid us from pronouncing definitively on the existence of a mind-independent external world or on the nature of causal powers. Their claim is rather that Hume believes that our minds are naturally ordered to assume the existence of an external world and causal powers, and that this assumption is necessary for navigation of common life, even despite the fact that these assumptions cannot hope to pass the verifiability or legitimacy tests posited by scepticism. Put differently, new Humeans claim that scepticism about the ultimate sufficiency of our metaphysical beliefs is mitigated by the fact that we are necessarily compelled to act and live as if these beliefs are true. It is here that the concept of natural belief enters as a feature of the human mind mitigating the practical conclusions to which scepticism might otherwise lead.

With this in mind I want now to turn to the accounts of natural belief found in Hume's texts, and particularly his discussion in the *Enquiry concerning Human Understanding* (Hume 2000, EHU; Hume 1978, SBN) Section 5, Part 2. In so doing, I especially want to isolate aspects of this account that were likely to have influenced Smith. Hume introduces this section by sharpening the question to which natural belief seems to be the answer. Up until now his question has been: what features of the mind enable a sceptic to navigate the world? His first answer, quite simply, is 'imagination': imagination is what enables us to conceive ideas beyond experience. But Hume recognizes that his answer to this question invites another. Imagination, as he repeatedly notes elsewhere, is 'arbitrary' when it goes beyond experience (see, for example, EHU 4.9–10; SBN 29–30), quickly finding itself in the land of whimsy. This is precisely the claim that introduces his account in EHU Section 5, Part 2, the first line of which notes that 'nothing is more free than the imagination of man', and that as a result of its 'unlimited power' to combine ideas, nothing is impossible for it to conceive (EHU 5.10; SBN 47). At this point, Hume seems backed into a corner: we need something more than mere ideas derived from the sensory impressions to get around in the world, but what we have, imagination, seems unreliable (at best). With this in mind Hume introduces his crucial distinction between 'fiction' and 'belief'.[8] To illustrate it, he explains that 'we can, in our conception, join the head of a man to the body of a horse; but it is not in our power to believe, that such an animal has ever really existed' (EHU 5.10; SBN 48). This sort of imagining he elsewhere calls the 'loose and indolent reveries of a castle-builder' (Hume 2007, T App. 3–4; SBN 624–5). Explicitly associating it with the poetic imagination, Hume insists that in such 'offspring of the fancy' one necessarily finds 'something weak and imperfect' (T 1.3.10.5–6; SBN 121–2 and T 1.3.10.10; SBN 630–1). Belief, on the other hand, goes beyond 'what the imagination alone is ever able to attain' (EHU 5.12; SBN 49) and thus must be fundamentally distinguished from 'mere reveries of the imagination' (T App. 2; SBN 624), 'mere fictions of the imagination' (T 1.3.5.4; SBN 628 and T 1.4.2.29; SBN 200–1 and EHU 5.13; SBN 50) or an 'illusion of the imagination' (T 1.4.7.6; SBN 267).

But what really differentiates reasonable belief from mere imagination? Hume in fact seems to give two answers. Neither answer, importantly, takes the form of insisting that reasonable beliefs somehow contain more truth than mere imaginings. Indeed, Hume is decidedly reluctant to endorse or challenge the content of these beliefs on this level at all. Thus rather than argue for either their substantive truth or falsity, Hume is more intent on examining belief from a phenomenological perspective. Consistent with his scepticism, Hume thus focuses much less on the normative question of the truth of reasonable beliefs than on the way beliefs are subjectively experienced by their possessor and how they practically shape his or her actions. Both inquiries reveal considerable differences between belief and mere illusive imaginings. In the first place, Hume appeals to our common experience of belief to argue that belief simply 'feels' different than the 'loose reveries of the fancy' (EHU 5.11; SBN 48). Our beliefs concerning matters of fact, he notes, simply have more strength and solidity and vivacity than any 'fictitious idea, that the fancy alone presents to us' (T 1.3.7.7; SBN 629). Thus the first difference between belief and imagined fictions lies not in their matter but in the *'manner'* in which we experience them (T 1.3.7.2; SBN 95 and T 1.3.7.7; SBN 628–9), and hence Hume's provisional conclusion that 'the sentiment of belief is nothing but a conception more intense and steady than what attends the mere fictions of the imagination' (EHU 5.13; SBN 50).

Hume is invested in this claim. But he also concedes its limits. As he admits, his aim in calling attention to the way in which belief is felt is less to set forth a 'definition' of belief than a *'description'* of it (EHU 5.12; SBN 49). But in what follows Hume does better. Thus at the end of EHU Section 5, Part 2, Hume offers his second reason for distinguishing belief from fiction, which concerns the function and the origin of our beliefs. His key claim on this front deserves to be quoted in full. A natural belief in causal powers, he writes, is

> so essential to the subsistence of all human creatures, it is not probable, that it could be trusted to the fallacious deductions of our reason, which is slow in its operations; appears not, in any degree, during the first years of infancy; and at best is, in every age and period of human life, extremely liable to error and mistake. It is more conformable to the ordinary wisdom of nature to secure so necessary an act of the mind, by some instinct or mechanical tendency, which may be infallible in its operations, may discover itself at the first appearance of life and thought, and may be independent of all the laboured deductions of the understanding. As nature has taught us the use of our limbs, without giving us the knowledge of the muscles and nerves, by which they are actuated; so has she implanted in us an instinct, which carries forward the thought in a correspondent course to that which she has established among external objects; though we are ignorant of those powers and forces, on which this regular course and succession of objects totally depends.
>
> (EHU 5.22; SBN 55)

Hume here touches on three fundamental aspects of natural belief to which we will have reason to return. The first is the ends of belief, which he identifies as the preservation of both self and species, in keeping with claims elsewhere concerning the necessity of belief 'to the subsistence of our species, and the regulation of our conduct' (EHU 5.21; SBN 55). The second is his claim that belief functions as a substitute for sluggish reason, itself in keeping with claims elsewhere that nature has deemed the belief on which our survival depends to be 'of too great importance to be trusted to our uncertain reasonings and speculations' (T 1.4.2.1; SBN 187). The third is his insistence that unlike fictions, which are always idle, belief is action-motivating – itself in keeping with the claim elsewhere that belief gives our judgments of reality 'more weight and influence; makes them appear of greater importance; enforces them in the mind; and renders them the governing principle of our actions' (EHU 5.12; SBN 49–50).

All told, Hume identifies three features as essential to natural belief. As summarized by Gaskin, such belief is (1) inherent to common life though questioned by sceptical philosophy; (2) ultimately incapable of rational justification; and (3) universally embraced as its absence would render ordinary life (indeed mere survival) impossible (Gaskin 1988 [1978]: 109, 116–19; cf. Tweyman 1986: 10–19; Kail 2007: 67–9). On these grounds, it's generally held that at least two ordinary beliefs – belief in the existence of a mind-independent external world and belief in causal powers – meet the criteria for natural belief. To these is sometimes added belief in the persistence of personal identity over time, and, more controversially, belief in God's existence.[9] Leaving aside the question of whether religious belief of any sort meets Hume's criteria for natural belief, it bears repeating that in all four cases, Hume's claim is never that these beliefs meet the standards of truth. His focus is consistently epistemological rather than metaphysical, and his consistent claim is rather that beliefs, irrespective of their ultimate truth, are inevitable and indeed indispensable elements of our mental architecture (see, for example, Richman 2007: 8; and, for a particularly clear and influential statement, Strawson 1989: esp. 10–15).

With this in mind, I want now to turn to Smith's *Theory of Moral Sentiments* (1976, TMS), and to do so in a way which I hope will justify the preceding exegesis of Hume. To reward patience in enduring that exegesis, we might begin by stating our main claim somewhat hyperbolically: namely, that Hume's conception of natural belief, described above, provides the key to understanding Smith's intention in at least three of the most important, most notorious, and most frequently misinterpreted passages in his corpus: the passage on his 'present inquiry' as a matter of fact and not a matter of right (TMS II.i.5.10 note), the passage on Christ's Atonement as revised in the 6th edition (TMS II.ii.3.12), and the passage on our reaction to the prospect of a 'fatherless world' (TMS VI.ii.3.2). Each of these passages has been repeatedly mined for Smith's stances on scepticism and theism. But these attempts are, I think, misguided. As I hope to show, in each case, so far from pronouncing on metaphysical questions, Smith is in fact engaged in epistemological inquiry, and specifically an inquiry into natural belief that employs a conceptual apparatus derived from his reading of Hume.[10]

In the first passage, Smith notoriously claims:

> the present inquiry is not concerning a matter of right, if I may say so, but concerning a matter of fact. We are not at present examining upon what principles a perfect being would approve of the punishment of bad actions; but upon what principles so weak and imperfect a creature as man actually and in fact approves of it.
>
> (TMS II.i.5.10 note)

This passage, as is well known, is almost universally taken as a profession of Smith's commitment in TMS to providing a value-neutral description of the phenomenology of morality as opposed to a normative inquiry into the nature of the good.[11] But however central the question of the normative vs. the descriptive is to TMS (and I believe it is central), this passage is the wrong place to look for insight. Smith's intention here is rather to provide an application of – and indeed an extension of – Hume's theory of natural belief. That Smith in fact has Hume's theory in mind here is signalled in several ways. First, Smith's claim that the present inquiry is a matter of fact is an echo of Hume's central statement on the nature of his inquiry into belief.[12] This similarity in their locutions suggests Smith's debt to Hume here, and what follows confirms it. In continuing, Smith restates two more of Hume's central claims on natural belief. First, the origin of our desire to see the unjust punished, he insists, is 'self-preservation, and the propagation of the species', here called 'the great ends which Nature seems to have proposed in the formation of all animals'. Second, Smith replicates Hume's account of how nature employs such a desire or belief to remedy reason's deficiencies. On the heels of noting the primacy of self-preservation and species-preservation, he thus explains that 'it has not been intrusted to the slow and uncertain determinations of our reason, to find out the proper means of bringing them about. Nature has directed us to the greater part of these by original and immediate instincts' – a repetition of his claim earlier in the paragraph that 'the Author of nature has not entrusted it to his reason' but to a form of 'immediate and instinctive approbation' (TMS II.i.5.10 note; cf. EHU 5.22; SBN 55).

On several fronts then, we find Smith here replicating Hume's theory of natural belief. But what in fact is the substantive natural belief in question? Here we find what I above called Smith's 'extension' of Hume's theory.[13] At TMS II.i.5.10 note, the category in question is the desire to see injustice punished. In what follows, Smith expands this to include a belief in the existence of a divinity that will punish injustice and reward justice in the afterlife. This of course goes well beyond anything Hume associated with natural belief.[14] Yet it is this belief – manifested in the fact that our violation of the rules of justice 'is naturally attended with the consciousness of deserving, and the dread of suffering punishment both from God and man' (TMS VII. iv.20) – that is the pre-eminent natural belief in Smith, one which he repeatedly invokes as a source of the commitment to justice necessary for the preservation and propagation of the species. In this way the 'wrath and anger of God' (TMS II.i.5.9 note) that forms the backdrop of TMS II.i.5.10 note, comes to take centre stage in our second passage, the revision in the 6th edition of the passage on Christ's Atonement. Here again it will be helpful to have the passage before us in full:

> For it well deserves to be taken notice of, that we are so far from imagining that injustice ought to be punished in this life, merely on account of the order of society, which cannot otherwise be maintained, that Nature teaches us to hope, and religion, we suppose, authorises us to expect, that it will be punished, even in a life to come. Our sense of its ill desert pursues it, if I may say so, even beyond the grave, though the example of its punishment there cannot serve to deter the rest of mankind, who see it not, who know it not, from being guilty of the like practices here. The justice of God, however, we think, still requires, that he should hereafter avenge the injuries of the widow and the fatherless, who are here so often insulted with impunity. In every religion, and in every superstition that the world has ever beheld, accordingly, there has been a Tartarus as well as an Elysium; a place provided for the punishment of the wicked, as well as one for the reward of the just.
>
> (TMS II.ii.3.12)

This is a second passage frequently invoked to bear more than it was intended to. As is again well known, this passage is almost universally regarded as Smith's reconsideration in the 6th edition of revealed religion and evidence of his displacement of Christianity for some sort of Stoicized natural religion.[15] Yet here again, the attempt to discover Smith's authentic views on scepticism and theism potentially misconstrues the passage's intent. To recover its intent we might do well to shift the emphasis from where it now lies. As it stands, interpretive emphasis tends to be on Smith's revised claim that 'we suppose' religion to second our beliefs (previous editions reading simply that 'religion authorises us to expect ... '), and his substitution for the claim about Christ with his remark on Elysium and Tartarus. But we'd do better to focus instead on the claims that do the real heavy lifting here, despite having been largely lost in the interpretive shuffle: that is, Smith's claims that 'nature teaches us to hope', and that 'every religion' insists on 'a place provided for the punishment of the wicked'.

On the first front, Smith's insistence that 'nature teaches us to hope' in the punishment of injustice in the afterlife is itself an explicit restatement and extension of Hume's theory of natural belief. The evidence for this lies in his argument earlier in TMS II.ii.3, for which TMS II.ii.3.12 is the conclusion. Here we again find Smith framing his discussion within Hume's horizons on two fronts. First, like Hume, Smith studiously avoids pronouncing on the truth of natural beliefs, and instead restricts his arguments to their origins and functions. Second, his argument replicates Hume's insistence on the necessity of natural beliefs for preservation, evident in the claims that society 'cannot subsist among those who are at all times ready to hurt and injure one another' and that 'the prevalence of injustice must utterly destroy' society (TMS II.ii.3.3), and lead it to 'crumble into atoms' (TMS II.ii.3.4). Smith's argument also replicates Hume's claim concerning the source of these beliefs: in order to enforce the observation of justice, 'Nature has implanted in the human breast that consciousness of ill-desert, those terrors of merited punishment which attend upon its violation, as the great safe-guards of the association of mankind, to protect the weak, to curb the violent, and to chastise the guilty' (TMS II.ii.3.4). These concerns are further reiterated in the notorious paragraph on final versus efficient causes that follows – another paragraph often parsed for evidence of Smith's theism or scepticism. But here again, Smith's concern is very different. Its first line makes clear that the question at issue is not the ultimate intelligibility of final causes, but the mechanisms designed 'for advancing the two great purposes of nature, the support of the individual, and the propagation of the species'. Accounting for these mechanisms, he goes on to suggest, requires not an investigation into metaphysical truth – that is, 'accounting for the operations of bodies' – but 'accounting for those of the mind'. Thus Smith signals that his aim, like Hume's, is to explain features of mind promoting species-preservation. In so doing he explicitly rejects the possibility that 'refined and enlightened reason' leads us to promote public well-being, suggesting instead that this is owed to 'natural principles' altogether different (TMS II.ii.3.5). He elaborates on these natural principles in what follows. Noting that 'society cannot subsist unless the laws of justice are tolerably observed', he examines several incorrect or incomplete accounts of such principles (TMS II.ii.3.6–8) in order to conclude in his own name that it is not 'consideration' that leads us to justice; after all, 'few men' reflect, but 'all men' hate 'fraud, perfidy, and injustice, and delight to see them punished' (TMS II.ii.3.9). The true 'natural principles' are thus non-rational and immediate. One of them is well known: the 'concern for that very individual who has been injured' (TMS II.ii.3.10) that leads Smith to ground justice in the sympathetic resentment felt by the spectator of innocent suffering (see, for example, TMS II.i.2.5 and TMS II.i.5.6 and esp. Haakonssen 1981: chs 5–6; and Pack and Schliesser 2006). But in these passages, he also lays out an alternative provenance, namely our natural, universal desire to 'call upon God to avenge, in another world, that crime which the injustice of mankind had neglected to chastise upon earth' (TMS II.ii.3.11).

With this in mind we might return to the Elysium and Tartarus sentence that replaced the original passage on Christ's Atonement. Two observations are commonly made about this new sentence: first, that the original material was 'omitted' from the 6th edition; and second, that the new sentence is 'dry' in comparison to the original.[16] Both claims are mistaken. First, far from dropping this material in the 6th edition, Smith redistributes it in the new passage on atonement (admittedly not Christ's) at TMS II.iii.3.4, and the new account of wisdom and virtue at TMS VI.iii.23–5, the latter focusing squarely on the main question of the 'dropped material': the proper stance of human imperfection before transcendent perfection.[17] Leaving these claims for a separate occasion, I want to focus now on the actual substituted passage. So far from tepid, Smith's claim concerning 'every religion' is better regarded as an invocation of the argument from universal consent which performs two distinct functions. First, Smith's claim that 'every religion' insists on belief in divine punishment of injustice is meant to serve as his empirical or socio-logical evidence for the universality of this natural belief, evidence which itself implicitly contests several central claims of Hume's *Natural History of Religion*. Second, by locating the most universal religious belief in the belief in divine punishment, Smith attests to its primacy as the proper core of religion.

This latter point deserves particular attention. Smith's complaints regard-ing the evils of religious zealotry and factionalism are well known. Much less understood or appreciated today is his understanding of 'the natural princi-ples of religion'; that is, religion in its uncorrupted state (TMS III.5.13). Smith's conception of natural belief in the punishment of injustice in the afterlife however affords an important window into his understanding of – to use Hume's phrase – 'true religion'. In particular, Smith goes to great lengths to emphasize the ineradicable nature of this belief, and indeed does so in an interestingly Humean manner. Hume is well known for having posited the problem of the 'sensible knave' who uses injustice to pursue his self-interest while free-riding on the justice of his neighbours. Hume's own response to this problem is that 'inward peace of mind, consciousness of integrity, a satisfactory review of our own conduct' will always be more highly valued by all 'ingenuous natures' than the material advantages that injustice affords (Hume 1998, EPM 9.22–3; SBN 283). But Smith uses his theory of natural belief to develop this claim into a considerably more pointed response. In his response to the knave, Smith insists that it is in fact the ineradicable persistence of our most fundamental natural belief that forms our best defence against the knave's injustice. For even if he should be successful in perpetrating his injustices, and even though 'he could be assured that no man was ever to know it, and could ever bring himself to believe that there was no God to revenge it, he would still feel enough [detestation and resentment of himself] to embitter the whole of his life' (TMS III.2.9). In this way Smith dramatically spells out the source of the threat to what Hume calls our 'inward peace of mind': namely the fear of divine retribution that leads us naturally 'to hope for his extraordinary favour and reward in the one case, and to dread his vengeance and punishment in the other' (TMS III.5.7).

I want now to turn to one final passage by way of conclusion, namely the passage on the psychological despair felt by the doubter who has come to entertain 'the very suspicion of a fatherless world' (TMS VI.ii.3.2). This is a powerful and rich paragraph, another example of one often parsed to justify one conclusion or another regarding Smith's scepticism or theism. But its claims, it would again seem, are limited to claims regarding the feeling of belief and disbelief. To bring these claims into the greatest possible relief, it may prove helpful to revisit Smith's most direct discussion of the operations of positive theistic belief, as found in TMS III.5. Here Smith's argument follows a now-familiar trajectory. It begins with his insistence on the magnitude of the duties of justice, as on them 'depends the very existence of human society, which would crumble into nothing if mankind were not generally impressed with a reverence for those important rules of conduct' (TMS III.5.2). Having again established the terms of debate as ones of survival or annihilation rather than truth or falsity, Smith then invokes Hume's claims for the source of natural beliefs that support these duties. The substantive belief he identifies as the belief 'that those important rules of morality are the commands and laws of the Deity, who will finally reward the obedient, and punish the transgressors of their duty'. Our 'reverence' for this belief, he then insists, is 'first impressed by nature, and afterwards confirmed by reasoning and philosophy' (TMS III.5.3). Again, even if the substance of this belief departs from Hume, his reason for its necessity is drawn directly from Hume: namely 'that the terrors of religion should thus enforce the natural sense of duty, was of too much importance to the happiness of mankind, for nature to leave it dependent upon the slowness and uncertainty of philosophical researches' (TMS III.5.4; cf. TMS III.2.7; TMS IV.2.7).

In what follows, Smith illustrates the practical benefits of this belief. In so doing, he also explains why the suspicion of a fatherless world feels so 'melancholy'. A fatherless world filled of mere matter in motion is unsettling not simply for its metaphysical implications. Rather, the fatherless world disturbs us because it lacks a means of gratifying our natural longing for justice. Thus Smith's key claim: when we

> despair of finding any force upon earth which can check the triumph of injustice, we naturally appeal to heaven, and hope, that the great Author of our nature will himself execute hereafter, what all the principles which he has given us for the direction of our conduct, prompt us to attempt even here; that he will complete the plan which he himself has thus taught us to begin; and will, in a life to come, render to every one according to the works which he has performed in this world.
>
> (TMS III.5.10)

Herein then lies the dual function of natural belief in divine punishment. First, fear of divine punishment shapes action in a politically salutary, justice-promoting way. In this sense, in keeping with a tradition extending from Plato to Rousseau, Smith demonstrates how the belief that 'we are always acting under the eye, and exposed to the punishment of God' serves as 'a motive capable of restraining the most headstrong passions' if rendered familiar and constant (TMS III.5.12). By rendering such belief natural, Smith shows how we might achieve Plato's ends without poetry and Rousseau's ends without compulsion.[18] Second, such belief gratifies longings central to our happiness but frequently disappointed on earth. In this sense, natural belief in a justice-loving God serves not merely as the ineradicable restraint on the sensible knave, but also as the ineradicable hope of the suffering just. Smith is well known for insisting that 'our happiness in this life' is

> upon many occasions, dependent upon the humble hope and expectation of a life to come: a hope and expectation deeply rooted in human nature; which can alone support its lofty ideas of its own dignity; can alone illuminate the dreary prospect of its continually approaching mortality, and maintain its cheerfulness under all the heaviest calamities to which, from the disorders of this life, it may sometimes be exposed.

False religion, that is, might send Calas to the rack, but natural religious belief 'can alone support' a good man in his suffering, and hence Smith's claim that 'the same great principle which can alone strike terror into triumphant vice, affords the only effectual consolation to disgraced and insulted innocence' (TMS III.2.33; TMS III.2.11–12). So strong indeed is the belief 'that there is a world to come, where exact justice will be done to every man', that even a doubter 'cannot possibly avoid wishing most earnestly and anxiously to believe it' (TMS III.2.33). Seen in this light, the melancholy of the fatherless world consists in its deprivation of the 'natural hopes and fears, and suspicions' that Smith insists are instrumental to the happiness of the just (TMS III.5.4).

The preceding has sought to offer a prolegomenon to a more sustained and more fully developed reconsideration of Smith's debts to Hume. Carrying it further – and specifically to an analysis of Smith's various studies of the nature and effects of the various 'deceptions' and 'illusions' and 'prejudices' and 'inventions' of the imagination – would, I think, be worthwhile (see TMS I.i.1.13, I.iii.2.2, III.2.5, IV.1.10; HA IV.52). For now, let me end by restating four advantages of the natural belief view as applied to Smith.

First, it illuminates a side of Smith's debts to Hume beyond debts to his scepticism and his views on imagination. In revealing his debts to Hume's naturalism it compels us to rethink which lessons he took from his ostensible surreptitious reading of the forbidden Hume at Balliol.

Second, it clarifies some of the most enigmatic passages in his corpus. In noting that their immediate point of reference is Hume's natural belief theory, it compels us to scale back certain of the more sweeping claims that have been made on their behalf.

Third, it calls attention to Smith's 'other' account of the origins of justice. Without denying the import of intersubjective sympathetic interaction, it calls attention to the alternative provenance of justice in natural belief in God's rewarding of justice and punishing of injustice.

Fourth, it offers a path through one of the thorniest thickets of Smith interpretation. Absolving us of having to pronounce on Smith's realism or anti-realism, theism or scepticism, it brings our interpretation in line with his identifiable aim of describing beliefs that are salutary and necessary, even if they cannot be legitimized rationally.

We might end by returning to the question with which we began. Is Smith a sceptic? No, not in any simple sense.[19] But if he's not a sceptic, what is he? The answer, I think, is that he's a sceptical realist.[20] Put slightly more polemically: not only is Smith not the 'old Hume', he may well stand closer to the 'new Hume' than Hume himself.

Acknowledgement

I am very grateful to the audience members at 'The Philosophy of Adam Smith' conference at Balliol College, Oxford, and at the Adam Smith Research Foundation's April 2009 meeting at the University of Glasgow, for their questions. I am particularly grateful to Eric Schliesser, Claudia Schmidt, Lauren Brubaker and Sam Fleischacker for their comments and suggestions on written versions of the essay.

Notes

1 In this vein see also the responses to Griswold in Fleischacker (2004: 21–2, 27), Schliesser (2005) and Hanley (2008: 225–9).

2 Raphael clearly has in mind religious scepticism if not epistemological scepticism proper, yet Smith scholarship, in its current state, tends to elide these. Important recent studies of Smith's conception of and debts to natural religion include Hill (2001), Waterman (2002) and Alvey (2004).

3 Smith's embrace of Hume's conception of the imagination's role in epistemological gap-filling and anxiety-soothing is now well appreciated. Compare Hume (2007) T 1.1.3;Hume (1978) SBN 8–10 and T 1.4.2.31–7; SBN 201–6 to Smith (1976) TMS I.i.1.2, V.1.2; and Smith (1980) HA II.7–8; and for development of these parallels, see esp. Skinner (1974), Raphael (1977: esp. 27–9, 34–7) and Griswold (2006: esp. 23, 26).

4 A helpful review of and response to the strong anti-realist reading is provided in Berry (2006: 121–4).

5 The closest to such an account that I've found in Smith scholarship are Haakonssen's claim that Smith holds 'a completely naturalistic theory of religious belief' in which religion is 'primarily a function and continuation of morality' (Haakonssen 1981: 75); and Broadie's claim that 'it is plain that Smith sees belief in a just God to be a *natural* phenomenon, and he is interested in the question of how such a belief stands in relation to the moral categories with which we operate' (Broadie 2006: 187). Both Haakonssen and Broadie however also explicitly insist on these same pages that Smithian morality does not require religion. Griswold uses the term 'natural belief' in a related but non-Humean context (Griswold 1999: 169).

6 My overview of this debate here is indebted to Read and Richman's (2007) opening essay (Richman 2007: esp. 6–8), in conjunction with supplemental suggestions made in Wright (2007) and Kail (2008: 442). The focus on the 'productive' and positive aspects of naturalism is helpfully developed in Broughton (2008: 425–6).

7 For major statements of the 'New Hume', see esp. the essays collected in Read and Richman (2007), as well as the major earlier statements of Kemp Smith (1941: esp. ch. 21), Wright (1983) and Strawson (1989).

8 A very helpful account of this distinction as drawn in the *Treatise* is provided in Morris (2006: 80–9).

9 On the first two beliefs, see Kemp Smith (1941: 455); on the third, see Tweyman (1986: 12). For challenges to the legitimacy of the fourth, see esp. Gaskin (1998: 120–31) and Kail (2007: 57, 71–2).

10 Put differently, I hope to illuminate the Humean commitments that explain why Smith, as Fleischacker rightly notes, 'neither affirms nor denies the ultimate truth of common-sense beliefs', but 'merely works within them' (Fleischacker 2004: 22). In a related vein, see Griswold's claim that Smith's aim is to 'enact scepticism' and by so doing move us beyond 'hopeless philosophical debates about ultimate metaphysical "realities"' and return us to the more promising inquiries available within the *theatrum mundi*' (Griswold 1999: 171–3). Particularly suggestive in this respect – and particularly relevant to the claims I wish to make here – is Berns' claim that 'for Smith the fact that we are induced by nature to hold certain beliefs is not in itself a warrant for the truth of those beliefs' (Berns 1994: 86 n.17).

11 The classic and most influential statements of this position are likely Cropsey (2001: 28) and Campbell (1971: 50–1). For a recent restatement, see, for example, Haakonssen and Winch (2006: 386). I argue for the reconsideration of the normative aspects of TMS as a whole at length in Hanley (2009: esp. ch. 2).

12 See T 1.4.2.38; SBN 206: 'We may begin by observing, that the difficulty in the present case is not concerning the matter of fact, or whether the mind forms such a conclusion concerning the continu'd existence of its perceptions, but only concerning the manner in which the conclusion is form'd, and principles from which is deriv'd.Both Smith and Hume thus explicitly restrict their 'present' discussions to the issue of where certain beliefs come from and how they work, specifically

separating their inquiries from questions of whether such beliefs might be true or good.

13 For an account of how Smith's conception of science may similarly be understood as an extension of Hume's views, see esp. Raphael (1977: 29). More relevant though to my present claim is Martin's helpful account of how Smith here is 'extending Hume's theory of natural judgments to the moral realm' (Martin 1990: 114).

14 Though cf. the crucial discussion of this point at EHU 11.28; SBN 147, to which Lauren Brubaker has helpfully called my attention. Yet Hume here emphasizes that such a belief, no matter how salutary, is a 'prejudice', which points in a different direction from Smith's discussions, which emphasize the utility of such a belief for both political stability and individual happiness.

15 The classic and most influential statements is likely Raphael and Macfie (1976: 19–20). For a recent restatement, see, for example, McLean (2007: 56–7).

16 See, for example, Raphael and Macfie (1976: 19), which references the introduction to Eckstein's edition as the source of their claim. Raphael also goes so far as to claim, with regard to the passages on 'the hope of divine justice in a life to come', that 'Smith writes with such eloquence about this article of faith that it must represent his own view' (Raphael 2007: 99).

17 I treat these passages at length in Hanley (2009: ch. 6).

18 Cf. *Republic* 618b–19b and *Social Contract* IV.8.33.

19 Griswold's attribution of non-dogmatic scepticism to Smith is an important step in the right direction, especially as its qualifying adjective emphasizes Smith's recognition that 'we act as though commonsense moral realism were valid' (Griswold 1999: 165). This clearly dovetails, in a crucial sense, with the view that I mean to attribute to Smith. Where we differ is that Griswold tends to emphasize that our beliefs, while hardly arbitrary, are yet the products of the poetic imagination and hence distinctively human artefacts subject to considerable malleability, whereas I want to emphasize Smith's (and Hume's) claims that our fundamental beliefs, no matter how unverifiable, are bequeathed to us by nature, and hence decidedly less subject to our casual revision. On Griswold's view of the imagination, see especially Griswold (1999: 340); cf. Hanley (2008).

20 I'm deeply grateful to Nicholas Phillipson for putting this question to me in this form and thereby initiating the year of reflection and study that culminated in the present essay. My response to his question should however be set next to Schliesser's persuasive argument that Smith's position in 'The History of Astronomy' 'is not so much sceptical realist but moderate realist' with regard to 'the theory-independent existence of bodies in the heavens' (Schliesser 2005: 727; see also esp. 725–6). I suspect the two claims are compatible given the great difference, in Smith's estimation, between the nature of inquiry in moral philosophy and the nature of inquiry in natural philosophy.

Bibliography

Alvey, J. (2004) 'The secret, natural theological foundation of Adam Smith's work', *Journal of Markets and Morality*, 7: 335–61.

Berns, L. (1994) 'Aristotle and Adam Smith on justice: cooperation between ancients and moderns?', *Review of Metaphysics*, 48: 71–90.

Berry, C. (2006) 'Smith and science', in K. Haakonssen (ed.), *The Cambridge Companion to Adam Smith*, Cambridge: Cambridge University Press.

Broadie, A. (2006) 'Sympathy and the impartial spectator', in K. Haakonssen (ed.), *The Cambridge Companion to Adam Smith*, Cambridge: Cambridge University Press.

Broughton, J. (2008) 'Hume's naturalism and his scepticism', in E. Radcliffe (ed.), *A Companion to Hume*, London: Blackwell.

Campbell, T.D. (1971) *Adam Smith's Science of Morals*, London: George Allen and Unwin.

Cropsey, J. (2001 [1957]) *Polity and Economy; with Further Thoughts on the Principles of Adam Smith*, South Bend, IN: St. Augustine's Press.

Fleischacker, S. (2004) *On Adam Smith's* Wealth of Nations*: A Philosophical Companion*, Princeton, NJ: Princeton University Press.

Gaskin, J.C.A. (1988) *Hume's Philosophy of Religion*, 2nd edn (1st edn 1978) London: Macmillan.

Griswold, C.L. (1999) *Adam Smith and the Virtues of Enlightenment*, Cambridge: Cambridge University Press.

—— (2006) 'Imagination: morals, science, and arts', in K. Haakonssen (ed.), *The Cambridge Companion to Adam Smith*, Cambridge: Cambridge University Press.

Haakonssen, K. (1981) *The Science of a Legislator: The Natural Jurisprudence of David Hume and Adam Smith*, Cambridge: Cambridge University Press.

Haakonssen, K. and Winch, D. (2006) 'The legacy of Adam Smith', in K. Haakonssen (ed.), *The Cambridge Companion to Adam Smith*, Cambridge: Cambridge University Press.

Hanley, R.P. (2008) 'Language, literature and imagination', *The Adam Smith Review*, 4: 221–30, V. Brown (ed.), London and New York: Routledge.

—— (2009) *Adam Smith and the Character of Virtue*, Cambridge: Cambridge University Press.

Hill, L. (2001) 'The hidden theology of Adam Smith', *European Journal of the History of Economic Thought*, 8: 1–29.

Hume, D. (1978 [1777]) *Enquiries concerning Human Understanding and concerning the Principles of Morals*, L.A. Selby-Bigge (intro.) and P.H. Nidditch (rev'd), Oxford: Clarendon Press.

—— (1998 [1751]) *An Enquiry concerning the Principles of Morals*, T.L. Beauchamp (ed.), Oxford: Clarendon Press.

—— (2000 [1748])*An Enquiry concerning Human Understanding*, T.L. Beauchamp (ed.), Oxford: Clarendon Press.

—— (2007 [1739–40]) *A Treatise of Human Nature*, D.F. Norton and M.J. Norton (eds), Oxford: Clarendon Press.

Kail, P.J.E. (2007) *Projection and Realism in Hume's Philosophy*, Oxford: Oxford University Press.

—— (2008) 'Is Hume a realist or an anti-realist?', in E. Radcliffe (ed.), *A Companion to Hume*, London: Blackwell.

McLean, I. (2007 [2006]) *Adam Smith, Radical and Egalitarian: An Interpretation for the Twenty-First Century*, New York: Palgrave Macmillan.

Martin, M. (1990) 'Utility and morality: Adam Smith's critique of Hume', *Hume Studies*, 16: 107–20.

Morris, W.E. (2006) 'Belief, probability, normativity', in S. Traiger (ed.), *The Blackwell Guide to Hume's* Treatise, London: Blackwell.

Pack, S.J. and Schliesser, E. (2006) 'Smith's Humean criticism of Hume's account of the origin of justice', *Journal of the History of Philosophy*, 44: 47–63.

Raphael, D.D. (1977) ' "The true old Humean philosophy" and its influence on Adam Smith', in G.P. Morice (ed.), *David Hume: Bicentenary Papers*, Edinburgh: Edinburgh University Press.

—— (2007) *The Impartial Spectator: Adam Smith's Moral Philosophy*, Oxford: Oxford University Press.

Raphael, D.D. and Macfie, A.L. (1976) Introduction to A. Smith, *The Theory of Moral Sentiments*, Oxford: Clarendon Press.

Read, R. and Richman, K. (eds) (2007 [2000]) *The New Hume Debate*, London: Routledge.

Richman, K. (2007) 'Introduction', in R. Read and K. Richman (eds), *The New Hume Debate*, 2nd edn, London: Routledge.

Schliesser, E. (2005) 'Wonder in the face of scientific revolutions: Adam Smith on Newton's "proof" of Copernicanism', *British Journal for the History of Philosophy*, 13: 697–732.

Skinner, A.S. (1974) 'Adam Smith: science and the role of the imagination', in W.B. Todd (ed.), *Hume and the Enlightenment: Essays Presented to Ernest Campbell Mossner*, Edinburgh: Edinburgh University Press.

Smith, A. (1976) *The Theory of Moral Sentiments*, D.D. Raphael and A.L. Macfie (eds), Oxford: Clarendon Press.

—— (1980) 'The History of Astronomy', in W.P.D. Wightman (ed.), *Essays on Philosophical Subjects*, Oxford: Clarendon Press.

Smith, N.K. (1941) *The Philosophy of David Hume*, London: Macmillan.

Strawson, G. (1989) *The Secret Connexion: Causation, Realism, and David Hume*, Oxford: Oxford University Press.

Tweyman, S. (1986) *Scepticism and Belief in Hume's* Dialogues Concerning Natural Religion, The Hague: Martinus Nijhoff.

Waterman, A.M.C. (2002) 'Economics as theology: Adam Smith's *Wealth of Nations*', *Southern Economic Journal*, 68: 907–21.

Wright, J. (1983) *The Sceptical Realism of David Hume*, Minneapolis, MN: University of Minnesota Press.

—— (2007) 'Kemp Smith and the two kinds of naturalism in Hume's philosophy', in *New Essays on David Hume*, E. Mazza and E. Ronchetti (eds), Milan: Franco Angeli.

Adam Smith's solution to the paradox of tragedy

Arby Ted Siraki

I

Tragedy is a subject that has occupied the thoughts of many theorists since antiquity. Of special interest is the so-called 'paradox of tragedy' – the problem of why spectators derive pleasure from viewing distressing scenes – which became of central importance during the second half of the eighteenth century. Unlike many of his philosophically inclined contemporaries, Adam Smith never wrote an essay on tragedy. Dramatic theory and the theatre in general were, however, never far from his thoughts. In his biographical memoir of Smith, Dugald Stewart mentions that Smith was especially interested in 'the history of the theatre, both in ancient and modern times', and that drama and the theatre 'were a favourite topic of his conversation, and were intimately connected with his general principles of criticism' (Stewart 1980, 'Account' III.15). Furthermore, Stewart suggests that these topics were to be included in Smith's completed essay on the imitative arts. *The Theory of Moral Sentiments* also brims with allusions to the theatre and tragic drama.

In his later years, Smith wrote of a work he had 'upon the anvil', a 'sort of Philosophical History of all the different branches of Literature, of Philosophy, Poetry and Eloquence', which was never realized (Smith 1987, *Corr.* Letter 248 to Duc de la Rochefoucauld, 1 Nov. 1785). Unfortunately for posterity, on his deathbed Smith ordered no fewer than sixteen folio volumes of manuscripts to be destroyed, a request faithfully carried out by his literary executors, Hutton and Black, and it is impossible to say precisely what was burnt (Campbell and Skinner 1982: 223). Fortunately, in 1795, five years after Smith's death, *Essays on Philosophical Subjects* appeared, a collection of Smith's essays on various subjects, of which he apparently thought highly enough to preserve them. In addition, we now possess student lecture notes that were posthumously collected and published as *Lectures on Jurisprudence* and *Lectures on Rhetoric and Belles Lettres*. These essays, along with the two major works published in his lifetime, reveal Smith's comprehensive interdisciplinary interests. The pieces in *Essays on Philosophical Subjects* further demonstrate Smith's interest in aesthetics, a subject he also refers to in his two major works. In fact, some commentators have argued that for Smith,

The Philosophy of Adam Smith, The Adam Smith Review, 5: 213–230 © 2010 The International Adam Smith Society, ISSN 1743–5285, ISBN 978-0-415-56256-0.

virtually all human endeavour has an aesthetic impulse: the impetus to obtain trinkets, to engage in scientific and philosophical speculation, and to sympathize are all fundamentally aesthetic in nature.[1]

Given Smith's interest in drama and aesthetics, it does seem odd that he did not contribute at all to the mid-eighteenth-century debate on tragic pleasure. Scholars have pondered the absence of a Smithian tragic theory. J.C. Bryce asks, 'why does not Smith of all critics tackle the problem of the pleasure afforded by tragedy?' (Bryce 1983: 20). Gloria Vivenza similarly observes that '[n]owhere, if I am not mistaken, does Smith ... adequately treat the problem of the enjoyment afforded by tragedy' (Vivenza 2001: 164). This is all the more strange since Smith's close friend, David Hume, contributed a famous solution to the problem, and the period during which Smith flourished was a particularly fecund one for the subject. Perhaps Smith's projected, yet unrealized, 'Philosophical History' would have dealt with the problem. Regardless of the reason, we have no explicit statement from Smith on tragedy, apart from a few *obiter dicta*.

Despite this, I argue that we do have Smith's theory of tragedy, including his solution to the paradox of tragedy.[2] We need but to draw it out from *The Theory of Moral Sentiments* (TMS).[3] The central concept in TMS is 'sympathy', which is also Smith's solution to the paradox of tragedy. More specifically, it is the pleasure of mutual sympathy stressed in Smith's formulation that overcomes the negative emotions occasioned by distressing scenes. Smith differs from noteworthy eighteenth-century solutions by rejecting explanations based on self-interest and artifice or the consciousness of fiction. Smith dissolves the distinction between art and reality: his theory is hence better equipped to explain more immediate 'tragedies', such as executions; it also derives some of its pleasure from a recognition of moral beauty, which occurs during the ideal sympathetic exchange. This essay will trace the line of thought on the paradox of tragedy beginning with Hobbes, then describe Smith's own theory and situate it in the then ongoing debate, comparing and contrasting it to those popular in the eighteenth century, namely, those of Addison, Hume and Burke.

II

Though Thomas Hobbes did not directly theorize on tragedy, his views had long been influential among those who did.[4] Hobbes popularized the Lucretian 'return upon ourselves', that is, the pleasure inherent in the spectator's consciousness of immunity from perceived danger.[5] Lucretius opens the second book of his *The Nature of the Universe* (*De Rerum Natura*) thus:

> What joy it is, when out at sea the stormwinds are lashing the waters, to gaze from the shore at the heavy stress some other man is enduring! Not that anyone's afflictions are in themselves a source of delight; but to realize from what troubles you yourself are free is a joy indeed.
>
> (Lucretius 1951, II.1–5: 60)

Granted, Lucretius was not writing on tragedy, but this provided the source for one strain of thought on the subject of the paradox of tragedy since the Renaissance. In a passage in his *Human Nature*, Hobbes uses the same example as Lucretius:

> from what passion proceedeth it, that men take *pleasure* to *behold* from the shore the *danger* of them that are at sea in a tempest, or in fight, or from a safe castle to behold two armies charge one another in the field? It is certainly, in the whole sum, *joy*; else men would never flock to such a spectacle. Nevertheless there is in it both *joy* and *grief*: for as there is novelty and remembrance of our own security present, which is *delight*; so there is also *pity*, which is grief; but the delight is so far predominant, that men usually are content in such a case to be spectators of the misery of their friends.
>
> (Hobbes 1966, IX.19: 51–2)

Hobbes thus emphasizes the 'remembrance of our own security' as the delightful factor that overpowers the painful emotions. As one modern commentator has succinctly put it, Hobbes's solution is 'of the thank-God-it's-not me sort' (Feagin 1998: 449).

Joseph Addison was the first British eighteenth-century theorist of note to attempt an explanation of the pleasure derived from tragedy, and in many ways he follows the Hobbesian solution. Addison devoted several papers of *The Spectator* to tragedy in general,[6] but his solution to the paradox of tragedy occurs in his ninth paper in the series, 'The Pleasures of the Imagination'. Addison begins by asking why 'such passions as are very unpleasant at all other times, are very agreeable when excited by proper descriptions'. He argues that the spectator's pleasure does

> not arise so properly from the description of what is terrible, as from the reflection we make on our selves at the time of reading it. When we look on such hideous objects, we are not a little pleased to think we are in no danger of them. ... [O]ur pleasure does not flow so properly from the grief which such melancholy descriptions give us, as from the secret comparison which we make between our selves and the person who suffers. Such representations teach us to set a just value upon our own condition, and make us prize our good fortune which exempts us from the like calamities.
>
> (Addison 1982, No. 418: 393; spelling modernised)[7]

Like Hobbes, Addison emphasizes the spectator's security and 'secret comparison' between his own situation and that of the sufferer. However, he argues that distance is necessary for this reflection and its concomitant pleasure to occur; the reflection would be impossible if the scene in question were too close to us in time or space. Pleasure would be impossible in this case because

> the object presses too close upon our senses, and bears so hard upon us, that it does not gives us time or leisure to reflect on our selves. Our thoughts

are so intent upon the miseries of the sufferer, that we cannot turn them upon our own happiness.

(Addison 1982; No. 418: 394; spelling modernised)

What is important for Addison is the assumption that spectators (or readers) are conscious that what they are witnessing is a feigned representation. Thus, Addison tempers the Lucretian/Hobbesian emphasis on the self by arguing for the Aristotelian notion of the inherent pleasure of imitation: regardless of the object imitated, 'any thing that is disagreeable when looked upon, pleases us in apt description' (No. 418: 392).

David Hume offered his solution to the paradox of tragedy in his essay 'Of Tragedy', which was published along with other essays in 1757. Hume's solution to the paradox was relatively simple: it is the eloquence or artistry of the drama that converts the unpleasant emotions into pleasant ones. Hume writes:

> The genius required to paint objects in a lively manner, the art employed in collecting all the pathetic circumstances, the judgment displayed in disposing them: the exercise, I say, of these noble talents, together with the force of expression, and beauty of oratorial numbers, diffuse the highest satisfaction on the audience, and excite the most delightful movements. By this means, the uneasiness of the melancholy passions is not only overpowered and effaced by something stronger of an opposite kind; but the whole impulse of those passions is converted into pleasure ... The passion, though, perhaps, naturally, and when excited by the simple appearance of a real object, it may be painful; yet is so smoothed, and softened, and mollified, when raised by the finer arts, that it affords the highest entertainment.
>
> (Hume 1987: 219–20, 223)[8]

Hume offers two exceptions to the view expressed in this passage. First, like Addison, he argues that the 'passion' cannot be converted if the spectator be 'too deeply concerned in the events'. He offers the example of Lord Clarendon, a royalist, who 'hurries over the king's [Charles I's] death, without giving us one circumstance of it' for this very reason (223).[9] The other is Nicholas Rowe's drama *The Ambitious Stepmother*, a play that is 'too bloody and atrocious', which excites 'horror as will not soften into pleasure' (224).[10] Though he does not explicitly argue for the requisite consciousness of fiction, as Addison does, Hume's emphasis on eloquence (or art) presupposes fictional or at least mediated representations.

Edmund Burke's *Philosophical Enquiry into the Origin of Our Ideas of the Sublime and Beautiful* appeared in the same year as Hume's essay. A comprehensive treatise on aesthetics, it nonetheless discusses tragic pleasure briefly. Burke begins by noting that we are never 'indifferent spectators' and that it is chiefly through sympathy that 'poetry, painting, and the other affecting arts, transfuse their passions from one breast to another, and are often capable of grafting a delight on wretchedness, misery, and death itself'. Burke takes issue with those theories which attribute the pleasure either to relief that the 'story is no more than a fiction' or to the consciousness 'of our own freedom from the evils which we see represented'. Burke disagrees because such theorists mistakenly attribute such pleasure to 'the reasoning faculty' when in fact the pleasure arises 'from the mechanical structure of our bodies, or from the natural frame and constitution of our minds' (Burke 1998, I.xiii: 91).

Unlike Addison and Hume, Burke maintains 'the comparative weakness of the imitative arts', and contends that 'we shall be much mistaken if we attribute any considerable part of our satisfaction in a tragedy to a consideration that tragedy is a deceit'. In fact, Burke unequivocally states that the nearer a tragedy 'approaches reality, the more perfect is its power'. Thus, not only does Burke blur the distinction between art and the reality, he privileges the latter. In fact, in a bold passage Burke claims that the announcement of an execution during 'the most sublime and affecting tragedy' would empty the theatre, an idea with which neither Addison nor Hume could agree (I.xv: 93).

Burke argues that 'we have a degree of delight, and that no small one, in the real misfortunes and pains of others' (I.xiv: 92). He goes further still by suggesting that 'there is no spectacle we so eagerly pursue, as that of some uncommon and grievous calamity; so that whether the misfortune is before our eyes, or whether they are turned back to it in history, it always touches with delight' (I.xv: 93). Though it seems as if Burke is endorsing the Hobbesian/Lucretian view, this is not the case: Burke believes in the benevolent nature of this attraction since it is grounded in providence, and it compels us never to be indifferent:[11]

> [A]s our Creator has designed that we should be united by the bond of sympathy, he has strengthened that bond by a proportionable delight; and there most where our sympathy is most wanted, in the distresses of others. If this passion was simply painful, we would shun with the greatest care all persons and places that could excite such a passion.
>
> (Burke 1998, I.xiv: 92–3)

Thus Burke's solution is more 'benevolent' than those of Hobbes and Addison, and it dismisses the role of art and the consciousness of fiction in the pleasure of tragedy.

III

Solutions to the paradox of tragedy predicated on self-love were moribund by the second or third decade of the eighteenth century, to be replaced by more 'sympathetic' and benevolent theories, of which Burke's is one (Wasserman 1947: 297). Smith's theory follows this 'benevolent' trend of thinking on the subject. Unsurprisingly perhaps, Smith's solution to the paradox of tragic pleasure is sympathy, not the (in)famous Lucretian 'return upon ourselves'. Smith begins TMS by explaining the principle of sympathy, which is common to everyone. Like Burke in his *Philosophical Enquiry*, Smith in *The Theory of Moral Sentiments* takes as a given that all people, even the most selfish, are possessed of principles 'which interest [them] in the fortune of others' (Smith 1976, TMS I.i.1.1). We thus have a natural capacity for sympathy, which Smith uses in the broader sense of 'our fellow-feeling with any passion whatever' (TMS I.i.1.5). However, because of the epistemological gap that exists between human beings, we can never 'know' what another person feels: it is 'by the imagination only that we can form any conception' of what are the sensations of, say, 'our brother upon the rack' (I.i.1.2). Thus, this sympathy occurs in the imagination as opposed to the body. Further, a spectator's sympathy arises from the facts, not the emotions displayed: '[s]ympathy, therefore, does not arise so much from the view of the passions, as from that of the situation which excites it'. Thus, spectators are capable of 'sympathizing' with the dead and mentally challenged, and feeling sentiments of which those 'sufferers' are incapable (I.i.1.10).

Though Smith uses the term sympathy in a broad sense, he expatiates on manifestations of distress and grief more than anything else: we are 'more anxious to communicate to our friends our disagreeable than our agreeable passions ... we derive still more satisfaction from their sympathy with the former than from that with the latter' (TMS I.i.2.3). This is because, according to Smith, sympathy is the only balm for one who is afflicted with grief or any other unpleasant emotion: 'the sweetness of his [the spectator's] sympathy more than compensates the bitterness of that sorrow ... The bitter and painful emotions of grief and resentment more strongly require the healing consolation of sympathy' (I.i.2.4–5). According to Smith, 'nothing pleases us more than to observe in other men a fellow-feeling with all the emotions of our own breast ... [The] correspondence of the sentiments of others with our own appears to be a cause of pleasure' (I.i.2.1–2). Because of the gap that exists between human beings, this sympathy can never be ideal; complete unison between the sentiments of the spectator and those of the sufferer can never be achieved (I.i.4.7). Though unison of sentiments is impossible, however, the sufferer longs for the closest possible 'concord' (Smith's word) of sentiments, and for this reason attempts to 'flatten' his passions so that a spectator may enter into them (I.i.4.7–8).

In TMS, Smith comes very close to saying that our experiences of real-life distress and tragedy are the same, or at least very similar. As Charles Griswold observes, '[f]rom the beginning, Smith compares human life to spectacles represented in plays' (Griswold 1999: 65). Indeed, very early on in his description of sympathy, Smith implicitly conflates the two spheres

> Whatever is the passion which arises from any object in the person principally concerned, an analogous emotion springs up, at the thought

of his situation, in the breast of every attentive spectator. Our joy for the deliverance of those heroes of tragedy or romance who interest us, is as sincere as our grief for their distress.

(TMS I.i.1.4)

Similarly, Smith says later that '[o]ur sympathy … with deep distress, is very strong and very sincere. It is unnecessary to give an instance. We weep even at the feigned representation of a tragedy' (I.ii.5.4). In an energetic passage that articulates his anti-exhibitionist (or 'Stoical') preference, Smith writes:

> We are disgusted with that clamorous grief, which, without any delicacy, calls upon our compassion with sighs and tears and importunate lamentations. But we reverence that reserved, that silent and majestic sorrow, which discovers itself only in the swelling of eyes, in the quivering of the lips and cheeks … . It imposes the like silence upon us.
>
> (TMS I.i.5.3)

This passage resembles something one would expect to find in a treatise on tragedy. Not only does Smith cite more literary texts than philosophical ones in TMS (with the exception of Part VII), but he frequently clarifies his moral theory using illustrations from tragedies, even when sympathy is not discussed (see TMS I.ii.1.7–11, I.ii.2.3–4, I.ii.3.2, I.iii.1.9, I.iii.2.2, II.iii.3.5, III.6.12, VI.ii.1.21–2).

Although Smith does not use the term 'tragedy' to describe real-life situations, he attenuates or dissolves the distinction between real and feigned spectacles, and stresses the pleasure of mutual sympathy. Thus, for Smith, the consciousness of fiction[12] and imitation do not account for the pleasure of tragedy, or are at most irrelevant since this pleasure occurs in real life. Smith is compelled to repudiate categorically theories of pleasure centering on the self, and tries several times to demonstrate that sympathy, which, as some would argue, itself may be pleasurable owing to considerations of self-love, is in fact completely selfless.[13] Smith cannot agree with the argument of self-love advanced by Lucretius, Hobbes and Addison:

> We run not only to congratulate the successful, but to condole with the afflicted … The plaintive voice of misery, when heard at a distance, will not allow us to be indifferent about the person from whom it comes. As soon as it strikes our ear, it interests us in his fortune, and, if continued, forces us almost involuntarily to fly to his assistance.
>
> (TMS I.i.2.6, I.ii.3.5)

Like Burke, Smith argues that human beings are never indifferent, but are instinctively compelled to be interested in the distresses of others and to attempt to relieve them using the only means available: sympathy.

Smith's dialogue with Hume is very fruitful, and clarifies Smith's position on the subject of tragic pleasure. Not only were they friends in regular communication with each other, but Hume made no secret of his objection to Smith's 'answer'. In a letter to Smith, Hume wrote:

> I wish you had more particularly and fully proved, that all kinds of sympathy are necessarily agreeable. This is the hinge of your system, and yet you only mention [it once] ... Now it would appear that there is a disagreeable sympathy, as well as an agreeable ... It is always thought a difficult problem to account for the pleasure, received from the tears and grief and sympathy of tragedy; which would not be the case, if all sympathy was agreeable. An hospital would be a more entertaining place than a ball. I am afraid ... this proposition has escaped you, or rather is interwove with your reasonings in that place.
>
> (*Corr.* Letter 36, 28 July 1759; spelling modernised)

It is worth noting Hume's invocation of the paradox of tragedy, which could not have been far from Smith's mind in this context. In addition, though Smith never mentions Hume's essay on tragedy in his works or correspondence, he almost certainly had read it.[14] Smith responded to Hume in his footnote to the second edition of TMS:

> It has been objected to me that as I found the sentiment of approbation, which is always agreeable, upon sympathy, it is inconsistent with my system to admit any disagreeable sympathy. I answer, that in the sentiment of approbation there are two things to be taken notice of; first, the sympathetic passion of the spectator; and, secondly, the emotion which arises from his observing the perfect coincidence between this sympathetic passion in himself, and the original passion in the person principally concerned. This last emotion, in which the sentiment of approbation properly consists, is always agreeable and delightful. The other may either be agreeable or disagreeable... .
>
> (TMS I.iii.1.9, n.)

Smith devotes the second chapter of Part I ('The Pleasure of Mutual Sympathy') to this concept, but Hume is correct to point out that the idea is implied rather than vigorously stated. Smith's footnote thus clarifies and elaborates what was already there.[15] This footnote in response to the objection of a friend is itself the 'hinge' on which Smith's solution to the paradox of tragedy lies. Thus, regardless of what one is witnessing, the concord of sympathy is *always* agreeable; disagreeable sympathy is an impossibility for Smith. In the same letter, Hume suggested that Smith respond to the objection only if it 'appear[ed] to be of any weight' (*Corr.* Letter 36). Smith clearly thought the addition was warranted.

Hume's solution to the paradox of tragedy, which, as we have seen, hinges on eloquence, assumes that one is witnessing an artificial representation.

As Alex Neill suggests, Hume's essay fails to take into account 'third-rate' tragedies (Neill 1999: 119). In other words, Hume's formula cannot account for plays that are not well-written, nor can it account for 'immediate' tragedies, that is, non-fictional tragic representations that are closer to the spectator in time and/or space, such as recent war narratives or documentary tragedies.[16] For Hume, eloquence is the catalyst that converts or, to use his own word, 'overpowers' the negative emotions and renders them pleasurable. For Smith, by contrast, art or linguistic considerations do not play a part: the concord of sympathy is what 'overpowers' the unpleasant emotions. The pleasure of mutual sympathy can occur in real life or in a feigned tragedy: Smith's formulation is better equipped to explain the pleasure derived from real-life situations as well as forms that attenuate the distinction between the real and non-real, namely, traumatic narratives which are closer to the spectators in time and/or space.

As Smith dissolves the distinction between art and reality, or distance and immediacy, there are no exceptions to the pleasure that sympathy can afford. Addison claimed that the 'secret comparison' spectators make is precluded when a scene is immediately before them, and, as noted earlier, Hume also argued that the painful passions cannot be converted into pleasure if the spectator be 'too deeply concerned in the events'. For Smith, however, we can feel a pleasurable sympathy in practically any circumstance. Many of Smith's examples demonstrating sympathy press very closely, including a brother on the rack (TMS I.i.1.1), and a man whose leg had just been blown off by a cannon shot (TMS III.3.26). Whatever the spectator's feelings about the horror of these situations themselves, for Smith, he or she can derive a certain pleasure from observing that the manifested emotions of the sufferers in those situations are apt: the concord of feelings between sufferer and spectator remains pleasurable even here – affords, indeed, 'almost the only agreeable sensation' that the sufferer is 'capable of receiving' in such circumstances (TMS I.i.2.2). Like Burke, Smith says that we can feel sympathetic pleasure even at a public execution (TMS I.iii.2.10), something that Addison's and Hume's solutions preclude.[17]

It is important to stress that the imagination is central to sympathy in representations *and* real life: for Smith, real life is judged as a tragedy and tragedies as real life. However, at times it appears that Smith distinguishes between real life and tragedies. Smith argues '[t]he loss of a leg may generally be regarded as a more real calamity than the loss of a mistress. It would be a ridiculous tragedy, however, of which the catastrophe was to turn upon a loss of that kind. A misfortune of the other kind, how frivolous soever it may appear to be, has given occasion to many a fine one' and '[w]hat a tragedy would that be of which the distress consisted in a colic! Yet no pain is more exquisite' (TMS I.ii.1.7, I.ii.1.11). However, Smith makes this distinction only to emphasize his claim that spectators cannot sympathize with bodily distress, whether in real life or a tragedy: 'And this is the case of all the passions which take their origin from the body: they excite either no sympathy at all, or such a degree of it, as is altogether disproportioned to the violence of what is felt by the sufferer' (TMS I.ii.1.5). A person who lost a leg in front of our eyes would not elicit sympathy, unless that person demonstrated a Stoic fortitude that we could admire (TMS I.ii.1.12). Smith illustrates this by using the example of hunger: spectators cannot sympathize with the hunger felt by the people they read about in the journal of a sea voyage; since they 'do not grow hungry by reading the description, [they] cannot properly, even in this case, be said to sympathize with their hunger' (TMS I.ii.1.1). However, spectators 'can sympathize with the distress which excessive hunger occasions ... [and] readily conceive the grief, the fear and consternation' (TMS I.ii.1.1). In other words, spectators can sympathize with the distresses or feelings that 'take their origin from the imagination' (TMS I.ii.1.6). In the same way, a spectator may sympathize with the fears or fortitude of one who is about to be executed, but not that person's potential physical distress (TMS I.iii.2.10).

The possible aesthetic relation between *The Theory of Moral Sentiments* and Burke's *Philosophical Enquiry* has not been explored in any detail.[18] J.T. Boulton,[19] Earl Wasserman[20] and Walter John Hipple[21] all briefly mention Smith *vis-à-vis* Burke. However, none of these critics, nor anyone since, has gone beyond merely mentioning a possible connection. Burke not only received a gift of TMS from Hume soon after its publication, but he later expressed his thanks for the gift and for the privilege of Smith's acquaintance (*Corr.* Letter 38, 10 Sept. 1759). In addition, in 1759 in the *Annual Register* a fulsome review of Smith's work appeared that has been unanimously attributed to Burke. Burke praises Smith's system as 'one of the most beautiful fabrics of moral theory, that has perhaps ever appeared' (Burke 2000 [1759]: 77–8). Unfortunately, neither Burke's letter nor his review makes any connection to his or any other aesthetics. What is significant, however, is the conclusion of Burke's review: it reproduces the whole first chapter of TMS, 'Of Sympathy', so that readers may observe 'the basis of [Smith's] theory' (Burke 2000 [1759]: 78). This makes perfect sense since Burke introduces the term 'sympathy' in his very brief exposition on tragedy in his *Philosophical Enquiry*. Whereas Burke had spent perhaps two pages on the subject in his discussion of tragedy without going into any detail as to the mechanism of sympathy, Smith expatiates on this concept, which ends up correcting and illuminating Burke's exposition.

Though Hume's solution to the problem was very different from Smith's, Burke's treatment appears at first glance to be very similar. Hipple groups Burke and Smith together, given their insistence on 'instinctive delight'. This 'instinctive delight' was advocated by Burke and others, but to characterize Smith thus is a little inaccurate since his formulation of sympathy is far more complex. Burke's solution, grounded as it is in sympathy, is very mechanistic: his entire book, in fact, is partly a reaction against Lockeans and rationalists, that is, those who believed that there are no innate ideas and that human beings are ruled by reason and are in conscious control of themselves.

It is unclear whether Smith had Burke's aesthetics in mind while he was writing TMS, although that seems likely.[22] Smith's solution to the paradox of tragedy, like Burke's, is the pleasure of sympathy, but his construction of the concept is far more elaborate and less mechanistic.

Smith differed from his predecessors by insisting that sympathy, even in our narrower sense of compassion, is not an automatic, 'knee-jerk' reaction. The Abbé Du Bos, for instance, who was well-known and appreciated in Britain, wrote:

> Les larmes d'un inconnu nous émeuvent même avant que nous sachions le sujet qui le fait pleurer. Les cris d'un homme qui ne tient à nous que par l'humanité, nous font voler à son secours par un mouvement machinal qui précède toute délibération.
>
> (Du Bos, *Réflexions Critiques sur la Poésie et sur la Peinture*, 1719, I.39, cited in Marshall 1986: 169)[23]

These theorists argued that, in Smith's words, sentiments are 'transfused from one man to another, instantaneously, and antecedent to any knowledge of what excited them in the person principally concerned' (TMS I.i.1.6). Conversely, Smith's moral theory is less 'instantaneous' and takes into account the mediating function of the imagination. Sympathy is only possible through an act of the imagination since it is only thus that we can come close to bridging the epistemological gap that exists between human beings.

Smith's emphasis on 'imagination', however, should not obscure the rational component of his construction: Smith's requisite act of the imagination entails a process of determining whether the sentiments on display seem fit for their object. As mentioned earlier, Smith's sympathy requires a knowledge of facts and context to reach such a decision, which is more important than any manifestations of emotion. It is for this reason that sympathy, in Smith's sense, is very broad, in a way Smith himself recognized: a spectator is capable of sympathizing with someone's grief, for instance, even if the sufferer does not really feel any (recall the possibility of sympathizing with the dead). Thus, Smith's construction of sympathy is more deliberate, conscious and mediated than Burke's: it requires an act of judgment and distance.

Unlike Burke, Smith affords us an apparatus for judging good from bad 'artificial' tragedies. In the same way that a spectator would judge the passions of a real-life sufferer, a spectator would likewise judge the passions of, say, Hamlet, and determine whether the sentiments felt and expressed are appropriate. 'Approbation' is a key component of Smith's construction of sympathy, which Burke's formulation lacks. Smith writes: '[t]o approve of the passions of another, therefore, as suitable to their objects, is the same thing as to observe that we entirely sympathize with them' (TMS I.i.3.1). As approbation is commensurate with sympathy, it is therefore subject to the same pleasure as sympathy. This perhaps explains Smith's denunciation of the abrogation of the dramatic unities of time and place in *Lectures on Rhetoric and Belles Lettres*. He does not complain about their absence on aesthetic grounds, but epistemological ones:

> Tis not then from the interruption of the deception that the bad effect of such transgressions of the unity of time proceed; It is rather from the uneasiness we feel in being kept in the dark with regard to what happened in so long a time. ... Many important events must have passed in that time which we know nothing of.
>
> (Smith 1983, LRBL ii.86–7)

Smith argues that the violation of the unity of place has the same failing: '[i]n this case the distance is so great that we are anxious to know what has happened in the intervall betwixt them' (LRBL ii.89). As mentioned earlier, Smith stresses that it is not the manifested emotions which lead to sympathy, but a knowledge of the context and facts that occasioned them. Smith here follows his 'never to be forgotten' teacher Francis Hutcheson,[24] who remarked:

> another strong reason of this [the attraction to tragedies], is the moral Beauty of the Characters and Actions which we love to behold. For I doubt, whether any Audience would be pleas'd to see fictitious Scenes of Misery, if they were kept strangers to the moral Qualitys of the Sufferers, or their Characters and Action. As in such a case, there would be no Beauty to raise Desire of seeing such Representations, I fancy we would not expose our selves to Pain alone, from Misery which we knew to be fictitious.
>
> (Hutcheson 2004, II.5.8: 160)

Hutcheson then argues that it is because of this attraction to moral beauty that people flocked to see the gladiators. A spectator in possession of all the relevant facts viewing a morally 'beautiful' character will be better able to approve of that character and thus feel the sympathetic pleasure. Though Smith dispenses with some of Hutcheson's ideas, most notably the 'moral sense', his debt to his teacher here is clear.

Smith stresses the 'Stoical' aspect of his construction of sympathy, linking sympathy to other people's reactions to pains rather than to the pains themselves. Admiration, which is 'complete sympathy and approbation, mixed and animated with wonder or surprise' occurs during the ideal sympathetic exchange. Smith illustrates this idea using the example of Cato Uticensis, a tragic hero popular in the eighteenth century, whose fortitude and tranquillity in the face of adversity and 'the necessity of destroying himself' provides a 'spectacle which even the gods themselves might behold with pleasure and admiration' (TMS I.iii.1.13). Smith insists that sympathy is not mere compassion: for sympathy to occur, approbation or admiration must be present. It is for this reason that it is possible to sympathize with a man whose leg has just been blown off by a cannon shot: spectators cannot sympathize with his physical pain, but they can sympathize with and approve of or admire his reaction to that calamity. Though Burke does not use the word 'compassion', his use of the word 'sympathy' is roughly synonymous with it. For Smith, sympathy in our narrower sense is not enough: Smith's tragic theory of course involves this, but requires approbation, as does his moral theory in general.

Like Hutcheson, then, Smith does not merely privilege pity or compassion, but unlike many of his contemporaries, he emphasizes the morally constructive function of tragedy. As a modern reader, Hathaway bemoans the eighteenth-century

> patent concern with empirical psychologizing. The average critic then was so intent upon discovering the spectator's reaction to a work of art that he lost sight of the work of art itself. Especially he lost sight of moral problems … [and] it did not often occur to him that our pleasure from tragedy is somehow connected with our attitudes toward the moral problems to which we are introduced by a tragedy.
>
> (Hathaway 1947: 688)

Smith's solution, though based on sympathy, avoids this problem by adding a pleasurable moral dimension that was lacking previously.

IV

Smith's solution to the paradox of tragedy, whether satisfactory or not, has been overlooked by literary-aesthetic history. Whether his solution was influential or not is difficult to tell, especially since it seems to have escaped his contemporaries.[25] Smith formulated his own theory, which elaborates on Burke's brief exposition, and which also fits into the debate at the time: Smith can be situated in one of two lines of thought on the subject during the century, namely, the 'benevolent' line, which was predicated on sympathy. Smith, however, does not merely follow his predecessors: the uniqueness of his solution lies in his more complex construction of sympathy, which requires the mediation of the imagination and ratiocination. Again, why Smith never wrote a piece devoted to the subject – or, if he did write such a piece, why it has not survived – remains unclear. What is clear is that such ideas were never far from Smith's mind, and we can infer from the writings he did publish his solution to the paradox of tragedy.

Acknowledgements

I would like to thank Samuel Fleischacker and Kathryn Sutherland for their useful comments and questions. My thanks are also due to Frans De Bruyn, whose suggestions were instrumental in clarifying some of the ideas presented here.

Notes

1 Charles Griswold has argued that, for Smith, '[a]ll of commerce depends on the love of beauty', and that Smith's pleasure of sympathy is 'what one might call aesthetic, because it consists in the apprehension of harmony [and] symmetry' (1999: 331, 111). John R. Harrison similarly concludes that 'aesthetic considerations and the faculty of imagination played a considerable role in the formation of Smith's philosophical system' (1995: 91).

2 Though scholars have missed Smith's contribution to tragic theory, this is not to say that they have completely overlooked or neglected the dramatic dimension of *The Theory of Moral Sentiments*. Jonas Barish observes that in *The Theory of Moral Sentiments*, 'we are in the theater' (1981: 245). David Marshall has demonstrated that Smith's spectatorial morality is structured dramatically (1986: 168–92). Charles Griswold also makes several observations on the theatricality of TMS, noting that, at the start of the book, 'the curtain goes up ... and the play begins' and that '[f]rom the beginning, Smith compares human life to spectacles represented in plays' (1999: 44, 65; see also pp. 48–68). For brief discussions of TMS in a similar context, see the essays by Fludernik (2001) and Murray (2003).

3 Like Smith, Thomas Hobbes never wrote directly on tragedy, but this has not prevented posterity from constructing a 'Hobbesian' tragic theory. See C.D. Thorpe (1940: 143–4), and Marvin Carlson, who remarks on Hobbes's contributions (1993: 129). The reader will discover more of Smith's dramatic theory in TMS than anywhere else. I argue elsewhere for Smith's comprehensive tragic theory, but for reasons of space and coherence, this essay will only examine his solution to the problem of tragic pleasure.

4 Baxter Hathaway traces the first application of Hobbes's ideas to tragic theory to Paul Hamelius's remarks in *Die Kritik der englischen Literatur des 17 und 18 Jahrhunderts*, published in 1897 (Hathaway 1947: 674).

5 For the reception and use of the Lucretian doctrine in Europe from the Renaissance onwards, see Hathaway (1947). The Lucretian explanation was adopted as early as 1586 by Malespini, and continued well into the eighteenth century, despite opposition from well-known dissenting voices. Hathaway cites John Dennis, Joseph Trapp, L'Abbé du Bos and John Upton, among others, as theorists who subscribed to the idea (1947: 676–83).

6 See Nos. 39, 40, 42, 44.

7 Francis Hutcheson similarly argued that the best tragedies are those that occasion pity yet never make spectators repine at providence (Hutcheson 1972 [1728], I.iii.V.3: 73).

8 Though he does not expatiate on tragedy, Alexander Gerard follows Hume in emphasizing the consciousness of fiction as a requirement for enjoying tragedy, in addition to the classic Aristotelian/Addisonian emphasis on the implicit pleasure of imitation. See Gerard's *An Essay on Taste* (1759, I.iv: 54–5).

9 Hume goes on to remark that this same subject would seem 'the most pathetic and most interesting, and, by consequence, the most agreeable' to readers who were not as close in time to it (Hume 1987: 223–4).

10 The views of Smith and Hume on tragic decorum fall outside the scope of this essay, but it is worth noting briefly that Smith would probably agree with Horace's famous prohibition ('Ne pueros coram populo Medea trucidet ... ' ['Medea should not butcher her children in front of the audience']) and Hume's objection to the graphic violence in Rowe's drama. However, Smith's greatest objection would not be aesthetic: he would merely deem such scenes as unnecessary since we cannot sympathize with physical pain, much less graphic violence. The contextual facts and sentiments of the suffering agent are enough.

11 Nearly a decade later, Kames wrote in his *Elements of Criticism*, 'sympathy, tho' painful, is attractive, and attaches us to an object in distress, the opposition of self-love notwithstanding, which would prompt us to fly from it. And by this curious mechanism it is, that persons of any degree of sensibility are attracted by affliction still more than by joy' (2005, 1.447: 309).

12 Samuel Johnson's solution, like those of Addison and Hume, rests on this assumption: '[t]he delight of tragedy proceeds from our consciousness of fiction; if we thought murders and treasons real, they would please no more' (Johnson 1978 [1765]: 312).

13 In a section of the text, in which Smith argues against 'Mr. Hobbes, and many of his followers' (Pufendorf and Mandeville are meant) (TMS VII.iii.1.1), Smith defends his construction of sympathy from charges of self-love:

> Sympathy, however, cannot, in any sense, be regarded as a selfish principle. When I sympathize with your sorrow or your indignation, it may be pretended, indeed, that my emotion is founded in self-love ... When I condole with you for the loss of your only son, in order to enter into your grief I do not consider what I, a person of such a character and profession, should suffer, if I had a son, and if that son was unfortunately to die: but I consider what I should suffer if I was really you, and I not only change circumstances with you, but I change persons and characters. My grief, therefore, is entirely upon your account, and not in the least upon my own. It is not, therefore, in the least selfish. ... A man may sympathize with a woman in child-bed; though it is impossible that he should conceive himself as suffering her pains in his own proper person and character.
>
> (TMS VII.iii.1.4)

14 In one of his many letters to Smith, Hume informs him of the publication of his 'Dissertations', including the essay on tragedy, and that Smith 'ha[d] read all the Dissertations in Manuscript' (*Corr.* Letter 22, March 1757).

15 In a draft of the footnoted response to Hume, Smith offers a musical metaphor to clarify the pleasure of mutual sympathy, which again reveals the comprehensive aesthetic basis of his thought: '[t]wo sounds, I suppose, may, each of them taken singly, be austere, and yet, if they are perfect concords, the perception of their harmony and coincidence may be agreeable' (TMS I.iii.1.9 n.).

16 In a recent article, Stacie Friend challenges the assumption 'that it is a prerequisite of our taking pleasure in tragedy that the story be either fictional or, if non-fiction, then non-transparently represented (as by actors)'. She argues that 'documentaries – in particular, non-fiction films that do not use actors – could produce tragic pleasure' (2007: 184). Smith's solution anticipates such arguments.

17 I am indebted to Samuel Fleischacker, who helped me tackle this potentially problematic crux of Smith's argument.

18 It is worth mentioning Luke Gibbons (2003) who compares and contrasts the two constructions of sympathy *vis-à-vis* colonialism and the 'Celtic' anxiety of conforming to Britishness.

19 In his introduction to Burke's *Enquiry*, Boulton points briefly to a possible connection, stating that Smith's construction of sympathy 'echoes Burke, though giving greater prominence to the term "imagination"' (1958: xlii)

20 Wasserman writes: '[l]ittle was added to Burke's theory by the other critics of the eighteenth century, but until the early nineteenth century the doctrine of sympathy was almost consistently called upon to explain the pleasures of tragedy. ... Burke's explanation was occasionally modified, and sometimes it was blended with others; but it served Adam Smith ... and many others' (1947: 299–300).

21 Hipple writes that Hume could not 'assent to an explanation grounding our enjoyment on an instinctive delight in compassion – a notion advanced by Burke, Adam Smith, Blair, Lord Kames, Bishop Hurd, Campbell, and a host of lesser lights' (1957: 50).

22 If a letter written by Dugald Stewart to one of Burke's biographers, James Prior, is to be trusted, Smith 'expressed at Glasgow upon the publication of Burke's book on the *Sublime and Beautiful*, that the author of that book would be a great acquisition to the College if he would accept of a chair' (Prior 1824: 37). Bonar's (1932) catalogue of Smith's library lists the ninth edition of Burke's *Philosophical Enquiry* of 1782. However, this need not prove that Smith was not familiar with the work earlier: Smith's library contains none of the novels of Samuel Richardson or Marie-Jeanne Riccoboni, yet he speaks highly of their moral fictions (TMS III.3.14).

23 'The tears of a stranger move us even before we know what is making him weep. The cries of a man who is only related to us through common humanity make us fly to his aid via a mechanical impulse that precedes all deliberation.' The translation is mine.

24 *Corr.* Letter 274 to Archibald Davidson, 16 Nov. 1787.

25 It is worth pointing out briefly that two German contemporaries of Smith, Gotthold Ephraim Lessing and Johann Gottfried Herder (2006), incorporated his ideas into their dramatic theory (Raphael and Macfie 1976: 29–30). What they said is beyond the scope of this essay, but it is worth noting that Lessing's *Laocoön* (1985) quotes Part I of TMS while discussing dramatic representations.

Bibliography

Addison, J. (1982) *Selections from the Tatler and the Spectator*, Angus Ross (ed.), London: Penguin Books.

Barish, J. (1981) *The Antitheatrical Prejudice*, Berkeley, CA: University of California Press.

Bonar, J. (1932) *A Catalogue of the Library of Adam Smith*, 2nd edn, London: Macmillan & Co.

Boulton, J.T. (1958) 'Introduction' in E. Burke, *A Philosophical Enquiry into the Origin of our Ideas of the Sublime and Beautiful*, London: Routledge & Kegan Paul.

Bryce, J.C. (1983) Introduction into A. Smith, *Lectures on Rhetoric and Belles Lettres*, Oxford: Clarendon Press; Liberty Press imprint, 1985.

Burke, E. (1998 [1757]) *A Philosophical Enquiry into the Origin of Our Ideas of the Sublime and Beautiful*, D. Womersley (ed.), London: Penguin Books.

—— (2000 [1759]) Review of A. Smith, *The Theory of Moral Sentiments*, *Annual Register*, 1759: 484–9; reprinted in *Adam Smith: Critical Responses* (2000), H. Mizuta (ed.), vol. 1, London: Routledge, pp. 78–81.

Campbell, R.H. and Skinner, A.S. (1982) *Adam Smith*, New York: St Martin's.

Carlson, M. (1993) *Theories of the Theatre: A Historical and Critical Survey from the Greeks to the Present*, expanded edn, Ithaca, NY: Cornell University Press.

Feagin, S.L. (1998) 'Tragedy', in E. Craig (ed.), *The Routledge Encyclopedia of Philosophy*, vol. 9, London: Routledge, pp. 447–52.

Fludernik, M. (2001) 'Spectacle, theatre, and sympathy in *Caleb Williams*', *Eighteenth-Century Fiction*, 14: 1–30.

Friend, S. (2007) 'The pleasures of documentary tragedy', *British Journal of Aesthetics*, 47: 184–98.

Gerard, A. (1759) *An Essay on Taste*, London: A. Millar.

Gibbons, L. (2003) *Edmund Burke and Ireland*, Cambridge: Cambridge University Press.

Griswold, C.L. (1999) *Adam Smith and the Virtues of Enlightenment*, Cambridge: Cambridge University Press.

Harrison, J.R. (1995) 'Imagination and aesthetics in Adam Smith's epistemology and moral philosophy', *Contributions to Political Economy*, 14: 91–112.

Hathaway, B. (1947) 'The Lucretian "return upon ourselves" in eighteenth-century theories of tragedy', *PMLA*, 62: 672–89.

Herder, J.G. (2006) *Critical Forests, or Reflections on the Art and Science of the Beautiful: First Grove, Dedicated to Mr. Lessing's* Laocoön, in *Selected Writings on Aesthetics*, trans. G. Moore (ed.), Princeton, NJ: Princeton University Press, pp. 51–176.

Hipple, W.J., Jr (1957) *The Beautiful, the Sublime, & the Picturesque in Eighteenth-Century Aesthetic Theory*, Carbondale, IL: Southern Illinois University Press.

Hobbes, T. (1966) *Human Nature*, in Sir William Molesworth (ed.), *The English Works of Thomas Hobbes*, vol. IV, London: John Bohn.

Hume, D. (1987 [1757]) 'Of Tragedy', in E.F. Miller (ed.), *Essays Moral, Political, and Literary*, Indianapolis: Liberty Press, pp. 216–25.

Hutcheson, F. (1972 [1728]) *An Essay on the Nature and Conduct of the Passions and Affections*, Menston, Yorkshire: Scolar Press.

—— (2004 [1725]) *An Inquiry into the Original of Our Ideas of Beauty and Virtue*, Wolfgang Leidhold (ed.), Indianapolis: Liberty Press.

Johnson, S. (1978 [1765]) 'Preface to Shakespeare', in F. Brady and W.K. Wimsatt (eds), *Samuel Johnson: Selected Poetry and Prose*, Berkeley, CA: University of California Press, pp. 299–336.

Kames, H.H. (2005) *Elements of Criticism*, P. Jones (ed.), 2 vols, Indianapolis, IN: Liberty Press.

Lessing, G.E. (1985) *Laocoön, or the Limits of Painting and Poetry*, in *German Aesthetic and Literary Criticism: Wincklemann, Lessing, Hamann, Herder, Schiller, Goethe*, H.B. Nisbet (ed. and trans.), Cambridge: Cambridge University Press, pp. 59–133.

Lucretius (1951) *The Nature of the Universe*, R.E. Latham (trans.), Harmondsworth: Penguin Books.

Marshall, D. (1986) *The Figure of Theater: Shaftesbury, Defoe, Adam Smith, and George Eliot*, New York: Columbia University Press.

Murray, J. (2003) 'Governing economic man: Joanna Baillie's theatre of utility', *ELH*, 70: 1043–65.

Neill, A. (1999) 'Hume's "singular phaenomenon"', *British Journal of Aesthetics*, 39: 112–25.

Prior, J. (1824) *Memoir of the Life and Character of the Right Honourable Edmund Burke*, London: Baldwin, Cradock, and Joy.

Raphael, D.D. and Macfie, A.L. (1976) Introduction to A. Smith, *The Theory of Moral Sentiments*, Oxford: Clarendon Press; Liberty Press imprint, 1982.

Smith, A. (1976) *The Theory of Moral Sentiments*, D.D. Raphael and A.L Macfie (eds), Oxford: Clarendon Press; Liberty Press imprint, 1982.

—— (1980) *Essays on Philosophical Subjects*, W.P.D. Wightman and J.C. Bryce (eds), Oxford: Clarendon Press; Liberty Press imprint, 1982.

—— (1983) *Lectures on Rhetoric and Belles Lettres*, J.C. Bryce (ed.), Oxford: Clarendon Press; Liberty Press imprint, 1985.

—— (1987) *Correspondence of Adam Smith*, E.C. Mossner and I.S. Ross (eds), Oxford: Clarendon Press.

Stewart, D. (1980) 'Account of the Life and Writings of Adam Smith, LL.D', ed. I.S. Ross, in W.P.D. Wightman and J.C. Bryce (eds), *Essays on Philosophical Subjects*, Oxford: Clarendon Press, pp. 269–351; Liberty Press imprint, 1982.

Thorpe, C.D. (1940) *The Aesthetic Theory of Thomas Hobbes*, Ann Arbor, MI: University of Michigan Press.

Vivenza, G. (2001) *Adam Smith and the Classics: The Classical Heritage in Adam Smith's Thought*, Oxford: Oxford University Press.

Wasserman, E.R. (1947) 'The pleasures of tragedy', *ELH*, 14: 283–307.

Smithian intrinsic value

Patrick R. Frierson

G.E. Moore coined the phrase and developed the concept of intrinsic value at the beginning of the twentieth century (Moore 1902, 1912);[1] it has continued to influence ethical theory ever since (Ross 1930; Audi 2004; Lemos 1994; T. Smith 1998; Zimmerman 2007. Cf. D'Arms and Jacobsen 2000; Rabinowicz and Rønnow-Rasmussen 2004). Lately, intrinsic value has dominated discussions in applied ethics, especially environmental ethics, where it plays central but contested roles in establishing moral considerability for non-human entities. As one environmental philosopher put it, 'How to discover intrinsic value in nature is *the* defining problem for environmental ethics' (Callicott 1999: 241).[2] 'Intrinsic value' also plays roles in ordinary ethical debates about topics as diverse as abortion, modern art, and whether to go to college.[3] However, the notion is often used with imprecision. Christine Korsgaard (1996: 250) rightly distinguishes between 'intrinsic' value, which a thing 'has ... in itself' (vs. extrinsic value), and 'final' value, being 'valued for its own sake' (vs. instrumental value). These are different concepts, but 'intrinsic value' is often used for both.

There are three main senses of intrinsic value: non-instrumental, non-relational and trumping value. Something has non-instrumental value if pursued for its own sake, making it an 'an end-in-itself' in Aristotle's sense, rather than 'a means to something else' (*Nicomachean Ethics*, 1097a). Non-relational value is the Moorean value that something has 'solely in virtue of its intrinsic properties' (O'Neill 2001: 165; cf. Korsgaard 1996: 249–74; Moore 1902, 1912; Ross 1930), independent of relations to other things. Finally, trumping value is that by virtue of which something overrides other considerations; Kant calls it 'dignity', which 'is raised above all price and therefore admits of no equivalent' (Kant 1900–, 4: 434).

Common to all senses of intrinsic value is the implication that intrinsic value implies moral considerability. For Aristotle, that something is an end-in-itself gives it a privileged place within ethics. Although Aristotle allows that one might not promote certain ends-in-themselves when other ends are more pressing, ends-in-themselves are *worth pursuing* for their own sakes, other things being equal. For Moore, non-relational value is *the* basic category of moral considerability; 'moral laws ... are merely statements that certain

The Philosophy of Adam Smith, The Adam Smith Review, 5: 231–249 © 2010 The International Adam Smith Society, ISSN 1743–5285, ISBN 978-0-415-56256-0.

actions will have ... effects [with intrinsic value]' (Moore 1902: §89). And trumping values 'trump' precisely within moral deliberation.

This essay develops a Smithian account of intrinsic value. I show how Smith's *Theory of Moral Sentiments* (Smith 1976a, TMS) provides a normative framework for a rich 'proper-attitude' account of value. I then show that Smith can account for all three sorts of intrinsic value. I end by suggesting an even richer Smithian approach to intrinsic value that accounts for the wide variety of values implicit in proper attitudes.

Smithian value

Smith's approach to value is part of a family of proper-attitude theories of value, according to which *things have value just in case they are objects of proper valuing attitudes*. Proper-attitude theories are distinct from both *subjectivism* about value, according to which things have value just in case they are valued, and *objectivism* about value, according to which the value of a thing is an objective property independent of attitudes that anyone might take towards it. Like subjectivism, proper-attitude theories ascribe value because something is valued, which helps make transparent the connection between values and human interests and desires. But like objectivism, proper-attitude theories are normative rather than merely psychological and thus can straightforwardly accommodate the possibility of error about value.

This general description of proper-attitude theories can be made specific by identifying relevant normative attitudes and criteria for evaluating propriety. Christine Korsgaard's neo-Kantian view of value, for example, takes rationality to be the basis of propriety and choice as the only (or primary) value-conferring attitude (Korsgaard 1996). Alternatively, Elizabeth Anderson includes a wide range of favourable attitudes and lays out a social approach for determining propriety (Anderson 1993: 93f.). One could even transform this proper-attitude account into subjectivism by claiming that all actual attitudes are proper, or into objectivism by claiming that valuing attitudes are proper only if responsive to objective value-properties. The rest of this section uses Smith's TMS to specify a distinctively *Smithian* theory of value.

The range of evaluable attitudes

For Smith, any possible human attitude is morally evaluable and potentially value-conferring. Smith includes attitudes such as love, hate, gratitude, anger, hunger, esteem, and even 'small vexations' (TMS I.ii.5.3); passions like hunger that 'take their origin from the body' (TMS I.ii.1); and those like infatuation or one's interest in one's 'own studies' (TMS II.ii.2.6) that 'take their origin from a particular turn or habit of the imagination' (TMS II.ii.2). He distinguishes among 'unsocial passions' like anger, hatred or resentment (TMS I.ii.3), 'social passions' like love, benevolence and esteem (TMS I.ii.4), and 'selfish passions' like grief, joy, uneasiness and satisfaction, 'when conceived upon account of our own private good or bad fortune' (TMS I.ii.5.1).

The broad range of Smith's account is an important advantage over alternative proper-attitude theories. Many have criticized rational desire theories such as Korsgaard's that limit evaluable attitudes to those oriented towards bringing about a state of affairs (Korsgaard 1996: 226) because '[t]here is much that we judge normatively and regulate by norms other than action, for example, reasoning, ... emotions, responses, feelings, ... and attitudes ... Respect ... cherishing, and sympathy ... are all ways of valuing something intrinsically which do not reduce to valuing the state of that thing's existence' (Darwall 2003: 478, 482. See too Anderson 1993:129–30; Gibbard 1990; Nussbaum 1990, 2001; Solomon 1976). Smith's moral theory rejects an emphasis on intentional action at its core by focusing not on agents but on 'person[s] principally concerned' (TMS I.i.3.1). Such persons can be agents but are often those *to whom* something happens; attitudes judged proper or improper are often passive *responses*. Grief and sorrow (primarily passive) along with animosity and generosity (primarily active) are capable of moral evaluation (see TMS I.i.3.3), and Smith mentions admiration for a poem or amusement at a joke as examples of valuing attitudes that can be proper or improper (TMS I.i.3.3). Of course, attitudes often cause actions, which can then be evaluated, but because attitudes are Smith's primary locus of evaluation, he includes passive responses within ethics. This extension not only seems ethically appropriate in that we can and do appraise people's responsive attitudes, but it also provides a richer normative basis for thinking about value; something can have value even if no one aims or even ought to aim to 'bring it about'.

Like Smith and unlike Korsgaard, Elizabeth Anderson defends a pluralist approach to value according to which a wide variety of different attitudes confer value on their objects. But Anderson's resistance to rational desire models of value leads her to limit her pluralism in ways that Smith does not. Smith sees *all* human attitudes as potentially value-conferring, while for Anderson desire itself is not a source of value (Anderson 1993: 130). Thus Smith can, with Korsgaard, see mere desire to realize a state of affairs – if proper – as conferring value on that state of affairs, but also recognize values of objects that cannot be 'realized or brought about'. such as the Grand Canyon (through awe) or other people (through respect, grief, love, and even hatred and resentment). By being open to value from any quarter, Smith's ethics provides for a full range of sorts of value.

Propriety

For Smith, an attitude is proper when a well-informed, attentive and impartial spectator can sympathize with it. Smith begins by observing that human beings sympathize by attentively imagining themselves in another's situation and responding emotionally to that imaginative change of place

(See Campbell 1971; Fleischacker 2004; Frierson 2006; Griswold 1999; Otteson 2002). Judgments of propriety are based on mutual sympathy between spectator and 'person principally concerned':

> WHEN the original passions of the person principally concerned are in perfect concord with the sympathetic emotions of the spectator, they necessarily appear to this last just and proper ... . To approve of the passions of another ... is the same thing as to observe that we entirely sympathize with them; ...
>
> (TMS I.i.3.1)

One soon learns, however, that people sympathize to different degrees due to inattentiveness, partiality or prejudice. One thus learns to judge propriety of sentiments – one's own and others' – by appealing not to particular spectators' sympathy but to sympathetic responses that would be present in attentive, well-informed and impartial spectators (TMS III.2.36).[4] Attitudes are judged proper if impartial spectators attentively imagining themselves in the place of the person principally concerned would have those attitudes.

It is important here to clarify two points. First, 'impartial' does not mean purely rational or distant from concrete particulars of life (see Griswold 1999; Campbell 1971).[5] Smith's impartial spectator is not an 'ideal observer' who is dispassionate in the sense that 'he is incapable of experiencing ... such emotions as jealousy, self-love, ... and others which are directed towards particular individuals as such' (Firth 1952: 55). The impartial spectator is *sympathetic*, imaginatively entering into particular situations and responding emotionally, and thus must be 'rich in feeling' (Nussbaum 1990: 338). The spectator's impartiality requires not apathy but only that one's emotional response be entirely sympathetic, not tainted by one's own personal interests. Such impartiality makes possible the 'concord' of sentiments that determines propriety.

Second, Smith's impartial spectator does not have transcendent access to a realm of moral values on the basis of which to make ethical evaluations. The mechanism for evaluating the propriety of attitudes is the impartial spectator, who appeals only to her own sentiments. When one seeks to determine the propriety of an attitude, one imagines oneself as impartially, attentively and vividly as possible in the place of the person principally concerned, and one reacts to that situation. One must be attentive to relevant features of the situation, lest sympathy or its lack be due to ignorance rather than impropriety. And one must abstract from or eliminate partial considerations that affect one's emotional response to the imaginative change of place. But features of situations do not carry normativity with them; normativity comes through affective responses of attentive spectators free from partiality.[6]

Smith builds several nuances into this account. He discusses custom's role in corrupting sentiments, and he outlines the importance of general rules to alleviate the effects of unseen prejudice in one's judgments of propriety.

He derives notions of 'merit and demerit' – and thereby justice – from propriety, and he discusses the origin of 'duty'. But the essence of his account, the sympathetic response of impartial and attentive spectators, is sufficient for a Smithian theory of value. Something has value, for Smith, whenever it is the object of a valuing attitude with which impartial spectators can sympathize.

This Smithian account of value avoids pitfalls of both objectivist and subjectivist theories of value. Because Smith does not ground the propriety of valuing attitudes on pre-existing 'objective' values, his account is free from metaphysical and meta-ethical worries (for example, about queerness: see Mackie 1977) that come with adherence to moral realism. But the impartial spectator also frees this account from subjectivism, since someone valuing something is insufficient for ascribing it value. The impartial spectator incorporates normative constraints that allow Smith to insist that certain valuing attitudes are called for, even if no actual person feels them, and other valuings are wrong, even if widely felt. Smith's critiques of slavery in his time (see TMS V.2.9; Smith 1976b, WN I.viii.41, III.ii.9, IV.ix.47) and his extended discussion of the approval of infanticide by 'almost all the states of Greece, even among the polite and civilized Athenians' (TMS V.2.13–16; WN Intro. 4, I.viii.24) provide excellent examples of anti-subjectivism.

The details of Smith's account of propriety highlight further ways in which Smith's theory is distinct from alternatives, such as those of Korsgaard and Anderson. On Korsgaard's account of value, reflection on what can be a rational object of desire leads to the conclusion that only the capacity to value is unconditionally valuable and other goods have value by virtue of being objects of a properly constrained valuing will (see Korsgaard 1996: 240). For this Kantian, universalist approach, one can determine a priori what has intrinsic or unconditional value. By contrast, Smith's approach is particularist, sentimental and social. While Smith allows for the development of general rules, value-ascription is ultimately context-specific. It might turn out that human beings are always ascribed value, but one cannot know this through a priori reflection on the mere process of valuing. To discern whether something has value, one must actually imagine oneself in the place of the person principally concerned, responding to the concrete particulars of that person's situation. Moreover, one responds to particulars not through reason alone, but with one's whole self. Value is not a matter of *thinking* through what ought to have value but a matter of *feeling* value when one is made fully aware of the relevant features and freed from one's partiality. Finally, because Smith is acutely aware of the tendency to partiality and because there is no a priori, rationalist method for deducing value, Smith's ethics requires intensive engagement with others in concrete dialogue and interaction in order to discern hidden partiality and better imagine others' situations.

In these respects, Elizabeth Anderson's approach is more Smithian. Anderson emphasizes the importance of 'non-propositional' attitudes (1993: 129), attention to particular details, and the role of social life in determining what has value. But Anderson's account is importantly different from Smith's in two respects. First, Anderson builds into her account a sub-stantive moral realism that Smith foregoes. She argues against any naturalism that would:

> try to substitute for the question: do these facts *merit* this attitude? the question: do these facts *cause* this attitude? ... [N]o matter how the facts are presented to a person however naturalistically constituted, she always has room to ask whether her resulting attitudes are rational or merited or endorsable.
>
> (Anderson 1993: 139)

For Smith, by contrast, what it *means* to ask whether someone's attitudes (including one's own) are endorsable or merited is simply to ask whether impartially imagining oneself in the place of that person *actually causes* one to feel those attitudes. Contra Anderson, for Smith there is no room for well-informed, impartial spectators to ask whether their sympathetic attitudes are rational. (Of course, one can always ask whether one is well-informed and impartial.) And Smith therefore has no need to appeal to realist 'norms for feeling' (Anderson 1993: 139) that would be prior to feelings themselves.

Paradoxically, Anderson's 'realism' about value leads her to an account of value that is pluralist and even relativist in ways that Smith's naturalism lets him avoid. Without a well-defined stance from which to question attitudes' propriety, Anderson's approach is social to the point that the 'objective valid[ity]' of a value is established by a 'process of justification' in which 'participants can reach significant agreement or progress on the matters under discussion' (Anderson 1993: 93). Whereas Smith posits an ideal (the hypothe-tical stance of impartial and well-informed spectators), Anderson has only concrete discussions in the context of various norms of interaction (Anderson 1993: 93). Thus Smith ascribes 'objectivity' to values only when all impartial spectators 'entirely sympathize with them' (TMS I.i.3.1), while Anderson allows that even when conversations about divergent values give rise to 'the response [of] sticking to one's guns' there can still be an improved under-standing of one's values that gives 'a legitimate claim to objectivity' (Anderson 1993: 97), such that opposed sets of values could *both* emerge with an 'objective' status out of rational dialogue. Smith's impartial spectator thus provides both a naturalist alternative to Anderson's realism and a universalist alternative to Anderson's moderate relativism about objectivity.

From value to *intrinsic* value

Even if Smith provides an account of *value* that is neither crudely subjectivist nor queerly objectivist, this conception might not make sense of *intrinsic* value. This section shows how Smith can account for the three sorts of intrinsic value of greatest relevance to contemporary value-theory.

Non-instrumental value

Smith's approach to non-instrumental value is straightforward and provides a general framework for any proper-attitude approach to intrinsic value: *things have non – instrumental (intrinsic) value just in case they are objects of proper, non – instrumentally (intrinsically) valuing attitudes.* Any proper-attitude account can be extended to cover any form of intrinsic value if, on that account, there is a proper attitude that ascribes that sort of intrinsic value to its objects. In this context, non-instrumental value is particularly easy for proper-attitude theories to accommodate. As Aristotle argued with respect to desire in his *Nicomachean Ethics*, instrumental goods are desired as means to *something*, and proper instrumental desires must be oriented towards the pursuit of something desired non-instrumentally. Smith adds that even goods that are valuable for further ends are often properly valued for their own sakes as well:

> With regard to all those ends [e.g. social-, self- or species-preservation] which, upon account of their peculiar importance, may be regarded ... as favourite ends of nature, she has ... not only endowed mankind with an appetite for the end which she proposes, but likewise with an appetite for the means [e.g. punishment, food or sex] by which alone this end can be brought about, *for their own sakes*, and independent of their tendency to produce it.
>
> (TMS II.i.5.10 note; emphasis added)

The appetite for various goods 'for their own sakes' includes goods essential for societies and individuals to thrive, but also other goods (Smith is not being exhaustive here).

Non-instrumentally-valuing attitudes are not limited to desire. Martha Nussbaum provides an excellent example of non-instrumental valuing in describing grief over her mother's death (Nussbaum 2001:19–88):

> My mother has died. It strikes me ... that a person of enormous value ... is there no longer. It seemed to me as if a nail from the world had entered my insides; it also felt as if life had suddenly a large rip or tear in it, a gaping hole.
>
> (Nussbaum 2001: 39)

Nussbaum's mother strikes her as having 'intrinsic worth or value' that is inconsistent with seeing her mother 'simply as [a] tool ... of [her] own satisfaction' (Nussbaum 2001: 31).

Of course, other emotional responses – missing a thing, or being upset at its loss – ascribe objects only instrumental value. When my bicycle was stolen, I missed it (and felt some resentment towards its thief), but I did not *grieve* over it. Were I to have felt anything resembling grief, this would have indicated that the bike had what we generally call 'sentimental value', which is a sort of non-instrumental value.

Grief is not unique in taking its objects to have non-instrumental value. One generally feels grief for what one loves, and love too values non-instrumentally. Likewise awe, delight and cherishing generally value non-instrumentally. Even when felt towards something that has instrumental value – say, the Hoover Dam – awe transcends and abstracts from instrumental value. Negative attitudes, too, can be non-instrumental. Hatred and resentment do not generally view their objects instrumentally. One who seeks revenge does not generally do so for the sake of further ends; resentment and hatred precisely consist in seeking another's harm *for its own sake*.[7] Of course, one can take instrumentally valuing attitudes towards objects. One might desire wealth for the sake of pleasure or feel sadness over the loss of something because it was particularly useful. One might have hope or fear directed towards objects of merely instrumental value. But many attitudes, from grief, love and awe to hatred and resentment, generally value objects non-instrumentally.

For a Smithian account of non-instrumental value, showing that attitudes ascribe non-instrumental value is insufficient. This would be adequate for subjectivist accounts, but it is all too clear that people sometimes *improperly* value things non-instrumentally. Smith describes those who 'ruin themselves by laying out money on trinkets ... which might ... be very well spared' (TMS IV.i.6) and one could multiply examples. Children who throw tantrums when denied desired toys, even when given equivalent ones, improperly ascribe intrinsic value. Adults who intrinsically value money are further from propriety, since money's value is *essentially* instrumental. Awe towards ordinary pebbles or grief at pruning trees are improper valuing attitudes. Failing to feel awe at the Grand Canyon or grief at a beloved parent's death reflect improper attitudinal deficiencies. The fact that one has or fails to have particular attitudes towards something is insufficient for determining its intrinsic value. What matters is what attitudes towards an object are *proper*.

Still, given that some attitudes value non-instrumentally, one need only explain when those attitudes are proper to complete one's account of non-instrumental value. Applying Smith's account of propriety requires looking at details of particular cases, but even my brief account of Nussbaum's grief over her mother indicates that one can at least partially sympathize with this grief. And while full assessments would require becoming well-informed about relevant details, there are strong presumptions in favour of *some* Smithian, non-instrumentally-valuing attitudes, including not merely desires for food and sex but also love for caring parents and grief at the death of loved ones.

Non-relational value

Even something with non-instrumental value might lack non-relational value. Something has non-relational value if its value does not depend upon its relationship to anything else. The precluded dependence could be instrumental, as when the value of gold depends upon its capacity to purchase goods, but value might also depend upon *relationships* non-instrumentally, as with the special value of children to their parents or the value of a benefactor due to past benefits. In these cases, value is non-instrumental but still relational.[8] Nussbaum's grief over her mother exemplifies such value:

> What inspires grief is the death of someone ... who has been an important part of one's own life. This does not mean that the emotions view these objects simply as tools or instruments of the agent's own satisfaction; they may be invested with intrinsic worth or value, as indeed my mother surely was. ... But what makes the emotion centre around this particular mother ... is that she is *my* mother, a part of my life.
>
> (Nussbaum 2001: 31)

This example makes clear the distinction between instrumental and relative goodness. Many valuing attitudes – filial love, gratitude and grief – are appropriate with respect to parents to a degree that would be inappropriate with respect to others. These attitudes do not ascribe *instrumental* value to one's parents. To love or feel gratitude towards parents only for what they can do for one would be deeply *im*proper. But these attitudes are proper only because of a relationship between their object and oneself. They are deeply *relational* valuings, and one's parents' value is, in that sense, a relational value.

Gratitude is the paradigm case of non-instrumental, relational valuing. Hobbes famously defended the importance of gratitude for instrumental reasons (cf. Hobbes 1996 [1651]: 105), but Smith is much closer to the mark, seeing gratitude as a 'sentiment, which ... *immediately* and directly prompts us to reward ... another' who has benefited oneself (TMS II.i.1.2; emphasis added). Gratitude is an immediate response to benevolence, involves immediate concern for another's well-being, and takes this other's well-being as an end-in-itself. But gratitude is nonetheless relational. One properly feels gratitude towards only those by whom one is 'assisted, protected, relieved' or benefited in some other way (TMS II.i.2.4).

Unfortunately, while Nussbaum rightly distinguishes non-relational from non-instrumental value, she uses the relational nature of her grief to argue that *all* emotions are 'eudaimonistic' (Nussbaum 2001: 31) in the sense that although 'they insist on the real importance of their object', 'they also ... have to do with me and my own, my plans and goals, what is important in my own conception ... of what it is for me to live well' (Nussbaum 2001: 33):

> Let us now return to my central example. My mother has died ... [A] person of enormous value, who was central in my life, is there no longer. ... [This emotion] is evaluative and eudaimonistic; it does not just

assert 'Betty Craven is dead'. Central to the [grief] is my mother's enormous importance, both in herself and as an element in my life.

(Nussbaum 2001: 39)

Nussbaum's self-analysis here is (I suspect) accurate and insightful. The emotional force of 'my mother is dead' is completely different from the emotional force of 'Betty Craven is dead'. The grief wrapped up with former ascribes importance to its object both non-instrumentally and in relation to oneself. This grief is, as Nussbaum puts it, eudaimonistic.

But Nussbaum goes too far in using this analysis for emotion in general or even grief in general. Images of war or disease, especially when victims are children, inspire grief. News reports of tragedy and even cold statistics can inspire grief in one sufficiently attentive, who has not grown callous, who is willing to deeply reflect on the news. To some extent, these feelings may be due to a sense of distant community, that we are all in this world together. To some extent, they may be due to associations with those closer to one's own life, stirring up fear or sadness at future dangers or past misfortune. To some extent, one might connect them with oneself through a sort of self-oriented sympathy with others, where one grieves over the pain that one feels in contemplating those situations. But it is proper to feel grief at others' tragedies even when those others have no special importance in one's life. Innocent lives lost provoke grief, and in grief one ascribes to those lives 'enormous importance', an importance that is often simply in-itself and not at all 'as an element in my life'.

Of course, the attitudes that ascribe value non-relationally will be different – in degree and often in kind – from those that ascribe value relationally. Grief at the death of a parent is different, and properly so, from grief at the death of a stranger. Love for one's children differs from love for parents, lovers and strangers in need. But love is proper in all of these cases, and love for strangers in need will at most be very weakly relational, and it will not – or at least need not – involve any appeal to the role of those strangers in one's life. In that sense, attitudes can properly ascribe value non-relationally, and proper-attitude theories of value can explain objects' non-relational value.

But there are two ways in which non-relational value poses special problems for a *Smithian* conception of non-relational value. First, Smith's particularism[9] seems to preclude the universality required for non-relational value. As G.E. Moore explained, 'it is impossible for what is strictly one and the same thing to possess [non-relational] value at one time, or in one set of circumstances, and not to possess it in another' (Moore 1922: 260). Second, accounts of value that tie objects' values to humans' *attitudes towards* those objects seem to make those values *relative* to human beings, and hence relational.

Fortunately, both problems are alleviated by making an important distinction between the *situation-dependence of attitudes* (reflected in Smith's particularism) and *attitudes of situation-dependent value*. The propriety of ascrib*ing* value may be situation dependent, but the value thus properly ascribed need not be. Smith even emphasizes that while every attitude's propriety is situational, values ascribed by those attitudes are typically *not* based on relations to oneself. 'Passion[s] excited by objects peculiarly related to ourselves' (TMS I.ii.Intro.1) are merely one sort of passion among others, and Smith specifically highlights the pleasure that impartial spectators take in 'affections ... towards those who are not peculiarly connected with ourselves' (TMS I.ii.4.1). The situation-dependence of an attitude is not the same as an attitude of situation-dependent value.

To illustrate: grief at the suffering of young innocents ascribes value to others independent of their relation to oneself or to anything else. The grief-value of suffering innocents is non-relational. Nonetheless, the *attitude* of grief over innocents is deeply situation-dependent. Grief is proper when one becomes aware of suffering, especially when suffering is particularly needless and one's awareness particularly vivid, but such grief is usually not proper at the birthday party of a neighbour's child. This impropriety is due neither to the fact that no innocents are dying (unfortunately, they are, in large numbers) nor even to one's ignorance of that fact (one may be far from ignorant). But the situation calls for something else, for putting one's grief to the side, for enjoying the festivities of the moment. This situation-dependence affects the propriety of feeling the attitude; it is not constitutive of the attitude's content. The fact that feeling grief is inappropriate in certain contexts does not mean that grief, when properly felt, ascribes contextual value to its objects. Grief ought not have the form, 'innocents' suffering leaves a vacant hole in our world ... unless I get to go to a birthday party'.[10]

Like grief, attitudes such as resentment or gratitude are situation-dependent in that one ought not to feel intense resentment at global injustice while at the birthday party of a neighbour's child, nor gratitude for a promotion when comforting a grieving friend. Unlike grief, however, these attitudes also properly ascribe situation-dependent value to their objects. Resentment 'prompt[s] us to desire ... that [the object of our resentment] should be punished ... upon account of that particular injury which he had done to us' (TMS II.i.1.6). And gratitude seeks good for another *because the other has done good to oneself* (TMS II.i.1.5). The value (either positive or negative) of the objects of gratitude and resentment is situation-dependent value.

Like grief, gratitude and resentment, respect for persons and awe at the Grand Canyon are proper attitudes that are situation-dependent. But like grief and unlike gratitude and resentment, they are not attitudes of situation-dependent value. One wandering alone through a vast and beautiful wilderness need not consciously have respect for persons, and one not in the presence of or contemplating the Grand Canyon need not feel awe. But when in the right context, these attitudes ascribe situation-*in*dependent value to their objects. One who truly respects another person ascribes to her a value that does not depend upon situation. Likewise, one in awe sees the Grand Canyon as being awesome *simpliciter*. The Grand Canyon is awesome not simply because of situational properties (its place in space or time, its designation as a National Park, its being viewed by me, and so on), but in-itself. Situational prompts[11] may be needed to activate awe, but the awesomeness one ascribes when those prompts are present does not depend upon those prompts. Proper awe at the Grand Canyon ought not have the form, 'With me standing here on its edge, this Canyon is pretty awesome.'

The distinction between situation-dependent attitudes and attitudes of situation-dependent value is related to another distinction that is crucial for explaining the sense in which Smithian intrinsic value is non-relational. Moore developed the notion of intrinsic value to defend *meta-ethical* realism about value. Smith's proper-attitude theory is offered precisely as an alternative to this meta-ethics, but Smith can still accommodate *normatively* non-relational value. Normatively non-relational value is value that an object has by virtue of being the proper object of a valuing attitude, where the attitude that one ought to take towards the object ought to be taken without regard any relations between that object and anything else. A non-relational *meta-ethical theory* of value, unlike this normative non-relationality, does not pick out a particular sort of value. Rather, it posits that things have value independently of any relations, including normative ones, to human beings. While Smith could support some forms of meta-ethical non-relationalism about value (for example, the idea that the value of a thing need not depend upon its *actual* relation to any other *actual* beings), proper-attitude theories are designed precisely to offer an alternative to meta-ethically non-relational (objectivist or realist) treatments of value. And this section has shown – contra Moore – how non-realist meta-ethics can justify normatively non-relational values.

Trumping value

Things with non-instrumental value need not have trumping value. I may value a painting non-instrumentally, but still be willing to sell the painting if I need money. The fact that my appreciation of the painting is non-instrumental does not imply that it trumps other values (including instrumental values such as the desire for money).[12] Even something with non-relational value, like 'consciousness of a beautiful object' (Moore's example, 1902: §18, ¶2)[13] need not have trumping value; I might perfectly well deny that consciousness (to myself or another) for the sake of something else. Nonetheless, one can develop proper-attitude explanations of trumping value similar to those for other sorts of intrinsic value. Certain attitudes ascribe trumping value to their objects, and when such attitudes are proper, their objects have trumping value. The appreciation one has for paintings does not generally imply trumping value, but the distinctive sort of appreciation – approaching reverence – that one has for historically, culturally or artistically unique and important paintings does. One can properly appreciate a fine painting and still sell it, but one's appreciation of Raphael's *Sistine Madonna* would be insufficient, and hence improper, if it did not imply at least some prima facie trumping value of that painting over other concerns. More obviously, respect for others and love for parents or children are not only non-instrumental, but trumping. Proper objects of reverence, awe, respect or love often have trumping value.

As in the case of non-relational value, Smith's particularism seems to collide with the generality of trumping-value claims. And again, one can distinguish the situation-dependence of valuing attitudes from attitudes of situation-dependent value. But trumping values are situation-independent in a way that complicates this simple solution. When grieving over suffering innocents, one ascribes non-relational value to them. As already noted, there are circumstances in which such grief is inappropriate, such as when at a neighbour's party. In principle, there is nothing in our account so far that would preclude the judgment that grief, respect and concern for innocents is equally inappropriate when deciding whether or not to go to war, or to alleviate suffering, or compensate victims. To decide whether or not these attitudes – which ascribe non-relational value to their objects – are called for, it seems necessary to evaluate each situation in particular. Because the propriety of these valuing attitudes is situation-dependent, the values ascribed by them do not automatically warrant certain attitudes in every situation.

But trumping value is precisely supposed to cut short or override certain sorts of deliberation about attitudes' propriety. When one sees an object as having trumping value, one sees it as the sort of object that requires certain attitudes even when, in many circumstances, one might otherwise have concluded that the proper attitude towards that object was quite different. For example, insofar as one respects human beings in a way that ascribes trumping value to them, one sees them as having a kind of value that requires respect even when circumstances might seem to demand a diminution of that respect. Whereas one could ascribe non-relational value to people and still allow circumstances to regulate the propriety of respecting them in particular cases, one who ascribes trumping value precisely takes such value to govern actions and attitudes regardless of circumstances. Of course, the degree of 'trumping' can vary. Dworkin's notion of 'rights-as-trumps' ascribes individuals value that trumps aggregate social goods (see Dworkin 1977, 1984). Callicott, in environmental contexts, articulates a sense of prima facie trumping value that allows such values to 'be overridden by considerations of ... aggregate utility' (Callicott 2002: 14; cf. Callicott 1999: 245–6). One could develop a range of degrees of trumping value, from weak prima facie trumpingness in a limited range of situations to absolute trumping value over all situations.[14] In every case, however, the ascription of trumping value precludes the *situation-dependence of valuing attitudes*, at least over some range of situations.

In that context, the distinction that proved so helpful for non-relational value is insufficient for making sense of trumping value. Towards objects with trumping value, valuing attitudes must be properly situation-independent, but Smith's particularism seems to rule out judging *any* attitudes as proper for *all* situations.[15] Smith mitigates his particularism, however, and provides for robust trumping values through an account of *general rules*, the need for which Smith explains using an example:

> The man of furious resentment, if he was to listen to the dictates of that passion, would perhaps regard the death of his enemy, as but a small compensation for the wrong, he imagines, he has received; which, however, may be no more than a very slight provocation. ... [T]he fury of his own temper may be such, that had this been the first time in which he considered such an action, he would undoubtedly have determined it to be quite ... proper, and what every impartial spectator would approve of.
>
> (TMS III.4.12)

Smith mentions this 'man of furious resentment' as an example of 'self-deceit' (TMS III.4): 'the violence and injustice of our own selfish passions are sometimes sufficient to induce the man within the breast [our attempted impartial view of ourselves] to make a report very different from what the real circumstances of the case are capable of authorizing' (TMS III.4.1). Even 'when the action is over ... and the passions which prompted it have subsided', although 'we can enter more coolly into the sentiments of the impartial spectator', we 'often purposely turn away our view from those circumstances which might render the judgment [of ourselves] unfavourable' because 'it is so disagreeable to think ill of ourselves' (TMS III.4.4). The ideal standpoint from which one ought to evaluate objects' values is difficult, especially when interests are particularly acute. Because people misjudge values that interfere with their interests, we should develop general rules based on truly impartial judgments. With the furious man:

> unless his education has been very singular, he has laid it down to himself as an inviolable rule, to abstain from ['sanguinary revenges'] upon all occasions. This rule preserves its authority with him, and renders him incapable of being guilty of such a violence. ... [R]everence for the rule ... checks the impetuosity of his passion, and helps him to correct the too partial views which self-love might otherwise suggest ...
>
> (TMS III.4.12)

General rules based upon particular but impartial judgments trump particular judgments in contexts where partiality causes self-deception.

The trumpingness of general rules explains trumping *value* in two ways. First, general rules provide a one-step-removed proper-attitude account of value. General rules are constructed from analyses of proper attitudes, and insofar as the *rule* ascribes value to an object, that object will have trumping value. The greater the generality of the rule, the more robust the trumping value. Where values are liable to be systematically misjudged through interested self-deception, one should ascribe absolute trumping values. Second, this account of general rules explains the nature of *attitudes* that properly ascribe trumping value to their objects. Taking a rule to be authoritative involves adopting an attitude towards the objects governed by the rule. An attitude that attributes trumping value to an object leads us to see that object *as* falling under general rules. So, for example, respect ascribes *trumping* value to a person insofar as one sees one's respect as an attitude called for whether or not it seems proper to one at the time, that is, as an attitude governed by a general rule. An object of this attitude – a person – will then be an object to which certain general rules apply.

This Smithian account of trumping values seems, in one sense, weak. Because general rules 'are ultimately founded upon experience of what, *in particular instances,* our moral faculties ... approve of' (TMS III.4.8; emphasis added), trumping values are in principle revisable in the light of further reflection on particular cases. But this revisibility does not imply that values do not trump, only that one's judgments that they trump are revisable. Willingness to revise judgments requires acceptance of one's own limited perspective, not diminution of an object's value. Moreover, Smith's account of trumping value helpfully shows why it is so important: it limits casuistry, preventing one from seeking ways around requirements to respect something's value. This need for clear lines comes from our tendency to *mis*use casuistry (a tendency so universal that 'sophistry' is given by the OED as a synonym for casuistry). Ascribing trumping value via Smithian general rules not only provides for robust conceptions of trumping, but also shows what it really is to hold a trumpingly valuing attitude towards something and why such attitudes are so important in human life.

Conclusion

This essay started by noting that 'intrinsic value' can refer to at least three distinct sorts of value, and I have shown that Smith's proper-attitude theory of value can make sense of these core senses of intrinsic value. But the notion of intrinsic value can be enriched even further; Smith provides for what we might call 'thick' intrinsic values. The general idea of thick ethical concepts (see Williams 1985) is that notions such as cruelty, disloyalty, humility and generosity are less abstract and more descriptive than more 'reflective' ethical concepts such as 'good' or 'right'. For Bernard Williams, thick concepts are better candidates for 'convergence' (1985: 140f.) because they have a more substantive connection to the world. For example, one can get wide agreement that torturing animals is 'cruel' without prior agreement about whether such action is 'wrong'. 'Cruelty' describes the action and ascribes normative weight to it, but it assigns normative weight in a thick way.

Proper-attitude theories can extend this notion of thick concepts into discussions of value while avoiding Williams's relativism about thick conceptual schemes. 'Value' and 'intrinsic value' are thin concepts, abstract and lacking natural descriptive sense. Proper-attitude theories thicken value concepts because they understand values as reflecting specific, potentially thick, normative attitudes. Thick value-terms would include 'awesome', 'piteous', 'lovable', 'fearsome' and 'worthy of gratitude'. Calling the Grand Canyon 'awesome' or suffering children 'piteous' is more descriptive, less controversial and better connected to normative claims about attitudes than saying that they have 'intrinsic value'.[16] In other words, Smithian intrinsic value is pluralist (cf. Anderson 1993: 98–103). Distinguishing non-instrumental, trumping, and non-relational value begins to highlight that pluralism, but the full range of thick intrinsic values – awesomeness; fearsomeness; worthiness of respect, grief or gratitude – describe intrinsic values more accurately and foster more productive ethical dialogue than abstract debates about intrinsic value itself.

Smith's proper-attitude account of thick values also shows how thick and thin value concepts can relate to one another. For Smith, value concepts are thick in that ascriptions of value are based on particular attitudes. They are even irreducibly thick because there is no fixed rule for deciding which descriptive accounts warrant particular attitudinal responses. But Smithian thick value judgments connect to thin concepts in three important ways. First, Smithian propriety is a thin concept. Second, one can abstract thin notions of intrinsic value from more specific ones, as I did in the previous section; and these abstract notions may play roles in explaining concrete ethical judgments. Finally, for Smith, one arbitrates disputes about thick values by means of the thin concept of the impartial spectator. Smith thus avoids the relativistic implications that pervade Williams's use of thick values (and that affect even Anderson's more modest value-pluralism).

The result is a Smithian theory in which proper objects of various valuing attitudes have value. Because of the ways these attitudes ascribe value to objects, one can abstract different sorts of intrinsic value, including but not limited to the non-instrumental, non-relational and trumping values that play such important roles in contemporary ethics.

Notes

1 Prior to Moore, the term 'intrinsic value' was primarily used – as it was by Smith (cf. WN IV.ii.4) – in economic contexts, to distinguish the nominal value of a thing (especially coins) from its 'intrinsic value' (for example, real weight of coins).

2 Defenders of intrinsic value in environmental ethics include Callicott, Rolston, Naess and Agar. Critics include Weston, Hargrove, Norton, Regan, Gruen and Light.

3 For references to intrinsic value in relation to abortion, see Dworkin (2004). For relation to modern art, see: http://query.nytimes.com/gst/fullpage.html?res=9F02E5D7103FF934A25751C1A9669C8B63 (accessed 2 Sept. 2008). Relating to going to college, see: http://essay.blogs.nytimes.com/2007/09/24/why-college-matters-7/ (accessed 2 Sept. 2008).

4 Smith assumes that the reactions of truly impartial and attentive spectators will be the same. See Heath (1995: 452) and Frierson (2006).

5 My contrast of Smith with Firth largely follows Griswold (1999), but I take Smith's impartial spectator to be more ideal than Griswold does in that I see the impartial spectator as primarily an imaginative construct.

6 Some Smithian expressions might seem to imply that impartial spectators respond to objective values. Smith says, for example, that a spectator should 'approve of the passions of another ... *as suitable to their objects*' (TMS I.i.3.1; emphasis added). But even here, he makes clear that this approval is based on the spectator's sympathetic response, not vice versa:

> WHEN the original passions of the person principally concerned are in perfect concord with the sympathetic emotions of the spectator, they necessarily appear to this last just and proper, and suitable to their objects ... .To approve of the passions of another ... as suitable to their objects, is the same thing as to observe that we entirely sympathize with them; ...
>
> (TMS I.i.3.1)

Passions being suitable to their objects amounts to no more than that impartial spectators fully sympathize with them.

7 Alice MacLachlan discusses Smith's view of resentment in detail at pp. 161–77, this volume.

8 Something's relationship to something else might give it value by virtue of the value of that to which it is related, such as Smith's example of gratitude towards 'the plank upon which [one] had just escaped from a shipwreck' (TMS II.iii.1.2). But relational value might not depend upon the relata's *value*, as in parental love. Although parents see their parental relationship as central to their children's value for them, they should not see their own *value* as the source of their children's value. This account of non-relational value differs from Anderson's, according to which 'the judgment that x is intrinsically valuable entails that ... x is properly intrinsically valued, independent of the propriety of valuing any other particular thing' (Anderson 1993: 3). Insofar as children are properly valued by their parents, independent of the propriety of valuing any other particular thing but only because of their relation to their parents, they lack intrinsic (non-relational) value.

9 Even general rules in ethics 'are ultimately founded upon experience of what, *in particular instances*, our moral faculties ... approve of' (TMS III.4.8; emphasis added). Regarding particularism, cf. Dancy (2004), Hooker and Little (2001). Regarding *Smith's* particularism, cf. Griswold (1999), Fleischacker (2004), Frierson (2006).

10 The grief-value ascribed to dead innocents is situation-dependent in another sense. If the innocents over whom one grieves have not actually suffered, then not only is .it improper for one to feel an attitude of grief, but the innocents lack the property ascribed to them in grief. They lack the value of being-worthy-of-being-grieved-over. One might quite properly say, 'the suffering of these children leaves a vacant hole in our world, unless, of course, they haven't really suffered'. In *this* sense, grief is an attitude of situation-dependent value. Of course, there is a derivative sense in which they still have this value. Insofar as they are such that one ought to grieve over them were they to suffer or die, we can say that they are grief-worthy in this secondary sense.

11 Dancy's discussion of 'enabling conditions' (Dancy 2003: 637) complements the account here.

12 The independence of trumping and non-instrumental value is in principle reciprocal. Someone might ascribe trumping value to her biological life, for example, while still seeing life as merely a means – but an absolutely necessary one – to other goods. In fact, anything perceived as a necessary means to all other goods will be trumping, whether or not it is valuable for-its-own-sake.

13 This might seem to be relational, since consciousness of an object seems to relate to the person with it. Moore's point, though, is that we take others' consciousness of beauty to be valuable, without any relationship between that consciousness and ourselves (or anything else).

14 Orthodox Kantians go far in the latter direction, though even Kantians need not insist that one actually feel respect for every human being all the time. Some theological conceptions of reverence for God might be trumping in this most absolute sense, where God would literally *always* require reverence.
15 It might turn out, even within Smith's particularist account, that some objects will properly give rise to valuing attitudes in all situations. But the ascription of trumping-value requires more than this inductive approach. The ascription of trumping-value requires that one can affirm the universal propriety of an attitude independently of actually examining every situation.
16 Although knowing that the Grand Canyon is awesome or a child piteous does not give rise to immediate action-plans – it does not directly tell us what to do with the Grand Canyon or the child – it provides substantially more guidance than simply saying that it has intrinsic value.

Bibliography

Anderson, E. (1993) *Value in Ethics and Economics*, Cambridge, MA: Harvard University Press.
Audi, R. (2004) *The Good in the Right: A Theory of Intuition and Intrinsic Value*, Princeton, N.J.: Princeton University Press.
Callicott, J.B. (1999) *Beyond the Land Ethic*, Albany, NY: State University of New York Press.
—— (2002) 'The pragmatic power and promise of theoretical environmental ethics: forging a new discourse', *Environmental Values*, 11: 3–25.
Campbell, T.D. (1971) *Adam Smith's Science of Morals*, Totowa, NJ: Rowan & Littlefield.
D'Arms, J. and Jacobsen, D. (2000) 'The moralistic fallacy: on the "appropriateness" of emotions', *Philosophy and Phenomenological Research*, 61: 65–90.
Dancy, J. (2003) 'Are there organic unities?', *Ethics*, 113: 629–50.
—— (2004) *Ethics without Principles*, Oxford: Oxford University Press.
Darwall, S. (2003) 'Moore, normativity, and intrinsic value', *Ethics*, 113: 468–89.
Dworkin, R. (1977) *Taking Rights Seriously*, Cambridge, MA: Harvard University Press.
—— (1984) *Law's Empire*, Cambridge, MA: Belknap Press.
—— (2004) *Life's Dominion*, New York: Vintage.
Firth, R. (1952) 'Ethical absolutism and the ideal observer theory', *Philosophy and Phenomenological Research* 12: 317–45.
Fleischacker, S. (2004) *On Adam Smith's* Wealth of Nations: *A Philosophical Companion*, Princeton, NJ: Princeton University Press.
Frierson, P. (2006) 'Applying Adam Smith: a step towards Smithian environmental virtue ethics', in E. Schliesser and L. Montes (eds), *New Voices On Adam Smith*, London: Routledge, pp. 140–67.
Gibbard, A. (1990) *Wise Choices, Apt Feelings*, Cambridge, MA: Harvard University Press.
Griswold, C.L. (1999) *Adam Smith and the Virtues of Enlightenment*, New York: Cambridge University Press.
Heath, E. (1995) 'The commerce of sympathy: Adam Smith on the emergence of morals', *Journal of the History of Philosophy*, 33: 447–66.
Hobbes, T. (1996 [1651]) *Leviathan*, R. Tuck (ed.), Cambridge, Cambridge University Press.

Hooker, B. and Little, M.O. (eds) (2001) *Moral Particularism*, Oxford: Oxford University Press.

Kant, I. (1900–) *Kants Gesammelte Schriften*, Royal Prussian Academy of Sciences (ed.), (Berlin: Georg Reimer) and later by the German Academy of Sciences (Berlin: de Gruyter).

Korsgaard, C. (1996) *Creating the Kingdom of Ends*, Cambridge: Cambridge University Press.

Lemos, N. (1994) *Intrinsic Value: Concept and Warrant*, Cambridge: Cambridge University Press.

Mackie, J. (1977) *Ethics*, Harmondsworth: Penguin.

Moore, G.E. (1902) *Principia Ethica*, Buffalo, NY: Prometheus Books.

—— (1912) *Ethics*, London: Oxford University Press.

—— (1922) *Philosophical Studies*, London: Routledge & Kegan Paul.

Nussbaum, M. (1990) *Love's Knowledge: Essays on Philosophy and Literature*, Oxford: Oxford University Press.

—— (2001) *Upheavals of Thought: The Intelligence of Emotions*, Cambridge: Cambridge University Press.

O'Neill, J. (2001) 'Meta-ethics', in D. Jamieson (ed.), *A Companion to Environmental Philosophy*, Oxford: Blackwell.

Otteson, J.R. (2002) *Adam Smith's Marketplace of Life*, Cambridge: Cambridge University Press.

Rabinowitz, W. and Rønnow-Rasmussen, T. (2004) 'The strike of the demon: on fitting pro-attitudes and value', *Ethics*, 114: 391–424.

Ross, W.D. (1930) *The Right and the Good*, Oxford: Oxford University Press; reprint, Hackett Publishing, 1988.

Smith, A. (1976a) *The Theory of Moral Sentiments*, D.D. Raphael and A.L. Macfie (eds), Oxford: Clarendon Press; Liberty Press imprint, 1982.

—— (1976b) *An Inquiry into the Nature and Causes of the Wealth of Nations*, R.H. Campbell and A.S. Skinner (eds), Oxford: Clarendon Press.

Smith, T. (1998) 'Intrinsic value: look-say ethics', *Journal of Value Inquiry*, 32: 539–53.

Solomon, R. (1976) *The Passions*, Garden City, NY: Anchor Press/Doubleday.

Williams, B. (1985) *Ethics and the Limits of Philosophy*, Cambridge, MA: Harvard University Press.

Zimmerman, M. (2007) 'Intrinsic vs. extrinsic value', *Stanford Encyclopedia of Philosophy*, available: http://plato.stanford.edu/entries/value-intrinsic-extrinsic/ (accessed 25 April 2009).

Memoir on Adam Smith's life

Adam Smith's smile

His years at Balliol College, 1740–46, in retrospect*

Ian Simpson Ross

It is a great honour to be invited to speak to you here this evening about Smith's time as a member of Balliol College. I will discuss some of his experiences at the personal level, and touch on what he made of them from an institutional point of view.

In his latter days, according to the obituary of Smith published in the *St James's Chronicle* on 31 July 1790, just fourteen days after his death, he smiled when he saw beef smoking on his table. When asked to interpret his smile, he would always tell a story about the first day he dined at Balliol. Possibly this was 4 July 1740, when he was admitted to the College as a seventeen-year-old Snell Exhibitioner elected by Glasgow University. Succumbing to absence of mind, he neglected his food, and a servitor noticing this 'desired him to fall to, for he had never seen such a piece of beef in Scotland'. Smith's 'smile', I think, came from rueful recognition that he was, and had always been, an absent-minded fellow, even in the presence of food. Also, I think, it was a smile at the memory of the Englishman's presumption that the food he served must be superior to Scottish fare. Enrolled at wealthy Oxford, Smith came to realize that its vaunted education fell noticeably short, at that time, of what could be obtained at a much poorer Glasgow.

This judgment is reflected in the first letter we have from Smith at Balliol. He is writing on 24 August 1740 to his cousin and guardian, William Smith, secretary and steward to that powerful but conflicted personality, the 2nd Duke of Argyll (Iain Ruadh nan Cath [Red John of the Battles]: 1678–1743). The address given is Bruton Street, where at No. 27 was to be found the Duke's London house in the vicinity of Parliament. We may speculate that Adam Smith visited there when he came down from Oxford, and heard from his cousin about the exciting political news of the Duke's opposition in his last years to Prime Minister Walpole. In the letter to hand, Adam thanks his cousin, obviously something of a father-figure, for his good advice. What did he advise, we wonder? Maybe something along these lines: 'just smile at the delusions of the English about their effortless superiority, and get the best you can out of their Southern speech, conversation, ideas and publications, then maybe you'll excel them as a thinker, teacher and writer'. The letter continues that the money William sent is most useful, because of the 'extraordinary

The Philosophy of Adam Smith, The Adam Smith Review, 5: 253–259 © 2010 The International Adam Smith Society, ISSN 1743–5285, ISBN 978-0-415-56256-0.

and most extravagant fees' demanded by the College and University at matriculation. Adam then permits himself a sharp comment on his situation: 'It will be his own fault if anyone should endanger his health at Oxford by excessive Study, our only business here being to go to prayers twice a day, and to lectures twice a week' (Smith 1987, *Corr.* Letter 1).

Young Smith's words about endangering health by excessive study at Oxford came back to haunt him, as will be discussed. Regarding public prayers, it is likely he was already sceptical about their efficacy by the time he left Glasgow. Also, he seems to have been averse to preparing himself for ordination and a career in the Scottish Episcopalian ministry as the Snell foundation had originally required (Stones 1984: 190). As for the state of the 'ancient universities' of Europe, Smith claimed in 1774 he had looked carefully into the constitution and history of several of them, not excluding Oxford, and found the greater part sunk into 'degradation and contempt'. The reasons, he thought, were high salaries given to professors 'without regard to diligence and success in their professions', and luring students with bursaries to enter universities to get degrees as passports to professions, whether the instruction on offer was or was not worth receiving (*Corr.* Letter 143). Smith was not opposed to high wages, just to drawing them without commensurate effort. Also, we can believe he thought universities providing bursaries to attract students should monitor their programmes responsibly.

Recently, an economics professor and a dean of a business college in the United States (Leathers and Raines 2007) have looked into the case Smith presents in the *Wealth of Nations* for what they call 'market-based "reforms" of higher education' (p.136), involving the prescription of fee income for university staff based on free student choice of their teachers, and have satisfied themselves that it is 'weakened by contradictions, qualifications and incomplete attention to the institutional functions of universities' (p.137). They believe that anecdotal evidence from Glasgow University, which Smith indicated was operating successfully under the right system, revealed faculty were paid 'assured salaries' and there was 'relatively little student-consumer sovereignty' (p.137). It may be, however, that these modern commentators are so focused on the issue of the compensation regime, that they lose track of its relationship with other sides of Smith's argument about the university reforms needed at the Oxford of his time. They do not examine the evidence, for instance, about the pervasive weak teaching and publication record at Balliol (Jones 2005: ch. 13), on the one hand, and the likely causes being found in slack supervision, absence of fair competition for fellowships, and assurance of income without evidence of performance. At Glasgow, on the other hand, there was the notably strong instruction and innovative scholarly achievement of a significant number of the professors, whose ability was assessed for preferment, though patronage was certainly an element in the process, and whose assured income was small, but could be increased by the fees of students drawn to their lectures. To some extent, an academic marketplace analogy holds here, not so much in terms of wages for the providers of higher education, perhaps, as in the competition among them for distinction in their fields. Most eighteenth-century Scottish students were constrained by economic opportunity, but they could, and did, vote with their feet about which of the five universities in their country (St Andrews, Glasgow, King's College and Marischal at Aberdeen, and Edinburgh: each with low fees) they wished to attend, drawn by the fame of the teachers. Eminent professors vied for reputation based on performance in the lecture hall or in print, or both, and they trained effectively candidates for the professions, vocational careers, or business life needed in their country and abroad: teachers, ministers, lawyers, doctors, scientists, technologists, and a cadre mainly of the gentry, but sometimes not, who entered public life, or were commanders in the armed services, or became entrepreneurs and improvers of estates. Glasgow and the other Scottish universities drew students from England (and Ireland) in this era, on the basis of a judgment expressed by the MP, Sir Gilbert Elliot, in 1758: 'I find every thinking man here [London] begins to discover the very absurd constitution of the English Universitys, without knowing what to do better' (*Corr.* Letter 27). The institutions north of the Tweed, for all their faults, had some workable answers to this predicament.

Smith mentions the educational weakness at Oxford University specifically in the *Wealth of Nations*, in relation to his argument that it is in each man's interest to live as much at ease as possible, and if someone's rewards are the same whether he performs or does not perform an onerous duty, he will either neglect it or perform it as slackly as his superiors permit. If the superior authority resides in a college of which he is a member, and the other members are teachers, they will agree among themselves to overlook one man's neglect of his duty, if each is allowed to neglect his own. Thus it came about, Smith reasoned, that 'Oxford professors had given up even the pretence of teaching for many years' (Smith 1976, WN V.i.f.7–8).

Regarding the curriculum, it seems that Smith included Oxford among the 'learned societies' that 'have chosen to remain, for a very long time, the sanctuaries in which exploded systems and obsolete prejudices found shelter and protection, after they had been hunted out of every other corner of the world' (WN V.i.f.34). The practice at his College of teaching the 'exploded system' of Aristotle's physics and his scholastic commentators would strike Smith in retrospect as an intellectual swindle, and it continued long enough. The philosopher Sir William Hamilton was still complaining about it as a Snell Exhibitioner in 1809:

> I am so plagued by these foolish lectures of the [Balliol] College tutors. ... Aristotle today, ditto to-morrow, and I believe if the ideas furnished by Aristotle to these numskulls were taken away, it would be doubtful whether there remained a single notion. I am quite tired of such uniformity of study.
>
> (Veitch 1869: 30)

Smith thought this procedure demeaned those who taught it, and those obliged to submit to it as students by the necessity of obtaining a qualification to practise a profession:

> if the teacher happens to be a man of sense, it must be an unpleasant thing to him to be conscious, while he is lecturing his students, that he is either speaking or reading nonsense, or what is little better than nonsense. It must too be unpleasant to him to observe that the greater part of his students desert his lectures; or perhaps attend upon them with plain enough marks of neglect, contempt, and derision.
>
> (WN V.i.f.14)

To avoid such derision, so Smith noted in WN, the teacher falls back on the expedient of reading with the students a book in a 'foreign and dead language', and making them interpret it to him, then 'by now and then making an occasional remark upon it, he may flatter himself that he is giving a lecture'. A very little effort and learning will allow him to do this without making himself ridiculous, and college discipline will force students to attend such a 'sham-lecture' regularly (WN V.i.f.14).

A specific instance of a 'sham-lecture' of the kind described in general terms in WN is found in printed submissions circulated by and about a rebellious Balliol student named James Cochrane, who was elected to a Snell Exhibition in 1767, and engaged in a dispute in 1772 about his stipend, and the charges imposed on him for tuition. He criticized in forthright terms, for example, the approach to teaching of Samuel Love, a Fellow elected in 1768:

> Do you dignify with the Name of a Lecture, your sitting silently in a Chair, and hearing the Undergraduates construe, sometimes right and sometimes wrong, and render an English Word for a Latin Word as faithfully as you can do? If this be the Case, can there be a more base Prostitution of such a Lecture, and may not the Understanding and Taste be equally improved by reading over the Dictionary? Indeed, what are all the Public Lectures at Balliol which are read? In Geometry, for Instance. Have they advanced farther than the 7th Proposition of the 1st Book of Euclid through the Whole of this Long Term? To finish a Book of Euclid in the Course of many Years is a Phaenomenon almost unknown at Balliol. Yet, if Mr Love will compare what he does with what he ought to do, as directed by the College Statutes, he will find his deficiency astonishing.
>
> (cited in Jones 2005: 166–7)

Love's excuses seem less than reassuring: he began his course late in the term, and there were only two lectures a week (a point Smith had made to his guardian in 1740). The twenty or thirty students who attended lectures included beginners, which required a slow pace, and a public execution had drawn away attenders from one lecture. Love did point out in his own defence that he gave a 'private lecture' in his own room to make up for the 'deficiency and absence' in students who should have benefited from the 'public lectures' in Hall (details found in a bound volume in the Balliol Library, Jones 2005: 166–7). This seems a far cry from the fare provided at Glasgow.

In opposition to the tendency towards slackness at Balliol, Smith advocated giving rein to the force of 'rivalship and emulation' to render excellency an object of ambition, and occasion the 'very greatest exertion' (WN V.i.f.4), in scholarship, we may add, as in every other domain. It must have been galling for Smith to hand over the cash he had in short supply, for the travesty of higher education he encountered at Oxford in the 1740s.

In Glasgow, he had been accustomed to listen to exhilarating lectures on moral philosophy, introducing enlightened theories about ethics, justice and economics, given in English by that vibrant personality, Francis Hutcheson (Scott 1900), and to study with the genial Robert Simson, one of the foremost mathematicians in Europe, the advanced geometry that supported Newton's planetary mechanics (Rankin 1995, Guicciardini 2005).

To be sure, though Smith was fortunate in being taught by these professors; Glasgow was not, on the whole, a heavenly city of eighteenth-century philosophers. Renouncing the kind of 'enthusiastic fit' felt by Imlac when aggrandizing his profession of poet in Johnson's *Rasselas* (ch. xi), I should report soberly what William Leechman, newly elected Glasgow Professor of Divinity, wrote on 9 March 1744, to an English dissenting minister, George Benson, who had been a fellow-student under Hutcheson:

> I don't believe it is possible for one in your situation to imagine what height bigotry and nonsense in Religion prevails in this Country, especially in this part of it: There is not one Man in the Presbytery of Glasgow, with whom I can use any freedom in discoursing on Religion, or from whom I can expect friendship in the present affair [he was facing a heresy trial], except an intimate Companion, who is quite disregarded by the Rest of them. From this view of my present Situation, you may easily perceive how difficult a task it is to preach pure and genuine Christianity, and at the same [time] not to expose myself to the fury of Bigots. There is the utmost care taken to watch every word pronounced by me. The Zealots have always some Secret Spies among the Students to give proper Information, of what is taught on every Subject.
> (Manchester: John Rylands Library, Benson Collection)

One possible motivation for Smith's acceptance of a Snell Exhibition was to remove himself from this atmosphere.

Understandably, when he was faced with neglect at Balliol, or the sterile neo-Aristotelianism that was taught, Smith fell back on the expedient of teaching himself. In one direction, I believe he continued the study of

Newtonian science he had begun at Glasgow, and was tracing its antecedents, a project which gave rise to his 'History of Astronomy' (in Smith 1980, EPS). In 1773, he described this text to Hume as a 'fragment of an intended juvenile work' (*Corr.* Letter 137), which would seem to push it back to his Balliol years, or soon afterwards, but likely enough before he became a freelance instructor in Edinburgh, 1748–51, and delivered lectures of evident maturity on rhetoric, jurisprudence and the history of science. One outcome of his study of science is to be found in the Letter on the state of learning in Europe which, according to his first biographer, Dugald Stewart (1980 [1794]), Smith addressed in 1756 to the editors of the first *Edinburgh Review* (EPS: 230, 242–56). There he presented his assessment of the originality and genius of leading English scientists of an earlier generation, such as Boyle and Newton, also the capacity of contemporary French men of letters for organizing and presenting scientific and other knowledge. As well, he indicated there was an opening for the Scottish literati to advance social science through achieving originality of thought, and combining this with its systematic exposition (Lomonaco 2002). The key to this process was what the Balliol of his time apparently lacked: incentives for, and competition among, intellectuals to excel in their fields, and exercise of responsible judgment about their performance.

Dugald Stewart also identifies the second major focus of his subject's autodidacticism. He reports that Hutcheson's lectures directed Smith to the 'study of human nature in all its branches, more particularly of the political history of mankind', and that he devoted himself to this study from the time of his removal to Oxford (1980 I. 8). Smith's self-improvement programme extended to developing his translation skills in ancient and modern languages. He must also have begun investigation of the 'civil history' of Europe covered in the extensive 'history of historians' he presented in his rhetoric lectures (Smith 1983, LRBL Lecture XIX, ii. 45–73), which he was delivering two years after leaving Balliol. Europe's 'civil history' as Smith understood it is further reflected in the account he gives in WN of the feudal barons, once so turbulent, forgetting their inheritance of martial spirit and adherence to faction, and giving themselves up to luxury and control by the authority of the day (WN III.iv.10, 17). In addition, he reveals (at WN V.i.g.25) how the same causes which destroyed the great barons, destroyed, though at a faster rate, in the same manner the whole temporal power of the clergy (Ross 2005).

In the course of these studies, it appears, Smith came upon Hume's Treatise of Human Nature, which resulted in a clash with the Balliol authorities, in this instance every bit as bigoted as the Glasgow Presbytery: 'We have heard that the heads of the college thought proper to visit his chamber, and finding Hume's Treatise on Human Nature, then recently published [1739–40], the reverend inquisitors seized that heretical book, and severely reprimanded the young philosopher' ([John Leslie; identified in Nangle 1955] 1797: 60). Not all Balliol dons in Smith's time were so reactionary, and one of them, Charles Godwyn, owned the *Treatise* and other books by Hume, bequeathing them with the rest of his extensive library to the Bodleian. Smith reflects knowledge of Hume's teaching in the *Treatise* about the imagination in relation to theory-building, in that early text, the 'History of Astronomy', and it is clear that Hume's thought was an abiding inspiration for him. It is possible, too, that Hume's early ideas about creating a 'science of man' inspired in Smith at Oxford, or fairly soon thereafter, the ambition to create a sequence of linked works that would constitute a 'system' of the moral universe equivalent to Newton's 'system of the [natural] world' (Ross 2004).

There was a cost in loss of health for Smith, however, in his excessive addiction to self-directed study at Balliol. On 19 November 1743, he wrote to his mother, surely causing her great alarm: 'I am just recovered of a violent fit of laziness, which has confined me to my elbow chair these three months' (*Corr.* Letter 5). In the next letter that survives, dated 2 July 1744, he attributes to 'laziness' his failure to write more often to his mother, and describes some physical symptoms: 'an inveterate scurvy and shaking of the head', which he professes to have cured by taking tar-water, a remedy 'very much in vogue here at present for almost all diseases' (*Corr.* Letter 6). This refers to the widespread response to Bishop Berkeley's sensational best-seller, *Philosophical Reflexions ... Concerning the Virtues of Tar-Water* (1901 [1744]), which claimed that 'lives hardly worth living for bad appetites, low spirits, restless nights, wasting pains and anxieties, might be rendered easy and comfortable' by this remedy (Berkeley 1901: iii.179). Smith later acknowledged his skin disease and head shaking continued as long as he could remember anything, and that in the end tar-water failed him.

The symptoms he describes resemble those recorded by Hume when he had a kind of nervous breakdown in 1729, brought on, so he believed, by excessive ardour in study, and seeking to embrace a repressive Stoic regimen (Hume 1932, vol. i, pp.13–17; M.A. Stewart 2005: 29–30). It is conceivable that Smith at Oxford, neglected by the dons, apart from incurring their censure, and avoiding physical exercise – no cricketing for him, unlike Samuel Johnson, or boating on the Isis, as far as we know, a pursuit engaged in by Hamilton – read himself into a lethargy of spirits, accompanied by involuntary shaking of the head, and skin eruptions. This might be the 'Disease of the Learned' which Hume felt had afflicted him. Otherwise, research on diet at eighteenth-century Balliol might reveal a physical cause of Smith's illness.

In Smith's last year at Oxford, there was increased tension, which he must have felt, between the Scottish Snell Exhibitioners, who were at that time Presbyterians and Hanoverians, and the long-lived Master, Theophilus Leigh (in office 1726–85), who was a devoted Anglican high churchman and Jacobite sympathiser, enthusiasms he passed on to his granddaughter, Jane Austen, and which are found reflected in her *Juvenilia* (2006; Harman 2008). Dr Leigh among others at the College probably showed pleasure at the news of the successful opening stages in 1745 of the Jacobite Rising under Bonnie Prince Charlie, and displeasure at the withdrawal from England, then final defeat of the Prince's army in April 1746. Smith and the other Scots scholars would feel great alarm about the fate of their relatives at the outbreak of civil war in their homeland, and commensurate relief at the collapse of Jacobite insurgency. As well, the Snell Exhibitioners believed that the College wrung out more from the revenues of the bequest than was lawful, and as a group, including Smith, they complained to Glasgow University about this state affairs. Leigh replied by informing them that since they disliked the College, they could leave. Smith apparently took him at his word, and departed from Oxford in the third week of August 1746.

Subsequently, Adam Smith befriended for a number of years a student of his at Glasgow, David Callander of Westertown (1742–98), who was a Snell Exhibitioner from 1760 to 1771. This individual stated to a collector of biographical materials named George Chalmers, that Smith 'did not like Balliol and left in disgust' (Edinburgh University Library, Laing MSS, II.451/2, ff. 429–34; Raphael 1992: 93). I do not believe this is the last word about Smith and Balliol. The College allowed Smith to be admitted to the Faculty of Civil Law in January 1744, and thus escape from the career path of ordination (Jones and Sander 2009). Also, he was permitted to retain his Snell Exhibition *in absentia* until he resigned it on 4 February 1749 (*Corr.* Letter 7), though it is doubtful whether he would continue to draw £40 p.a. (perhaps something like £4,000 in 2006, see Sher 2006: xxv). In addition, Smith made lasting friendships at Balliol with other Snell scholars, one being James Menteath, who became a curate in Adderbury, near Banbury, then rector of All Saints in Barrowby, Lincolnshire, and planned to return to Scotland in 1785. When he heard of this, Smith wrote: 'You are now, except one or two old Cousins, the oldest friend I have now remaining in the world, and it gives me the most unspeakable satisfaction to think that I have some chance of ending my days in your Society and neighbourhood' (*Corr.* Letter 243).

Dr John Jones, the most recent historian of Balliol, has recorded the results of his study of Theophilus Leigh's papers, finding in them an indication that in his old age he supported efforts to replace the lax practices of the College, of which Smith had complained, with firmer regulation of teaching and study (Jones 2005: 173). In time, the contribution of Snell Exhibitioners to the intellectual life of Balliol was recognised, and when necessary reforms were put through for the conduct of College affairs in the early nineteenth century, these men won a share of the open and competitive Fellowships. Also, the most able and rivalrous students among them enjoyed major success in the University's final Honours examination system, established in 1800 in large part through the efforts of a Master of Balliol, John Parsons (Jones 2005: 177). In time, as well, Balliol acknowledged Adam Smith as one of the greatest sons of the House. Marking this, the College placed in the Senior Common Room what Professor Alec Macfie (1956) regarded as the 'rather over-dramatized bust' of him (dated 1851) by Baron Carlo Marochetti, a sculptor much admired by Queen Victoria. Balliol would be gratified when the political economist and MP, Thorold Rogers (1823–90), drew attention to the significance of Smith's years at the College, in the preface to his scholarly edition of WN (1869). Balliol Economics dons presumably concurred in the requirement for many years that Oxford students of their subject should read WN. Adam Smith's recurrent smile at the memory of his first dinner in the Old Hall was a premonition of all that better feeling.

Note

* This is an expanded version of the after-dinner talk given at Balliol College on 6 January 2009.

Bibliography

Austen, J. (2006) *Juvenilia*, P. Sabor (ed.), The Cambridge Edition of the Works of Jane Austen, Cambridge: Cambridge University Press.

Berkeley, G. (1901 [1744]) *Philosophical Works*, vol. iii: *Philosophical Reflexions and Inquiries Concerning the Virtues of Tar-Water* [later named *Siris*], Oxford: Clarendon Press.

Edinburgh Univ. Library, Laing MSS, II.451/2, ff. 429–34 – notes made by George Chalmers (1742–1825) of information about Adam Smith given to him by David Callander of Westertown.

Guicciardini, N. (2005) 'The Auctoris Praefatio to Newton's *Principia*: geometry and mechanics in the Newtonian mathematical school', in E. Mazza and E. Ronchetti (eds), *Instruction and Amusement: La ragioni del'Illuminismo britannico*, Padua: Il Poligrafo, pp. 115–25.

Harman, C. (2008) 'Partiality and prejudice: rhe young Jane Austen's "hatred of all those people whose parties or principles do not suit with mine"', *Times Literary Supplement*, 1 Feb., 14–15.

Hume, D. (1932) *The Letters*, J.Y.T. Greig (ed.), Oxford: Clarendon Press; reprinted, 1969.

—— (2000 [1739–40]) *Treatise of Human Nature*, D.F. Norton and M.J. Norton (eds), Oxford: Oxford University Press.

Jones, J. (2005) *Balliol College: A History*, 2nd edn, Oxford: Oxford University Press.

—— and Sander, A. (2009) *Catalogue of an Exhibition arranged for a Conference of the International Adam Smith Society*, at Balliol College, January.

Leathers, C.G. and Raines, J.P. (2007) 'Adam Smith's (weak) case for fee incomes for university faculty and student-consumer sovereignty', *The Adam Smith Review*, 3: 119–57, V. Brown (ed.), London and New York: Routledge.

[Leslie, J.] (1797) Review of A. Smith, *Essays on Philosophical Subjects*, 1795, *Monthly Review*, 22: 57–68.

Lomonaco, J. (2002) 'Adam Smith's "Letter to the Authors of the Edinburgh Review"', *Journal of the History of Ideas*, 63: 659–76.

Macfie, A.L. (1956) Appendix on the Muir Portrait of Adam Smith and Other Portraits, in C.R. Fay, *Adam Smith and the Scotland of His Day*, Cambridge: Cambridge University Press.

Manchester: John Rylands Library, Benson Collection: William Leechman to George Benson, 9 March 1744.

Nangle, B.C. (1955) *The Monthly Review, Second Series 1790–1815: Indexes of Contributors and Articles*, Oxford: Clarendon Press.

Rankin, R.A. (1995) 'Robert Simson'. http://www-history.mcs.st-andrews.ac.uk. Biographies/Simson.html

Raphael, D.D. (1992) 'Adam Smith 1790: the man recalled; the philosopher revived', in P. Jones and A.S. Skinner (eds), *Adam Smith Reviewed*, Edinburgh: Edinburgh University Press.

Ross, I.S. (2004) ' "Great Works upon the anvil" in 1785: Adam Smith's projected corpus of philosophy', *The Adam Smith Review*, 1: 40–59, V. Brown (ed.), London and New York: Routledge.

—— (2005) 'Italian background to Smith's *Wealth of Nations*: historiography and political economy', in E. Mazza and E. Ronchetti (eds), *Instruction and Amusement: La ragioni del'Illuminismo britannico*, Padua: Il Poligrafo, pp. 267–87.

St James's Chronicle (1790) Obituary of Adam Smith, 31 July.

Scott, W.R. (1900) *Francis Hutcheson: His Life, Teaching, and Position in the History of Philosophy*, Cambridge: Cambridge University Press.

Sher, R.B. (2006) *The Enlightenment and the Book: Scottish Authors and Their Publishers in Eighteenth-Century Britain, Ireland & America*, Chicago: University of Chicago Press.

Smith, A (1869) *An Inquiry into the Nature and Causes of the Wealth of Nations*, J.E. Thorold Rogers (ed.), Oxford: Clarendon Press; revised edn, 1880.

—— (1976) *An Inquiry into the Nature and Causes of the Wealth of Nations*, R.H. Campbell and A.S. Skinner (eds), W.B. Todd (textual ed.), Oxford: Clarendon Press.

—— (1980) *Essays on Philosophical Subjects*, W.P.D. Wightman and J.C. Bryce (eds), D.D. Raphael and A.S. Skinner (gen. eds), Oxford: Clarendon Press.

—— (1983) *Lectures on Rhetoric and Belles Lettres*, J.C. Bryce (ed.), Oxford: Clarendon Press.

—— (1987) *Correspondence of Adam Smith*, E.C. Mossner and I. S. Ross (eds), 2nd edn, Oxford: Clarendon Press.

Stewart, D. (1980) 'Account of the Life and Writings of Adam Smith, LL.D.', I.S. Ross (ed.), in Adam Smith (1980), pp. 263–351.

Stewart, M.A. (2005) 'Hume's intellectual development, 1711–52', in M. Frasca-Spada and P.J.E. Kail (eds), *Impressions of Hume*, Oxford: Clarendon Press, pp. 11–58.

Stones, L. (1984) 'The Life and Career of John Snell (c. 1629–79)', in D. Sellar (ed.), *Miscellany Two*, Edinburgh: The Stair Society.

Veitch, J. (1869) *Memoir of Sir William Hamilton, Bart*, Edinburgh and London: Blackwood.

Index

Made in the USA
Middletown, DE
02 November 2017